SUBJUGATION AND BONDAGE

SUBJUGATION AND BONDAGE

Critical Essays on Slavery and Social Philosophy

TOMMY L. LOTT

ROWMAN & LITTLEFIELD PUBLISHERS, INC.
Lanham • Boulder • New York • Oxford

ROWMAN & LITTLEFIELD PUBLISHERS, INC.

Published in the United States of America
by Rowman & Littlefield Publishers, Inc.
4720 Boston Way, Lanham, Maryland 20706

12 Hid's Copse Road
Cumnor Hill, Oxford OX2 9JJ, England

British Library Cataloguing in Publication Information Available

Library of Congress Cataloging-in-Publication Data

Subjugation and bondage : critical essays on slavery and social
   philosophy / [edited by] Tommy L. Lott.
      p. cm.
   Includes bibliographical references and index.
   ISBN 0-8476-8777-5 (cloth : alk paper).—ISBN 0-8476-8778-3 (pbk: alk paper)
   1. Slavery. 2. Social sciences—Philosophy. I. Lott, Tommy Lee,
1946– .
HT891.S83 1998
306.3′62—dc21   97-35950
                                                              CIP

ISBN 0-8476-8777-5 (cloth: alk paper)
ISBN 0-8476-8778-3 (pbk: alk paper)

Printed in the United States of America

♾ ™ The paper used in this publication meets the minimum requirements of
American National Standard for Information Sciences—Permanence of Paper
for Printed Library Materials, ANSI Z39.48–1984.

*For my mother Bertha Bayonne Lott Stance and
my grandfather Richard Bayonne.*

CONTENTS

CONTENTS

FOREWORD

I n this fine collection Tommy Lott has brought together essays by analytical philosophers on issues of slavery and social philosophy. Recently, there has been a movement in American colleges and universities to include issues about race, ethnicity, and gender in required humanities courses, and to identify works by women, Asians, Africans, Native Americans, and members of minority communities in America and Europe for the reading lists of such courses. This movement has provoked a loud and powerful reaction, the premise of which is that letting these issues and writers into the curriculum will force out deeper issues and better writers. My experience suggests that premise is quite false.

Throughout the 1980s I taught, with the help of a variety of guest lecturers and postdoctoral teaching fellows, a course affectionately known as Philosophy 5B, the winter quarter of the Stanford Philosophy Department's three-quarter sequence, "Ideas in Western Culture." This sequence satisfied a university distribution requirement for freshmen; to do so it had to cover a list of familiar classics. Given the period of time we covered, it seemed only natural to consider Mary Wollstonecraft's *Vindication of the Rights of Women* along with Rousseau, and Equiano's *Travels* along with Locke's *Second Treatise*. Far from driving out important issues, these works helped to focus attention on important philosophical issues and to deepen the student's understanding of historical events. In retrospect, the practice of teaching Locke and Rousseau without Equiano and Wollstonecraft, or lecturing on the Reformation and Enlightenment without paying attention to the slave trade and the literature to which it gave rise, seems bizarre.

It is true, if unfortunate, that students do not have time to read everything. In our course, Thomas More's *Utopia* and Luther's *On Christian Liberty* moved off the reading list when Wollstonecraft and

Equiano moved in. One need not imply that these are negligible works, to point out that such a change does not amount to abandoning the accumulated wisdom of Western culture, or to closing the American mind.

The experience of teaching Equiano's *Travels* and other slave narratives convinced many of those involved in the course that these narratives constitute a rich literature that has much to offer courses in the humanities. In particular, analytical philosphers can benefit greatly from the careful study of such works as a literature full of philosophical themes and they in turn can help provide a conceptually rich approach to this literature that will help teachers throughout the humanities. Slavery itself is about as settled as a moral issue gets. Even the present turn away from liberal values has not produced advocates of it. But the philosophical issues involved with slavery are by no means fully understood, much less resolved. Ethical issues remain concerning what, exactly, the evil of slavery consists, as do metaphysical issues about what it is to be an individual, and the nature and value of freedom. There are even issues in the philosophy of language, about the nature of categories and classification, and how language enables categories of little or no intrinsic scientific interest to gain causal powers and psychological and social importance.

The essays in this collection highlight some of the work that has been done on these topics. I am pleased to see that four of the contributors, Tommy Lott, Julius Moravcsik, Bill Uzgalis, and Julie Ward, are veterans of Philosophy 5B. This collection should help produce a generation of humanists for whom the institution of slavery is a natural topic for a humanities course, to whom the literature provoked by that institution is as familiar as that inspired by the Reformation or the Industrial Revolution. These scholars will teach courses that will open the American mind to the true philosophical, moral, and historical richness of its intellectual tradition.

John Perry,
Stanford University

Acknowledgments

R esearch for this book was supported by a Ford Postdoctoral Fellowship for Minorities. I owe a special thanks to Dean Ewart Thomas and John Perry for bringing me to Stanford to work on this project.

"Necessary Identities" by Bernard Williams. Originally published in Bernard Williams, *Shame and Necessity* (Berkeley: University of California Press, 1993), pp. 103–29. Reprinted by permission of the author and University of California Press.

"Locke and the Legal Obligations of Black Americans" by Bill E. Lawson. Originally published in *Public Affairs Quarterly* 3 (July 1989): pp. 49–63. Reprinted by permission.

"The Master-Slave Dialectic: Hegal vs. Douglass" by Cynthia Willett. Originally published in Cynthia Willett, *Maternal Ethics and Other Slave Moralities* (New York: Routledge, 1995), chaps. 4, 5, and 6. Reprinted by permission of the author and Routledge.

"Paternalism and Slavery" by Howard McGary. Originally published in Howard McGary and Bill E. Lawson, *Between Slavery and Freedom: Philosophy and American Slavery* (Bloomington: Indiana University Press, 1992), pp. 16–34. Reprinted by permission of the author and Indiana University Press.

"What Is Wrong with Slavery" by R. M. Hare. Originally published in *Philosophy and Public Affairs* 8 (1979): pp. 103–21. Reprinted by permission of the author and Princeton University Press.

"Slavery and Surrogacy" by Anita L. Allen. Originally published as "Surrogacy, Slavery, and Ownership of Life" in *Harvard Journal of Law and Public Policy* 13 (1990), pp. 139–49, and "The Black Surrogate Mother" in *Harvard BlackLetter Journal* 8 (Spring 1991): pp. 17–31. Reprinted by permission.

"American Slavery and the Holocaust: Their Ideologies Compared" by Laurence Thomas. Originally published in *Public Affairs Quarterly* 5 (April 1991): pp. 191–120. Reprinted by permission.

"The Arc of the Moral Universe" by Joshua Cohen. Originally published in *Philosophy and Public Affairs* 26 (Spring 1997): pp. 91–134. Reprinted by permission of the author and Princeton University Press.

INTRODUCTION

I t has been more than a century since the official abolition of
slavery in the New World, yet historians and social scientists
continue their heated moral debates on the subject.[1] Given the
frequent invocation of the views of historical philosophers, from Aristotle to Hegel, in arguments on all sides of these debates, it is
rather surprising that contemporary philosophers only rarely have
shown interest in addressing the important moral questions raised
by slavery. This volume aims to provide a selection of recent philosophical essays that explores a wide variety of moral concerns regarding slavery as an institutionalized social practice.

Many of the questions on slavery that have attracted the interest
of contemporary philosophers were prominent in the political
thought of the Enlightenment. Over half of the essays included here
present novel interpretations of some of these views. In some cases
explicit comparisons are drawn between the arguments given by ex-
slaves and certain political theories that may have been an influence.
By considering the slaves' critical appropriation of Enlightenment
views, the ambiguous implications of various notions of consent, liberty, and natural rights are examined from the slaves' perspective.

The influence of Enlightenment thought regarding slavery extends far beyond the abolitionist movement. Locke's ambivalence
towards slavery continues to frame philosophical discussions in current social and political theory. Traces of his argument are evident,
for instance, in the justification of slavery John Rawls presents in *A
Theory of Justice*. According to Rawls,

> [S]lavery and serfdom, in their familiar forms anyway, are toler-
> able only when they relieve even worse injustices. There may
> be transition cases where enslavement is better than current
> practice. For example, suppose that city-states that previously

have not taken prisoners of war but have always put captives to death agree by treaty to hold prisoners as slaves instead. . . . [I]t may be that under these conditions, since all run the risk of capture in war, this form of slavery is less unjust than present custom.[2]

While rejecting the utilitarian justification, Rawls permits slavery under extreme circumstances where it serves as a substitute for death. Following Locke, he stipulates that slavery must not be hereditary and that it must be only temporarily institutionalized, adding his own provision that this practice is to be established by agreement between "the free citizens of more or less equal city-states." Even on Rawls's liberal view the practice of slavery is both condemned and condoned. The essays included here on contemporary issues critically examine the source of this ambiguity in the liberal tradition. Many of the authors presume that, although slavery is undoubtedly an evil social practice, its moral assessment stands in need of a more nuanced treatment. Some of the authors address the question of what is wrong with slavery by critically examining, and in some cases endorsing, certain principles derived from Marxism, communitarianism, paternalism, utilitarianism, moral realism, and jurisprudence.

Slavery and the Enlightenment

How much does our rejection of slavery as unjust depend on modern conceptions that were not available in the ancient world? In contrast with Plato and other ancient thinkers, Aristotle's view of slavery was prominent in early modern thought. Despite abundant criticism from modern philosophers, his famous defense of slavery as a necessary social institution remained influential among Southern apologists.[3] Bernard Williams argues that Aristotle's commitment to showing that there are some people for whom it is natural that they, rather than someone else, should be slaves indicates how, within the framework of Aristotle's justification, the question of justice can arise in cases where slavery has been imposed arbitrarily. Aristotle assimilated the condition of slaves to the condition of women to establish that being a slave was a necessary identity grounded in nature. Williams cites the fact that, in the case of women, the idea that there was by nature a position to be filled, and there were people who by nature occupied it, was a conventional view among the Greeks. If we distinguish biological from social identity, being a woman was considered a necessary identity, whereas being a slave was considered a matter of "bad luck"—a condition imposed by force. Williams points out that Aristotle believed that if the practice of slavery were properly conducted, "slaves would become what women actually were."

That slavery is imposed by force suggests that it is unjust and not natural. Williams maintains that what distinguishes modern liberalism from the ancient world is not the view that slavery was unjust; rather, it is the rejection of the idea of necessary social identities. Since the Enlightenment, a framework of social justice has been constructed that allows us to hold all social roles open to question and avoid relying on notions of luck and necessity to justify the subordination of women and slaves.

It has been widely acknowledged among historians that John Locke was a major influence on Jefferson and the American founding fathers.[4] To what extent, however, were they influenced by Locke's view of slavery? Although Jefferson had condemned the practice of slavery as a violation of human rights in the original version of the Declaration of Independence, in *Notes on Virginia* he expressed a view of American slaves as racially inferior.[5] Did Locke perhaps share Jefferson's ambivalence towards the American slave? The question of whether Locke's justification of slavery applies to the enslavement of African Americans has been a matter of debate among Locke scholars. This question ties in with the question of whether he was racist. Ironically, these concerns have been countered by raising the question of whether his ideas influenced the abolitionists and, perhaps indirectly, the writing of slave narratives. Some scholars believe that Locke's political doctrine should be taken to imply that, even today, African Americans are not obligated to obey the law.

In his essay on Frederick Douglass, Bernard Boxill examines Locke's account of self-evident moral propositions to determine whether his moral epistemology entails racism and elitism. Boxill rejects the interpretation of Locke as a racist but concludes that his view is not elitist. Boxill locates the source of Locke's elitism in his view of property. He points out that Locke believed most people will be propertyless, and this suggests they will be too distracted by ceaseless toil to have time to discover the truths of morality. He turns to Frederick Douglass's discussion of human nature to find a version of Locke's moral epistemology that avoids this elitism. An alternative to Locke's doctrine of the malleability of human nature can be discovered in Douglass's view. Boxill argues that, by rejecting Locke's account of property, and by subscribing to a different view of human nature, Douglass could endorse the egalitarian tendencies in Locke's moral epistemology, in particular, the view that human rights are self-evident, without embracing any of his elitist conclusions.

Although Boxill exonerates Locke's account from the charge of racism, some commentators are less certain of whether Locke had a racial view that provided the grounds for a justification of African-American slavery.[6] Bill Uzgalis sustains Boxill's interpretation. He defends Locke against this charge by maintaining that there is no evidence that Locke had an empirical theory of African racial inferiority or a moral theory that justified the enslavement of Africans. Uzgalis partly supports this conclusion by reexamining the standard interpretation of Locke's account of slavery in the second of the *Two Treatises on Government*. According to Uzgalis, Locke was in a position to know that his account was incompatible with the practice of slavery in America, and given this, his account should be understood to implicitly reject that particular form of slavery.

The question of whether Locke's political theory contributed to the abolitionist crusade against slavery has interesting implications for the widely acknowledged fact that the slaves' view, expressed in autobiographies, was a central component of this crusade. Uzgalis's claim must be squared with a careful reading of narratives by ex-slaves. In her essay on the two black British abolitionists, Olaudah Equiano and Ottobah Cugoano, Julie Ward argues that their writings show clear traces of influence by the abolitionist views of the period. She distinguishes between the metaphysical, biological, and economic aspects of their arguments to show the structural similarity with arguments by other abolitionists. She highlights the similarity of key passages drawn from the publications of Granville Sharp,

Thomas Clarkson, and James Ramsay, as evidence of their influence on Equiano and Cugoano. Ward concludes that it is no surprise that some of the ex-slaves who wrote about their plight relied upon natural-rights theories to challenge the moral basis of slavery.

Given the central importance of the slaves' critical stance towards the justification of slavery, there is no reason to privilege the philosophic views of the master over those held by slaves in coming to grips with Enlightenment doctrine. In my essay on early Enlightenment views of slavery, I examine critically the theory of natural rights presented by Hobbes and Locke. I indicate the shortcomings of their account of the injustice of slavery by reference to criticisms, contained in slave testimonies, of their notions of coercion and liberty. The overlap of slavery and servitude, I argue, allows the natural rights theories of Hobbes and Locke to condone benign forms of slavery. Hence, such theories cannot provide an adequate ground on which to condemn slavery as inherently evil.

The many criticisms of Locke's account of slavery notwithstanding, some philosophers believe that the value of his political theory is undiminished for understanding many current social issues relevant to African Americans. In his essay on the legal obligations of African Americans, Bill Lawson argues that Locke's account of the state of nature can be employed to establish a ground for the political obligation of African Americans. He examines critically the suggestion that, since slavery, African Americans have been in a state of nature vis-à-vis the United States government. Lawson rejects this suggestion by interpreting Locke's account of the sovereign's misuse and abuse of power in connection with an important distinction between the dissolution of government and the dissolution of society. According to Locke, political obligations cease only when the society dissolves. Lawson points out that since Reconstruction, American society has not dissolved and concludes on Lockean grounds that African Americans must be viewed as citizens with legal obligations.

While Douglass's abolitionist arguments show traces of the Enlightenment doctrine of natural rights, his account of the relationship between master and slave can be instructively compared with Hegel's parable. In her essay on the master/slave dialectic, Cynthia Willett employs Douglass's account to object to Hegel's paradigm of the master-slave relationship, arguing that it cannot be applied to the experience of African American slaves. She maintains that, because Douglass, unlike Hegel, viewed slavery from the slaves' perspective, there are significant differences in their respective accounts. On her reading of *My Bondage and My Freedom* Douglass constructs a version of the dialectic in which Hegelian notions of selfhood and freedom are replaced. She points out that Douglass rejected a crucial presupposition of the Hegelian model, namely, that slaves are the mirror reversal of the master.

Contemporary Issues

Slavery is often employed in moral theory as a paradigm of social injustice. This practice must be called into question given that it presupposes common agreement regarding the moral status of slavery. Social scientists, such as Robert Fogel, have maintained that the idea that slavery was wrong stands in need of factual support.[7] Unfortunately, the harshness of Fogel's proclamation has overshadowed his insight. Nonetheless, philosophers have heeded his point that the question of what is wrong with slavery has a variety of answers that rest on contingent matters.

In his essay on the moral assessment of slavery, Julius Moravcsik opposes the rights-based theory, preferring instead to assign responsibility for slavery to communities as well as individuals. He takes the question of slavery's evilness to be open and to be decided in varying contexts, but nonetheless insists that it should be viewed as always having evil effects on both individuals and communities. He argues that our moral assessment of slavery must take into account a constellation of ingredients that varies from context to context. Moravcsik captures this variety by explicating the conceptual core of the notion of slavery in terms of principles derived from a normative communitarian theory.

Howard McGary elaborates Moravcsik's dissatisfaction with liberal doctrine by examining critically the paternalistic model some historians have used to explain slavery. He points out that even historians, such as Genovese, who oppose and condemn slavery nonetheless believe that it was paternalistic.[8] Genovese has maintained that paternalism accounts for the slaveholder's need to rationalize his use of coercion, as well as his need to establish a relationship that undermined the solidarity of slaves. McGary points out that the reason paternalistic explanations have been so pervasive in explaining or evaluating slavery and the plight of oppressed groups is that utilitarian principles that could justify slavery have been unacceptable to liberals. Paternalistic explanations tend to diminish the evils of slavery because they are closely connected with excuses and justifications that mask the exploitation involved. McGary considers several versions of the paternalistic model to show why all paternalistic defenses of slavery fail. He draws upon the narrative of Solomon Northup to present the example of black women slaves as a counterinstance to the paternalistic model, arguing that the practice of selling the offspring of female slaves does not fit such an account.

McGary's worry that less harsh forms of slavery can be justified on paternalistic grounds leads him to reject utilitarianism. In his essay on the wrongness of slavery R. M. Hare takes to be empirical the question of whether on utilitarian principles all forms of slavery are wrong and leaves open the possibility of accepting certain benign cases. He proposes to meet the objection to utilitarianism based on imaginary cases on the empirical ground that such cases are highly unlikely to occur and that further, if such a case did occur, to accept it would be of little consequence. He argues that we need not abandon our intuitive principle condemning slavery by accepting such cases. The standard cases of slavery do not pose an objection to utilitarianism for two reasons. First of all, good empirical grounds usually exist on which to show that utility is not maximum. Second, there is a good utilitarian justification for adopting this principle in the actual world. Hare concludes that slavery is wrong on utilitarian grounds because it, in fact, will almost always cause misery.

Philosophers opposed to surrogacy sometimes rely on the idea that slavery is inherently wrong. Their opposition to surrogacy stems from a sense that it may be evil because its practice is tantamount to the immorality of slavery. The question then is whether surrogacy is a form of slavery. Anita Allen argues that the experience of American slavery is instructive for present efforts to determine the legal and moral status of surrogacy. She views the opposition to surrogacy and the opposition to slavery as having analogous features.

Although she denies that surrogacy is a form of slavery, she insists that the experience of African American women under the system of American slavery is relevant to the controversy surrounding surrogacy's legal and moral status. Allen begins with the assumption that slavery is a paradigm of patent immorality and illegality. She draws the analogy with surrogacy by focusing on the surrogate mother's reproductive function, arguing that the role of gestator is a kind of enslavement. The racial factor in the landmark Anna Johnson case, in which Johnson's legal status as the black mother of a white child was denied, lends credence to this analogy. Allen condemns surrogacy as an intolerable practice that treats women's wombs as commodities and denies them respect as equals. The parallel she draws between surrogacy and slavery is substantiated by the similarity between Anna Johnson's legal battle to gain custody of her offspring and the legal case of a slave woman who sued for her own freedom and then for the right to own her own child. She spells out the analogy between slavery and surrogacy to set up her argument for a social policy of treating surrogacy contracts as unenforceable.

Laurence Thomas compares African American slavery, as a nineteenth-century form of oppression, with the twentieth-century Jewish Holocaust to highlight their underlying ideological differences. Thomas points out that the aims and practices in each case were vastly different, especially with regard to the oppressor's concept of the victim. He argues that because slavery and the Holocaust were such radically dissimilar institutions, it makes no sense to view one as more evil than the other. He cites three major differences between American slavery and the Holocaust. First, the Holocaust was totally coercive in that Jews were never trusted, whereas slaves were sometimes given roles and duties that presupposed a high level of trust. Second, Jews were subjected to genocide, a plight much different from the natal alienation suffered by African slaves severed from their cultural roots. Third, Jews were considered irredeemably evil, unlike black slaves who were viewed as a group of amoral simpletons. There was a sense in which these different conceptions led to different practices. The benevolent treatment of slaves, including sexual relations, was not inconsistent with the slavemaster's view of them, whereas these practices were inconceivable under the Nazi concept of the Jew. Thomas concludes that slavery and the Holocaust were two different forms of evil in the sense that there were evils in the Holocaust that have no parallel in slavery.

Slavery and the Holocaust reveal the brutal side of Enlightenment notions of historical progress guided by Enlightenment principles. With an eye to current debates on moral realism and moral objectivity, Joshua Cohen examines the question of whether the injustice of slavery limited its viability as a social institution. He takes the moral claim "slavery is unjust" to state a fact that moral reasoning will consider, namely, the conflict between slavery and the legitimate interests of slaves in material well-being, autonomy, and dignity. He defends the claim that the injustice of slavery contributed to its demise.

Relying on slave testimony, Cohen emphasizes the role of slave resistance in bringing this about. By reference to a range of activity that indicates agency, he insists that the lack of publicly acknowledged rights exaggerated the slaves' real situation and that slaves were commonly able to do what the law denied them the right to do. The "phenomenology of compliance" requires qualifications that acknowledge that the slaves did not simply embrace dominant religious views, but developed syncretistic versions. Indeed, slaves embraced the language and moral ideals of the dominant culture in order to assert their rights. On Cohen's account in applying the moral norms of the dominant culture to themselves they had to advance a divergent interpretation of these norms.

Cohen's assessment is grounded on a careful reading of slave narratives. His use of the insight provided by these narratives to address questions raised by contemporary moral realists shows that the moral thought that slaves presented amounted to much more than a critique of the views held by European philosophers. That some of these narratives remain very appealing to philosophers interested in extending moral thought concerning slavery to issues in social philosophy demonstrates the continuing significance of the slaves' perspective to Western moral discourse.

Notes

1. See Robert William Fogel and Stanley Engerman, *Time on the Cross: The Economics of American Negro Slavery* (Boston: Little, Brown and Co., 1974); Paul A. David,

Herbert G. Gutman, Richard Sutch, Peter Temin, and David Wright, *Reckoning with Slavery: A Critical Study in the Quantitative History of American Negro Slavery* (New York: Oxford University Press, 1976); and Herbert Gutman, *Slavery and the Numbers Game: A Critique of "Time on the Cross"* (Urbana: University of Illinois Press, 1975). See also Darlene Clark Hine, ed., *The State of Afro-American History* (Baton Rouge: Louisiana State University Press, 1986); and Vera Rubin and Arthur Tuden, eds., *Comparative Perspectives on Slavery in New World Plantation Societies* (New York: The New York Academy of Sciences, 1977).

2. John Rawls, *A Theory of Justice* (Cambridge: Harvard University Press, 1971), 248.

3. For example, George Fitzhugh, *Cannibals All! or Slaves without Masters* (1856; rpt. Cambridge: Harvard University Press, 1960). See also the essays collected in *Slavery Defended: The Views of the Old South*, Eric L. McKitrick, ed. (Englewood Cliffs: Prentice-Hall, 1965).

4. See Bernard Bailyn, *The Ideological Origins of the American Revolution* (Cambridge: Harvard University Press, Belknap Press, 1967), 232–46; James Oakes, *Slavery and Freedom: An Interpretation of the Old South* (New York: Vintage, 1990), 61–79; and David Byron Davis, *The Problem of Slavery in the Age of Revolution 1770–1823* (Ithaca: Cornell University Press, 1975), 169–84.

5. Thomas Jefferson, "Notes on the State of Virginia" (1784), in Adrienne Koch and William Peden, eds., *The Life and Selected Writings of Thomas Jefferson* (New York, 1944), 261.

6. See Wayne Glausser, "Three Approaches to Locke and the Slave Trade," *Journal of the History of Ideas*, 51 (April-June 1990).

7. Robert William Fogel, *Without Consent or Contract: The Rise and Fall of American Slavery* (New York: W. W. Norton, 1989), 388–417.

8. Eugene Genovese, *Roll, Jordan, Roll* (New York: Pantheon, 1974).

1

Necessary Identities

Bernard Williams

A t this point, we are between two necessities. The Homeric, tragic, in particular Sophoclean, characters are represented to us as experiencing a necessity to act in certain ways, a conviction that they must do certain things. I have suggested that we should understand this in terms of the mechanisms of shame.[1] The source of the necessity is in the agent, an internalized other whose view the agent can respect. Indeed he can identify with this figure, and the respect is to that extent self-respect; but at the same time the figure remains a genuine other, the embodiment of a real social expectation. At the extreme, the sense of this necessity lies in the thought that one could not live and look others in the eye if one did certain things: a thought which may be to varying degrees figurative but can also be in a deadly sense literal, as it was with Ajax. These necessities are internal, grounded in the *ēthos,* the projects, the individual nature of the agent, and in the way he conceives the relation of his life to other people's.

Contrasted with this, at the other end of the universe, as one might say, is a divine necessity. In the Greek world this was not conceived as a unitary world-historical or redemptive enterprise, as it has been by Jews and Christians. When Homer says at the beginning of the *Iliad* that the anger came about, and many were killed, "and the plan of Zeus was fulfilled,"[2] it was not a plan for the world: it was not even a plan for the whole Trojan War, and anyway (as Homer frequently reminds us)[3] the Trojan War was not the whole world.

1

For the Greeks, divine necessity did not even consist of one plan for one individual, except in very special cases. But the world did contain various forces that could make certain outcomes necessary for the individual: they were necessary outcomes because they were, simply, unavoidable. Those divine necessities were purposive, in the sense that events were shaped towards a particular outcome. Sometimes, though not always, they were purposed as well, in the sense that they were designed by a supernatural agency that had a motive. Those external, divine, necessities, and some of the thoughts that go with them, will be the concern of the next chapter.[4]

Agents, typically, are not fully conscious of those supernatural necessities in advance. They may have a sense that there is a necessity involved, but not be sure what it is; for them, the outcome may, at the time, seem like luck. That is the sense in which, in the *Ajax* (803), Tekmessa, trying to prevent Ajax killing himself within the day—the oracle has said that he will live if he survives the day—can ask her friends "to stand in the way of a necessary chance," *anangkaias tuchēs*.

That phrase, in that connection, unnervingly combines most of the thoughts available about supernatural necessity. But Tekmessa had already used that same phrase earlier in the play (485 seq.), indeed in some such sense, but also with a more everyday meaning. She had said to Ajax that there is no greater evil for human beings than "necessary chance," and she cited her own case: she had a free and rich father, but now she is a slave. "So it was decided by the gods, perhaps, and above all, by your hand": and the move from an indeterminate speculation about the gods to a very definite assertion about Ajax brings with it a shift in the idea of an *anangkaia tuchē*. Her bad luck may possibly have been written in the stars, but it was quite certainly imposed on her by force, and it is continued by the threat or presence of force, even if in Tekmessa's own case her attitude to Ajax had put that to one side. This kind of necessity is certainly not hidden from the victim. Indeed, it most usually operates because it is offered clearly to the victim, in the form of a present threat; though if the threat is carried out and the agent is physically coerced, his consciousness may not matter any longer— what happens just happens to him. *Bia*, force, and *kratos*, physical constraint—a pair personified at the beginning of the *Prometheus*

Vinctus, as they are in Hesiod—were well known to be the bearers of a certain kind of *anangkē,* necessity. (A shrine of Bia and Anangke on the way up to the Acrocorinth is mentioned by Pausanias.)[5] Thucydides deploys the word in a sinister plural when he says that the Athenians were very exacting to their subjects who failed to pay the tribute, making themselves objectionable by applying *tas anangkas* to unwilling people (I.99).

Coercion may be both the cause and the effect of bad luck, and a paradigm of bad luck throughout the ancient world was being taken into slavery by military conquest, as Hecuba said in the *Iliad* had happened to some of her sons, "whom at times swift-footed Achilles captured, and he would sell them as slaves far across the unresting salt water into Samos, and Imbros, and Lemnos in the gloom of the mists."[6] And this was what, famously, Hector most regretted when he anticipated the fall of Troy: "None of it troubles me," he says to Andromache, "so much as the thought of you, when some bronze-armoured Achaian leads you off, taking away your day of liberty, in tears; and in Argos you must work at the loom of another . . . all unwilling, but strong will be the necessity upon you."[7]

In this chapter I shall be concerned first with some consequences in the world of ideas of this very basic kind of disaster and of slavery more generally; more generally still, with the Greeks' recognition that in their world one's whole life, all the ways in which one was treated, one's ethical identity, might depend on a chance.

My concern here is quite particularly with what I called at the beginning of this study the philosophical understanding of a historical phenomenon. Much is known about ancient slavery, and much is not known; unfortunately, much of what is known is not known to me. What I have to say about it is not meant to add to our understanding of it as a social institution, but rather to try to help us understand some things that some Greeks said about it. I hope that this may also help us to understand better our own rejection of it, and of certain other Greek practices, as unjust. In particular, this raises a basic question that we have met before and shall come to again, of how far our rejection of that institution, and of other ancient practices that we see as unjust, depends on modern conceptions that were not available in the ancient world.

Greek and Roman slavery was, as Moses Finley stressed,[8] a novel

3

invention, and its pattern has been rare in history. There was in fact a range of different institutions, which are distinguished by modern theory and to some extent were distinguished in antiquity itself. The helots in Sparta, though they were regarded by many as slaves, were not chattel slaves but an entire subject people, perhaps best classified as "state serfs"; they were notorious for being ready to revolt.[9]

Slaves in Athens, however, were chattel slaves in the fullest sense, pieces of individual property—"living property," in the phrase of Aristotle, who with his usual capacity to find an interesting point of ordinary language philosophy in an unlikely place, remarks that while a master can of course say that another man is his slave, equally a slave can say that another man is his master: but only a master can say of another man that he is *his*.[10] In their own persons slaves had no legal rights, and in particular none in the area of marriage or family law. Some slaves were allowed to live together as couples, but any such connection and the association of slaves and their children were frequently broken up, a practice that seems not to have been challenged until the fourth century A.D.[11] Slaves were, of course, sexually available to their owners.[12]

It was important for the ideology of this institution that the slaves were mostly barbarians, people who did not speak Greek, usually from the north and the northeast. (In the fifth and early fourth centuries Athens had a police force consisting of Scythian slaves, who lived in tents and were the subject of a great deal of humour).[13] The supply of slaves had to be renewed, and this was by no means necessarily a matter of regular warfare. The skills involved in capturing people to be slaves are said by Aristotle to be "a kind of hunting"; being a slave trader was regarded as both dangerous and unpopular.[14]

One of the paradoxes of chattel slavery, in the ancient world as in other cases, was the varying social distance between free and slave to be found in different aspects of life. In Greece, the free and the slaves worked side by side. Xenophon says "those who can do so buy slaves so that they can have fellow workers." As Finley has pointed out,[15] there were no slave employments as such, except domestic service and, usually, mining; the only entirely free employments were law, politics, and military service (but not in the navy). We know from the accounts the status of eighty-six workmen who worked on the construction of the Erechtheum at the end of the fifth century: twenty-four citizens, forty-two metics, and twenty slaves, all skilled craftsmen, and those on a daily wage were all paid the same.

Yet at the same time the slave was set apart from the free, in particular by the violence that surrounded his life. The slave was called (as elsewhere) "boy," *pais,* and it was a joke that *pais* came from *paiein,* "to beat."[16] Public slaves, at least, were marked with a brand, which, as Xenophon observed, made them harder to steal than money.[17] The overwhelming difference between free and slave, Demosthenes remarked, was that the slave was answerable with his or her body. Evidence from slaves was acceptable in the courts solely on condition that it had been extracted under torture. In a speech of Lysias, a man's reluctance to allow his slave concubine to be tortured is cited as evidence against him.[18]

Modern experience shows that it is possible for people to work next to each other who have startlingly different sets of rights, and social identities that require them to be treated in quite different ways. What made ancient slavery even more remarkable was the ready way in which a person could change from one of these identities to another. Some were born slaves, but you could become a slave from being free, by being captured, and this, as we have already seen, was a well-known calamity, a piece of ill luck. But equally, you could cease to be a slave, by manumission. In Rome, slaves were manumitted into citizenship, but this was not so among the Greeks: in Athens, a manumitted slave was a metic, a resident alien, a status that carried fewer rights than being a citizen but was already a world away from being a slave. Manumission, which at least from the fourth century B.C. was fairly common, involved an extraordinary transition: as one scholar has put it, the freed slave was transformed from an object to a subject of rights, the most complete metamorphosis one can imagine.[19]

In later antiquity the law of slavery was complex, and its attempts to mitigate some of the arbitrary features seem sometimes only to add another arbitrariness to the system, that of lawyers. Under Roman law, if a woman conceived as a free person but had become a slave by the time that she gave birth, the child was recognized as free: the *Digest* smugly remarks, "The mother's adversity should not

5

prejudice a child in the womb."[20] From the beginning, the arbitrariness of slavery was recognised. Some people, it is clear, went on to conclude from this that it was difficult to defend. Not many of their opinions have been preserved, but there are some famous verses that say: "If someone is a slave, he has the same flesh, for no one was ever born a slave by nature: it is chance that has enslaved his body." A similar thought is attributed to the Messenian Oration of Alcidamas (who was a pupil of Gorgias and a contemporary of Isocrates): "God let everyone set out as free people; nature never made anyone a slave."[21] As a nineteenth-century commentator on Aristotle remarked,

> it was just the facility of the transition from slavery to freedom and from freedom to slavery, and the dependence of men's status on accident and superior force and the will of men . . . that would give rise to the view that it was based on convention, not nature.[22]

To say that something was conventional was not necessarily to say that it was unjust; it did not necessarily imply this conclusion even in the period in the late fifth century when oppositions between nature and convention played a particularly large part in discussions of questions in politics and ethics. Slavery, however, was not merely conventional but arbitrary in its impact, and granted that it was intensely unpleasant for the slaves (which no one was disposed to deny, at least until the high-minded accommodations of later Stoicism), it was not hard to reach the conclusion summarized by Aristotle in his most lapidary manner:

> But to some people, holding slaves [*despozein*, "to be their master"] is against nature (for it is by convention that one man is a slave and another is free, and in nature there is no difference); therefore it is not just, either; since it is imposed by force [*biaion gar*].[23]

In the first book of the *Politics*, Aristotle notoriously tried to answer this charge and to show that slavery was in some sense natural. His attempt has not been well received by modern critics, who have been struck by the fact that various things he says in the course of it are not entirely consistent with each other or with things he says

6

elsewhere.[24] Some of these inconsistencies are clearly ideological products, the results of trying to square the ethical circle. Thus, he compares the subordination of slave to master with that of body to soul. (The analogy is not even with the relation of emotion to reason; that comparison is reserved for the relations of women to men.) But at the same time he has to allow that slaves have enough reason to understand what they are told. They are in many ways, as he says more than once, like domestic animals, but they are (bizarrely enough) domestic animals who interpret instructions, obey through the understanding, and display better or worse characters. Yet again, the master and the slave should, ideally, be friends; elsewhere Aristotle is less clear about this possibility and says only that one can be friends with a slave "*qua* man but not *qua* slave,"[25] a more than usually evasive deployment of one of his least satisfactory philosophical devices. These inconsistencies and strains are revealing. However, there is also something revealing about the way in which modern commentators have seized upon them. They are obviously embarrassed by the philosopher's conclusions and are relieved to discover in his argument any sign that he may have been embarrassed himself; at the very least, they are glad to find an encouragement from within to detach these positions from the body of his work. As opposed to Plato, who is manifestly and professedly offensive to liberal and democratic opinion, Aristotle can be seen as expressing a more generous and accommodating humanism, and there is a strong motivation to find a center to that outlook that will push to one side his less congenial opinions. There are motives, too, provided by his methods. No one expects to write, or be, like Plato. Aristotle, though, even when one has dimly recognized the extent of his genius, can seem to provide a comforting assurance to philosophers about the possibility of their subject, in the form of an omnipresent judiciousness, which, in itself, is only too easy to imitate.

In fact, Aristotle's argument about slavery is not an aberration in his work at all. It is, certainly, very unlike other people's treatment of the institution, but the ways in which it is untypical deeply express Aristotle's own view of the world. It is incoherent, but this is so not simply because of what slavery was, but because of Aristotle's own demands on how it was to be understood. I shall consider his argument in some detail, and this is relevant to my purpose in more than

7

one way. It will help us, I hope, to understand the Greek outlook on slavery and, perhaps, our own views of justice. It will also illustrate the truth that if there is something worse than accepting slavery, it consists in defending it.

I have tried in earlier chapters to show that the outlook of the Greeks, particularly of archaic and fifth-century Greeks, is nearer to our own than is often thought.[26] Moreover, we must not assume that the progress of philosophy, the theoretical constructions of Plato and Aristotle, always brought us nearer to what we can understand as an adequate grasp of the matters in question. Here is another example of that point, very different from those that we have encountered before. The Greeks had the institution of chattel slavery, and their way of life, as it actually functioned, presupposed it. (It is a different question whether as an abstract economic necessity they needed it: the point is simply that, granted the actual state of affairs, no way of life was accessible to them that preserved what was worthwhile to them and did without slavery.) Almost all of them took it for granted. But that did not mean that they had no ways of expressing what was wrong with it. A few did so in general and abstract terms, as we have seen. There were also the less theoretical complaints of slaves themselves, frequent in drama and, certainly, in everyday life. It is not hard to say what is bad about the life of a slave, and slaves everywhere have said it. Equally, free people in the Greek world were able to see what an arbitrary calamity it was for someone to become a slave. What they found it much harder to do, once they had the system, was to imagine their world without it. For the same reason, they did not take too seriously the complaints of the slaves. They had nothing to put in the place of the system, and granted the system, it would be surprising if slaves did not complain, and in those terms. What the Greeks were not generally committed to, however, was the idea that if the system were both properly run and properly understood, no one, including the slaves, would have reason to complain. This is the conclusion that Aristotle offered.

A recent writer has said that the debate whether slavery was natural was not about the question "whether there should be slaves, but why there should be."[27] In a way this is right, but it simplifies the issues. Aristotle, and no doubt almost everyone else who discussed the issue, thought that if there was a question whether there should be slaves, it had a quick answer: they were necessary. He thought they were a technological necessity: he explicitly allows, but only at the level of pre-science fiction, that if there were self-propelling tools that could perform the tasks, "either at our bidding or itself perceiving the need," there would be no need of slaves. He is himself not entirely consistent about how necessary slaves are; they are certainly necessary to the household, but with regard to agriculture, while slaves are certainly best, he concedes later in the *Politics* that other arrangements are possible.[28] However, in general he supposes them to be necessary; and this already yields one sense in which he might say that slavery is natural. It is necessary for life in the *polis*, and the *polis* is a natural form of association: it is the natural condition of human beings to live in such a community, with an appropriate division of labor.

If we grant the premises, Aristotle has already shown why there should be slaves; indeed, he has even shown, in a sense, why it is natural that there should be. But he has not yet even started to argue for that conclusion in his own distinctive sense, and the further step he has to take makes it very clear what he aims to do. What he has shown so far, on his own assumptions, is that some people have to be in the power of other people. This in no way determines who should be in whose power. All we have is that it is necessary and natural that some people should be masters of others; so far, it could be arbitrary which people were which. But if it is arbitrary, then this, as he said, might support the charge of injustice.

Worse—or, at least, worse from Aristotle's general point of view—is the consideration that to leave a blank at this point might generate a conflict within the account of what is natural. Central to Aristotle's thought is a contrast between what is natural and, on the other hand, what is *biaion*, that which is produced by constraint or force applied from outside. In Aristotle's physics this yields the theory of the natural motions of the elements: air and fire move upwards, water and earth downwards, according to their natures, unless they are constrained to move otherwise. For Aristotle's science, the "natural tendencies" of things were basically connected with what sorts of things they were. Human beings also have natural tendencies, and what goes against such a tendency is *biaion* and involves force or constraint.

9

The same thing is true, to a considerable extent, the other way round: in a healthy, uncorrupted, and adult individual, behavior that systematically requires constraint in order to elicit it is not natural. But if slavery is arbitrarily imposed, it will require such force: no person who could live a free person's life would want to be a slave. This shows that the life of a slave, for the person who has to lead it, would not be natural. So if we cannot get any farther, the argument from above, as we might call it, that it is natural that there should be slaves, is met by a contrary argument from below, that nobody is naturally a slave. It is vital to the question whether slavery could be seen as a "natural" institution that there are two issues here. If the argument to that conclusion could get only to the point it has reached so far, the theory of slavery as a natural arrangement would turn out to be (roughly) what modern mathematics calls omega-inconsistent: it would be natural and necessary that someone should be a slave, but for each person, it would not be natural that he or she should be one.

Aristotle thus has to take the next step, which yields his distinctive conclusion. He argues not merely that it is natural that someone or other should be a slave, but that there are people for whom it is natural that they, rather than someone else, should be slaves. In fact, all that Aristotle has to show, and he is careful to point this out,[29] is that there are pairs of people naturally related as master to slave. But since the slaver's task is identified in terms of being an implement or a workhorse and the condition of being a slave is absolute,[30] sharp distinctions have to be found between slaves and nonslaves. Physical differences are invoked, between the crouching posture natural to a slave and the upright posture of a free man. This is archaic aristocratic material, going back, for instance, to Theognis: "A slave's head is never upright, but always bent, and he has a slanting neck. A rose or a hyacinth never comes from a sea-onion: no more does a free child from a slave woman." But the important point for Aristotle is the supposed mental superiority of masters to slaves. Not surprisingly, he has problems in adjusting this to the required physical differences, as also to any plausible understanding of the observed reality. He admits that there is considerable miscasting as things are:

Nature aims to make the bodies of free men differ from those of slaves, the latter adapted in strength to necessary employment, the former upright and not suited to such work. . . . But the opposite often happens, and some people have the bodies of free men and others the souls.[31]

The last sentence of this passage is a disaster: it has to accommodate falsehoods he needs to say, and other things he needs not to say (for instance, that there are free men who should be recast as slaves), and it has collapsed under the pressure, generating a great debate among scholars about how, even syntactically, it is to be taken. These ideas, together with a familiar set of Greek prejudices about the slavish nature of barbarians, are the ancestors of the physiognomic and other ideological myths that have been notorious in modern times.[32]

The idea that slavery was natural, so to speak, *all the way down,* and that the argument from above, that slavery was necessary to the type of community in which human life could best develop, was met by an argument from below, that there existed people for whom the role was not contrary to nature and involved no real constraint: these ideas did not have much future in antiquity. They were to be called upon again, much later, in connection with the directly racist ideology of modern slavery, even if there they played a secondary role to Scripture ("learned embroidery" is Finley's phrase for them).[33]

Later antiquity seems rather to have given up the question of slavery as a problem in political philosophy in favor of edifying attempts to show that slavery was not really harmful to the slave; in particular, that real freedom was freedom of the spirit, and that this could be attained as well, perhaps better, by slaves. One of the most explicit, certainly one of the more repulsive, expositions of this attitude is offered by Seneca:

It is a mistake to think that slavery goes all the way down into a man. The better part of him remains outside it. The body belongs to the master and is subject to him, but the soul is autonomous, and is so free that it cannot be held by any prison. . . . It is the body that luck has given over to the master; this he buys and sells; that interior part cannot be handed over as property.

11

This view and its various Christian relatives are manifestly very different from Aristotle's,[34] because they invoke a dualism, or some similar picture of human beings, by which the most essential characteristics and interests of people transcend the empirical social world and its misfortunes. Aristotle did not have such a picture. But these views, and his, do share an objective: to sustain the belief that life cannot be ultimately or structurally unjust. Seneca and his various associates can let the social world be unjust, because they can, in accordance with one or another of their fantasies, suppose that one can get out of it. Aristotle knew that one could not get out of it, and his fantasy had to be that however imperfect it was likely in practice to be, at least it was not structurally unjust—the world could not be such that the best development of some people necessarily involved the coercion of others against their nature.

The earlier Greeks were not involved in either of those illusions. They were not particularly disposed to think of slavery as unjust, but that was not because they thought of it as a just institution. If they had thought of it as a just institution, they would also have thought that the slaves themselves—free people captured into slavery, for instance—would have been mistaken to complain about it. So it is now with judicial punishment: those who regard it as a just institution think that those who are properly subjected to it have basically no reason to complain. The earlier Greeks thought no such thing about slavery. On the contrary, being captured into slavery was a paradigm of disaster, of which any rational person would complain; and by the same token, they recognized the complaints as indeed complaints, objections made by rational people. Slavery, in most people's eyes, was not just, but necessary. Because it was necessary, it was not, as an institution, seen as unjust either: to say that it was unjust would imply that ideally, at least, it should cease to exist, and few, if any, could see how that might be. If as an institution it was not seen as either just or unjust, there was not much to be said about its justice, and indeed it has often been noticed that in extant Greek literature there are very few discussions at all of the justice of slavery.

The Greek world recognized the simple truth that slavery rested on coercion. Aristotle's attempt to justify the institution, in the literal sense of conferring justice on it rather than accepting that it was necessary, required him to deny this simple truth. Coercion, the *biaion,* is against nature, and if slavery, properly conducted, could be natural, then it would not be, in the deepest sense, coercive. It would be optimistic to have hoped that if slavery were properly conducted it would not involve violence at all; the point would be, rather, that even if violence had to be directed to a natural slave, it need not be in the deepest sense coercive, because slavery, properly allocated, would be a necessary identity. Aristotle's argument, of course, merely sets the task; it does not provide the intellectual negotiations and evasions that would be needed in real life to see slavery in that light, and to change it from being what it had always been seen to be, a contingent and uniquely brutal disaster for its victims. As I have already said, antiquity did not persist in any attempt to find those materials, and it is not surprising.

At least in the case of slaves, Aristotle thought that his case needed some argument. The subordination of women to men, on the other hand, receives at the crucial point in the *Politics* only a phrase: "A slave does not have the deliberative faculty at all, while a woman has it, but it lacks authority."[35] The argument is of basically the same shape as that about slaves: there is a need for the division of roles, and nature provides the casting. But the downwards and upwards movements of the argument in this case virtually coincide, since Aristotle seemingly thinks that less needs to be provided and also that the observed facts clearly provide it. This was merely received opinion, and what was in the case of slavery a peculiar and strained conclusion of Aristotle's, that there were people who by nature filled the required role, was the conventional view with regard to women. There was by nature a position to be filled, and there were people who by nature occupied it. In trying to show that being a slave was a necessary identity, Aristotle was, up to a point, suggesting that if slavery were properly conducted, slaves would become what women actually were.

In the role that Aristotle allocated to women, and in what he said about them, he followed prejudices familiar not only among the Greeks, and they hardly need to be catalogued. Not every Athenian, and still less every Greek, accepted the very restrictive description of a woman's role given in the famous passage of Pericles' Funeral Speech, to the effect that the greatest glory of women lay in not being talked about by men for good or ill, and it has been claimed that a woman's life could be more free than has generally been supposed. Some important facts are unclear—for instance, it is still not agreed whether women went to the theater. Moreover, the effects of segregation, as Kenneth Dover has pointed out, must have varied between social classes. But, whatever the details, it is clear that a respectable woman's life was to a great degree confined to the house.[36]

Athenian women were not citizens, but the "women of Attica." At the same time, there was a relevant difference between being such a woman and not being so, since the Periclean rule required a male citizen to be *ex amphoin aston*—as it cannot quite be translated, "a citizen on both sides."[37] Their duties lay within the house, and contrasts between *oikos* and *polis*, private and public, were deeply involved in the representation of the relations between women and men; the understanding of those contrasts itself varied, with the result, as Sally Humphreys has noted, that *oikos* is itself an ideological word.[38]

As Dover has reminded us, almost every surviving word of classical Greek was written by men.[39] Nevertheless, complaints about the treatment of women, indeed complaints that their treatment was unfair, are by no means unknown. Already in the *Odyssey* Calypso complains about the double standard that is applied to gods and to goddesses with respect to sexual relations with mortals: "You are jealous," she says to the god, "and you resent goddeses sleeping with men, though you do it with mortal women."[40] A woman in a fragment of Sophocles complains of how they are nothing, are sold into marriage and moved around at their husbands' will.[41] The most famous—they might almost be called systematic—objections are those of Euripedes's Medea. She is something of a special case,[42] but more generally Aristophanes could make Euripides say that in his plays women spoke. It is interesting that Euripides has been thought by some people to be a feminist, and by others a misogynist: we should perhaps entertain the bleak possibility that he was both.[43]

There is a famous remark, which according to the tradition was ascribed by the biographer Hermippus to Thales (that is to say, to some indeterminate sage), though others ascribed it to Socrates: that there were three things for which he gave thanks to luck—that he had been born a human being and not a beast, a man and not a

14

woman, and a Greek and not a barbarian. (It is a partial inversion of this triad that Aeschylus's Agamemnon invokes when he refuses to walk on the carpet, where he distinguishes himself first from a woman, then from a barbarian, finally from a god.)[44]

But what sort of luck is this? What exactly is the object of the gratitude? Thales—let us call him that—doubtless knew what he meant, more or less, when he said that he was thankful that he was not a woman, and it may seem a philosophical absurdity to press heavily on such a familiar kind of thought. But notions of luck, of justice, and of identity are very tightly enmeshed in this area, and a certain amount of pressure is needed to extract them. One thing at any rate is clear: whatever Thales meant, he was not referring to a real possibility avoided. He had no way of supposing, as a risk he had managed to escape, that he, that very Thales, might have been a woman.

Ancient theories of generation gave no support to the idea that someone who was a man might have been a woman. Those theories themselves are ideological, if not quite straightforwardly so. The kind of theory to be found in Aristotle and elaborated later in Galen superficially expresses male-centered ideas. By contrast with the Hippocratic theory over which it prevailed, it ascribes no active or distinctive role to the female. It represents the female parent as a receptacle rather than a contributor, matter rather than form; it also sees the female child as a spoiled or less than perfect male, a fetus to which not enough heat had been applied to dry it off properly or, in particular, to extrude the genital organs. But it is a very striking fact, as Peter Brown has pointed out, that these ideas were not of a kind to reassure a belief in unquestionable male distinctness. Sexual bimorphism came out as a matter of degree and of accidents, rather than an unambiguous signal of incommensurability; indeed, as Thomas Laqueur has shown, the emphasis in traditional studies of anatomy was quite remarkably directed towards supposed homologies between the male and female reproductive systems. (The first detailed female skeleton in an anatomy book appeared only towards the end of the eighteenth century.)[45] So from a purely biological standpoint, Aristotelian or Galenian medicine might be thought to come nearer than modern theory does to the idea that one might have been born to the other gender—if the father's sperm had been a bit cooler, for instance. But it would still not come near enough. Even if it were an accident that a male came from that copulation rather than a female, and that was an accident simply of degree rather than of the identity of a component, as it is now understood, it was still not an accident that befell *that person,* and Aristotle, for one, never for a moment thinks of it in those terms; just as he thinks that if something is a lion, it is necessarily a lion, so if someone is male, he is necessarily male.

An indication that no one was disposed to deny this thought may perhaps be found in quite a different direction. There was in Greek mythology one figure, Teiresias, for whom belonging to one gender had not excluded belonging to the other. There is more than one version of his myth.[46] The one relevant here is that as a young man he saw two serpents copulating. He killed one and turned into a woman. He was told by Apollo that if he saw the same scene and killed the other, he would turn back; after some time, he did encounter the scene again and did revert to being a man. Hera and Zeus quarrelled on the question whether men or women derived more pleasure from sex, and asked the uniquely qualified Teiresias, who said that of ten parts, the woman enjoyed nine and the man one, which agreed with Zeus. Hera, angry, blinded him. But Zeus gave him the gift of divination and a life lasting seven generations.

This is an old myth, going back to the Hesiodic *Melampodia.*[47] Teiresias's prophetic powers are closely connected in the myth to his sexual history; in Euripides's *Bacchae,* moreover, where Teiresias plays a significant if not very dignified part, there is emphasis on bisexual aspects of the god Dionysus and of his worship.[48] Yet at no point here, or in other plays in which he appears, or in any other extant tragedy is Teiresias's mythical history mentioned. One must surely suppose that the tragedians knew the myth, which survived into later antiquity. Perhaps we may conjecture that despite the psychological power of the myth, it lacked any public significance. The idea of having two sexual histories belonged only to the world of personal fantasy; the field of tragedy, which is also a field of social interaction, is so powerfully structured by the distinctions between men and women that this mythical peculiarity of Teiresias remains, so far as we know, quite irrelevant to it.

The triad of things from which a free Greek male distinguished himself more usually took the form not of *animal, woman, barbarian,* but of *barbarian, woman, slave,* and in that form it remained very powerful for centuries.[49] It was also in that form a good deal more socially relevant. If Thales had given thanks to luck that he was not a slave, he would have been thanking the goddess for a very different and more comprehensible intervention than that which saved him (or somebody) from being a woman. In fact, to thank her that he had not been born a slave would be only part of the message. He would have to thank her further for not making him a slave subsequently. In the matter of his not being a slave, it was not merely in some indeterminate sense luck, but very definitely and comprehensibly his luck, that things had turned out better than they might have done. It was not *his* luck that he was not a woman, and no one ever seriously supposed that it was. Being a woman really was a necessary identity; being a slave or a free man, despite Aristotle's desperate efforts to the contrary, was not. That is why, as I put it before, his attempt can be seen as an attempt to assimilate the condition of a slave to that of a woman.

A lot of conventional practice, now and in the past, has made the assimilation the other way round. In expressing aspirations for a better state of affairs, we acknowledge that being a woman is a necessary identity, but distinguish that biological identity from a social one, in terms such as a distinction between sex and gender.[50] Our aim is that no one should be a slave, but it is not anyone's aim, even the most radical, that no one should be a woman: it is a question of the social construction of what it is to be a woman. The double idea that there should be a sharp and unchanging distribution of roles and that females and males were designed to fill those roles has managed to find a remarkable range of political philosophies ready to accommodate it, including some supposedly devoted to ideals of abstract equality. It was no peculiarity of Aristotle, or of his Greek predecessors, to construe a genuinely necessary sexual identity as a naturally given social identity.

There had, indeed, been one famous exception, Plato, who had argued in the *Republic* that women should not be excluded from performing any role in his ideal state, in particular that of a Guardian, simply because they were women. Plato's opinion seems to have been that as a matter of fact women were not talented for mathematics or ruling; but the question, he insisted, did concern their talents and not their sex.[51] For Aristotle, this argument might as well never have been put, but it is not hard to see the reason. Plato's argument is intimately connected in the *Republic* with his proposal that among the Guardians the family should be abolished. For Aristotle the family was a natural institution that one could not conceive of abolishing, and he took it for granted that the traditional role of women was essentially involved in that natural institution.

The role of women could be taken for granted by most Greeks as natural, except for a few Utopians such as Plato or intellectual malcontents such as Euripides. Both tragedy and comedy show, in different ways, that it was not at all unimaginable that women should act differently, but those passages only serve to reveal, and perhaps they helped to reinforce, the standard assumption that there was nothing arbitrary or coercive about the traditional arrangements. With slavery it was different, for while it structured to an immense degree the relations between people in the ancient world, they themselves recognized its arbitrariness and violence.

Except for Aristotle (and he spoke less for existing arrangements than for some indeterminate improvement of them) the Greeks saw what slavery involved, and regarded being a slave as a paradigm of bad luck: *anangkaia tuchē*, the bad luck of being in a condition imposed and sustained by force. "Bad luck" was not a notion that they standardly applied to being a woman. In part, this was because it was not a matter of luck, except at the level of a wish that could be represented by such thoughts as Thales's gratitude. It was also not seen, most of the time and in particular by men, as so bad. It was, for instance, less overtly coercive.

Our attitudes to these matters are different from the Greeks' (though I recognise that the "we" embraced by that "our" is less extensive in the case of women than in the case of slavery). But exactly how are they different? In particular, how far do we need, in rejecting those Greek ideas and practices, ethical ideas that were not available to the Greeks themselves? In the case of slavery, it may be that we deploy ethical ideas against it that the Greeks did not have, but we do not need to do so in order to reject it. It was no secret to the Greeks, as I have said, why it was unenviable bad luck to be in the power of another. Moreover, they recognized how arbitrary the impact of that luck was. Those thoughts could provide the materials for the claim that slavery was unjust—*biaion gar*, in the pungent phrase of Aristotle's I quoted earlier, "because it was imposed by force." But slavery was taken to be necessary—necessary, that is to say, to sustaining the kind of political, social, and cultural life that free Greeks enjoyed. Most people did not suppose that because slavery was necessary, it was therefore just; this, as Aristotle very clearly saw, would not be enough, and a further argument would be needed, one that he hopelessly tried to find. The effect of the necessity was, rather, that life proceeded on the basis of slavery and left no space, effectively, for the question of its justice to be raised.

Once the question is raised, it is quite hard not to see slavery as unjust, indeed as a paradigm of injustice, in the light of considerations basically available to the Greeks themselves. (What really needed new materials, of a scriptural and systematically racist kind, were the attempts to justify slavery in the modern world, when the question of its justice had for a long time already been raised.) We, now, have no difficulty in seeing slavery as unjust: we have economic arrangements and a conception of a society of citizens with which slavery is straightforwardly incompatible. This may stir a reflex of cultural self-congratulation, or at least satisfaction that in some dimensions there is progress.[52] But the main feature of the Greek attitude to slavery, I have suggested, was not a morally primitive belief in its justice, but the fact that considerations of justice and injustice were immobilized by the demands of what was seen as social and economic necessity. That phenomenon has not so much been eliminated from modern life as shifted to different places.

We have social practices in relation to which we are in a situation much like that of the Greeks with slavery. We recognize arbitrary and brutal ways in which people are handled by society, ways that are conditioned, often, by no more than exposure to luck. We have the intellectual resources to regard the situation of these people, and the systems that allow these things, as unjust, but are uncertain whether to do so, partly because we have seen the corruption and collapse of supposedly alternative systems, partly because we have no settled opinion on the question about which Aristotle tried to contrive a settled opinion, how far the existence of a worthwhile life for some people involves the imposition of suffering on others.

With regard to women, the relations between ancient and modern prejudice are different. For one thing, modern prejudice is to a much vaster extent the same as ancient. Quite apart from the fact that prejudice based on traditional religious conceptions flourishes in the contemporary world, the idea that gender roles are imposed by nature is alive in "modern," scientistic forms. In particular, the more crassly unreflective contributions of sociobiology to this subject represent little more than continuations of Aristotelian anthropology by other means. This is concealed by the fact that it is not Aristotelian *biology* that is being presented. Precisely because it is based on natural selection theory, sociobiology feels confident of being immunized against teleology and against the Aristotelian spirit that reads the universe on an analogy to intelligent construction. But it is not in virtue of its patterns of biological explanation that Aristotelian assumptions have their hold on this style of thinking, but in the more general assumption that there is some relatively simple fit between social gender roles, on the one hand, and, on the other, nature as it is to be biologically understood (however that may be). Changing the picture of nature does not necessarily remove the assumption that nature has something to tell us, in fairly unambiguous terms, about what social roles should be and how they should be distributed.

As we have already seen in several connections, the idea that there was a harmonious fit between social roles, the structure of the human mind, and nature was by no means a belief that all Greeks held, and in its most complete and comforting form it was almost an Aristotelian speciality, one that was to prove immeasurably influential. Other Greeks had more disrupted and disquieting images of the relations of human life to the cosmos, and not simply because they were sophists or skeptics. A sense of the opacity or inscrutability of things was expressed by earlier writers such as Pindar, and while this could minister to social passivity, the *amēchania* of the archaic world that Dodds memorably captured in the phrase "God's in his Heaven, all's wrong with the world,"[53] it certainly did not speak to any encouraging idea of the harmony of humanity and nature.

In many comparisons between the ancient world and the modern world it is assumed that in the ancient world social roles were understood to be rooted in nature. Indeed, it is often thought to be a special mark of modern societies, distinguishing them from all earlier ones, that they have lost this idea. These assumptions are made equally by those who are favourably disposed to modernity and by those who are not. For those critical of the modern world, the loss of the idea leads to alienation and a feeling that human beings have been unroofed and robbed of a harmony between themselves and their world. Those who salute the power of modern enlightenment, on the other hand, find a liberating force in the recognition that any social role can be held up to human criticism and that no such necessities are dictated to us by nature. A central feature of modern liberal conceptions of social justice can indeed be expressed by saying that they altogether deny the existence of necessary social identities.

There are several reasons why it is so readily assumed that a major difference between modern liberal societies and their predecessors can be found in their accepting or rejecting the idea of necessary social identities. Much of the intellectual machinery needed to discuss the question is of course a modern invention, including the idea, consciously expressed, of a social role; discussion is influenced, moreover, by certain general theories about the nature of authority in traditional societies. Above all, a huge shadow is cast, at least onto European and American conceptions, by Aristotelianized Christianity. But if we look to the ancient Greeks, and in particular look behind Aristotle, we can see that it is to a significant extent untrue that the presence or absence of the idea of necessary identities makes the difference between their outlooks on society and our own. It is untrue, above all, with respect to one of the fundamental and most striking social contrasts between them and ourselves, the attitude to slavery. The institution of slavery in the ancient world involved a very conspicuous and important social role. Most people were no doubt disposed to think that it was "natural" just in the sense that the best development of social life required it, but few thought that it was natural in the sense most closely associated with nature and with these interpretations, namely, with regard to the ways in which the role was allocated. Few, that is to say, seriously thought of it as a necessary identity, a role dealt out to an individual by nature speaking a social language.

Modern liberal thought rejects all necessary social identities, but

21

it is not this element in its outlook that distinguishes its attitude to slavery from that of most ancient Greeks. With regard to slavery, as opposed to their attitudes towards women, two concepts particularly governed their thoughts: economic or cultural necessity and individual bad luck. Obviously we do not apply those concepts, as the Greeks did, in such a way that we accept slavery. But we do apply those concepts very extensively to our social experience, and they are still hard at work in the modern world. The real difference in these respects between modern liberal ideas and the outlook of most Greeks lies rather in this, that liberalism demands—more realistically speaking, it hopes—that those concepts, necessity and luck, should not *take the place of* considerations of justice. If an individual's place in society is to be determined by forces of economic and cultural necessity and by that individual's luck, and if, in particular, those elements are going to determine the extent to which he or she is to be (effectively, if not by overt coercion) in the power of others, then the hope is that all this should happen within the framework of institutions that guarantee the justice of these processes and of their outcome. Even if we cannot, and perhaps should not, cancel all effects of mere necessity and luck, at least we hope that they can be placed within a framework that raises the question of justice and can answer it in such a way that the necessities will not be radically coercive and the luck will be no worse than luck.

Modern liberalism already stands at some distance from the ancient world not only in rejecting altogether the idea of a necessary identity, but in setting this problem. It has given itself the task of constructing a framework of social justice to control necessity and chance, in the sense both of mitigating their effects on the individual and of showing that what cannot be mitigated is not unjust. It is a distinctively modern achievement to have set the problem. However, we shall not know how great our distance really is from the ancient world until we are in a position to claim, not merely that there is this task, but that we have some hope of carrying it out.

Notes

1. Editor's note: The author's reference is to Bernard Williams, *Shame and Necessity* (Berkeley: University of California Press, 1993), chap. 4.

2. Homer, *Iliad*, trans. Richmond Lattimore (Chicago: University of Chicago Press, 1951), Book I, chap. 5; compare Williams, *Shame and Necessity*, chap. 3, n. 5.

3. Homer often refers to elsewhere, above all where the heroes have come from, for example, *Il*. 18.101–2, 9.393–94; to past time and peace time, as in the activities described in the similes and the description of the shield in book 18; and to future time, as in the account, 12.13–34, of how Poseidon and Apollo after the war swept away all traces of the Greek wall, and in Hector's challenge, 7.67–91, which links the future to his own deeds, when he speaks of a man who in time to come may see from his boat the tomb of a hero who died long before, killed by Hector, τὸ δ᾽ ἐμὸν κλέος οὔ ποτ᾽ ὀλεῖται.

4. Editor's note: The author's reference is to Williams, *Shame and Necessity*, chap. 6.

5. Hesiod, *Theogony*, ed. Martin L. West (Oxford: Clarendon Press, 1966), 385 seq. West, ad loc., mentions the passage from Pausanias, 2.4.6. προσάγοντες τὰς ἀνάγκας Thucydides 1.99.1.

6. *Il*. 24.750–53. However, the standard practice on capturing a city was rather to kill the men and enslave the women; on this and the present passage, see James M. Redfield, *Nature and Culture in the Iliad* (Chicago: University of Chicago Press, 1975), p. 120. This occurred in historical times, for example, in the Peloponnesian War: for Scione in 421 B.C. see Thuc. 5.32.1; and there is the case of Melos, 416 B.C., famous from the dialogue in Thucydides book 5. A man can be a slave among a foreign people in the *Odyssey:* 14.272, 297.

7. *Il*. 6.450 seq.

8. For example, Moses I. Finley, *Ancient Slavery and Modern Ideology* (New York: Viking Press, 1980), 67. I am heavily indebted to this and other work by Finley on this subject.

9. Plato assimilated them to slaves in *Leg*. 776B seq.; they were called ἡ δουλεία in a treaty between Sparta and Athens of 421 B.C., reported by Thucydides, 5.23.3. For the terms of the conditions on the Messenians, see Pausanias 4.14. G. E. M. de Ste. Croix claims that they were "state serfs" in "Slavery and Other Forms of Unfree Labour" in *Slavery and Other Forms of Unfree Labour*, Léonie Archer, ed. (London: Routledge, 1988). The ephors, on taking office each year, had to make a declaration of war on the helots so that they became official enemies of the state and could be killed as necessary without incurring pollution (Plutarch, *Lycurgus* 28.7). De Ste. Croix has remarked (p. 24) that this extraordinary practice of a government's formally declaring war on its own work force is probably unparalleled. For their readiness to revolt, compare, among others, Thuc. 4.80.3, Aristotle, *Politics* 1269a38–39.

10. Arist. *Pol*. 1253b32, 1254a9.

11. Quem patrem, qui servos est? Plautus, *Captivi* 574, quoted by Finley, *Ancient Slavery*, 75. Practice was by no means everywhere the same. The Gortynian code in

Crete allowed marriage between a free woman and a man who was not free (but perhaps not the converse); this example is cited by R. F. Willetts in a discussion of the situation in Argos in the early fifth century: "The Servile Interregnum at Argos," *Hermes* 87 (1959).

12. In Rome compare Horace, *Serm.* 1.2.116–19; and the remarks of Seneca the Elder *(Controversiae* 4 praef. 10) on passive buggery, that it is *impudicitia* in the free, a necessity for a slave, and an *officium* for a freedman.

13. For example, Aristophanes, *Thesmophoriazusae* 930–1125; *Lysistrata* 435–52. Other material in Thomas Wiedemann, *Greek and Roman Slavery* (Baltimore: Johns Hopkins University Press, 1981).

14. Compare Aristophanes, *Plutus* 520 seq. "A species of hunting or war": Arist. *Pol.* 1255b37.

15. Xenophon, *Memorabilia* 2.3.3. Finley, *Ancient Slavery*, 81; the Erechtheum, 101. It seems that master sculptors, master painters, and architects were now slaves: for the last, see James Coulton, *Ancient Greek Architects at Work* (Ithaca: Cornell University Press, 1977), chap. 1. (I owe this point to Mr. Andrew Stewart.)

16. Aristophanes, *Vesp.* 1297–98, 1307.

17. σεσημασμένα τῷ δημοσίῳ σημάντρῳ *Poroi* 4.21. Xenophon is proposing a new departure in the state ownership of slaves, but he must be referring to a familiar practice. Aristophanes, *Av.* 760 is compatible with the brand being applied just to recaptured runaways.

18. Dem. 22.3; Antiphon, *I Tetral.* 2.7; Aristotle, *Rhetoric* 1376b31 seq.; Lysias 4.10–17.

19. E. Levy, quoted by Finley, *Ancient Slavery*, 97.

20. Digest 1.5.5 [Marcianus].

21. The first fragment was attributed to the comic writer Philemon, of the fourth century B.C., by Kock (frag. 95), but in this he followed, after Meineke, an error made by Rutgers in 1618 in copying out the name of a Roman collection, the so-called *Comparison of Menander and Philistion:* see Rudolf Kassel and Colin Austin, *Poetue comici Graeci* (Berlin: DeGruyter, 1983), 7:317. The author and the date of the verses are unknown.

Alcidamas ap. schol. Arist. *Rhet.* 1.13.3: ἐλευθέρους ἀφῆκε πάντας θεός, οὐδένα δοῦλον ἡ φύσις πεποίηκεν. The translation attempts to capture two senses of ἀφῆκε, "sent out " and "set free."

22. W. L. Newman, *The Politics of Aristotle,* vol. 1 (Oxford: Clarendon, 1887), 139–42.

23. *Pol.* 1253b20–23.

24. For an attempt to show that Aristotle's argument is at least successful on his own premises, see W. Fortenbaugh, "Aristotle on Slaves and Women," in *Articles on Aristotle,* vol. 2, J. Barnes, M. Schofield, and R. Sorabji, eds. (London: Duckworth, 1977); well criticised by Nicholas D. Smith, "Aristotle's Theory of Natural Slavery,"

Phoenix 37 (1983). See also Malcolm Schofield, "Ideology and Philosophy in Aristotle's Theory of Slavery," in G. Patzig, ed., *Aristotele's "Politik,"* XI Symposium Aristotelicum.

25. *Pol.* 1255b13; *EN* 1161b5.

26. Editor's note: The reference is to the author's discussion of these issues in *Shame and Necessity*, chaps. 1–4.

27. R. G. Mulgan, *Aristotle's Political Theory* (Oxford: Clarendon Press, 1977), 43–44.

28. *Pol.* 1254b fin., 1330a25.

29. Note the order of the derivation at 1254a15–17 and the question that immediately follows at the start of chapter 5. Hegel, in this as in many other respects, was following Aristotle when he gave a deeper content to the obvious fact that slavery is a relational concept.

30. At 1259b34 seq. Aristotle has to make a special point that there are no degrees of command and obedience. Inasmuch as this is not just a verbal point, it is the product of assuming that the institution needed must be slavery.

31. Theognis 535; *Pol.* 1254b27 seq.

32. Compare Aristotle's own argument that barbarians do not observe the differences between slaves and woman and treat women like slaves, because everyone among them is like a slave: 1252a34 seq. For the commonplace about slavish barbarians, compare Euripides, *Helen* 246 (the verse Aristotle quotes is *IA* 1400). For various implications of the word βάρβαρος, and what peoples were counted as barbarian, compare Helen H. Bacon, *Barbarians in Greek Tragedy* (New Haven: Yale University Press, 1961). On some physiognomic materials in the Aristotelian corpus, see G. E. R. Lloyd, *Science, Folklore and Ideology* (Cambridge: Cambridge University Press, 1983), 22–25. For the "scientific" investigation in modern times of physical traits of the kinds in question, see Stephen Jay Gould, *The Mismeasure of Man* (New York: W. W. Norton, 1982).

33. Finley, 18.

34. Seneca, *Ben.* 3.20. The view that Christianity was responsible for the abolition of ancient slavery—or indeed was notably opposed to it—was attacked by John Millar in 1771, destroyed by Overbeck in 1875; see Finley, 14.

35. 1260a12–13. "Lacks authority" is a standard translation for ἄκυρον: it has the disadvantage of its not even looking as though the phrase provided a reason. The word can sustain a more neutral sense of inefficacy: at *GA* 772b28 it means "impotent."

36. The remark in the Funeral Speech is at Thuc. 2.45.2. For differing views of the situation, see A. W. Gomme, "The Position of Women in Athens in the Fifth and Fourth Centuries," *Classical Philology* 20 (1925); and John J. Gould, "Law, Custom and Myth: Aspects of the Social Position of Women in Classical Athens," *Journal of Hellenic Studies* 100 (1980). Source materials can be found in Mary R. Lefkowitz

and Maureen B. Fant, *Women's Life in Greece and Rome* (London: Duckworth, 1982).
Kenneth J. Dover, *Greek Popular Morality in the Time of Plato and Aristotle* (Berkeley:
University of California Press, 1974), 95 seq., gives a helpful summary with references, and for a useful outline with bibliography see Helene P. Foley, "Attitudes to
Women in Greece" in *The Civilization of the Ancient Mediterranean*, Michael Grant
and Rachael Kitzinger, eds. (New York: Scribner's, 1988); Eva C. Keuls, *The Reign
of the Phallus* (New York: Scribner's, 1985), emphasizes Athenian males' fear of
women.

37. See Nicole Loraux, *Les enfants d'Athéna* (Paris, 1981); John K. Davies, "Athenian Citizenship," *Classical Journal* 73 (1977): cited by Simon Goldhill, *Reading
Greek Tragedy* (New York: Cambridge University Press, 1986), 58, who stresses the
degree of anxiety generated by questions of citizenship.

38. See Sarah C. Humphreys, *The Family, Women and Death* (London: Routledge,
1983), chap. 1. Humphreys also discusses in this connection the representation of
women in tragedy, which is of course a very striking feature of the genre (of the
surviving plays, only one, the *Philoctetes,* has no female character). On this see also
the very suggestive discussion by Nicole Loraux, *Façons tragiques de tuer une femme*
(Paris, 1985), translated by Anthony Forster as *Tragic Ways of Killing a Woman* (Cambridge: Harvard University Press, 1987).

39. Dover, *Greek Popular Morality,* 95.

40. Homer, *Odyssey* 5.117 seq.; "resent" renders ἀγάασθαι (119, 122), which is
also the word for the attitude that the gods had towards Odysseus and Penelope
being together and enjoying their youth. *Od.* 23.211.

41. A. Nauck, *Tragicorum Graecorum fragmenta,* 2nd ed. (Leipzig 1889), Frag. 524.
Helene P. Foley, *Ritual Irony: Poetry and Sacrifice in Euripides* (Ithaca: Cornell University Press, 1985), 87, comments that this passage brings marriage very near to
slavery.

42. Recent work has brought out the unique character of Medea's final apotheo-
sis, and the conflict of "male" and "female" elements in her character: Bernard
Knox, "The *Medea* of Euripides," *Yale Classical Studies* 25 (1977), reprinted in Bernard Knox, *Word and Action* (Baltimore: Johns Hopkins University Press, 1979); Ann
Norris Michelini, *Euripides and the Tragic Tradition* (Madison, University of Wisconsin Press, 1987), 87 al.; Helene P. Foley, "Medea's Divided Self," *Classical Antiquity*
8 (1989). Her famous final speech has been much discussed in connection with
questions of ἀκρασία and the Platonic division of the soul: for an interesting discussion of Stoic views, see Christopher Gill, "Did Chrysippus Understand Medea?"
Phronesis 28 (1983).

For some scholars, the famous final speech does not belong to the play. Their
proposals offer a striking example of the pretensions of textual criticism when it is
not controlled by a sense of its function. The whole of *Medea* 1056–80 was deleted
by Bergk as spurious, and in this he is followed by Diggle in the latest Oxford text,

who refers us to an article by M. Reeve, "Euripides *Medea* 1021–1080," *Classical Quarterly* n.s. 22 (1972). The passage does present some difficulties of dramatic interpretation. One of the more serious is in fact soluble, if 1079 θυμὸς δὲ κρείσσων τῶν ἐμῶν βουλευμάτων is understood to mean not "my anger is stronger than my reasonings"—βουλεύματα up to this point has always referred to Medea's murderous plans—but "my anger is in charge of my plans": see Hans Diller, "ΘΥΜΟΣ ΔΕ ΚΡΕΙΣΣΩΝ ΤΩΝ ΕΜΩΝ ΒΟΥΛΕΥΜΑΤΩΝ," *Hermes* 94 (1966), supported by G. R. Stanton, "The End of Medea's Monologue: Euripides *Medea* 1078–80," *Rheinisches Museum*, N.F. 130 (1987), replying in particular to H. Lloyd Jones, "Euripides *Medea* 1056–80," *Wurzburger Jahrbuch fur die Altertumswissenschaft*, N.F. 6 (1980). The present concern, however, is not with this or any other particular proposal. The point—and it is a fundamental one—is that even if there are unsolved difficulties of interpretation, it is quite inappropriate to mark the fact by parentheses meaning that the entire passage (a passage well known in antiquity and offering few difficulties at a purely linguistic level) is not part of the play. As Fraenkel wisely said, "when a careful examination of the language and the style has produced no evidence of a corruption and yet the sense remains obscure, then there may be a case, not for putting a dagger against the passage, but for admitting the limits of our comprehension" (*Aeschylus Agamemnon*, vol. I, ix).

In this case, moreover, reflection is called for on what constitutes a difficulty, and whether the notions of "coherence" that the critics so freely deploy are those appropriate to Euripides and this text. M. Reeve, "Euripides *Medea* 1021–1080," *Classical Quarterly* n.s. 22 (1972): 58, remarkably and revealingly says, referring to an editor who condemned the passage, "If Medea is swaying to and fro, Muller has every right to insist that the audience should know at each moment exactly what is in her mind." For a sensitive treatment, comparing the speech (in particular, the sense in which it is a monologue) with Seneca, *Medea* 893–977, see Christopher Gill, "Two Monologues of Self-Division," in *Homo Viator: Classical Essays for John Bramble*, Michael Whitby, P. Hardie, and Mary Whitby, eds. (Bristol: Bristol Classical: Oak Park, Ill.: Bolehazy-Carducci, 1987).

43. Aristophanes, *Ran*. 949–50. See now Anton Powell, ed., *Euripides, Women and Sexuality* (London: Routledge, 1990).

44. Hermippus: Diog. Laert. 1.33. Aesch. *Ag*. 918 seq.

45. Peter Brown, *The Body and Society: Men, Women, and Sexual Renunciation in Early Christianity* (New York: Columbia University Press, 1988), 9 seq.; Thomas Laqueur, "Orgasm, Generation, and the Politics of Reproductive Biology," *Representations* 14 (1986); and see now Laqueur's *Making Sex: Body and Gender from the Greeks to Freud* (Cambridge: Harvard University Press, 1990) For various theories of the female role in reproduction, and other material on the attitude of Greek medicine to women, see Lloyd, *Science, Folklore, and Ideology*, 58–111. It has been remarked that Aristotle's theory of the generation of females is rather oddly related to his

general teleology: an essential element in the reproductive economy depends on something going wrong roughly 50 percent of the time. It may be relevant to this anomaly that there is an ethical connection at this point: see Williams, *Shame and Necessity*, 161.

46. I am indebted to Luc Brisson, *Le mythe de Tirèsias* (Leiden 1976).

47. Frag. Hes. 275, Reinhold Merkelbach and Martin L. West, eds., *Fragmenta Hesiodea* (Oxford 1967), 136 seq. Compare Hyginus, *Fab.* 75; Ovid, *Metamorphoses* 3.316–39. Brisson refers to the idea that in the animal kingdom the Teiresian analogy is the hyena, which was thought to be male one year and female the next (Aelian, *NA* 1.25); the story, often repeated, that it had both organs of sex is dismissed by Aristotle, *GA* 757a2–14.

48. τὸν θηλύμορφον ξένον Euripides, *Bacchae* 353; compare 453 seq. Teiresias's persona in the play is interestingly discussed by Paul Roth, "Teiresias as *Mantis* and Intellectual in Euripides' *Bacchae,*" *Transactions of the American Philological Association*, vol. 114 (1984). For Teiresias's role elsewhere, see Rebecca W. Bushnell, *Prophesying Tragedy: Sign and Voice in Sophocles' Theban Plays* (Ithaca: Cornell University Press, 1988), 56.

49. See, for the second century A.D., Peter Brown, *The Body and Society*, 9, with references on the importance of the threefold division.

50. The distinction of sex and gender can itself be criticised from a radical point of view as encouraging a too easy distinction between nature and convention, and an assumption that the body simply belongs to the former. See Carole Pateman, "Sex and Power," *Ethics* 100 (1990), particularly 401–2.

51. There has been a good deal of debate in recent years about the extent and depth of Plato's feminism: for a helpful discussion, see Gregory Vlastos, "Was Plato a Feminist?" *Times Literary Supplement* (March 1989):17–23. For a negative view, see Julia Annas, "Plato's *Republic* and Feminism," *Philosophy* 51 (1976).

52. Complacency in this direction is not necessarily suppressed, and may merely be concealed, by relativism. "Unjust for us" still sounds like an improvement.

53. E. R. Dodds, *The Greeks and the Irrational* (Berkeley: University of California Press, 1951), 32. Editor's note: The author's reference is to *Shame and Necessity*, chap. 6.

2

RADICAL IMPLICATIONS OF LOCKE'S MORAL THEORY: THE VIEWS OF FREDERICK DOUGLASS

Bernard R. Boxill

I

My discussion begins with Locke's claim that "Morality is capable of Demonstration, as well as Mathematics."[1] Locke took this to mean that all true principles of morality can be deduced from a few self-evident propositions. To place "Morality among the sciences capable of Demonstration," he wrote, implied that "from self-evident Propositions, by necessary Consequences, as incontestable as those in Mathematics, the measures of right and wrong might be made out, to any one that will apply himself to the same Indifference and Attention to the one, as he does to the other of these Sciences."[2]

If we assume that the self-evident propositions that form the basis of moral science include some moral propositions, this raises a difficulty, because Locke denied that any moral propositions were self-evident. According to Locke, because "there cannot any one moral Rule be propos'd, whereof a Man may not justly demand a Reason," it is "perfectly ridiculous and absurd" that such a rule can be innate, "or so much as self-evident."[3] I set this difficulty aside on the assumption that Locke was confusing what he called a "mark" of self-evidence with self-evidence itself. Locke noted that "Universal and ready assent, upon hearing and understanding the Terms, is . . . a mark of self-evidence," but that knowledge is self-evident when an agreement or disagreement of ideas "is perceived immediately by itself, without the intervention or help of any other."[4] Supposing that self-evident propositions need not bear this mark of self-evidence, Locke's apparent rejection of self-evident moral rules may have really been a concession that self-evident moral rules fail to bear the mark of self-evidence.

Since a self-evident proposition can fail to bear the mark of self-evidence only if people fail to understand what the terms in it mean, the above commits Locke to the view that there is considerable confusion about the meaning of moral terms. In fact, Locke firmly believed this to be the case, arguing that although the words expressing moral ideas remain the same, the ideas themselves "may change in the same Man; and 'tis very seldom, that they are not different in different Persons."[5] According to Locke, this was because of two peculiarities of moral ideas. The first was that unlike, for example, mathematics, "we have no sensible marks that resemble them, whereby we can set them down" to help fix their meaning. The second, and here again Locke compares morality to mathematics, was that "moral Ideas are commonly more complex than those of the Figures ordinarily considered in Mathematics."[6]

II

Given that there can be self-evident moral rules, the next step is to determine the self-evident moral rules from which morality is to be deduced. In the *Second Treatise* Locke cites one possible self-evident moral rule capable of helping to form the foundation of his moral geometry. According to Locke, there is, "nothing more evident, than that Creatures of the same species and rank promiscuously born to all the same advantages of Nature, and the use of the same faculties, should also be equal one amongst another without Subordination or Subjection."[7] This is obviously a moral claim, or rule. The word "should" leaves no doubt about this. Further, assuming that a proposition is self-evident if there is nothing more evident than it, he seems to be saying that it is a self-evident moral rule that creatures with the same faculties should not subject or subordinate each other.

I emphasize three points. First, the proposition is not a tautology. Locke is not saying that those with the same rights to freedom should not subject or subordinate one another. Locke is saying that creatures with the same faculties, that is, the same natural powers of perception, understanding, reason, will, and so on, have the same rights to freedom and therefore should not subject or subordinate one another.[8] It is especially important for Locke's rule that reason, or the power to understand moral rules, is among the faculties that the creatures all have. Otherwise, the rule would not only fail to be self-evident, it would also fail to be true. Since to be bound by moral rules, one must have reason enough to understand them, creatures that do not have reason cannot be bound by moral rules.

Second, when Locke enunciates his rule, he is not committing a "naturalistic fallacy," or trying to deduce an "ought" from an "is." Although he does affirm a connection between man's natural properties—his faculties—and his rights and duties, the connection is not made by a definition or an inference, but by a moral rule. Third, while Locke says that this rule is self-evident, he does not commit himself to the view that all or most people will assent to it. As we saw, he views a proposition as self-evident if it affirms an agreement or disagreement of ideas that can be perceived to be true without appeal to other ideas even if many people do not perceive it to be true.

The moral rule that creatures with the same faculties (including reason) should not subject or subordinate one another can be interpreted quite broadly. Locke apparently understood it to forbid these creatures from harming each other, where evidently "harming" is also understood quite broadly. "Reason," he says, "teaches all Mankind, who will but consult it, that being all equal and independent, no one ought to harm another in his Life, Health, Liberty, or Possessions."[9] Later, Locke further extends the rule to say that the creatures must preserve each other. According to Locke, "being furnished with like Faculties . . . Every one . . . when his own Preservation comes not in competition, ought he, as much as he can, to preserve the rest of Mankind."[10] In the *First Treatise* the point is put strongly. "Charity," Locke writes, "gives every Man a Title to so much out of another's plenty, as will keep him from extreme want, where he has no means to subsist otherwise."[11]

III

There is a difficulty with Locke's rule. As I said earlier, one of the faculties that he must assume is possessed by all the creatures bound by the rule is sufficient reason to understand and follow the rule. But Locke was skeptical about the rationality of some human beings. He wrote that "it is impossible with any certainty, to affirm, that all Men are rational."[12] And he denied in particular that all men have enough reason to understand and follow the law of nature. According to Locke, some men, "because of a hidden defect of nature, have a keenness of mind too weak to allow them to unearth these hidden secrets of nature," and again that "some men are born defective of mind, as well as sight, who need some guide, who do not know in what direction to move."[13]

There is a further problem. Locke's rule says that creatures of the same "species" should not subject and subordinate each other; but how do we tell when creatures are of the same species? If we can tell only with great difficulty, the rule may not be very helpful. Take the human species. To know what creatures are included in the human species, we must know what human nature is. But Locke is clear that we do not know what human nature is. Answering his own question, "Wherein . . . consists the precise and unmovable Boundaries of that Species [Man]?" Locke wrote, "'Tis plain . . . there is *no* such thing *made by Nature,* and established by Her amongst Men. . . . if several Men were to be asked, concerning some oddly shaped Foetus as soon as born, whether it were a *Man* or no, 'tis past doubt, one should meet with different Answers. . . . And so far are we from certainly knowing what a *Man* is; though, perhaps, it will be judged great Ignorance to make any doubt about it. And yet, I think, I may say, that the certain Boundaries of that Species, are so far from being determined, . . . that very material Doubts may still arise about it."[14]

IV

Some years ago H. M. Bracken charged that Locke's theory supports elitism and racism.[15] He based the charge of racism on Locke's skepticism about human nature noted above, which follows from his skepticism about our knowledge of essences. According to Locke, we do not know the "real essences" of substances, which he defined as "that real constitution of any Thing, which is the foundation of all those Properties, that are constantly found to co-exist."[16] Denied knowledge of the real essences of things, we have to make do with "nominal essences" that are man-made collections of simple ideas often found together.[17] According to Locke, nothing in nature compels us to include or exclude in nominal essences any of the simple ideas we notice together. Thus on his account, "the boundaries of the Species . . . are made by Men."[18]

Not surprisingly from Locke's account it follows that different people do not have the same nominal essences of things. This applies in particular to Man. Locke writes, "He that annexes the name Man, to a complex idea, made up of Sense and spontaneous Motion, join'd to a Body of such a shape, has thereby one Essence of the Species Man: And he that, upon farther examination, adds rationality, has another Essence of the Species he calls Man: By which means, the same individual will be true Man to the one, which is not so to the other."[19]

Bracken argues that because Locke thus "provides a model which permits us to count skin color as a nominally essential property of men," he is "a pivotal figure in the development of modern racism."[20] This is not implausible. According to Locke's model, we construct nominal essences according to our "fancy," and it was certainly to the fancy, to speak nothing of profit, for Europeans, at least, to include skin color in the nominal essence of Man. Further, given his investments in the slave trade, and his explicit endorsement of black slavery in *The Fundamental Constitution of Carolina,* I think that we may reasonably suspect that Locke himself was not opposed to the racist use of his theory.

Let us now consider the charge of elitism. Here Bracken's argument is less plausible. It depends on Locke's rejection of innate ideas. Locke argued that at birth the mind is "white Paper, void of all Characters; without any ideas." Bracken infers that this "blank tablet" model of the mind "carries with it the need for a group which will be charged with 'writing' on the blank tablets," and "has helped justify the creation and growth of an elite class of experts who handle human programming."²¹ This inference is invalid. It is possible that each person should write on his or her own blank tablet. Locke suggests this himself. He maintained that if people employed their faculties they would discover the law of nature without any help from experts. It can be proved, he wrote, that "man, should he make right use of his reason and native faculties with which he is provided by nature, can arrive at a knowledge of this law without a teacher to instruct him; without a tutor to teach him his duty."²²

Locke further suggests that his rejection of innate ideas helps to undermine the pretenses of elitism. According to Locke, the doctrine of innate ideas encourages people to believe that propositions they take for granted are true because they are innate, and this takes "them off from the use of their own Reason and Judgment . . . In which posture of blind Credulity they might be more easily governed by, and made useful to some sort of Men, who had the skill and office to principle and guide them."²³ This is persuasive, at least, insofar as the doctrine of innate ideas implies that we know innate ideas easily, simply by looking into our hearts. By contrast his own view that even "universal Truths" are "discovered by the application of those faculties, that were fitted by Nature to receive and judge of them" encouraged people to think for themselves, and, as Locke himself argues, this is a barrier to elitism.²⁴

Nevertheless, Locke's moral and political theory is elitist. Thus, while he allowed that everyone could know the law of nature, he denied that everyone did, concluding that on this question, "we must consult not the majority of mankind, but the sounder and more perceptive part."²⁵ Presumably on grounds like this, he limited political participation to what he believed were the sounder and more perceptive part of mankind.

How did Locke manage to arrive at these conclusions? To answer this question we must consider some of his broader views of human nature and society.

Locke's egoistic view of human nature suggests that people have a tendency both to ignore and to be ignorant of the law of nature. In the *Second Treatise* Locke writes: "For though the Law of Nature be plain and intelligible to all rational Creatures; yet Men being biassed by their Interest, as well as ignorant for want of study of it, are not apt to allow of it as a Law binding to them in the application of it to their particular Cases."[26] Now since this view is that all people are egoistic, it does not distinguish between people, and consequently does not, by itself, have elitist implications; but Locke combines it with a second view about human nature, and the resulting combination does have elitist implications.

That second view is Locke's well-known doctrine of the malleability of human nature. According to Locke, other than the innate desires for self-preservation and pleasure, all human desires are acquired by association and conditioning. This leads directly to the theory that all virtue and vice are the result of association and conditioning. Now this theory may seem unobjectionable, except perhaps to those who believe in original sin or in the natural goodness of human beings; but on the assumption that the innate desires for pleasure and self-preservation are egoistic, it strongly suggests that virtue is the result either of lucky accident or a system of rewards and punishments carefully devised to develop virtue, and this suggestion has definite elitist implications. For if it is true, probably only a few are likely to acquire virtue; the majority who acquire their habits in a haphazard way will probably acquire vices. And Locke believed that the vices are among the main reasons why people fail to see the law of nature. Thus, in the early *Questions Concerning the Law of Nature*, Locke writes, "I allow that reason is granted to all by nature, and I affirm that there exists a law of nature, knowable by reason. But it does not follow necessarily from this that it is known to each and all, for some make no use of this light, but love the darkness. . . . Some men who are . . . nurtured in vices scarcely distinguish between good and evil, since evil occupations, growing strong with the passage of time, have led them into strange dispositions, and bad habits have corrupted their principles."[27] In the *Essay* he expands on this, speaking generally of knowledge, but also specifically of ethics. There are people, Locke notes, who in the "hot pursuit of pleasure, or constant drudgery in business," do not think of morals. Others through "laziness . . . or a particular aversion for Books" fail to know what they ought. And still others refuse to learn "out of fear that an impartial enquiry would not favour those opinions, which best suit their Prejudices, Lives, and Designs," and so "content themselves without examination, to take upon trust, what they find convenient, and in fashion."[28]

Locke was aware that egoism and the accidents of conditioning were not the only causes of moral ignorance and vice. In particular, he saw that certain social institutions caused widespread moral ignorance; but he could not use this straightaway to justify elitism, for he was clear that some of these institutions were unjust and avoidable or remediable. For example, he noted that in some countries, people are "cooped in close, by the Laws of their Countries, and the strict guards of those, whose Interest it is to keep them ignorant, lest, knowing more, they should believe less in them."[29] But Locke also believed that some of the social institutions that caused widespread moral ignorance were just, or at least unavoidable.

According to Locke, "a great part of Mankind are, by the natural and unalterable State of Things in this World and the Constitution of humane Affairs, unavoidably given over to invincible ignorance of those Proofs, on which others build. . . . The greatest part of Men, having much to do to get the Means of Living, are not in a Condition to look after those of learned and laborious Enquiries."[30] It is true that following this passage, Locke asks, "Are the greatest part of Mankind, by the necessity of their Condition, subjected to unavoidable Ignorance in those Things, which are of the greatest Importance to them?" (by which he means morality) and answers, "No Man is so wholly taken up with the Attendance on the means of Living, as to have no spare Time at all to think of his Soul."[31] But it remains that according to his account, the "natural and unalterable State of Things in this World" denies most people time to discover the truths of morality. This firmly suggests that the majority must look to the enlightened minority for guidance on how to live.

The key to Locke's position here is his theory of property. According to that theory, a relatively small number of people have justly appropriated or acquired the world's wealth, leaving the majority with no property but only with their talents and persons.[32] If this is correct, the majority is—unavoidably, and without injustice— condemned to ceaseless toil and ignorance.

V

These, then, are the charges of racism and elitism against Locke's theory. They have been fiercely denounced, but they have not been answered.[33] I propose to reexamine the issue here. I argue that, in a perfectly straightforward way, Locke's theory does not countenance racism. The question of elitism is more ambiguous. As I suggested, the clearly egalitarian tendencies of Locke's moral epistemology are subverted by his theories of human nature and his theory of property, which together lead him to conclude that society is unavoidably and without injustice so structured that most are condemned to moral ignorance. It is these theories that make him an elitist. Nevertheless, even though he holds different theories of property and human nature, the overall tendency of his thought is egalitarian. I will try to justify this claim by a consideration of the arguments of Frederick Douglass.

Let us first consider the charge of racism. As we have seen, critics complain that Locke's claim that we have no knowledge of real essences makes him a key figure in the development of racism because it allowed for the racist theory that whiteness was an essential quality of human beings. This complaint, however, is unjustified. Locke's theory has the resources for blocking any attempt to exploit it for racist purposes, a conclusion that emerges from a consideration of how Douglass handled the charge that the Negro was not human.

Douglass usually responded to this charge by arguing that the Negro was human. His arguments emphasized that Negroes were rational, corporeal, and vulnerable to various afflictions and dangers, just like white people. Since these qualities were sufficient for inclusion in the moral family, if not in the human family, Douglass's response amounted to the claim that it was irrelevant to Negroes' moral standing whether or not they were human or whether or not they were of the same species as Whites. That this was indeed Douglass's view is particularly clear in his response to the claim that Negroes and Whites had different origins. Although Douglass said he believed that this claim was false, he maintained that it was in any case irrelevant to the Negroes' moral status, given that Negroes and whites have the same "essential characteristics."[34]

Locke's epistemology implies that he would agree with Douglass. Locke is clear that being human is not essential for inclusion in the moral family and that what is essential is rationality and corporeality. According to Locke, "For as to Substances, when concerned in moral Discourses, their divers Natures are not so much enquir'd into as supposed; v.g. when we say that *Man is subject to Law:* We mean nothing by Man, but a corporeal rational Creature: . . . And therefore, whether a Child or a Changeling be a *Man* in a physical Sense, may amongst the Naturalists be disputable as it will, it concerns not at all the *moral* Man, as I call him, which is this immovable unchangeable *Idea, a corporeal rational Being.*"[35] He nails this point down with the following remark: "For were there a Monkey, or any other Creature to be found, that had the use of Reason, to such a degree, as to be able to understand general Signs, and to deduce Consequences about general *Ideas,* he would no doubt be subject to Law, and, in that Sense, be a *Man,* how much soever he differ'd in Shape from others of that Name."[36]

Now let us consider the charge of elitism. Douglass shared many of Locke's views on morality and moral epistemology. This is not surprising. Douglass was a keen student of the American system of government, and Locke decisively influenced the Founding Fathers who designed the American system of government. For example, the resemblance has often been noted between the passage from section four of the *Second Treatise* already quoted, and the sentence in the *Declaration of Independence,* "We hold these truths to be self-evident, that all men are created equal, that they are endowed by their Creator with certain unalienable rights, that among these are Life, Liberty, and the pursuit of Happiness." Douglass fastened especially on the self-evidence of the right to liberty. He explicitly declared that this right was "self-evident," and that "No argument, no researches into mouldy records, no learned disquisitions, are necessary to establish it."[37] We should distinguish two claims in this sentence: first, the moral claim that all people have rights to liberty, and more generally, natural or human rights; second, the epistemological claim that it is self-evident that people have these rights.

Let us begin with the second claim. Douglass not only agreed with Locke on the self-evidence of human rights, he also followed Locke in allowing that the self-evidence of these rights does not mean that everyone acknowledges them. Indeed, he tended to cite the same reasons for the widespread ignorance of morality as Locke did, though he used different examples to illustrate them. Thus, while he agreed with Locke that selfishness was one of the main reasons people fail to see the law of nature, he illustrated this with the example of the slavemasters: Although the law of nature is "easily rendered appreciable to the faculty of reason in man," he wrote, selfishness moves the slaveholder to deny that the slave has these rights.[38] Similarly, where Locke argued that many governments kept citizens ignorant so as to rule them more easily, Douglass argued that the slavemaster kept slaves ignorant for the same reason. As he recounts, his master forbade him to read on the ground that "Learning will spoil the best nigger in the world."[39] And where Locke noted that in ordinary society, toil and hunger, business and social advancement all tend to distract men and women from knowledge of the moral law, Douglass pointed out that in slavery, the whip had the same result. As he put it, "Beat and cuff your slave, keep him hungry and spiritless, and he will follow the chain of his master like a dog; but feed and clothe him well,—work him moderately—surround him with physical comfort,—and dreams of freedom intrude. Give him a bad master, and he aspires to a good master; give him a good master, and he wishes to become his own master. Such is human nature. You may hurl a man so low, beneath the level of his kind, that he loses all just ideas of his natural position; but elevate him a little, and the clear conception of rights rises to life and power, and leads him onward."[40]

Although Douglass thus agreed with Locke that moral ignorance was widespread, he did not follow him in drawing elitist conclusions from this. As we saw, Locke suggested that the vote should be restricted to the sounder and more perceptive part of humanity. Douglass, on the other hand, insisted on the vote for every adult, including newly freed slaves and women. How can we explain the difference? Part of the answer lies in the first of the two claims that Douglass fastened on from the *Declaration of Independence*, namely, the moral claim that all people have human rights. Though this claim repeats Locke's view that people have human rights, it does not follow that Douglass agreed with Locke on what these rights were. As I suggested, Locke arrived at elitist conclusions because he conceived of the right to property in such a way as to justify the conclusion that the majority was unavoidably and without injustice condemned to toil and ignorance. Accordingly, if Douglass rejected Locke's account of the right to property, the egalitarian tendencies inherent in the moral epistemology he shared with Locke, in particular the view that human rights are self-evident, would lead him to reject the latter's elitist conclusions.

I will not develop this line here, but rather examine a reason that is less obvious and more interesting. It is almost certainly one reason why Douglass did not follow Locke into elitism. This concerns their differing views on human nature. The most important of those differences concerned the malleability of human nature, and in particular the desire for liberty. I assume that Locke and Douglass meant the same thing by the word "liberty," in Locke's words, "not to be subject to the inconstant, uncertain, unknown, arbitrary will of another Man."[41] However, where Locke's views implied that slaves could be and probably were conditioned not to desire liberty, Douglass thought that this desire dominated the life and imagination of the slave. This difference goes a long way toward explaining why Locke was an elitist, and Douglass was an egalitarian.

Let us first consider Locke's position. Locke often suggested that the desire for liberty is innate.[42] Further, even if the desire is not innate, his theory of human malleability implied that in normal circumstances most people would acquire a desire for liberty. Locke maintained that "The first and strongest desire God Planted in Men, and wrought into the very Principles of their Nature (was) . . . that of Self-preservation" and that "Nature . . . has put into Man a desire of Happiness and an aversion to Misery."[43] He also believed that self-preservation and happiness are insecure if one is not at liberty.[44] Given that it is rational to desire the best means to secure one's strongest and deepest desires, these views imply that Locke would have agreed that it was rational for human beings to desire liberty. Finally, assuming that in normal circumstances rational desires tend to be reinforced, it follows that Locke would also have agreed that people in normal circumstances either acquire a desire for liberty or have their innate desire for liberty reinforced. However—and this is the crucial point—Locke's theory of human malleability implies that in abnormal or contrived circumstances, the desire for liberty may not be reinforced, and people may lose this desire if it is innate or never acquire it in the first place. Indeed, the theory implies that in appropriate circumstances, people may be conditioned to acquire a desire for servitude. Locke did not comment on this, but Rousseau did. According to Rousseau, "Slaves lose everything in their chains, even the desire to be rid of them. They love their servitude."[45] And many, including some blacks, thought this was true of black slaves in America. As the Black Nationalist Martin Delany lamented, "A continuance in any position . . . begets an adaptation and reconciliation of the mind to such position" and may lead the slave to "become a lover of his master, and learn to forgive him for continual deeds of maltreatment and abuse."[46]

Douglass's experience suggested that Locke's theory of human malleability was mistaken. According to Douglass, every effort was made to condition the slaves not to desire liberty. The standard strategy was to punish them severely for any attempt to escape, the object being to make them associate freedom with pain. Another was to give them freedom temporarily and then encourage them to indulge in those "wild and low sports, peculiar to semi-civilized people"—typically drunkenness—to make them disgusted with freedom.[47] Yet contrary to what the malleability theory would have led one to conclude, Douglass insisted that the slaves continued to desire liberty.

He reached this conclusion for two reasons. The first was his view, based on his own experience and on extensive observation, that slavery was necessarily cruel. Douglass was aware of dissenting voices; some people, he knew, opined that slavery did not have to be cruel. Refuting their conjectures with the bloody facts of the institution, Douglass argued that its invariable cruelty pointed to the slaves' inextinguishable desire to be free. Slavery had to be cruel, Douglass contended, because only in this way could the slave be distracted from thoughts of liberty. He was relying here on a distinction between being distracted from the desire for liberty, and being conditioned out of the desire for liberty. Douglass admitted that the slave can be distracted from his desire for liberty. As he put it, "When I was looking for the blow about to be inflicted on my head, I was not thinking of my liberty; it was my life."[48] But he denied that the slave could be *conditioned* out of his desire for liberty. If the slave were conditioned out of his desire for liberty, presumably he would not desire liberty even when he was not desperately hungry, afraid for his life, or thinking of the blow about to fall. But according to Douglass, as soon as the slave was not distracted in these ways, he began yearning for liberty.[49]

The second reason Douglass believed that the slaves desired liberty lay in his conviction that the slaves were *always* unhappy. He was aware that some people believed that many slaves were happy and that unhappy slaves were the result of abuses of the institution. But he argued that those who believed this had been misled. A keener eye would see that slaves were always unhappy no matter how comfortable their surroundings. This suggested to him that the slaves longed for liberty.

Douglass's postulation of a universal and practically ineradicable desire for liberty suggests that he saw the case for the right to liberty differently from Locke. According to Locke, if we have the same faculties we ought not to subject or subordinate one another. This seems to be a generalization argument: Each person makes a claim against others and is logically required to recognize the like claims others make against him. In the present argument, the claim is presumably that others should not take away his liberty.[50] On Locke's view, this claim is based on the fact that liberty is an essential condition for self-preservation, the desire for which is the strongest nature has planted in us. Assuming that this is sound, the generalization argument says that each person is logically required to recognize the claim of others against him that he not take away their liberty. My suggestion is that if Douglass is right that people always actually desire liberty, a generalization argument for a right to liberty could be based on that desire, not, as in Locke's argument, on the fact that it is a condition for self-preservation.

If my interpretation is correct it helps to explain one of Douglass's most striking and characteristic arguments. I have argued that, on his account, the right to liberty is based on a desire for liberty. This suggests a more particular reason why some people may fail to see the self-evident fact that all people have natural rights to liberty. Suppose that some people *display* no desire for liberty. Although it would not follow that these people do not desire liberty, and therefore have no right to liberty, their failure to display a desire for liberty could lead an observer to these conclusions. Douglass had this possibility very much in mind. He wrote, "the very submission of the slave to his chains is held as an evidence of his fitness to be a

RADICAL IMPLICATIONS OF LOCKE'S MORAL THEORY

slave; it is regarded as one of the strongest proofs of the divinity of slavery, that the negro tamely submits to his fetters. His very non-resistance . . . is quoted as proof of his cowardice, and his unwillingness to suffer and to sacrifice for his liberty."[51]

Further, if slaves who submit to slavery tempt their masters to believe that they do not desire, and have no right to liberty, they are themselves also tempted to believe the same thing. Introspection may not enable a person to know what his desires are. His behavior can lead him to doubt whether he has certain desires or how strong these desires are. This is especially the case in the desire for liberty. As Douglass claimed, submitting to slavery in order to save one's life is justifiable. But he also suggested that to have a right to freedom, a person must desire it enough to "suffer and sacrifice," and even "peril" his life for it. Consider, then, the predicament of a slave who submits to slavery in order to save his life. Is the likelihood of death great enough to justify his submission? Or are the chances of escape and freedom great enough to justify periling his life for his freedom? These are obviously difficult things for him to know.

But if the slave who submits gives others an excuse for believing that he does not desire liberty, and consequently has no right to it, the slave who rebels explodes that excuse. Similarly, if the slave who submits comes to doubt that he desires and has a right to liberty, the slave who rebels and perils his life for his freedom explodes that doubt. Douglass encouraged slave rebellions for precisely these reasons. "Every slavehunter who meets a bloody death in his infernal business," he wrote, "is an argument in favor of the manhood of our race."[52]

If Douglass was correct, slave rebellion was to be encouraged not simply because it could help the slaves regain their freedom, but also because it was morally regenerative, helping both the slaves and their masters to see the self-evident moral truth about themselves. This has radically egalitarian implications. It does not present moral reform as coming from above, from the educated and comfortable classes, but on the contrary, as coming from below, from what was supposedly the least educated, most benighted segment of society.

Douglass's theory does not propose to defend slavery against its most serious criticism—that it morally corrupts the slave. We must distinguish malleability from corruptibility. Douglass denied that slavery moulded slaves until they were fit for slavery. But he did not deny that it corrupted them. His point was that though they were indeed morally corrupted by slavery, they still possessed within themselves a sort of fail-safe mechanism that could lead to their moral rebirth and that slavery itself would trigger that mechanism. The most important part of this mechanism was their inextinguishable desire for freedom. Although suppressed and forgotten, it was the hidden cause of slave rebellions, which although driven by the most primitive and amoral desires, could lead slaves to a realization of their moral equality. Let us consider Douglass's argument, which is based on his own experience.

Douglass had been sent to a Mr. Covey for "breaking." Through overwork and beatings, Covey, on Douglass's own admission, had "succeeded in breaking" him. He was, again on his own admission, "transformed to a brute!"[53] What did he mean by that? If our earlier discussion was right, he could not have meant that he had actually lost his desire for liberty. Rather, he must have meant that while looking for the blow to fall, he never thought about liberty or actively desired it. But Douglass says he was transformed back to a man because of a "battle" with Covey. What caused him to fight back? Douglass says he did so when "I had reached the point at which I was not afraid to die."[54] I do not think Douglass meant that he had reached a point at which he said, with Patrick Henry, "Give me liberty, or give me death." A person who says this knows he desires liberty. He has not been transformed to a brute. But Douglass allowed that he had been transformed to a brute; though he still desired liberty, he was distracted from thoughts of it and did not know that he desired it. I think Douglass meant simply that he had reached the point when he preferred to die rather than continue suffering pain. Let me try to describe the process.

Douglass allowed the existence of at least three innate desires: the desire for liberty; the desire to secure pleasure and avoid pain; and the desire to avoid death. As noted, he described how the slavemaster used the slaves' desire to avoid pain and death in order to distract them from the desire for liberty. Through overwork, starvation, punishment, and the threat of death, the slave could be distracted from thoughts of liberty. But the slave also desired to avoid pain, and to avoid the pain necessary to distract him from thoughts of liberty, he could be driven to risk his death. When this happened, he would attack the cause of his pain, that is, he would rebel.[55]

In this process the slave's desire to avoid pain is the immediate cause of his rebellion. But it is not the ultimate cause. The ultimate, though hidden, cause of the slave's rebellion is his desire for liberty. If the slave did not desire liberty, the master would not have to distract him from thoughts of it and consequently would not have to inflict great pain on him. But if the master did not inflict great pain on the slave, the slave would not be driven to risk his life, and consequently would not rebel.

If this argument is sound, then, though the desire for liberty is the ultimate cause of the slave's rebellion, it is not the reason he rebels. He rebels to avoid pain. How then can his rebellion help him to rediscover his desire for liberty? Why, in Douglass's words, had his fight with Covey "rekindled in my breast the smouldering embers of liberty"?[56]

One explanation is that Douglass won the fight. This may seem supported by Douglass's claim, "A man without force is without the essential dignity of humanity. Human nature is so constituted, that it cannot honor a helpless man, though it can pity him, and even this it cannot do long if signs of power do not arise."[57] On this account, Douglass's fight with Covey had the consequences he said it had because it showed him that he had the power to defend himself. But this is not a satisfactory explanation. The power to win fights cannot be essential to dignity, though I suspect it helps to sustain something that is. A person without the power to win fights and defend himself may find it difficult to hang on to whatever is essential to dignity, but it cannot be itself what is essential to dignity. Otherwise, we must conclude that the weak and infirm literally cannot have dignity, which seems false.

A more plausible explanation rests on the fact that the fight brought an end to his whippings. Douglass tells us that after the fight he "was never fairly whipped" again; it was, he said, "the end of the brutification to which slavery had subjected me."[58] Given that brutification, or the constant fear of whipping, distracted him from thoughts of liberty, the fight with Covey may have transformed Douglass back to a man because by bringing an end to his whippings, it allowed him to dwell again on liberty. I think that this was in fact Douglass's argument. As he put it, "When a slave cannot be flogged, he is more than half free."[59] Part of his meaning may have been that a slave who is not flogged will not be distracted from thoughts of freedom, and, by dreaming of freedom, will be more likely to seize every opportunity to gain it and therefore more likely to do so. But I think that he also meant the deeper point that a slave who dreams of freedom, and knows therefore that he desires it, will see the self-evident moral fact that he has a right to freedom and is the moral equal of others.

This argument does not make slavery less of the outrage than it is. When Douglass spoke of a slave who could not be flogged, he did not mean it literally. Rather, he was speaking of slaves who could not be flogged in the sense that, if the master tried to whip them, he would have to kill them. Slaves who were known to be of this sort often escaped floggings if the master preferred to keep them alive for his work. But if the master thought the slave expendable, his rebellion would gain him only the escape of death.

Notes

1. John Locke, *An Essay Concerning Human Understanding*, ed. Peter H. Nidditch (Oxford: Clarendon Press, 1975), book 3, chap. 11, sec. 16, p. 516. I will refer to this work as *An Essay*. Numbers following *An Essay* will refer to book, chapter, section, and pages.

2. *An Essay*, 4, 3, 18: 549. See also, 4, 12, 8: 643.

3. *An Essay*, 1, 3, 4: 68.

4. *An Essay*, 1, 2, 18: 58 and 4, 7, 2: 591.

5. *An Essay*, 4, 3, 19: 550.

6. *An Essay*, 4, 3, 19: 550.

7. John Locke, *Two Treatises of Government*, ed. Peter Laslett (Cambridge: Cambridge University Press, 1988) book 2, chap. 2, sec. 4, p. 269. I will refer to this work as *Two Treatises*. Numbers following *Two Treatises* will refer to book, chapter, section, and pages.

8. See *An Essay*, 2, 11, 14: 161, and 2, 21, 17: 242.

9. *Two Treatises*, 2, 2, 6: 271.

10. *Two Treatises*, 2, 2, 6: 271.

11. *Two Treatises*, 1, 4, 42: 170.

12. *An Essay* IV, VI, 4: 580.

13. John Locke, *Questions Concerning the Law of Nature*, ed. Robert Horwitz, Jenny Strauss Clay, and Diskin Clay (Ithaca: Cornell University Press, 1990), pp. 111 and 217. Henceforth referred to as *Questions*.

14. *An Essay,* 3, 6, 27: 454–55.

15. See, for example, H. M. Bracken, "Essence, Accident and Race," *Hermathena* 116 (Winter 1973): 81–96; and, "Philosophy and Racism," *Philosophia* (Israel) 8, (November 1978): 241–60. See also Winthrop D. Jordan, *White Over Black* (Baltimore: Penguin Books, 1968), 235.

16. *An Essay,* 3, 6, 9: 444 and 3, 6, 6: 442.

17. *An Essay,* 2, 6, 26: 453.

18. *An Essay,* 3, 6, 37: 462. Further, the choice of what is included "depends upon the various Care, Industry, or Fancy of him that makes it." *An Essay,* 3, 6, 29: 456.

19. *An Essay,* 3, 6, 26: 453.

20. "Philosophy and Racism," 243.

21. *An Essay,* 2, 1, 2: 104; "Philosophy and Racism," 251.

22. *Questions,* 124, 125.

23. *An Essay,* 1, 4, 24: 102.

24. *An Essay,* 1, 4, 24: 102.

25. John Locke, *Questions Concerning the Law of Nature,* 111. See also p. 137 where he claims that those who "make proper use" of the "light of nature" to discover the law of nature are "very few in number."

26. *Two Treatises,* 2, 9, 124: 351. See also, 2, 2, 6: 271. I admit that the above is not unambiguous. Locke does not quite say that all men are rational and see the *Law of Nature.* Yet this surely seems implied.

27. *Questions,* 109. See also pages 125, 135, 165.

28. *An Essay,* 4, 20, 6: 710.

29. *An Essay,* 4, 20, 4: 708, 709.

30. *An Essay,* 4, 20, 2: 207.

31. *An Essay,* 4, 20, 3: 707, 708.

32. *Two Treatises,* 2, 2, 5.

33. See Geoffrey Sampson, *Liberty and Language* (Oxford: Oxford University Press, 1979); John Searle, "The Rules of the Language Game," *Times Literary Supplement,* 10 September 1976; and Kathy Squadrito, "Locke's View of Essence and Its Relation to Racism: A Reply to Professor Bracken," *The Locke Newsletter.*

34. Frederick Douglass, "The Claims of the Negro Ethnologically Considered," in *The Life and Writings of Frederick Douglass,* vol. 2, ed. Philip S. Foner (New York: International Publishers, 1975), 307.

35. *An Essay,* 3, 11, 16: 516, 517.

36. *An Essay,* 3, 11, 16: 516.

37. Frederick Douglass, "Lecture on Slavery," ed. Foner, *Life and Writings,* vol. 2, 141.

38. "The Anti-Slavery Movement," ed. Foner, *Life and Writings,* vol. 2, 355.

39. Frederick Douglass, *The Life and Times of Frederick Douglass* (New York, Collier, 1962), 79.

40. Frederick Douglass, *My Bondage and My Freedom* (New York: Dover Publications, 1969), 263–64.

41. *Two Treatises*, 2, 4, 22: 324.

42. See, for example, John Locke, *Some Thoughts Concerning Education*, ed. John W. Youlton and Jean S. Youlton (Oxford: Oxford University Press, 1989), secs. 35, 41, and 103.

43. *Two Treatises*, 1, 9, 88: 206, and *An Essay* 1, 3, 3: 67.

44. *Two Treatises*, 2, 3, 17: 279.

45. Jean Jacques Rousseau, *On the Social Contract*, ed. Roger D. Masters and trans., Judith R. Masters (New York: St. Martin's, 1978), book 1, chapter 11: 48.

46. Martin R. Delany, "The Condition, Elevation and Emigration of the Colored People of the United States," in Howard Brotz, ed., *Negro Social and Political Thought: 1850–1920* (New York: Basic Books, 1966), 96.

47. My Bondage and My Freedom, 255–56.

48. *Life and Writings*, vol. 1, 157.

49. See note 40. A comparison with Hobbes may help here. Hobbes allows that our desire to aggress on others may be suppressed from fear of death. But he denies that we can ever be conditioned out of our desire to aggress on others.

50. *Two Treatises*, 2, 3, 17: 279.

51. "Speech on John Brown," ed. Foner, *Life and Writings*, vol. 2, 534. See also "Is it Wise and Right to Kill a Kidnapper?" in Foner, 287. Douglass says there, "submission . . . becomes an argument in the mouths of the community, that Negroes are, by nature, only fit for slavery; that slavery is their normal condition . . . their unwillingness to peril their own lives, by shooting down their pursuers, is already quoted against them, as marking them out as an inferior race." Of course, though Douglass allowed that the slavemaster may have believed that the slave did not desire liberty, he did not allow that this belief could be honest. It could not be honest because the slavemaster himself, by his punishments and threats, brought it about that the slave displayed little desire for freedom. And from Locke himself we can make sense of the idea of dishonest belief. As Locke observed, "some out of fear that an impartial enquiry would not favour those opinions which best suit their Prejudices, Lives, and Designs, content themselves without examination, to take upon trust, what they find convenient, and in fashion." *An Essay*, 4, 20, 6: 710.

52. "Is it Right and Wise to Kill a Kidnapper?" ed. Foner, *Life and Writings*, vol. 2, 287.

53. Douglass, *Life and Times*, 124.

54. *Life and Times*, 143.

55. *Life and Times*, 143.

56. *Life and Times*, 143.

57. *Life and Times*, 143.

58. *Life and Times*, 143.

59. *Life and Times*, 143.

3

"... THE SAME TYRANNICAL PRINCIPLE": LOCKE'S LEGACY ON SLAVERY

William Uzgalis

No matter in what shape it comes, whether from the mouth of a king who seeks to bestride the people of his own nation and live by the fruit of their labor, or from one race of men as an apology for enslaving another race, it is the same tyrannical principle.

—Abraham Lincoln

Abraham Lincoln clearly believed that the same argument that condemned absolute monarchy, condemned also the practices and institutions of African American slavery, for they represented ". . . the same tyrannical principle." There were pragmatic political reasons for Lincoln to link slavery with the unpopular doctrine of absolute monarchy. Yet Lincoln also claimed to have found in the Declaration of Independence, which he regarded as the founding document of the United States, a condemnation not only of absolute monarchy but of slavery as well. I believe we can trace the origins of this dual condemnation of royal tyrants and slave masters even farther back, to John Locke's *Second Treatise of Civil Government*.

In chapter 4 of the *Second Treatise of Civil Government*, Locke sets forth a theory of slavery. There has been an extraordinary degree of controversy over the purpose for which this theory was crafted. M. Seliger, for example, believes that Locke is seeking to justify African American slavery. He writes that ". . . in accordance with the opinions and practices of his time, the justification of slavery makes sense only in connexion with colonial conquest."[1] Such a view seems to be reinforced by Locke's extensive involvement through Lord Shaftesbury with trade, colonial affairs, the slave trade, and African American slavery. Richard Farr, in contrast, holds that the theory of slavery was not intended to deal with African American slavery at all. Rather, it was part of Locke's attack on absolute monarchy during the Exclusion controversy and that in this battle "the shores of Africa and America were out of sight and out of mind."[2] Farr persuasively shows that Locke's theory of slavery cannot be used to justify or legitimize African American slavery. The incompatibility of the theory of slavery in the *Second Treatise* with the practice of African American slavery, however, raises some new questions.

There seems to be a contradiction between Locke's conduct as a colonial administrator and his theory in the *Second Treatise*. Farr, for example, while arguing that Locke's theory of slavery in the *Second Treatise* condemns the practices and institutions of seventeenth-century slavery, holds that Locke was "most certainly guilty of avoiding the moral issues raised by the enslavement of black Africans. He averted his eyes from the glaring contradictions between his theories and Afro-American slavery." Farr goes on to endorse John Dunn's remark that "what we confront here is not an example of bland but deliberate moral rationalization on Locke's part but one of immoral evasion."[3] The picture Farr paints is of a philosopher with a general moral theory who neither says nor does anything about a particularly glaring violation of that theory in which he himself is to some degree involved. In the face of this violation Locke remained, in Farr's words, "inert, frozen, speechless."[4] What then are we to say about the *Second Treatise* and Locke's conduct?

The thesis of this paper is that we may regard the machinery of the *Second Treatise of Civil Government* as an implicit rejection of the practices and institutions of African American slavery as well as the royal absolutism of the Stuarts. Locke's intention to show the illegitimacy of royal absolutism is largely uncontroversial, though its application to his account of slavery may be somewhat more so. Hence, the chief focus of this paper is on the claim that Locke is implicitly condemning African American slavery. The argument for this conclusion is fairly simple. First, if Locke's theory of slavery in the *Second Treatise* is applied to the practices and institutions of African American slavery it condemns these practices as completely illegitimate. Second, Locke was in a position to know perfectly well that his theory would yield these results in respect to these practices and institutions. These two considerations alone produce a *prima facie* case that the theory of the *Second Treatise* is an implicit rejection of the practices and institutions of African American slavery.[5] The remaining points are aimed at staving off efforts to qualify one or the other of these first two points so as to weaken the force of the *prima facie* case or, indeed, reverse its import. The standard way of avoiding this conclusion, by claiming that Locke was a racist in the sense that he holds some theory about the inferiority of other races, can be persuasively refuted from Locke's philosophical works. Further, while the theory of slavery was primarily crafted to combat the doctrines of absolute monarchy, the theory of slavery and the doctrine of natural rights were intended as general theories that could thus be applied to both Africa and America as well as England. When we put these points together, we are left with the strong impression that while Locke's theory of slavery makes no explicit mention of the practices and institutions of African American slavery, it is an implicit rejection of those practices and institutions. Finally, I consider what is to be said about Locke's conduct and the use to which the legacy of the *Second Treatise* was put in the eighteenth century and beyond.

Locke's theory is incompatible with African American slavery.

The basic reason Locke's theory of slavery in the *Second Treatise* is incompatible with the practices and institutions of seventeenth-century slavery is that it is a minimalist theory of slavery. Such a theory allows very few people to be enslaved by sharply restricting the conditions under which legitimate slavery may occur. Any theory designed to justify the practices and institutions of seventeenth-century slavery would have to be much less restrictive than Locke's theory.

We may begin by noting the connection between Locke's theory of slavery and his doctrine of just wars. In a just war, one resists the attempts of an aggressor to violate one's natural rights to life, liberty, health, and property. An aggressor in such a war who wins, wins an unjust war. Any people he may take captive and enslave are unjustly and illegitimately enslaved. Only if those who are defending themselves against such aggression win the war and capture the aggressor do they have the right to legitimately enslave the aggressor. The aggressor, by violating the natural rights of human beings, has reduced himself from a man to the level of a beast. Thus, the aggressor has forfeited his rights as a human being. These are the polecats and tigers of Locke's state of nature. The emphasis on just wars as the sole basis for legitimate slavery is absolutely crucial to Locke's theory. If one were to change the theory so that it is simply prisoners taken in war, whether just or unjust, who may be enslaved, this change would entail disastrous consequences for the central and crucial rejection of the doctrine that might makes right in the *Second Treatise*.[6] Locke seeks to show that government which "is the product of force and violence," and in which "men live together by no other rules but that of beasts, where the strongest carries it . . . is the foundation for perpetual disorder and mischief, tumult, sedition and rebellion" (2T, 4).[7] But rulers are often those who are strongest, and Locke's view was clearly that an absolute sovereign might well hold power *as if* he were lord and his subjects his slaves. The chief role of Locke's minimalist theory of slavery in the *Second Treatise* was to turn this relation around so that it would never be legitimate for the sovereign violating the rights of his people to be master and the people slaves; while a people whose rights had been systematically violated by a sovereign (thus creating sedition, tumult, and rebellion) could legitimately kill or enslave that sovereign. This reversal, which makes the king of England and his ministers subject to legitimate enslavement, is surely one of the prettiest ironies in the literature of political philosophy. The connection between aggression against natural rights and legitimate slavery by itself is arguably enough to render most of the forcible seizures of people and their sale into slavery in the period of the slave trade illegitimate on Locke's account. There is no basis in the theory of the *Second Treatise* to justify the claim that the seizure of Africans either directly by

Europeans or by Africans at the instigation of Europeans amounted to just wars.[8]

While the crucial and fundamental point about Locke's theory of slavery that renders it incompatible with African American slavery is its connections with just wars and his doctrines of natural rights, there are more restrictions that make it even less plausible to consider that Locke's theory of slavery could be used to justify African American slavery. First, the lawful conqueror has slave rights only over those who "actually assisted, concurred, or consented to that unjust force" (2T, 179). Principally this means combatants and government officials. "All the rest are innocent"—noncombatants, wives, and children. Women and children were among those who were transported on the slave ships in large numbers. The largest implication of the claim that the conqueror has slave rights only over those who actually used or consented in the use of unjust force is that a whole population cannot be enslaved, for: "the people have given to their government no Power to do so unjust a thing, such as to make an unjust war (for they never had such a Power in themselves)" (2T, 129).

In truth, on Locke's theory, the only way in which one can legitimately become a slave is by engaging in unjust aggression, thus violating the natural rights to life, liberty, health, and property of others, losing this unjust war, and agreeing to serve the just victor rather than be put to death. Locke did not regard liberty as a property. One cannot, therefore, legitimately sell oneself into slavery. Locke's theory was more constrained than, say, those of Molina or Suarez on both the point about the enslavement of whole peoples and about selling oneself into slavery.[9]

Third, slavery cannot extend to future generations. Children born of slaves cannot themselves be retained as slaves, for slavery "reaches no further than the Persons" of those who acted unjustly, and thus it "dies with them" (2T, 189). Slaves' children have committed no injstice, no act deserving of death. So hereditary slavery, or the institution of slavery is positively unjust.

There are further constraints regarding the property of slaves. The lawful conqueror has no right to the possessions of the conquered people, except insofar as to "make reparation for damages received . . . and the charges of war" (2T, 180, 182). Depending on the economic plenty or penury of the enslaved people, Locke even states that no seizure of possessions is just if wives and children have more "presssing and preferable Title" (2T, 183). The seizure of land itself is explicitly excluded by this constraint, for land is by right the inheritable property of future innocent generations, especially "in any part of the world, where all the land is possessed, and none lies waste" (2T, 184). This is an important constraint to keep in mind when considering the arguments of those who hold that Locke endorses colonial conquest and the seizure of Indian lands.

Given all these constraints on Locke's theory of slavery, it clearly will not justify or legitimize the practices and institutions of seven-teenth-century slave trading and slave holding.[10] In fact, the pretty irony noted above, the reversal of who may be legitimately enslaved, can be applied to the situation of African American slaves. Thus those innocent people who were captured, sold, transported, and worked on plantations and in other capacities, and whose children were held as slaves, could have appealed to violations of the Lockean constraints on legitimate slavery noted above to justify resistance, rebellion, and, indeed, the death or enslavement of their tyrannical masters, be these black African slave traders, officers or sailors on slave ships, or plantation owners or their minions.

Locke knew his theory would not justify Afro-American slavery.

Once one accepts the point that Locke's theory of slavery implicitly condemns the practices and institutions of seventeenth-century Afri-can American slavery, then most of the points made about Locke's life that show how at various points before the writing of the *Second Treatise,* Locke was involved with and knowledgeable about the slave trade and the prctices and institutions of the Afro-American slave trade appear in a new perspective. I will recall only some of these points about Locke's life, particularly those relevant to the thesis of this paper. Locke was a collector of traveller's tales and had a great interest in the accounts of explorers and adventurers. He collected such travel books and was interested in the customs of peoples throughout the world. These travellers' tales amounted to the an-thropology of the time. Besides this sort of learning, however, Locke was an active participant in the affairs of the American colonies and in British trade, including the slave trade. Farr notes that in "the service of Anthony Ashley Cooper, later the first Earl of Shaftesbury, one of Locke's principal duties was the overseeing of colonial matters."[11] In 1668 Locke was appointed secretary to the Lords Proprietors of Carolina, of whom Lord Ashley was a founding member. Locke played a part in the writing of the *Fundamental Constitution of the Carolinas* in 1669.[12] This document declares that "every freedman of Carolina shall have absolute power and authority over his negro slaves." Locke, along with his patron Shaftesbury and many others, bought shares in the original subscription for the Royal Africa Company in 1671, which he later sold at a profit in 1675. The Royal Africa Company was the company which carried on the British slave trade.[13] In 1672 Ashley, now the first Earl of Shaftesbury, convinced Charles II to found a Council of Trade and Foreign Plantations. Shaftesbury was its president, and in the next year Locke became its secretary. "Characteristically, Locke performed his tasks meticulously, fully informed himself about colonial trade and plantation life."[14] As Shaftesbury's secretary, Locke oversaw Ashley's voluminous papers and correspondences on colonial matters. As Farr also points out, Locke "also kept his own correspondence with many in the New World, especially with his friend, Sir Peter Colleton, slave owner in Barbados."

In this correspondence Locke drew up a bibliography of "writers of Carolina" for Colleton's inspection. For his part, Colleton supplied Locke with information about all manner of things. For Locke's medical curiosities, Colleton informed him of herbal cures for yaws and gonorrhea in slaves. For Locke and Ashley's financial interest, Colleton advised investing in fishing, planting, and timber.[15]

After Shaftesbury's flight and death in 1683, Locke himself was forced to flee to Holland. Among his friends on the continent were Furley and Le Clerc, who were both early abolitionists. He remained on the continent until 1688, when he returned to England with the flight of James II and the ascension of William and Mary to the throne. In 1689 and 1690 the *Essay Concerning Human Understanding,* the *Two Treatises of Civil Government* and the *Letters Concerning Tolera-*

tion were all published. Locke did not acknowledge his authorship of the *Two Treatises* and the *Letters* until his death.

Locke again became a member of a new Board of Trade instituted by King William in 1696. He resigned in 1700 with the fall of Lord Sommers. In the meantime, however, Locke shaped policy in various areas and he was once again concerned in detail with the practices and institutions of the seventeenth-century slave trade and African American and Indian slavery. As Farr notes, in considering all these facts and others, ". . . when Locke died in 1704, precious few Englishmen could have boasted of equalling his intimate knowledge of colonial life, foreign peoples, or slavery and the slave trade."[16]

All of this information about Locke's life and his involvement with colonial administration and the slave trade has been used to bolster the claim that Locke's theory in the *Second Treatise* is aimed to support the practices and institutions of African American slavery. Once one accepts the fact that the theory is not compatible with such practices and institutions, one can draw another conclusion. The conclusion is that Locke *knew* that his theory was incompatible with the practices and institutions of African American slavery. This, in turn, leads to the conclusion that the theory is an implicit rejection of the practices and institutions of African American slavery. There are a variety of ways in which one might seek to avoid accepting this conclusion.

Locke was not a racist.

There are many explicit claims in the *Second Treatise* that make it plain that in discussing the state of nature Locke is talking about *all* men and about *mankind*. This being so, it would appear that blacks, Indians, or other peoples of color would have the same natural rights as anyone else, and the machinery that Locke uses to oppose absolute sovereignty would be of use to them in arguing that enslavement of those who have violated no one's rights is illegitimate. Those who maintain that Locke is justifying African American slavery in the *Second Treatise* must find some basis for claiming that Locke, at least implicitly, would deny the claim that blacks or other peoples of color had the same natural rights as white men. Such writers must hold that Locke was a racist in one form or another.

Farr makes a distinction between strong and weak racism. Weak racism is bigotry or racial prejudice. Strong racism is underwritten by theory and claims that blacks or other peoples of color deserve to be slaves because of their racial inferiority: ". . . racism in this stronger more theoretical sense entails both an *empirical* theory that explains black racial inferiority and a *moral* theory which justifies enslavement because of racial inferiority."[17] I shall consider each of these forms of racism in turn. In regard to weak racism, Farr notes that:

> We simply have *no* evidence about what Locke thought on this score. Neither his political works, nor his theological writings, nor his medical notes, nor his marginalia on travelogues supply any hints whatsoever. Locke surely never stopped to the embarrassing caricatures of black people, that for example David Hume later concocted. It is interesting that Locke had generous or nondisparaging things to say about other peoples of color, especially American Indians. He was intrigued by their customs and medical practices, fascinated by their sexual mores, convinced of their "native rustic reason," and praising of their form of government because they were founded on "consent and persuasion, [rather] than compulsion."[18]

Farr goes on to make the point that even if Locke were a racist in the weak sense, this would not imply that blacks or other peoples of color did not have a full complement of natural rights. The charge of weak racism is therefore irrelevant to any interpretation of the *Second Treatise* that seeks to show that blacks or other peoples of color do not have a full complement of natural rights.

A strong racist might hold that blacks and other peoples of color are not human beings. In that case, sentences about all men and mankind would have no application to them. They would stand outside the sphere of the state of nature. Such nonpersons would have no natural rights. We have good evidence that Locke did not hold this view. In the *Essay* at IV, 7, 16 Locke is making the point that such propositions as *What is is*, and *It is impossible for the same thing to be and not to be*, are dangerous and lead to falsehood where the terms they are applied to are complex ideas that allow for equivocation. As an example he cites the case of a child in England who can demonstrate to you *"that a Negro is not a Man,* because whiteness is one of the constant simple *Ideas* of the complex *Idea* he calls *Man,"* but this childish notion is clearly false.[19] This means that the sentences in the *Second Treatise* about all men and mankind do apply to blacks, Indians and other peoples of color.

Alternatively, perhaps, Locke could allow that such people were human, but were like children, incapable of using reason to grasp the law of nature. Or he might make appeals to the Aristotelian doctrine of natural slavery as Sepulveda did in Spain in his debate with Las Casas in the 1550s. Or perhaps he might claim that those who did not use their talents to actually acquire property would lose their complement of natural rights. A variety of authors hold that Locke is implicitly following this last strategy to exclude people of color from the domain of application of natural law and natural rights. Thus, Popkin writes:

> The degeneracy theory started to come into its own in the views of John Locke, for whom everyone was *created* equal, and endowed with the rights of life, liberty and property. Locke tried to remain within orthodox Christianity, and apparently accepted the biblical account of man's origins. However, the equality at creation and the endowment of natural rights no longer had to apply to seventeenth-century America, because (a) the Indians and the Africans were not properly using their land, and (b) they had been captured in "just wars" and so could be enslaved. Locke, who was one of the architects of English colonial policy (and the drafter of the *Constitution for the Carolinas*) saw the Indians as failing to mix their labors with the land, and thus failing to create property as an extension of their person. Hence they have no property due to their natural rights due to their own failings. They also had properly lost their own liberty "by some Act that deserves Death" (presumably opposing the Europeans) and hence could be enslaved. Their lands were waste lands. The Europeans were thus justified in turning them into property and enslaving the resisters.[20]

The passage on which this argument is largely based is 2T, 45. In this section, Locke remarks that in some parts of the world "(where the Increase of People and Stock, with the *Use of Money*) had made

Land scarce, and so of some Value," communities by laws settled the properties of private persons within them and by compacts settled the boundaries of states and kingdoms. Yet there are still ". . . *great Tracts of Ground* to be found, which (the Inhabitants thereof not having joyned with the rest of Mankind in the consent of the Use of their common Money) *lie waste,* and are more than the people who dwell on it do, or can make use of, and so still lie in common. 'Tho' this can scarce happen amongst that part of Mankind, that have consented to the use of Money."

Locke conceives of colonial expansion in America not as the seizure of Indian land, which would be unjust, but as the occupation of waste land, leaving "as much and as good" for the Indians. Nor is there any reason to suppose that Locke would deny that Indians had mixed their labor with some land and that it was properly theirs. He explicitly allows that the various fruits of the land which they take are their property. He explicitly allows that a contract between a European and an Indian in a state of nature holds good. He would also have been in a position to know that many Indian nations engaged in agriculture, thus mixing their labor with the land. There is thus little reason to suppose, as Seliger does, that Locke leaves it up to the Europeans to determine what is "waste land."[21] The distinctions made in the *Second Treatise* provide at least some objective basis for such judgments. As I noted above, one of the constraints on the just war doctrine is that the conqueror has very limited rights to the lands of the conquered.

Supposing, however, that the Indians were to oppose the settling of "waste land" by Europeans, they would then be engaging in unjust war (assuming that the "as much and as good" condition had been met) and one could legitimately conclude that they could be justly killed or enslaved on the theory of the *Second Treatise*. Still, the reason such Indians could be justly enslaved would not be the racist reason of simply opposing Europeans, but rather of engaging in war that would be unjust because it would violate the rights of property of those settling the waste land. This is clearly the most uncharitable consequence that can be legitimately drawn from the theory of the *Second Treatise*. It is interesting that we have some evidence that Locke, as a colonial administrator, was quite unwilling to draw this consequence. Popkin's reference to the *Constitution of the Carolinas* is ironic in this context. As Farr notes, Locke had a hand in drafting some temporary laws on the basis of the *Fundamental Constitution of the Carolinas*. "One law clarified the Lords Proprietors' desire to limit the extent of New World slavery, declaring that: 'no Indian upon any occasion or pretense whatever, is to be made a slave, or without his own consent to be carried out of our country.' "[22]

One striking aspect of this argument of Popkin and Seliger that deserves comment is that they extend the argument about waste lands and Indians to Africa and the taking of African slaves as if the two cases were identical. In fact the two cases are vastly different. Europeans in the seventeenth century were showing little interest in seizing African lands. When they went to Africa they wanted only one commodity: slaves. Thus, even if one were to grant to these authors their extremely ungenerous reading of 2T, 45 in regards to the occupation of waste lands in America, there is no basis for generalizing this argument to Africa or the slave trade and African American slavery.[23] Perhaps the assumption these authors are making is that Locke was a racist who would lump all peoples of color together for exploitation.

Another aspect of the argument is the claim that resisting Europeans is an "Act deserving of death." In his edition of the *Two Treatises of Civil Government* Peter Laslett claims that Locke viewed the depredations of the Royal Africa Company as just wars.[24] Presumably this claim depends on the truth of something like Popkin's claim that Locke viewed resistance to Europeans as "an Act that Deserves Death." On the whole, the view seems fairly ridiculous. Consider the logic of this claim in light of its integration into the theory of the *Second Treatise*. Europeans go to enslave Africans. Because the Africans resist their enslavement by Europeans they can justly be enslaved. Note, however, that had they not resisted, they would then have committed no crime that deserved death, and so their enslavement would have been unjust! This view also fails to deal with the point that by far the majority of Africans were originally seized by other Africans, and only later sold to Europeans. A recent commentator has also pointed out that Laslett is making unjustified use of his sources.[25] In regard to the stronger sense of racism, then, there simply is no evidence that Locke had an empirical theory of racial inferiority or a moral theory that would justify enslavement.[26] Thus there is little evidence to support the claim that Locke was a racist and thus little basis for the uncharitable reading of the *Second Treatise*. Let us turn to the views to which these authors think Locke is implicitly committed.

Seliger, like Popkin, focuses on the issues of the seizure of Indian lands. He holds that Locke's speaking of slavery in universally applicable terms "although the justification of slavery made sense only in connection with colonial conquest" and his failing to link colonial conquest with "the question of the universal applicability of natural law" shows "Locke's reluctance to frankly admit that in its entirety natural law is not equally applicable to the whole species of man."[27] Locke, as I have already suggested, had an excellent philosophical reason for making his theory of slavery universally applicable. If he had applied it only to peoples of color, it would not have applied to white Englishmen or their kings. Thus, it would have failed in the chief role it was designed to play in the *Second Treatise*. Farr has clearly refuted Seliger's claim that the justification of slavery makes sense only in connection with colonial conquest. Farr has demonstrated that the language of freedom and slavery was an important element in the rhetoric of the battle waged by the Whigs against the English monarchy.[28] Hans Aarsleff provides us with an answer to Seliger's claim that implicitly Locke holds that natural law does not apply to the whole species of man.

Aarsleff claims that Locke explicitly holds a "uniformity principle" about human nature. Aarsleff's view is that for Locke, all men possess reason but not everyone or even most men reach the highest attainments of reason. Aarsleff claims that for Locke, there are "varieties of human behavior and the uniformity of human nature underneath that variety." Aarsleff calls the uniformity of human nature underneath the varieties of behavior "the axiom of uniformity" and claims that it "is fundamental to his entire philosophy."[29] He cites a passage from the *Conduct of the Understanding:* "Men, I think, have been much the same for natural endowments, in all times. . . . "[30] The differences in human behavior come about because not all men make full use of their reason. This is the doctrine of the differential attainment and capacities of men. Since not all will reason well, there result difficulties in the state of nature that lead to the institution of civil government. Further, some with preeminent virtue in

61

this regard may come along and be the benefactors of the rest. About this Aarsleff quotes a passage having to do with Indians from the *Essay* IV, 12, 11. "Were the use of iron lost among us, we should in a few ages be unavoidably reduced to the wants and ignorance of the ancient savage *Americans,* whose natural endowments and provisions come no way short of those of the most flourishing and polite nations." The point to be drawn from Aarsleff is this. First, because of the uniformity of human nature, all men have the capacity to reason and thus a full complement of natural rights. Second, there will be great variations in the attainments of various cultures that in no way threaten the first point. Locke is not a degeneracy theorist who holds that such degeneracy deprives various groups of their natural rights. There is thus no basis to claim that the author of the *Second Treatise of Civil Government* implicitly excluded Blacks or other peoples of color from the application of natural law or held that such people do not have or have lost their natural rights.

Locke's theory is a general theory.

On the whole then, the case that Locke was a racist in the strong sense, and that the theory of slavery in the *Second Treatise* was crafted to justify the practices and institutions of African American slavery has no merit. What, then, are we to make of the incompatibility of the theory with the practices and institutions of African American slavery in the seventeenth century? Is Farr right that, in crafting the theory of slavery, Locke had his eye on local matters, and that the shores of Africa and America were out of sight? Did Locke, as Farr claims, avert his eyes from the glaring contradictions between his theories and the practices of seventeenth century African American slavery?

Farr's position contains much merit. It is plain that the provisions of the theory of slavery in the *Second Treatise* are aimed primarily at absolute sovereigns, and that some of the restrictions on conquest have no applicability to African American slavery at all. We might even grant that when Locke wrote the theory he was not thinking about how it would apply to African American slavery.[31] Nonetheless there are certain features of what Locke was doing that create a serious tension in this interpretation.

First, there is the passage that Popkin and Seliger make so much about colonial land expansion. If Locke was not thinking of America, what is this passage doing in the chapter "Of Property"? Locke often uses America and Indians as examples. It might be objected that these references to Indians and America are incidental, but this hardly seems to be the case. When Locke uses an Indian gaining property in the deer he is hunting, he is making it plain that Indians have a right to property in the fruits of the earth as much as Europeans (2T, 30). When he says: "Thus in the beginning the world was America, and more so than that now; for no such thing as money was anywhere known" (2T, 49), Locke is telling us that America is the paradigm of the state of nature. If so, then his account of natural rights, just wars, and slavery should apply (*pace* Popkin) to seventeenth-century America. It also follows that the shores of America were not (*pace* Farr) out of sight while Locke was engaged in his struggle with absolute monarchy.

Second, Locke was, as Farr claims, certainly engaged in a local fight. Still, as Farr himself notes, Locke's "overall program" was "to devise truly general theories, uncluttered by historical particulars."[32] If one has a truly general theory one ought to be able to apply its principles to situations not originally envisaged by the author of those principles and find either agreement or diagreement that they are being properly applied. This point is further enforced if we accept Ruth Grant's point that Locke's political terminology when it is normative involves *mixed modes* and *relations* rather than substances, then terms like *slavery* involve adequate ideas and precise definitions.[33] In such cases the question is not whether the term properly copies the archetype in the world (as in the case of substances) but whether things in the world correspond to the archetype in the mind.

Locke may well have been surprised, perhaps unpleasantly, when his friend William Molyneaux applied the principles of the *Second Treatise* to the case of Ireland. Still, there is little doubt that Molyneaux was correctly applying Locke's principles. This would require Locke (were he to be consistent) to either allow the justice of Molyneaux's case for self-rule in Ireland, or modify the principles of his book so as to block such an application. Unfortunately, we do not know what Locke and Molyneaux had to say to one another about

Molyneaux's book.[34] We do know that nowhere in print does Locke ever modify the principles of the *Second Treatise* so as to block their application to Ireland.[35] We do not know of anyone who confronted Locke about slavery in the way Molyneaux did about Ireland. Still, Locke says nothing in the *Second Treatise* that would prevent us from applying its principles to the slave trade or the institutions of African American slavery. It is also clear that these principles do apply in a substantive way to African American slavery. The theory tells us that, since these practices and institutions involve numerous cases of unjust aggression as well as massive violations of people's rights to life, liberty, health, and property, these institutions and practices are illegitimate.

What then are we to say of the contradiction between Locke's conduct as a colonial administrator, fostering and profiting from the slave trade and African American slavery, and the theory of slavery in the *Second Treatise* that would condemn the slave trade and African American slavery as a case of the stronger prevailing like beasts over the weaker? Much of Locke's knowledge and his engagement with colonial policy, the slave trade, and African American slavery came before Locke began to write the *Two Treatises of Civil Government.* Locke's involvement in the writing of the *Fundamental Constitution of the Carolinas,* his purchase of shares in the Royal Africa Company, and so forth might well lead one to conclude that at least up to 1675 Locke had few if any scruples or moral qualms about African American slavery or the slave trade. It was, however, only after all of this had happened that Locke along with Shaftesbury became embroiled in the Exclusion Controversy and that Locke came to write the *Two Treatises of Civil Government.* This makes it somewhat difficult to charge Locke with a contradiction between his actions in the late 1660s and early 1670s and a work that was presumably not begun until after 1675. Locke's views on toleration changed before 1667. His views about political freedom changed as a result of his involvement with the Exclusion crisis and his exile.[36] Thus, it is possible that Locke might have come to deplore his own support for slavery and the slave trade. It is possible that he might have come to do this as a result of thinking through the nature of slavery in writing the *Second Treatise.*[37]

Even if one accepts this point about chronology as partially defusing the conflict between Locke's actions as a colonial administrator and his philosophical account of legitimate slavery, there is still the period between 1696 and 1700 during which Locke served on King William's newly constituted Board of Trade and once again dealt with colonial affairs, the slave trade, and slavery. Here we are in a period after the writing of the *Second Treatise*. Presumably this is the only period where the contradiction between Locke's written works and his actions has full force.

Did Locke, as a member of the Board of Trade, avoid the moral issues raised by the enslavement of black Africans? In a certain sense, he clearly did. The Board of Trade, of which he was the most influential member, continued to implement British government policy on the slave trade and African American slavery.[38] These policies may have included Christianization of slaves and limiting the trade to the established monopoly, but they did not include abolition of the slave trade and the emancipation of slaves. Locke made, so far as we know, no attempt to use his immense prestige to change that policy in any radical way. Nor did he explicitly draw from the *Second Treatise* the implications about the illegitimacy of the slave trade and African American slavery that could reasonably be drawn from that work. He did not publicly denounce the slave trade or slavery and call for abolition and emancipation. Presumably, had he done such things, Farr and Dunn would not be accusing him of immoral evasion and avoiding the moral issues raised by the enslavement of black Africans. However, there are some considerations that may excuse to some degree, though perhaps not justify, Locke's conduct during this period.

The board had many pressing problems to deal with, including colonial government, piracy, poverty in England, and trade with Ireland.[39] The legitimacy of slavery was not recognized as one of these. It is fairly clear from the struggle that took place a century later to abolish the slave trade and emancipate the slaves that to raise this issue would have been to start a major battle. During this period Locke was a sick old man who was serving on the Board of Trade largely out of patriotic motives. He tried to resign in 1697 on account of his poor health. He stayed to please Lord Sommers. Locke may well have felt that he was in no condition to begin another great battle. He may have felt that to do so would have jeopardized his ability to achieve any of his goals as a member of the Board of Trade.

Another complication in judging how Locke should have acted given his theory of slavery in the *Second Treatise* is that during this period he was not admitting to being the author of the *Two Treatises*. He got angry at James Tyrrell, one of his lifelong friends, for spreading the report that he was the author of that work. He denied that he had written the book to another of his best friends, William Molyneaux. Presumably Locke had his reasons for denying his authorship of these works. John Dunn speculates that while Locke may not have clearly known himself why he acknowledged the authorship of the *Essay* but not of his political or religious works, "one likely reason is the simple recognition, strongly confirmed from 1690 onwards, that the difficulty of retaining control over opinions expressed in one work is greatly accentuated by juxtaposing them with related opinions on further topics in one or more other works."[40] On Dunn's view, Locke's primary objective was defending and improving the *Essay,* and this was made easier by not acknowledging the authorship of the other works.

Richard Ashcraft has another hypothesis about why the *Second Treatise* was published anonymously. Ashcraft holds that Locke, from the beginning of the Exclusion crisis on, was a member of the most radical wing of the Whig party. Ashcraft claims that Locke and other radicals were distressed to find that the convention that was called to legitimize William's kingship was abandoning the revolutionary principles of the radicals who had struggled against the Stuarts. The *Two Treatises* were published to give the radical interpretation of the Glorious Revolution and the struggle preceding it. Ashcraft also suggests that the radical character of the work would have been recognized by Locke's audience and that the work was published anonymously in order not to alienate Locke's friends amongst the palace Whigs.[41] If this interpretation is correct, Locke could hardly count on general agreement on the principles that he advances in the *Second Treatise* to make a case that slavery and the slave trade were illegitimate. If anything, drawing attention to such consequences (as in the case of Ireland) might lead people to reject the principles of the *Two Treatises* rather than to reject slavery. At any rate, given the decision to publish these works anonymously, Locke might well have been reluctant to raise issues that might result in his having to admit to being their author.

On the whole, I am inclined to hold that a more important point than how we should interpret the conflict between Locke's conduct and his theory in the *Second Treatise* is to recognize that the theory condemns the practices and institutions of seventeenth-century and eighteenth-century slaveholding and slave trading. About African American slavery Locke may have been inert but he was not speechless. Farr, I presume, does not count the *Second Treatise* as "speech" while I do. We should see Locke's theory of slavery as one of his legacies to the eighteenth century and afterwards. I use the word "legacy" advisedly. In his will Locke did acknowledge his authorship of the *Two Treatises*. If the theory of slavery of the *Second Treatise* implies that the practices and institutions of African American slavery are illegitimate, then this represents a positive moral statement about these issues: a legacy on political theory to the eighteenth century and beyond. Did Locke know that his theory had these implications? I believe that he must have known it did.

The influence of the *Second Treatise* was against slavery.

One last point worth considering is what effect the Lockean legacy of the theory of slavery in the *Second Treatise* had on later generations. If the thesis espoused by Popkin, Bracken, Seliger, and others were correct we might expect to find the *Second Treatise* being used to justify African American slavery during the eighteenth century. If, on the other hand, the theory is incompatible with the practices and institutions of African American slavery, we might expect to find the theory used to appeal for the abolition of slavery. The weight of the evidence is vastly in favor of the second hypothesis.[42]

John Dunn remarks of the *Second Treatise* that it enjoyed no great eclat after its publication. He continues:

All through the eighteenth century its reputation trailed that of his major philosophical work *An Essay Concerning Human Understanding*. In England its status as the outstanding exposition of the principles of 1688 derived more from the enormous esteem in which the *Essay* was held than any close reading of the

book itself. That the greatest of modern European philosophers should have written a work in defence of the revolution
was a sufficient recommendation. It was felt to contain principles of the most indubitable and parochial political orthodoxy
and its intellectual quality was guaranteed by the identity of its
author. It seemed to be above all an unexacting exposition of
the English way of conducting politics which made it so superior to that of any other community. It was this slackly ideological reading of the book which represented the characteristic
English understanding of it for most of the eighteenth century.[43]

Dunn's account of the reception of the *Second Treatise* might lead to
the conclusion that it exercised no influence, whether positive or
negative, in regard to slavery. Clearly, however, the abolitionist
movement in England was pervaded by the doctrine of natural
rights. Locke was perhaps the most influential contributor to the
acceptance of the doctrine by eighteenth-century Englishmen.
There was, however, a more specific influence. Caroline Robbins
attributes to a small group of Whig theoreticians a principle that
"extended the rights of Englishmen to all mankind." She continues:

> The right of conquest was no longer recognized. Conquest did
> not, according to these men, confer rights of long duration,
> nor did it deprive the conquered of their privileges as human
> beings. . . . The same process of thought began to modify old
> assumptions about slavery. These were not unaffected by the
> influence of the Quakers and the growth of humanitarianism.
> The role played by Hutcheson, James Foster, and Isaac Watts in
> preaching the doctrines expressed so forcibly by Molyneaux
> and Locke, and in influencing all sorts of people who the other
> groups did not affect was important.[44]

In the *London Magazine* for March 1738 we find A. R. supposing that
"*all* Mankind are equally *free born* . . . [and that] no Individual of the
Species, who may be deemed a *moral Agent,* can at any Time, or on
any Pretense whatsoever, consistent with Justice, be deprived of this
natural right excepting only those who by their *Crimes* have forfeited
not only *Liberty,* but even *Life.*" In the *Edinburgh Amusement* of No-

vember 30, 1769 we find a note from "An Enemy of Slavery" making points such as that prisoners of war cannot be made slaves and "that a free man cannot sell himself." Locke is not mentioned explicitly by these authors, but the ideas certainly are Lockean. Examples like these may not be numerous, but they show, I think, that the Lockean legacy concerning slavery may well have influenced some eighteenth-century abolitionists before the movement gained momentum towards the end of that century.

There is another writer who as far as I know has received little or no attention in regards to the Lockean legacy about slavery in the eighteenth century. This is Olaudah Equiano, who published his *Travels* in 1789. Equiano was born in Ebo, a dependency of the African Kingdom of Benin. He was kidnapped by African slavers and sold repeatedly until he came to the coast where he was shipped to the West Indies and sold again. In the course of his career as a slave he became educated on board ships and eventually managed to purchase his freedom from his master. In England he lectured extensively in favor of the abolition of the slave trade and emancipation of the slaves. His autobiography, one of the first of the slave narratives, was a best seller.

I do not know if Equiano had read Locke or his followers. He was an educated man; it is possible that he did. Even if he did not, however, the following passage would be of interest. Given that Equiano is writing late in the eighteenth century when he might have been influenced by Quakers or humanitarians, the affinities with Locke are particularly striking.

> Such a tendency has the slave trade to debauch men's minds and harden them to every feeling of humanity! For I will not suppose that the dealers in slaves are born worse than other men—No, it is the fatality of this mistaken avarice that it corrupts the milk of human kindness and turns it into gall. And had the pursuit of those men been different, they might have been as generous, as tender-hearted and just, as they are unfeeling, rapacious and cruel. Surely this traffic cannot be good, which spreads like a pestilence and taints what it touches! . . . which violates the first natural rights of mankind, equality and independency, and gives one man a dominion over his fellows

which God could never intend! . . . When you make men slaves you deprive them of half their virtue, you set them in your own conduct an example of fraud, rapine, and cruelty, and compel them to live with you in a state of war, and yet you complain that they are not honest or faithful![45]

While there are a variety of insightful and original comments in this passage about the paradoxes of slavery and the kinds of hypocrisy and double think it induces, one is also struck by the points of similarity between the analysis of slavery in this passage and Locke's *Second Treatise of Civil Government.* The Lockean notion that by violating the rights of other human beings, one ceases to be human and reduces oneself to the level of beasts is at least suggested by this passage. The Lockean notion that the systematic violation of natural rights amounts to a state of war is clearly enunciated. One also finds in this passage the claims for the natural equality of all men and that God gave no man dominion over another. What is only implicit in Equiano's use of the phrase "compel them to live in a state of war with you" is the Lockean doctrine of the legitimacy of resistance. In a book designed to promote abolition of the slave trade and the emancipation of the slaves, this omission was diplomatic. There are other similarities, but surely this is enough to make some interesting points. Perhaps Equiano was influenced by Locke or Locke's followers. If so, we have here an eighteenth-century use of Locke or his influence on behalf of abolition and emancipation by one of the victims of the slave trade and African American slavery. Either Equiano read Locke or his followers or he did not. In a way it doesn't matter. Surely those who read him and who had read Locke cannot but have been struck by the similarities. In a country where the *Second Treatise* was regarded highly, the similarities to the Lockean analysis may well have made this passage an especially effective piece of rhetoric.

Finally we come to the influence of Locke's legacy on slavery in America. Locke, like Bacon and Newton, was one of Thomas Jefferson's intellectual heroes. Jefferson had read both the *Essay Concerning Human Understanding* and the *Two Treatises of Civil Government.* There are strong parallels between the anti-monarchist argument of the Declaration of Independence and Locke's *Second Treatise of Civil*

Government.[46] If the interpretation of Locke on slavery that I have offered here is correct, in the 1850s, when Abraham Lincoln found in the anti-monarchist argument of the Declaration of Independence an antislavery argument, he was finding, whether he knew it or not, the Lockean legacy on slavery.[47]

Notes

1. M. Seliger, "Locke, Liberalism and Nationalism" in *John Locke: Problems and Perspectives,* ed. J. Yolton (Cambridge: Cambridge University Press, 1969), 28–29.

2. James Farr, " 'So Vile and Miserable an Estate'—The Problem of Slavery in Locke's Political Thought," *Political Theory* 14 (May 1986): 285.

3. Farr, 281.

4. Farr, 281.

5. Farr, 224. Farr comes close to giving the same argument. He remarks that Locke's ". . . theory is woefully inadequate as an account of Afro-American slavery and further *that Locke knew this.* Indeed, Locke's theory positively condemns seventeenth century slave practices and any ongoing institutions of slavery whatsoever." Farr goes on to argue, however, that Locke simply did not have African American slavery in mind when he crafted his theory. So, if Locke crafted his theory of slavery to deal with royal absolutism and did not have African American slavery in mind, and yet knew that it condemned seventeenth-century slave practice, what was Locke's attitude towards seventeenth-century slave practice? It is not clear to me what Farr's answer is to this question. It does not seem to me to be the one offered here, that Locke is implicitly rejecting the practices and institutions of African American slavery.

6. It is interesting to note that this position is one that is not universal among the Whigs. Sidney, for example, gloried in war and felt that conquest was a mark of divine favor.

7. Wayne Glausser in "Three Approaches to Locke and the Slave Trade," *Journal of the History of Ideas* 51 (April-June 1990), lists Leo Strauss and MacPherson as the main proponents of a view that sees Locke as a bourgeois advocate of acquisitive individualism and capitalism. These authors take chapter 5 (Of Property) of the *Second Treatise* as basic. Glausser treats these authors as advocates of his third or integral approach to Locke and slavery. On this approach, the justification of African American slavery flows naturally from Locke's philosophy. As Glausser remarks: "To those who believe wholly or partially in this version of Locke, his participation in slavery comes as no particular surprise. Protection against enslavement are less fundamental to his theory than provisions for capitalist growth." See "Three Approaches," 211. This seems to me the fundamental mistake of this interpretation

of the *Second Treatise.* Locke's primary goal in the *Second Treatise* is to distinguish between legitimate and illegitimate civil government. The basic distinction is that legitimate civil government protects the life, liberty, health, and property of its citizens, while illegitimate civil government does not, following rather the rule of the beasts. The protection of property is merely one feature of legitimate civil government, and the acquisition of property is surely limited and constrained by the necessity of not violating other people's rights to life, liberty, health, and property. Any interpretation that sees Locke as justifying the rule of the beasts, of which African American slavery is surely a fine example, is confusing the means and the ends in Lockean political philosophy. It becomes quite implausible when it becomes clear that its conclusion about slavery clashes with the fact that Locke has a theory of slavery that when applied to African American slavery condemns such slavery as unjust and illegitimate.

8. Laslett, Bracken, Popkin, Seliger, and Davis have all suggested that Locke would allow that such seizures by Europeans were just. The evidence against this claim is discussed later in this paper.

9. Richard Tuck, *Natural Rights Theories* (Cambridge: Cambridge University Press, 1979), 54–56.

10. Glausser claims that what he calls his third approach to Locke and slavery (this is the approach that he finds most "useful") sees Locke's "treatment of slavery . . . as part of the fabric of Lockean philosophy, however embarrassing that might be for modern admirers of one of the founding liberals." "Three Approaches," 199. (See note 7 as well.) He cites David Brion Davis's account in *The Problem of Slavery in Western Civilization* as the most successful version of this approach. He remarks that ". . . Davis attends to the specifics of Locke's slavery for war captives. Unlike torture or deviation theorists (Glausser's second approach), Davis sees this provision as a coherent part of his system" (214). What Glausser fails to note is that while Davis does indeed attend to the specifics of Locke's theory of slavery for war captives, Davis simply *assumes,* without any argument, that Locke's theory of *legitimate* slavery applies to African American slavery. Once one rejects this assumption it turns out that while Locke's theory of slavery is part of the fabric of his philosophy, there is nothing embarrassing about it. Glausser's own exploration of Locke's use of the term "common" does nothing to remedy this essential failure on Davis's part to provide any reason to believe that Locke's theory held African American slavery to be legitimate slavery.

11. Farr, 265.

12. How important a role Locke played in the composition of this document is a question. It is included in his *Collected Works,* and there is a letter from Sir Peter Colleton suggesting that Locke played a great part in the production of this document. Caroline Robbins, on the other hand, in *The Eighteenth Century Commonwealthmen* (Cambridge: Harvard University Press, 1961), 59, remarks that "Sometime

before July 1669, Ashley dictated to Locke *The Fundamental Laws of Carolina. . . .*" If this were so it would hardly show Locke to be a principal author of this document. Sir Leslie Stephen allows that the provisions of the *Constitutions of the Carolinas* "perhaps do not represent his opinions in all respects." John Murray, *English Thought in the Eighteenth Century*, vol. 2 (London, 1902), 139.

13. K. G. Davies, *The Royal Africa Company* (New York: Athenaeum, 1970), 58–65.

14. Farr, 267.

15. Farr, 266–67.

16. Farr, 269.

17. Farr, 278.

18. Farr, 277–78.

19. Various writers have justified calling Locke a racist, or claim that he is excluding blacks from the human race, on the basis of this passage. All of these attempts strike me as ill-conceived. Glausser, "Three Approaches," 213, speaking of this as well as other passages (one in which a child fears a *blackamoor* and one in which a child might mistake a Negro for the Devil) remarks: "Locke's choice of examples could make a modern reader uneasy . . . [This suggests] a prejudice already well rooted in English society." What these passages do *not* suggest is that Locke condones the mistakes of children or the well-rooted prejudices of English society.

Constantine Caffentzis in *Clipped Coins, Abused Words and Civil Government—John Locke's Philosophy of Money* (New York: Autonomedia, 1989), 194, asks about this passage: ". . . is it the fallaciousness of the argument or the falsity of the conclusion which Locke rejects?" The question suggests that while Locke may have rejected the *argument* for the conclusion that Blacks are not men, he may have accepted the truth of the conclusion on other grounds. This, as far as I can see, is not possible. The logic of the argument is impeccable. So, if Locke did not like the *argument,* it was because he rejected one or both of the premises as false. The two premises are the maxim, *it is impossible for the same thing to be and not to be,* and the child's claim about the world that all the men he has observed (in England) are white. Locke, as Caffentzis admits, is not rejecting the truth of the maxim, so he must be rejecting the child's claim. But if this is correct, then he is also rejecting the truth of the conclusion of the argument.

Caffentzis, after a long digression in which amongst other subjects he discusses Locke's antiessentialism and skepticism about the boundaries of species, concludes:

We now have reason for concluding that what Locke objected to was not so much the conclusion "a negro is not a man" but its *modality,* i.e. it is impossible for a negro to be a man. Locke finds such negative certainty impossible for any proposition involving substance terms like "man." Locke uses a child as a reasoner precisely to indicate the limited kind of evidence that he has concerning the conclusion, and the intellectual Megalomania which the Maxim leads to when badly employed.

This is an implausible interpretation. First, the conclusion in the passage has no modal term in it. It does not say that it is *impossible* for a Negro to be a man. Second, as I pointed out above, if Locke does not like the argument, then he must reject the truth of the conclusion, not its modality. How making a child "with the limited kind of evidence he has concerning the conclusion" contributes to distinguishing between a true proposition and false modality on partial evidence about the world and a general maxim completely eludes me. Using a child does make sense to me if the point is that reasoning based on the use of a general term produced by partial or incomplete induction (which would be characteristic of someone with little experience of the world) and thus false abstraction, together with a maxim will yield a false conclusion.

20. Popkin, 85. Popkin's argument is based on Bracken's and is similar to that of Seliger.

21. James Tully in "Rediscovering America: The *Two Treatises* and Aboriginal Rights," in *An Approach to Political Philosophy: Locke in Context* (Cambridge: Cambridge University Press, 1993), 137–78, has recently strengthened the argument that Locke advocates the seizure of Indian lands. He claims that Locke was the spokesman for a group of colonialists who favored seizing Indian lands on the grounds that they were not making proper use of the land in agriculture, and thus their land was "waste land." The three most important respects in which Tully strengthens the argument are these. First, he makes the point that by treating America as an example of the state of nature, Locke is denying that Indians have legitimate civil governments. Second, he argues that Locke holds that it is because of ineffective agricultural practices that Indian agricultural land can be regarded as waste land. Third, Tully cites colonial sources giving the same argument. In other respects, the argument seems essentially the same as that of Popkin and Seliger.

Tully says that in claiming that America is a state of nature (and thus denying the legitimacy of Indian civil governments), Locke is holding the same position as those colonists for whom he is speaking. But there is another possible source for Locke's claim that America is an example of a state of nature, and that source is Hobbes. In the *Leviathan*, chapter 13, in the famous section called *"The Incommodities of such a war,"* Hobbes remarks:

It may, peradventure be thought, there never was such a time, nor condition of war as this, and I believe it was never generally so, over all the world: but there are many places where they live so now. For the savage people in many places of America, except the government of small families, the concord whereof depends on natural lust, have no government at all, and live at this day in that brutish manner, as I said before.

If we compare this section with Locke II, 2, 14, and II, 5, 49 there is a fair parallel with this section of chapter 13 of the *Leviathan*. Hobbes, I assume, was not concerned about the colonial debate over expropriating Indian lands. So while Locke's point may well have the sinister implications that Tully finds in it, that may not have been his intention.

It seems to me that if Tully is right, and Locke was speaking for this group of colonists who wished to seize Indian agricultural lands on the basis that they were not being used effectively, this would have serious implications for his general theory of property that he might well not have found very acceptable. Could one landholder in England seize the land of another because they were not farming or grazing efficiently? It is, of course, possible that Locke did what Tully suggests without pondering the consequences.

22. Farr, 266.

23. Glausser, 209, notes that Farr raises the same objection as I am to the Popkin/Seliger argument and comments: "Although Locke and the English apparently did not envision grand settlements, they nevertheless saw Africa as a waste land that could be turned to more productive use." I would like to see the evidence that would support the claim that Locke saw Africa as a waste land that could be turned to more productive use. The notion that Englishmen in general, or the English government, would deny that there were civil governments in Africa seems to me even more difficult to demonstrate than the corresponding proposition about America.

24. John Locke, *Two Treatises of Government,* ed. Peter Laslett (Cambridge: Cambridge University Press, 1963), 325–26, n. to 2T. 24, lines 1–9.

25. Ruth W. Grant, *John Locke's Liberalism* (Chicago: University of Chicago Press, 1987), 68, n. 22.

26. There was a second empirical theory about the inferiority of blacks and other peoples of color. This was the polygenetic theory. For an account of the history of the polygenetic theory, see Popkin, 90–99. For the argument that Locke did not adopt the polygenetic theory, see Farr, 279–80.

27. Seliger, 28–29.

28. Farr, 282.

29. Hans Aarsleff, "The State of Nature and the Nature of Man" in *John Locke: Problems and Perspectives,* ed. John Yolton (Cambridge: Cambridge University Press, 1969), 103.

30. Quoted in Aarsleff, 103.

31. Caffentzis, 49, takes the same point a bit further. Having listed some of Locke's involvements with slavery and the slave trade he remarks: "Are we to 'accuse' Locke of blatant 'hypocrisy,' or, rather, of attributing a different significance to the word *slavery.* Surely his notion, and abhorrence, of slavery, did not extend to the African."

32. Farr, 274.

33. Ruth Grant, *John Locke's Liberalism* (Chicago: University of Chicago Press,

1987), 16–17, for the distinction between substances and mixed modes. On p. 22 she writes:

Locke's *Second Treatise,* then, is not a discussion of the art of government drawn from personal experience or from historical examples. Instead, it is the kind of demonstrative normative theory the possibility of which is argued for in the *Essay.* It is an analytical argument demonstrating the grounds for and extent of political rights and duties from the premise of all men's equal natural right to preservation. The *Second Treatise* defines relations; relations of ruler and ruled; master and slave, parent and child.

34. Patrick Kelly in "Locke and Molyneaux," in *Hermathena* (Summer 1979), 38–54 adduces evidence that Locke felt that Molyneaux's book was foolish and ill-timed, but there is no suggestion that Molyneaux was not applying the principles of the *Second Treatise* correctly.

35. This is a point made by Josiah Tucker in arguing that Molyneaux had correctly applied Locke's principles to Ireland. See the preface to Tucker's *A Treatise concerning Civil Government* (1781), in R. L. Shuyler, *Josiah Tucker, A Selection of his Economic and Political Writings* (New York: Columbia University Press, 1931), 407.

36. John Dunn, *Locke* (Oxford: Oxford University Press, 1984), 12–13.

37. There are many writers who have shown little or no awareness of this point about chronology. Farr, 281, for example, writes: "If he had any misgivings he surely suppressed them. *He invested alongside his patrons* and contributed to the steady development of the old colonial system" (my emphasis added).

38. While Locke was the most influential member of the Board of Trade, Cranston points out that this was a result of outwitting and outmaneuvering his rival William Blathwayt on the board. (See Maurice Cranston, *John Locke, A Biography* [Oxford: Oxford University Press, 1985], 406.) Thus Locke's control was not absolute by any means. It seems most unlikely that he could have succeeded in using the board to bring about drastic changes in the policy of the English government regarding slavery and the slave trade.

39. Cranston, 399.

40. Dunn, 16.

41. See Richard Ashcraft, *Revolutionary Politics and Locke's Two Treatises of Civil Government* (Princeton: Princeton University Press, 1986), 549–51 ff, 572–73, for the claims that there was a division in the Revolutionary party and the claim that Locke was on the radical edge of the party; and the postscript for the hypothesis about anonymous publication, 600–601.

42. I should note, however, that as John Dunn points out, there is some use of Locke's chapter "Of Property" by colonial writers to justify the seizure of Indian lands. See John Dunn, "The politics of Locke in England and America," in *John Locke: Problems and Perspectives,* ed. John Yolton (Cambridge: Cambridge University

Press, 1969), 71–72. This seems to have inspired Tully's article "Rediscovering America" cited above in n. 22.

43. Dunn, 57.

44. Robbins, 10–11.

45. Paul Edwards, ed., *Equiano's Travels* (Oxford: Heinemann, 1989), 73.

46. Carl Becker, *The Declaration of Independence* (New York: Random House, 1970), 78–79, speaking of the "political philosophy of nature and natural rights" remarks: "The Americans did not borrow it, they inherited it. The lineage is direct: Jefferson copied Locke and Locke quoted Hooker. In political theory and political practice, the American revolution drew its inspiration from the parliamentary struggle of the seventeenth century."

47. Gary Wills, *Lincoln at Gettysburg* (New York: Simon and Schuster, 1992), 98–101.

4

"THE MASTER'S TOOLS": ABOLITIONIST ARGUMENTS OF EQUIANO AND CUGOANO

Julie K. Ward

Introduction

So *speak you, and so do, as they that shall be judged by the law of liberty"* (James 2: 12). So began an essay by the British abolitionist Granville Sharp entitled "The Law of Liberty, or Royal Law, By Which All Mankind Shall Be Judged," published in London, 1776. The question could equally well be the opening lines of Ottobah Cugoano's work, *Thoughts and Sentiments on the Evil and Wicked Traffic of Slavery,* published in 1787, or of Olaudah Equiano's autobiography, *The Interesting Narrative of the Life of Olaudah Equiano, or Gustavus Vassa, The African,* published in 1789.[1] Both of the works presented powerful cases for the abolition of slavery that made use of arguments based on the notion of natural individual liberty. Alternatively, they employed Biblical texts concerning the origin of human beings as part of the justification for their abolitionist views. Typical of eighteenth-century abolitionist writings, these latter arguments appealed to the Judaeo-Christian tradition to argue for equality among all human beings, using the Biblical account of the common origin of humans in *Genesis.* On both grounds, one might compare the argumentation of these two African abolitionists, Equiano and Cugoano, to that of the leading eighteenth-century English abolitionists, namely, Granville Sharp, Thomas Clarkson, and James Ramsay. In fact, textual evidence supports the claim that Equiano and Cugoano adapted and made free use of the standard abolitionist arguments of their day. In Equiano's narrative, for example, is evidence that he read Thomas Clarkson's work, *An Essay on the Slavery and Commerce of the Human Species,* published in 1786, and agreed with the account on the origin of the differences in skin color that Clarkson offers.[2] Similarly, in Cugoano's work (published one year after Clarkson's tract), one finds arguments very close to those given by Clarkson in refuting the notion that Africans were descendents of Ham cursed by Noah and thus deserving of enslavement.[3]

Yet although both Cugoano and Equiano were undoubtedly influenced in their use of arguments by non-African English and American abolitionists, it would be wrong to suppose that their views were derivative, or were fashioned from them out of whole cloth. To begin with, one distinction is that having experienced slavery firsthand, Equiano and Cugoano lacked neither personal knowledge nor powerful conviction concerning its evils. At the level of composition and argumentation, one observes, then, a fundamental difference in their writings from those of the non-African abolitionists. Equiano and Cugoano employed the standard abolitionist assumptions and tropes of their time, but they synthesized them anew from the standpoint of their own experiences of slavery, thus devising wholly new formulations of the antislavery arguments. As a result of their efforts, we find Africans' argument and rhetoric influencing the direction of white English and American abolitionists. Thus, the question of influence must be admitted to be, at the very least, of equal contribution on the African side, acknowledging that both Equiano and Cugoano exerted force on the abolitionist movement. For example, Equiano knew Granville Sharp, the white English abolitionist, personally, and Equiano's detailed account to Sharp about the events aboard a slave ship motivated Sharp to become involved in the legal proceedings concerning certain of those events. These came to be known as the notorious Zong case of 1780, in which 132 sick slaves were thrown off the English slaveship, in order that the captain would be able to recover their value from the insurers, as the slaves were too ill to make it to market in the West Indies.[4] This information, relayed by Equiano to Sharp and from him to the Duke of Portland, became a *cause célèbre* of the abolitionist movement, "ringing the death knell of the English slave trade."[5]

Somewhat later, in a published letter of 1791, one Thomas Digges made the astonishing claim that Equiano himself was "the principal instrument in bringing about the motion for a repeal of the Slave-act."[6] Although it might be difficult to assess accurately the contribution of individual efforts on the abolitionist movement, as opposed to the effect of historical economic forces, for example, one indication that there was some basis to Digges's claim lay in the undoubted popularity of Equiano's and Cugoano's published works during this period in both Europe and America. Equiano's narrative, for example, ran through eight editions in Great Britain from 1789 to 1794, and twelve editions in America and Europe from 1791 to the mid-1800s. On the assumption, then, that the rate of reprints and range of sales indicated a high level of public interest in abolitionism, it seems reasonable to think that Cugoano's work in 1787 and Equiano's in 1789 provided direction and support for the antislavery debate in Parliament.[7] Having said this, it would be well to add that in considering the effects of slave narratives of this period, Equiano's work always stands out as that which appears to have had the most influence. Thus, we are naturally led to inquire how it was that this man, Olaudah Equiano, described in an English magazine article in 1792 as "the African, well-known . . . as the champion and advocate for procuring the suppression of the slave-trade," was able to accomplish such an objective.[8] In what follows, I shall examine the argumentative strategies that the African abolitionists, Equiano and Cugoano, made use of in their writings.

The Scope of the Arguments and the Metaphysical Arguments

In the works of both Equiano and Cugoano, one finds two general kinds of arguments against slavery: one is metaphysical in the sense that it appeals to some theory of human nature; the other is what one might call empirical. The metaphysical sort of arguments can be further broken down into two types, the first based on the Bibli-

81

cal notion of a common ancestor for all humans and the second on the idea of inalienable individual rights to life and liberty. The empirical arguments are of various sorts: they present reasons as to why Africans have dark skin, why slaves are not better off enslaved, and why England would profit by giving up the slave trade. Altogether, we find some five species of abolitionist arguments, which I shall call for the sake of brevity the Biblical, natural rights, biological, pragmatic, and economic arguments. All of these arguments, except that based on natural rights, are constructed in response to certain arguments made by antiabolitionists. Consequently, one gains a better appreciation of them if one first looks at the standard antiabolitionist views. This strategy is especially helpful in the case of Equiano since his book is a life narrative, not a philosophical tract, and his arguments are sometimes implicit, not spelled out as is the case in Cugoano's work.

One of the more interesting debates concerned the issue of the alleged inferiority of Africans to Europeans, a stock justification offered by antiabolitionists to support slavery. The antiabolitionists held that Africans were an inferior link in the chain of nature and so were "designed" for slavery, as the physical differences from Europeans in skin color, hair type, and so on, were supposed to show. This line of argumentation was supported by two separate strands of reasoning, one biological and one Biblical. Since the Biblical argument and its criticism featured prominently in both Equiano's and Cugoano's works, we shall turn first to these, postponing the examination of the biological arguments until later.

The basic antiabolitionist argument purporting to depend on Scriptural authority for the justifiation of slavery held that since Africans were the descendents of either Cain or Ham, both of whom were the recipients of curses, according to Biblical texts, they deserved to be enslaved.[9] To this reasoning, Cugoano gave the same response as the abolitionist Thomas Clarkson, namely, that the argument was either inapplicable or false.[10] For, first, if one attempts to establish that Africans are cursed because they are the descendents of Cain who is cursed, the argument fails because all of Cain's descendents are destroyed in the Flood. Alternatively, if we try to show that they are descended from Canaan, the son of Ham who is cursed by Noah, the argument again fails because there are no Biblical texts saying these descendents are black, and in any case, the descendents of Canaan, although cursed, are entirely destroyed.[11] Hence, according to Scriptural texts, the curse of Ham, like the curse of Cain, has already been fulfilled.[12] In a later, shortened edition of his work, Cugoano emphasized that since Africans were said to be the descendents of Cush, not of Canaan, who was cursed, the curse argument was not applicable to Africans to begin with.[13]

In addition to the negative arguments about Biblical evidence, in both editions of his work Cugoano included a positive argument based upon the Biblical notion of a common origin of all people. He argued that since all humans have a common ancestor and so are of one nature, it cannot be lawful or just for one people or nation to oppress and enslave another. To Cugoano, as to Equiano, it seemed clear that the God who made the world "made of one blood all the nations of men that dwell on all the face of the earth," from which they thought "we may justly infer, as there is no inferior species, but all of one blood, and of one nature, that there does not an inferiority subsist, or depend, on their colour, features, or form, . . . and consequently, . . . it could never be lawful and just for any nation, or people, to enslave one another."[14] This idea of a common origin of all humans constituted part of what is termed the monogenetic, as contrasted to the polygenetic view of the origin of racial differences, and will be examined in more detail later on.[15]

A second line of argumentation proposed by antiabolitionists drawing on Biblical sources concerned the so-called Mosaic law. In the eighteenth century, it was commonly argued that since the law of Moses permitted servitude, the Bible therefore condoned slavery and therefore, it was just to enslave people. To this line of reasoning, Cugoano replied that the kind of servitude that Moses' law allowed was not slavery, but a kind of bond-servitude in which the individual worked for the master for a specified length of time to regain the bond. Such servitude was not, he claimed, "contrary to natural liberties."[16] It is notable that here Cugoano makes his counter-argument depend upon an assumption concerning natural rights.

The natural-rights argument was perhaps the most powerful argumentative strategy employed by the abolitionists; it was frequently used, as above, in conjunction with the Biblical idea of a common genesis of all people.[17] The notion of individual natural rights had, of course, been successfully wielded by intellectuals and political radicals in the American and French revolutions. Now it was adroitly seized upon by abolitionists using it for their own purposes. The position was well stated by Equiano, who asserted: "slavery violates the first natural right of mankind, equality and independency, and gives man a dominion over his fellows which God could never intend."[18] Cugoano had in a similar manner argued that one of the grossest wrongs of slavery was that it infringed on "the natural and common rights and privileges of men."[19] From the standpoint of liberty, Cugoano offered a withering rejoinder to the claim of James Tobin, a Jamaican planter and slave owner, that some slaves were better off than some poor servants: "no free man, however poor, . . . would resign his liberty for that of a slave. . . . Brute creation in general may fare better than man and some dogs may refuse the crumbs that the distressed poor would be glad of; but the nature and situation of man is far superior to that of beasts."[20] Cugoano's statement that the nature and situation of humans was "superior to that of beasts" is, of course, ironically betrayed by the facts of the slave trade that revealed the terrible suffering of Africans at the hands of brutal and brutalized Europeans supporting a situation in which, as Equiano pointed out, neither party was admitted humanity.[21]

Second to the natural-rights argument, and falling under what were in essence the "metaphysical" arguments, one finds another polemic based upon the notion of the Biblical "Golden Rule." Both Equiano and Cugoano became Christian converts, and their conversion, placed alongside their firsthand experience of the cruelty of slavery, left them in disbelief as to how those who called themselves Christians could treat their fellow men so unjustly.[22] In one of Equiano's more impassioned lines, he queried: "O, ye nominal Christians! Might not an African ask you, learned you this from your God, who says unto you, '*Do unto all men as you would men should do unto you*'?"[23] Cugoano, too, made the argument that slavery was antithetical to the central maxims of Christianity, including the Golden Rule and the commandment, "Love your neighbor." These were, he claimed, "inconsistent and opposite to the ensnaring of others and taking away their liberty by slavery and oppression."[24] That Africans suffered such treatment at the hands of those calling themselves

Christians was underscored by Equiano's various examples of his treatment by non-Christians that was better than that by Christians.[25] Equiano not only made the point that those who enslaved him and others acted contrary to the spirit of Christianity, but the more subtle one that it was the institution of slavery itself that degraded and brutalized men so that they became capable of enslaving others.

Like Equiano and Cugoano, abolitionists such as Granville Sharp, James Ramsay, Thomas Clarkson, and Anthony Benezet emphasized the inconsistency between the Christian ideal of brotherly love and the practice of slavery to argue for the abolition of the institution.[26] For example, in a 1776 essay, Granville Sharp argued that the moral duties of the Bible reduced to two principles, love of God and love of neighbor, and that nothing could be considered lawful that contradicted either principle.[27] Further, he added that love of God cannot be considered prior to love of neighbor; rather, the two were reciprocal principles: a person could only follow one by observing the other.[28]

The Biological and Economic Arguments

Granville Sharp's work, *Tracts on Slavery and Liberty* (1776), provided various arguments aimed at the basic antiabolitionist argument that slavery was justified on Biblical grounds. Equiano's and Cugoano's works took up many of these arguments; their reflections, sometimes based on raw experience, demonstrated the inconsistency of slavery with Christian teachings. But offering Biblical injunctions against wronging others was of little use against those who disbelieved in the authority of the Bible, especially those who claimed to possess "scientific" evidence for the inferiority of Africans. This audience included a diverse set of individuals: French Enlightenment philosophers, Voltaire and Rousseau; Enlightenment thinkers, Kant and Hume; West Indian planters, like Edward Long; pseudoscientists, White and Soemmering; and in general, antiabolitionists looking for secular grounds to justify slavery.[29] This time, the alleged evidence supporting slavery was drawn from biological sources.[30]

By the mid-eighteenth century, European nations had been colonizing and enslaving peoples in the New World and Africa for almost three centuries, but now an interest in accounting for the physical differences between Native Americans and Africans from Europeans arose. The observed differences in skin color and other physical traits led Europeans to maintain a difference of races and to inquire into the origin of races. Generally, eighteenth-century racial views could be divided into monogenetic and polygenetic accounts.[31] The former held that all humans have a single, common origin (as attested by Biblical texts, according to Sharp, Ramsay, Cugoano, Equiano, and others), and that racial variations emerged later in human history, perhaps as a result of climate and other environmental factors. Polygenesis, in contrast, held that each race was a separate creation.[32] Perhaps surprisingly, neither view was the sole territory of the antiabolitionists, and both views had proponents who claimed Biblical and biological grounds for them. For example, monogenesis was claimed both by humanitarians arguing on Biblical grounds against slavery, and by those arguing on biological grounds against abolition. Polygenesis, holding that Africans were a distinct species from Europeans, was promoted largely, though not originally, on biological grounds in the eighteenth century. Although it might seem natural to us to suppose that a polygenecist would oppose the abolition of slavery, this was not necessarily the case. Clearly, even if one held that the human races were biologically distinct species, it did not logically follow that any one was inferior, or that any one was deserving of enslavement.

A common feature of the monogenetic theory, also called "degeneracy theory," was that variations in skin color and other superficial physiological differences were traits acquired over time due to various environmental factors, such as climate. This view followed the account of the French biologist, Buffon, who in his *Histoire Naturelle* (1749) maintained that climate was the origin of differences in skin color, and that darkness of skin was like a heritable suntan.[33] Beginning with the premise that the original skin color was white, Buffon reasoned that other races "have undergone various changes by the influence of climate, food, mode of living, epidemic diseases, and the mixture of dissimilar individuals."[34] According to Buffon's work—then taken to be based upon the most current empirical research—not only white skin, but European culture and society were assumed to represent the standards of beauty and civilization. Additionally, while nonwhite, non-European societies were thought to be degenerate, they were also thought to be remediable insofar as European culture could be extended to them. In contrast, polygenetic theory held that not only physical differences but also social and intellectual differences were fixed, thereby precluding the possibility that non-European cultures could be "improved." Most abolitionists, including (perhaps surprisingly) Cugoano and Equiano were monogenecists. One may suppose that the reason for holding to the monogenetic theory was that, in spite of presupposing a European standard of beauty and culture, the theory as a whole seemed more accommodating to non-Europeans by allowing for change. In this respect, monogenism might have provided a more "optimistic" account of racial differences: it was not a form of biological determinism, and so did not preclude the possibility of amelioration for non-European societies.[35] The polygenetic thinkers, in contrast, maintained that Africans were intellectually inferior to Europeans, and necessarily so. The strongly deterministic aspect of the polygenetic theory was evidenced in authors as distinguished as David Hume. We find Hume's endorsement of polygenesis in a much-cited footnote to his essay, "Of National Character":

There never was a civilized nation of any other complexion than white, nor even any individual eminent either in action or speculation. No ingenious manufactures amongst them, no arts, no sciences. . . . Such a uniform and constant difference could not happen if nature had not made an original distinction between these breeds of men.[36]

Notable in this passage is Hume's employment of the so-called "experimental method," a method of drawing inferences from observed cases. This methodology was used by followers of Hume who claimed to infer from physical and cultural differences to the conclusion that Africans had a different natural origin from Europeans.[37] The fact that Hume's method influenced subsequent thinkers along polygenetic lines is attested by its appearance in one canonical text of polygenism, a pseudoscientific work by Edward Long, a Jamaican plantation owner, entitled *A History of Jamaica*. In this work, published in 1774, Long credited Hume with the method of inference used.

About a decade later, one of England's leading abolitionists,

James Ramsay, explicitly attacked Hume's views and his method in a brilliant set of arguments showing the fallacies in his reasoning. In his *Essays on the Treatment and Conversion of African Slaves in the British Sugar Colonies* (1784), Ramsay sharply criticized Hume's views on Africans as "made without any competent knowledge of the subject" and that would, he stated, "appear to have no foundation, either in reason or nature."[38] Holding true to his word, Ramsay went on to demolish the polygenetic argument that differences in facial structure and skin color amount to inferiority in intelligence: genius comes in many shapes, Ramsay noted, "tall in Newton, bulky in Hume, slender in Voltaire," and therefore, it was senseless to equate shape with intelligence.[39] Hume might just as well deny intelligence to those who lacked his own corpulence, Ramsay drily observed, as to those who lacked his white skin.[40]

The biological polygenetic view of Long's *History of Jamaica* met with direct criticism from Ramsay and Clarkson and indirect criticism from Cugoano and Equiano. The thrust of Long's work was to establish that Africans were not the same species as Europeans. To this end, he sought to associate Africans with nonhuman animals: African children matured more quickly than whites; African women bore children more easily than white women; lastly, as the key argument, he argued that mulattos were sterile.[41] Since the biological definition of a species was that its members could produce fertile offspring, this was taken to be a conclusive piece of evidence for polygenesis. Ramsay first in 1784 and then Clarkson in 1785 attacked Long's arguments.[42] Likewise, Cugoano and Equiano responded to the polygenetic position by offering their view of a single origin of all humans and the climatic explanation for skin color, thus countering the pre-Adamite account of racial differences.[43] Yet Ramsay's work of 1784 contained the most thorough critique of the various biological arguments offered by Long. In general, Ramsay argued that biologists had not established a causal link between physical form and mental abilities. To support this conclusion, first, he denied that skull shape or size had been proven to bear any relation to intelligence.[44] Then he continued on to demolish the remains of Long's position by noting that even if Africans were a distinct species from whites, it did not follow that they were inferior.[45] And even if they were both distinct and inferior as a group, it did not follow that all individuals of the group were inferior. Finally, he argued, even if we were to grant that all Africans were inferior, as Long maintained, it did not follow from this that it was just to enslave them.[46] To this devasting set of arguments, Ramsay further argued that if Africans had indeed "been intended by nature" for slavery, as Long contended, they should possess many qualities they lack—such as not needing clothes or cooked food, and they should equally have been born lacking a desire for liberty.[47] Based on his own experience with African slaves, Ramsay confuted Long's assertion that slaves were lacking in intelligence. Slaves were as quick to learn, as intellectually capable as Europeans, Ramsay maintained; the fact that they seemed otherwise was solely due to their enslaved condition.[48] On a last ground, Ramsay contradicted the biological argument about the difference of races. Where Long and others had claimed as proof of the polygenist view that mulattos were sterile, he demonstrated this proof false with his own observations of racially mixed families.[49]

Having refuted the biologists' arguments concerning Africans' inferiority, the abolitionists needed to acocunt for incidental physical differences, such as skin color. This they accomplished by adopting Buffon's climatic explanation. Cugoano, making use of the same account as Clarkson, claimed that the differences in hair, facial structure, skin, and so on, were the result of humans being dispersed over the globe. He argued that just as their bodies differed according to climate, so, too, "their colors vary, in some degree, in a regular gradation from the equator towards either of the poles."[50] Against the polygenecists, Cugoano emphasized that the difference in skin color was "only incidental, and equally natural to all, and agreeable to their place of habitation."[51]

In addition to the explicitly biological arguments, Equiano and Cugoano, like other leading abolitionists, had to combat a related set of arguments connected to the notion of the "natural" inferiority of Africans. Typically, these arguments centered around claims to the effect that Africans were ignorant, unsociable people who enslaved each other, and it was then concluded that on account of their natural deficiencies, Africans would be better off enslaved by Europeans.[52] To this line of reasoning, Cugoano gave two arguments. First, he claimed that the premises were false: Africans were neither ignorant nor unsociable, nor did they use slaves as the Europeans did; hence, it was false that Africans were better off enslaved by Europeans. Second, he added that even if it were true that Africans were as antiabolitionists claimed, it would not be just grounds for enslaving them.[53] Equiano, though not replying directly to the "unsociability argument," provided fascinating indirect evidence to refute the antiabolitionist position by describing, over the first chapter of his work, the cultural richness of his people: "we are almost a nation of dancers, musicians, and poets."[54] In his description of his life among the Ibo before his abduction, Equiano emphasized that his society valued obedience to law, honor, fidelity, modesty, and frugality. In these accounts of his early life, one finds him carefully balancing the notion of Africans as rude barbarians embraced by the antiabolitionists.[55] In addition to the claims about natural inferiority, Equiano argued against those who maintained that African slaves were happier in their enslavement by contending that this allegation was simply empirically false. Throughout his work, he gave numerous examples of intentional cruelties to slaves on the part of slave owners, such as mutilation, rape, branding, burning, starvation, theft, division of families, and lack of decent living conditions that left no doubt about the nature of experienced slavery.[56]

To those antiabolitionists who argued, based on observations of Africans in slavery, that Africans showed their inferior nature by being idle, dishonest, and unfaithful, Equiano responded by showing in essence that they had mistaken cause for effect: the slaves' behavior was caused by the institution of slavery itself. Equiano's reasoning, similar to that presented by Mary Wollstonecraft in *The Vindication of the Rights of Women,* was that one cannot infer to the capacities (or nature) of a person, or group, if that person existed in deprivation, since it was precisely the state of deprivation that limited one's capacities.[57] The injustice of denying slaves a human existence and then blaming them for acting differently was not lost on Equiano, who exclaimed, "When you make men slaves you deprive them of half their virtue, you set them in your own conduct an example of fraud, rapine, and cruelty, and compel them to live with you in a state of war, and yet you complain that they are not honest or faithful! You stupefy them with stripes and think it necessary to keep them in a state of ignorance, and yet you assert that they are incapable of learning."[58]

Yet even if the antiabolitionists conceded the moral, Biblical, and biological arguments to their abolitionist opponents, they still possessed a further ground for the continuation of slavery, namely, the monetary value of the slave trade. The economic argument, that the slave trade was too valuable to England to allow abolition, provided sufficient reason for slavery for those who might otherwise have been swayed by the arguments of the abolitionists. The force and ubiquity of the economic argument seems to be the reason for Equiano appending a number of counterarguments concerning trade at the close of his narrative. At first, these arguments appended without connection to the previous chapter strike the reader of the narrative as ill-timed and out of context. But a suggestion as to their appropriateness can be made once the context for the economic arguments in favor of slavery is made explicit. The opportunity for further debate thus presented itself, and Equiano, an astute observer of the rhetorical strategies employed by his opponents, wanted to trade like with like.

The weight of the economic argument against abolition may be appreciated in some measure by noting that the opening up of the American continent to European and especially English manufactured goods was said by Adam Smith to constitute "one of the greatest events of mankind."[59] The so-called discovery of America and the West Indies led to the development of what came to be called "the triangular trade," in which England, France, and the American colonies supplied the ships, Africa the slaves, and the colonial plantations the raw products, the largest one being sugarcane from the West Indies.[60] According to the trading scheme, a ship never needed to sail without cargo; for example, a slave ship sailed from England to Africa with manufactured goods, where it exchanged the manufactured products for slaves, and it then sailed on to the West Indies, where it sold the slaves for raw products, such as sugar, rum, coffee, tobacco, and cocoa, which were transported back to England, or north to the American colonies for sale. For those slavers and planters involved in the trade, the financial gain was great; it is contended that entire fortunes of many English merchants were made in the slave trade, and this fact alone made its abolition unlikely, if not impossible.[61] As a consequence of the powerful economic interests involved, it is not surprising to find in Equiano's work, as in that of abolitionists like Ramsay and Clarkson, a series of arguments intended to persuade an audience primarily interested in maintaining the slave trade on financial grounds. The economic line of argumentation on the abolitionist side was, then, perhaps one of the most crucial in that its aim was to demonstrate that trade after abolition could be just as profitable as the trade in slaves. But to the antiabolitionist trading audience, the burden of proof lay at the feet of the abolitionists, for, as one scholar has noted, "it was no use saying it was an unholy or un-Christian occupation. It was a lucrative trade, and that was enough."[62]

In the last chapter of his narrative, Equiano offered an argument concerning the profitability to Great Britain of establishing trade with Africa not based upon slaves, but upon the exchange of English manufactured goods for colonial products. Equiano argued that since the African continent was rich in resources and the African population huge in relation to that of Great Britain, the need for manufactured items in Africa was essentially inexhaustible, and therefore, it would be even more profitable to the English to exchange their goods for raw products from the African continent than to exchange them for slaves.[63] Equiano might have read Ramsay's pamphlet, *An Inquiry into the Effects of Putting a Stop to the African Slave Trade* (1784), or *An Address on the Proposed Bill for the Abolition of the Slave Trade* (1788), where Ramsay makes essentially the same argument.[64] In both, he emphasized, like Equiano, that the size of the potential African market was so large that English manufacturing would be fully employed in supplying Africa alone. In addition, Ramsay argued that the new, nonslave trade would be more democratic since at present the trade was restricted to a few merchants, but after abolition, the trade would be wider and would include more kinds of merchants.[65] Of course, increased demand for manufactured goods would require the development of African nations, but once developed, Ramsay and Equiano argued, the trade with England, far from dropping off, would increase greatly.

Cugoano's economic argument, couched in more polemical language than that of Equiano, took up another side of the question: the relative cost of slave labor to that of free labor. Adam Smith had argued that free labor was cheaper than slave labor, and this claim was repeated by the abolitionists. Cugoano asserted that while the produce from slave labor brought immense wealth to Great Britain, "let that amount be what it will, there might be as much or more expected from the labour of an equal increase of free people. . . ."[66] The actual computation was provided by Ramsay in 1784, based on his calculations of sugar production in the West Indies; he argued that the greatest increase of cost to the slave owners arose from the amount necessary to acquire and maintain slaves. Therefore, slaves should be freed, he concluded, since they would be more productive as free workers, cost British planters less, increase their numbers without importation of new workers, and would themselves become consumers of British products.[67] The argument to the owners of colonial plantations, however, was fraught with difficulties since they had the most to lose with abolition, unlike the members of British Parliament to whom Equiano and Cugoano seem to have primarily directed their arguments. As Equiano remarked toward the end of his narrative, although planters generally complained that they could never recover the original purchase price of a slave through his or her labor, nevertheless they always refused to let their slaves go, even if they were offered one thousand pounds for them, and they continued to argue vehemently against abolition.[68] Such arguments could only be made to persuade English Parliamentary members rather than traders and plantation owners themselves.

As abolitionists, Equiano and Cugoano provided persuasive arguments of five kinds, Biblical, natural rights, biological, economic, and pragmatic. On three grounds at least, Biblical, biological, and pragmatic, the abolitionists clearly out-argued their opponents. The additional strategy of using an argument based on natural rights for abolition of slavery proved effective to intellectuals and parliamentarians, if less so to the planters themselves for whom the economic concerns were paramount. Yet the fact that Equiano and Cugoano successfully adapted various Enlightenment arguments—at least one of which was originally intended to establish the property rights of landed white men—and recast them for their own purposes would seem to undermine Audre Lorde's dictum, "the master's tools will never dismantle the master's house."[69]

JULIE K. WARD

Notes

1. Paul Edwards, in his introduction to *Cugoano's Thoughts and Sentiments on the Evils of Slavery* (1789, n.p.; reprint, London: 1969), notes that Cugoano's work contains evidence of a second, perhaps a third, hand. In contrast, Equiano's work is considered to be his own. Precisely who the other revisers of Cugoano's work are is not known, but textual evidence suggests that Equiano, a friend of Cugoano, may have been one. The evidence comes from comparison of passages in Cugoano's work with a report authored by Equiano, published 6 April, 1787 (see Edwards's introduction to *Cugoano's Thoughts and Sentiments,* viii–xi, and to *The Interesting Narrative of the Life of Olaudah Equiano,* hereafter, *Equiano's Travels* [1789; reprint, London: 1969], xxxiv–xxxvi).

2. *Equiano's Travels,* 40–41; Equiano quotes from Clarkson on the claim of one Dr. Mitchel that Spaniards in America became as dark as Indians as support for Clarkson's "natural cause" explanation of differences of skin color due to climate (p. 41).

3. Cugoano, *Thoughts and Sentiments on the Evil of Slavery,* hereafter, *Thoughts* (1787, n.p.; reprint, London: 1969), 33–37; compare Thomas Clarkson, *Essay on the Slavery and Commerce of the Human Species* (London: 1786), 178–86. Paul Edwards, in the introduction to the reprint of Cugoano's work (p. viii), notes that Cugoano may have found the argument either in Clarkson or in a letter from a Mr. Bryant to Granville Sharp (Sharp was a friend of Cugoano's); Bryant's letter to Sharp is contained in appendix 4 in Sharp's *Tracts on Slavery and Liberty* (1776, n.p., reprint, New York: 1969), 47–53. The letter to Sharp, dated 20 October, 1772, while it expresses the same view as does Clarkson, does not show a similar structure of argument to Cugoano's, but Clarkson's does; therefore, I suggest that the source for Cugoano is Clarkson, not Bryant. However, since scholars think that Cugoano's work shows evidence of other hands, and since there are signs that Equiano may have been one of the revisers of Cugoano's work, the argument may be Equiano's reading of Clarkson. See also note 1.

4. As Cugoano notes in his *Thoughts* (1969, 111), the Zong case became notorious because the captain threw the men overboard to lighten the load in bad weather, and then applied to the insurers for compensation for loss of property, arguing that the slaves were cargo just as much as horses were. See also Edwards's introduction to Cugoano's work, xv, and Charles Nichols, *Many Thousands Gone* (Bloomington: Indiana University Press, 1969), chap. 2.

5. John F. Bayliss, *Black Slave Narratives* (New York: Macmillan, 1970), 13.

6. Letter by Thomas Digges, in an appendix to Edwards's edition of *Equiano's Travels,* v. I. xii.

7. This period saw the birth of other slave narratives as well, including those of Ukawsaw Gronniosaw, John Marrant, David George, Boston King, and Venture

94

Smith; see Angelo Costanzo, *Surprising Narrative: Olaudah Equiano and the Beginnings of Black Autobiography* (New York: Greenwood Press, 1987), 5, 54.

8. *Gentlemen's Magazine* 1 (1792): 384.

9. See Genesis 4:15 (Cain), and Genesis 9:25–27 (Ham); see also Thomas Clarkson, *An Essay on the Slavery and Commerce of the Human Species,* hereafter *Essay* (London, n.p., 1788), 2d ed., 126–27.

10. Cugoano, *Thoughts,* 33–38. Edwards notes that Cugoano's argument follows that of Clarkson; see note 3. While we do not find this same line of argument in Equiano, we may infer that he had read Clarkson's work and agreed with the criticism he offered; thus, I take Cugoano to be representing the same view as Equiano on this point.

11. Cugoano notes that the Biblical texts support the idea that Africans are decendents of Cush (another of Ham's sons): "the Ethiopian can no more change his color than the leopard its spots . . . " (*Jeremiah* 13:23), where "Ethiopian" in Hebrew reads "descendant of Cush"; see Claron, *Essay* (1788), 127. See also Bryant's letter to Granville Sharp, 20 October, 1772, contained in Sharp, *Tracts on Slavery and Liberty* (London, n.p., 1776; reprint, Westport, Conn.: Negro University Press, 1969), appendix 4, 47–53.

12. Clarkson summarizes: "It appears that the argument is wholly inapplicable and false; it is false in its *application* because those who were the objects of the curse were a totally different people; it is false in its proof because no such distinguishing marks, as have been specified, are to be found in the divine writings; and if the proof could be made out, it would be *inapplicable,* as the curse has long been completed" (*Essay,* 1788, 130–31).

13. Cugoano, *Thoughts* (London: 1791), 13–17. This later edition is much shorter (46 pages), but contains the same basic six arguments against slavery of the 1787 edition; Edwards thinks, on the basis of stylistic evidence, that the later edition was actually written first, and expanded into the longer edition, but published later.

14. Cugoano, *Thoughts* (1791), 10–11; see also Equiano, *Equiano's Travels,* 30–32, 38–40.

15. For a thorough discussion of the two views, see Richard Popkin's "The Philosophical Bases of Modern Racism," *The High Road to Pyrrhonism,* Richard Popkin (San Diego: Austin Hill Press, 1980), 79–102.

16. Cugoano, *Thoughts* (1787), 40–44.

17. The eighteenth-century notion of natural rights was connected to the conception of a divine being, although the natural rights argument is logically dissociable from a belief in a divine being. As Equiano and Cugoano express the rights argument, it depends more upon the belief of a common creation of all humankind by God than upon a transcendent being that guarantees these rights. For the latter, see Jane Moore, "Sex, Slavery and Rights in Mary Wollstonecraft's Vindications," in *The Discourse of Slavery: Aphra Behn to Toni Morrison,* ed. Carl Plasa and Betty Ring (London: Routledge, 1994), chap. 2.

18. Equiano, *Equiano's Travels*, 224.

19. Cugoano, *Thoughts* (1787), 21.

20. Cugoano, *Thoughts* (1787), 17–18.

21. See Equiano, *Equiano's Travels*, 225–26, where he observes that slave owners treat their slaves brutally and also harm themselves. See also Alexander Falconbridge, *An Account of the Slave Trade on the Coast of Africa* (London, n.p., 1788).

22. On the issue of Equiano's conversion and the syncretistic aspect of his Christianity, see Paul Edwards and Rosalind Shaw, "The Invisible Chi in Equiano's *Interesting Narrative,"Journal of Religion in Africa* 19 (1989): 146–56.

23. Equiano, *Equiano's Travels*, 87.

24. Cugoano, *Thoughts* (1787), 4, see also 60–63.

25. See Equiano, *Equiano's Travels: the incidents concerning the Musquito Indians* (180–192) and being abused even once he has regained his freedom (194–209).

26. See Granville Sharp, *Tracts on Slavery and Liberty* (London, n.p., 1776); James Ramsay, *Essays on the Treatment and Conversion of African Slaves in the British Sugar Colonies* (London, 1784), hereafter, *Essays;* Thomas Clarkson, *An Essay on the Slavery and Commerce of the Human Species* (London, 1788); Anthony Benezet, *Some Historical Account of Guinea* (London, 1788).

27. Granville Sharp, "The Law of Liberty, or Royal Law, By Which All Mankind Shall Be Judged," *Tracts on Slavery and Liberty*, 8.

28. Granville Sharp, *Tracts*, 20. Sharp takes the crucial texts to be Paul's claim, "All the law is fulfilled in this: 'Thou shalt love thy neighbor as Thyself' " (*Galatians* 5:14), and "If we loveth one another, God dwelleth in us, and His love is perfected in us" (*I John* 4:12).

29. See Edward Long, *A History of Jamaica* (London, n.p., 1774); Charles White, *Regular Gradations in Man* (London, 1795), a work based on Long's polygenetic thesis; White's view about alleged mental inferiorities was also supported by S. T. von Soemmering, *Uber die Köperlich Verschiedenbeit des Negers vom Europaer* (Frankfurt, 1785); see also Philip D. Curtin, *The Image of Africa: British Idea and Action 1780–1850* (Madison: University of Wisconsin Press, 1964), 46.

30. For a good discussion on the history of the biological arguments, see Stephen Jay Gould, *The Mismeasure of Man* (New York: W. W. Norton, 1981), esp. chaps. 1–4.

31. See Philip D. Curtin, *The Image of Africa*, chap. 2; Richard Popkin, *High Road to Pyrrhonism*, 79–102.

32. See Philip Curtin, 40–42. The polygenetic view could be further divided into the pre-Adamite and co-Adamite accounts: the former held that Europeans were descendants of an earlier creation than Adam, based on a 1655 work, *Prae-Adamitae*, by Isaac LaPeyrere; the latter held that all races were created contemporaneously, but not with equal ability, based on an anonymous work of 1732, *Co-Adamitae*.

33. Montesquieu, *Spirit of the Laws*, gives an earlier version of the climate explanation, as did Linnaeus; see also Popkin, 86.

34. Buffon, *Histoire Naturelle* (1785), vol. 3, sec. 9, 207.

35. Clearly, the humanitarian abolitionists, including Sharp, Ramsay, Clarkson, Cugoano, and Equiano, hold the degeneracy account since they equally speak of the Biblical "single origin" and single nature of all humans.

36. Hume, *Philosophical Works of David Hume,* note to 1753 edition (London, n.p. 1898), v. III, 252.

37. See Popkin, 85, 93.

38. Ramsay, *Essays* (1784), 198.

39. Ramsay, *Essays* (1784), 213.

40. Ramsay, *Essays* (1784), 214.

41. See Curtin, 43–44.

42. 1785 is the date of Clarkson's dissertation, the *Essay on the Slavery and Commerce of the Human Species,* which was later published by Phillips in London, 1788.

43. Cugoano uses the same argument for the cause of skin color as does Clarkson in his *Essay,* 31–32, 44–47. Equiano notes (40–41) that he agrees with Clarkson's account.

44. Ramsay, *Essays* (1784), 212–14.

45. Clarkson, *Essay* (1788), gives the same argument, 131.

46. Ramsay, *Essays* (1784), 179–263. Clarkson, *Essay* (1788), 132, gives a clever reductio to the argument that skin color could be a basis for enslavement by noting that anyone who is lighter than another by a shade could enslave the other; thus, the residents of France, Spain, and England should beware of lighter northerners.

47. Ramsay, *Essays* (1784), 233–234.

48. Ramsay, *Essays* (1784), 244.

49. Ramsay, *Essays* (1784), 239–40. See also Clarkson, *Essay,* 132–33.

50. Cugoano, *Thoughts,* 31; cf. Cugoano, 31–32, 44–47.

51. Cugoano, *Thoughts,* 32.

52. This argument was endorsed by many English people, even by intellectuals, like Boswell; see Francis Adams, *Three Black Writers in Eighteenth Century England* (Belmont, Calif.: Wadsworth, 1971), 12.

53. Cugoano, *Thoughts,* 21–22, 25–28.

54. Equiano, *Equiano's Travels,* 10.

55. Equiano, *Equiano's Travels,* 6–12.

56. Equiano, *Equiano's Travels,* 205–26. In addition, Equiano points out the injustice of law in Barbados where a slave can be put to death by a master without any fine, but someone else intentionally killing a slave pays fifteen pounds sterling in fines.

57. Equiano, *Equiano's Travels,* 224–26; Wollstonecraft, *A Vindication of the Rights of Women* (1792; reprint New York: Penguin, 1986).

58. Equiano, *Equiano's Travels,* 224–25.

59. Quoted in Eric Williams, *Capitalism and Slavery* (New York, Capricorn Books,

1961), 51. Though the specific figures of the amount of wealth amassed vary (and vary over specific decades), even conservative estimates show that the slave trade was profitable. See, for example, Roger Anstey, *The Atlantic Slave Trade and British Abolition 1760–1810* (New Jersey: Humanities Press, 1975), chap. 2.

60. See Peter Hogg, *Slavery* (London: British Library booklets, 1979); Eric Williams (1961), 50–51.

61. See Williams, chap. 2. esp. 52–64. For a later, more conservative figure of the fortunes made, see Anstey, chap. 2, esp. 38–49.

62. Williams, 47.

63. Equiano, *Equiano's Travels*, 249–59, esp. p. 250; Equiano's argument here is expanded in his letter to Lord Hawkesbury of 13 March, 1788, which was later published by a committee in 1789; see Edwards's introduction to *Travels*, lix.

64. See Ramsay, *An Inquiry into the Effects of Putting a Stop to the African Slave Trade* (1784), 11–16; *An Address on the Proposed Bill for the Abolition of the Slave Trade* (1788), 5.

65. Ramsay, *An Inquiry into the Effects of Putting a Stop to the African Slave Trade*, 19.

66. Cugoano, *Thoughts,* 98, in Adams's edition (Belmont, 1971).

67. Ramsay, *Essays,* 110–17.

68. Equiano, *Equiano's Travels*, 203–204. In contrast to Equiano, Ramsay, *Essays,* 122–25, directed specific arguments to the planters including arguments that in the long term, abolition benefits them since laborers would be more productive, would not rely on them for their needs, would not pose losses when they died, and would not require an original expense to the owners.

69. Audre Lorde, "The Master's Tools Will Never Dismantle the Master's House," in *This Bridge Called My Back,* Cherrie Moraga and Gloria Anzaldua, eds. (New York: Kitchen Table: Women of Color Press, 1983), 99.

I would like to thank Tommy Lott, the editor of this volume, for his assistance. My thanks also to Cornell University Library and its Africana collection, where most of the research material for this paper was gathered.

5

EARLY
ENLIGHTENMENT
CONCEPTIONS OF THE
RIGHTS OF SLAVES

Tommy L. Lott

L ocke's justification of slavery seems inconsistent with his remark that "[s]lavery is so vile and miserable an Estate of
Man," unless we are reminded that many philosophers
condemn slavery as inherently evil, yet sometimes condone certain
relatively benign forms as justified.[1] Even the black British abolitionist, Olaudah Equiano, condoned the practice of slavery in Africa—
indeed, his own enslavement by fellow Africans, as though this was
more humane than the European enslavement of Africans.[2] To what
extent, however, can relatively benign forms of an unjust practice,
or institution, be condoned? The practice of slavery has varied
widely in different places and at different times, a consideration rendering difficult the task of giving a coherent account of its peculiar
injustice.[3] I want to examine more closely one influential account of
the injustice of slavery by considering the suggestion we find in early
Enlightenment philosophers, such as Hobbes and Locke, that slavery is a violation of natural rights. To the extent that this view condones relatively benign forms of slavery, under which certain rights

of slaves are respected, it seems inconsistent with the claim that slavery is inherently evil.

Utilitarians are especially worried about having to embrace a justification of relatively benign forms of slavery. On the supposition that such forms are virtually nonexistent, R. M. Hare proposed to meet this objection by accepting benign forms as, in principle, morally permissible.[4] Hare's proposal overlooks the fact that American slaves frequently included references to benign instances in their testimonies.[5] Black abolitionists such as Harriet Jacobs and Frederick Douglass presented their inside accounts of such benign instances as part of a general conception of slavery as a fundamentally evil institution.[6] From their perspective, so-called "benign" slavery is always relative within a context of harsher forms. Consequently, they would insist that even when a form of slavery is relatively benign, it is nonetheless to be condemned as inherently evil. Just as utilitarians have no ground on which to condemn relatively benign forms of slavery, natural-rights accounts of the injustice of slavery must face a similar difficulty, for, if certain forms of slavery and servitude are indistinguishable with regard to natural rights, the ground on which slavery is to be condemned is unclear.

Early Enlightenment accounts often relied on a natural-rights doctrine that condoned slavery. In *The Tempest*, Shakespeare presented a definitive version of the idea that slavery essentially involves physical bondage. He incorporated a parallel notion of servitude as a substitute for slavery into his view of slavery as a substitute for death. This notion recurs in Hobbes's account of slavery as a harsh form of involuntary servitude, leading him to conceive of servitude in terms of manumission from slavery. Although Hobbes provided a fairly good criterion by which to gauge the harshness of slavery, his natural-rights account of its injustice is inadequate. The coerced servitude he wanted to justify is indistinguishable from certain forms of slavery. Locke rejected Hobbes's account of dominion. His chief objection, however, is inconsistent with his own view of natural rights. In the end, what Locke offers is a slightly modified restatement of Hobbes's view. For both accounts, the trouble created by the overlap of certain forms of slavery and servitude warrants a reconsideration of the adequacy of their natural-rights doctrine as a ground on which to condemn slavery as inherently evil.

Preamble: Shakespeare on Slavery and Servitude

In Shakespeare's play *The Tempest*, the idea that enslavement can sometimes justifiably violate certain basic human rights exerts a strong influence on the initial exchange between Prospero (the master) and Caliban (the slave), issuing in a dispute in which Caliban proclaims his right to the island.[7] From Prospero's standpoint as ruler of the island, Caliban's sexual aggression towards Miranda provided sufficient reason for his forfeiture of the basic human rights he once had been accorded. Miranda, in turn, reinforces this justification of Caliban's enslavement by declaring that his misdeed deserved more than imprisonment, as if to suggest instead of permanent enslavement Caliban deserved the more stringent punishment of death. By comparison with the wrath Miranda had in mind, Prospero's enslavement of Caliban appears to be a relatively merciful substitute.

Shakespeare employed the idea of physical bondage to represent the harshness of slavery. This is quite vivid in his portrayal of two instances in the play. He represents Caliban's enslavement with an image of his being tied to a rock and Ariel's former enslavement by Caliban's mother, Sycorax, with an image of his imprisonment in the trunk of a pine tree.[8] These very concrete illustrations captured a strand of early Enlightenment thought regarding the injustice of slavery, namely, that it imposes an extreme physical restriction on the slave's freedom of bodily movement. Allowing Caliban to show initiative by speaking out and conspiring to rebel, Shakespeare apparently recognized that the injustice of Prospero's rather harsh imposition on Caliban required a justification. But what about Prospero's more benign imposition on Ariel, the servant who also registered a demand for his freedom?[9] Although Ariel's being at liberty from the physical restrictions of the tree trunk was rightly depicted as a greatly improved situation, his new status as Prospero's servant does not seem to amount to such a categorical difference that we should withhold our condemnation of Prospero's treatment of him. Given Ariel's status as a servant, there is some sense in which it may be improper to *refer* to him as a slave. However, with Prospero's coercive tactics in view, it does not seem entirely mistaken to consider Ariel to have remained in bondage—only now with greater liberties.

101

Shakespeare clearly intended to draw a contrast between Caliban's status as a slave and Ariel's status as a servant in the social arrangement he envisioned in the play.[10] The obvious physical difference between Ariel and Caliban seems to signify an equally obvious difference in the level of trust extended to each by Prospero. Indeed, Caliban's untrustworthiness warranted the physical restraint of a rock. Hence, as a nonmaterial spirit who was released from physical bondage in exchange for temporary servitude, Ariel was granted a certain liberty of physical movement denied to Caliban. Here we must guard against allowing the question of whether Shakespeare meant to justify their respective forms of servility to preclude a more fundamental question of whether he was right to think of slavery as primarily involving physical bondage such that a slave's mere release from physical restraint is sufficient to count as manumission.[11]

Although Ariel was not under any direct physical restraint, he was nonetheless wont to entreat Prospero to release him from his obligation of servitude. Given that both slavery and servitude required manumission, how far would Shakespeare have to go in assigning rights to Caliban before we stopped using the term "slave" to refer to him?[12] If Shakespeare had made manumission available to Caliban, the differences between Ariel and he would tend to converge. To see this we need only suppose what Caliban might have expected to happen if his conspiracy to take over the island had succeeded. The aim of his desire to install Stephano as his new master was to bring about a less harsh form of slavery, and perhaps even to create an opportunity for his manumission. Shakespeare closed off this option for Caliban, and thereby offered a justification of slavery, by employing Caliban's natural physical difference as a sign of the latent danger of his animal instincts—a danger that required Prospero's absolute dominion to guard against.

Manumission was not possible for Caliban because he was not conceived by Shakespeare as a full-fledged member of the human circle. It was because of Caliban's inability to be socially assimilated—or rather, domesticated—that he was shown to be justifiably treated as would any other beast of prey who is perceived to be a threat. Caliban's representation as a beast of prey was Shakespeare's way of logically constructing him as a "natural" slave, that is, as a subhuman creature who *deserved* to be enslaved.[13] Although Shakespeare's image of the slave as a potentially dangerous beast was a crucial component of his justification of colonial conquest, by allowing Caliban to question Prospero's authority, he displayed a curious ambivalence towards the rights of slaves. This ambivalence, which indicates Shakespeare's recognition of the inherent evil of slavery, lingered into the seventeenth century, bequeathing to subsequent thinkers such as Hobbes and Locke the task of reconciling their respective accounts of conquest with a more fully developed natural-rights doctrine.

Hobbes's Justification of Coerced Servitude

Hobbes quite strongly opposed the notion of a natural slave, although the target of his objection was Aristotle, rather than Shakespeare. Despite his criticisms, Hobbes's discussion of slavery owes much to Aristotle's influence. Aristotle aimed to show that the master-slave relationship is significantly different from the sovereign-subject relationship by presenting a political analysis of the household, including the husband-wife and parent-child relationships as well as the master-slave relationship. He set the stage for his view of the natural slave by first presenting rather straightforward paternalistic arguments to justify human dominion over animals and male dominion over females. Although Aristotle believed that on the whole slavery was justified, he was more interested in showing that, because household management is a form of monarchy involving domination by humans over animals, masters over servants, husbands over wives, and parents over children, it is much different from political rule by a sovereign in relation to free and equal people.[14] In his account of the various kinds of dominion, Hobbes employed this Aristotelian framework to draw a parallel between the justification of authority in the family household and the justification of authority in the state.

Hobbes rejected Aristotle's inegalitarian view, maintaining instead that social distinctions have no place in the state of nature where all men are equal. He objected to Aristotle's contention that some people, who lack reason, are more suited by nature to serve while others are more worthy to command "as if Master and Servant

103

were not introduced by consent of men, but by difference of Wit."¹⁵ Hobbes considered this view to be against reason, because whether men really are equal, or only think themselves equal, does not matter, since they "will not enter into conditions of Peace, but upon Equal termes."¹⁶ He appealed to experience to show that social inequalities were introduced by civil law and argued against Aristotle's view of the natural slave by assimilating the master-servant and the sovereign-subject relationships. Given the political parallel he drew between the natural rights of servants and subjects, he was constrained to treat the slave's right of resistance as no different than the subject's. With regard to natural rights, Hobbes's political theory can be understood to condemn slavery as inherently evil, especially slavery justified by arguments derived from Aristotle's idea of a natural slave.

It may seem strange that Hobbes held this view of slavery given that his general account of dominion is informed by a political realism that acknowledged sovereignty by acquisition to be, historically, the most common form of government.¹⁷ Although he spoke of dominion being acquired in several ways, the paradigm for his political theory was clearly what he referred to as "a *naturall* Government, which may also be call'd, *Acquired*, because it is that which is gotten by power, and naturall force."¹⁸ He described the state of nature as a situation in which a commonwealth arises through conquest, governed only by the principle of self-preservation. Unlike Aristotle, who invoked sexual differences in order to grant the natural dominion of men over women (and children), Hobbes did not make any such assumption in favor of men. Instead, after noting those instances in which women have the right of dominion, he argued that parental authority must be understood in terms of a tacit contract. In the state of nature, since the mother has the power (of nourishment) over the child, the child's obligation arises from the fact that she owes her life to the mother. This is not to suggest that Hobbes's thinking was entirely unbiased toward men, but, to his credit, he consistently maintained that parental dominion could only be justified in terms of civil law, which in turn is ultimately grounded on an appeal to self-preservation.¹⁹

Given the central role of conquest in Hobbes's account of the growth and development of the commonwealth, it is not surprising to find the principle of self-preservation underlying his notion of authorization. He tells us that, once family units have been formed in the state of nature, under the dominion of the father, some men will "use Violence, to make themselves Masters of other mens persons, wives, children, and cattel" (*Lev.* 13.7:88). A commonwealth arises by forcible acquisition when the master of one household subdues the master of another, whose members then become servants, or slaves. It is mainly for purposes of self-defense that one household will then join with other households to eventually become a commonwealth.

Unlike Aristotle, who argued for a distinction between a household and a commonwealth, Hobbes saw no essential difference between them. In the *Elements of Law* he spoke of "a little body politic" as being composed of "two persons, the one sovereign, which is called the master, or lord; the other subject, which is called the servant" (*EL* 2.3.2:128).[20] This move to conceptually converge household and commonwealth enabled Hobbes not only to draw a parallel between the master-servant relationship and the sovereign-subject relationship, but also permitted him to treat the two relationships as identical. Most importantly, however, it grounds his argument that the justification of dominion in both cases is identical, for, just as subdued servants are motivated by the desire for self-preservation to pledge obedience to a master, subdued subjects are similarly motivated to authorize a sovereign.

Although the right of dominion may be established in all cases "by force and naturall strength," there is an important difference between the case of dominion over slaves (and perhaps animals) and the various other cases (*DC* 7.10:120). In the case of slaves, especially war captives who were once a mortal enemy, self-preservation may sometimes dictate that they be held in captivity (or killed). Dominion of this sort is unauthorized in the sense that such captives have no obligation not to resist their conquerors. Hobbes's talk of the family as a household consisting of "a man, and his children, and servants together," which operates as a small scale commonwealth, stems from the idea that each member is to be understood as having entered into a contractual relationship whereby obedience to the father (or husband or master) is exchanged for protection. If the master of a household is unable to provide sufficient security against an invader, the members are at liberty to do what they think is necessary to save their own lives. According to Hobbes, "A *Son* also is freed from subjection on the same manner as a *subject* and *servant* are" (*DC* 9.7:124). As nonconsenting parties to the household arrangement, and hence nonmembers, slaves remain in a state-of-nature relationship with their masters, such that a master's right of conquest is always understood to be matched by a slave's right of resistance.[21]

Even with this moral distinction between the servant and the slave in mind, Hobbes was prone to view slavery as an extreme form of servitude. In keeping with the terminology of the Greeks and Romans, he preferred to speak of "two sorts of servants."[22] But there was a political reason as well for this construal, given that he wanted to assimilate the sovereign-subject relationship to the master-servant relationship. As I indicated, Hobbes generally distinguished slavery and servitude in terms of a contract between master and servant that, without the conditions of trust being met, is never understood to have been entered into by a slave. More specifically, he held that slaves "are absolutely in the power of their Masters" in two respects: (1) "[their] bodies are not in their own power" and (2) "[they] are brought and sold as Beasts." The harshness of the slave's condition is contrasted with that of servants, who hire themselves out to their masters "voluntarily" and "the Masters have no further right, then is contained in the Covenants made betwixt them" (*Lev.* 45.12:447). In terms of Hobbes's political theory, these remarks imply that the difference between slavery and servitude is much like the difference between the commonwealth created by institution, that is, when there is a "voluntary offer of subjection" and the commonwealth created by acquisition, that is, when there is a "yielding by compulsion" (*EL* 2.3.2:127). Unfortunately, Hobbes did not consistently maintain this view. In order to uphold the validity of coerced contracts, and thereby establish the legitimacy of sovereignty by acquisition, he argued that compelled acts are no less voluntary than uncompelled ones. But if compelled acts are nonetheless "voluntary," then the contrast between sovereignty by conquest and sovereignty by institution cannot be maintained.[23]

A similar contrast Hobbes wanted to draw between the slave and the servant in terms of voluntary action was equally fraught with

difficulty. Consider, for instance, his account of how a master acquires dominion over a servant:

And this Dominion is then acquired to the Victor, when the Vanquished, to avoyd the present stroke of death, covenanteth either in expresse words, or by other sufficient signes of the Will, that so long as his life, and the liberty of his body is allowed him, the Victor shall have the use thereof, at his pleasure. (*Lev.* 20.10:141)

This ritual of conquest, involving coerced consent, seems indistinguishable from an act of enslavement. But Hobbes goes on to stress the point that it is only "after such Covenant made, the Vanquished is a Servant, and not before: for by the word *Servant* . . . is not meant a Captive, which is kept in prison, or bonds" (*Lev.* 20.10:141). It is therefore not the conqueror's use of coercion that marks the crucial difference between slavery and servitude; rather, it is the fact that the servant *is not kept in prison, or bonds.* As a sign of the master's trust, corporal liberty is taken to be the earmark of a valid contract.

Hobbes allows dominion to be authorized on the basis of coercion as long as this does not involve a denial of corporal liberty to the vanquished party. He argued that since the aim of a captive giving consent to serve a master is "to avoyd death or bonds," a servant held in bondage could not be understood to have consented and, by an appeal to the principle of self-preservation, he sustained the enslaved servant's right of resistance. He remarked that the captive has "a right of delivering himself . . . by what means soever" (*EL* 2.3.3:128).[24] This general endorsement of the slave's inalienable right of defense is consistent with his political motivation for viewing slavery as a form of involuntary servitude. Both servants and slaves share the fact that their labor is assigned to them by their masters, and the fact that both *belong* to their masters. Servitude lapses into slavery, however, when a servant loses corporal liberty by being imprisoned or kept in bonds, for the contract between master and servant presupposes trust, which, if violated in this way, ends the servant's obligation to the master and transforms their relationship to master-slave.

The authority of the sovereign, or master, over the subject, or servant, is absolute with regard to a right to frame the will of subjects.

Hobbes maintained that the sovereign, or master, can do no injury to the subject, or servant, because obedience in both cases requires the latter to have subjected their wills.[25] Given that a sovereign can also be a master and a subject can also be a servant, the main difference between a free subject and a servant is that the former is obligated only to the commonwealth and has greater privileges regarding more "honorable" employment and possessions, whereas, in addition to having an obligation to the commonwealth, the latter is obligated to serve another subject and does not have any rights regarding proprietary matters.[26]

A master's authority and dominion over servants cannot be understood to allow enslavement for the same reason that a sovereign's authority and dominion over subjects cannot. Hobbes consistently extended his account of the inalienable right of defense to apply to servants in a household, as well as to subjects in a commonwealth. This political implication was captured in his remark that "Servants . . . are discharged of their servitude or subjection in the same manner that subjects are released of their allegiance in a commonwealth institutive" (*EL* 2.3.7:129).[27] The distinction he made between slavery and servitude in terms of corporal liberty indicates how he employed the notion of slavery to specify a limit to all contractual social arrangements, including the absolute authority of the sovereign. The right of resistance Hobbes grants to citizens of a commonwealth is the same inalienable right he extended to slaves.

Locke's Justification of Slavery

Locke's account of slavery is largely a restatement of Hobbes's view modified to accord with his own version of the social contract theory. His opposition to Hobbes's justification of sovereignty by conquest was, to a great extent, influenced by his view of absolutism as a form of enslavement.[28] Because his political theory sought to establish a greater limit than Hobbes's to the authority of the sovereign, as well as to the authority of the master of a family, his account of slavery displayed a quite different concern with the rights of slaves. He nonetheless adopted much of the same Aristotelian framework utilized by Hobbes. With regard to distinguishing the sovereign-sub-

ject relationship from those that obtain between a master and other members of a household, he was closer to Aristotle.

When Locke turned to a consideration of the master of a family with all of the subordinate relationships, namely, wife, children, servants, and slaves, he acknowledged that this household resembles in many ways "a little Commonwealth" (*TT*, 2.86:366). By direct contrast with Hobbes's attempt to assimilate the commonwealth to the family, Locke claimed that the master of a family has limited powers over everyone except the slave.[29] He agreed with Hobbes regarding the mother's right of dominion over children, which he also derived from the principle of self-preservation, but distinguished the obligation of children to honor their parents from a wholesale granting of parental authority. Parental authority is only required "by a tacit, and scarce avoidable consent" that entails only a limited duty of respect (*TT*, 2.74:360).

Hobbes's absolutist view is further modified in Locke's account of authority in a household. Although men rule the family "as the abler and the stronger," the wife nonetheless retains certain rights, such as the liberty to separate (*TT*, 2.82:364). He accepted Hobbes's account of the commonwealth developing from the growth of the family, beginning with the "Conjugal Society" based on a voluntary compact between men and women, yet he made clear that the power of the husband is "far from that of an absolute monarch" (*TT*, 2.82:364). He pointed out that even when the household is enlarged by the addition of servants, it will nonetheless fall short of a political society, whose chief end is the preservation of property.[30]

Despite these modifications, many of the basic tenets of Hobbes's doctrine were reproduced by Locke in his discussion of the difference between slavery and servitude. According to Locke, although slaves are "another sort of Servants," they differ from servants with regard to their status at citizens.[31] He held that slaves are not to be considered a part of civil society and, following Hobbes, further distinguished slaves from servants with regard to the latter's having contracts that specify a temporary granting of services for wages. But, contrary to Hobbes, Locke maintained that, having forfeited their lives, liberties, and estates, slaves who are war captives are justifiably subjected to "the Absolute Dominion and Arbitrary Power of their Masters" (*TT*, 2.85:366). Locke, however, insisted upon a stipulation that carried a quite significant political implication for the institution of slavery, namely, that this absolute dominion is limited only to those who have been subdued in a just war and does not extend to their children (*TT,* 2.189:440–41). Although this stipulation is consistent with Locke's political theory, as well as with his justification of slavery, he seems to have adduced it with an eye to countering Hobbes's view of hereditary servitude.[32]

Locke's justification of slavery was meant to be consistent with his general contractarian account of political obligation. Although he accepted Hobbes's distinction between servants and slaves in terms of a contract, unlike Hobbes Locke considered promises extorted by force to be invalid agreements. Hence, he believed that the subdued parties who have been coerced into a compact have no obligation. He described the condition of slavery as "the state of war continued between a lawful Conqueror, and a Captive" (*TT,* 2.24:325). By arguing that sovereignty by conquest is an illegitimate form of political authority, he objected both to Hobbes's account of the servant's obligation and to his general political theory.[33]

With regard to the rights and duties of servants and slaves, the disagreement between Hobbes and Locke stems from their different concepts of liberty. Hobbes defined liberty as freedom from external impediments, but, for Locke, this notion was much too narrow. He instead preferred to define liberty as "not to be subject to the inconsistent, uncertain, unknown, Arbitrary will of another Man" (*TT,* 2.22: 324). By expanding the notion of liberty to include a stipulation against the forced subjection of a person's will, Locke opposed Hobbes's contention that dominion can be authorized through some ritual of conquest whereby a compact is extorted. He maintained that such acts of submission do not count as consent.[34]

Here we must wonder how Locke could have expected to sustain this line of criticism given that his account of servitude seems to converge with Hobbes's on the matter of the servant's contractual obligation. Once he agreed with Hobbes that a servant's duties can be specified by contract, Locke was in no position to deny the extension of this right to slaves as well. Locke's criticism of extorted promises suggests that from his perspective, Hobbes's coerced servants can be viewed as contracted slaves. Despite Locke's moral objection to the coercion that plays such a vital role in Hobbes's account of dominion, his adherence to the contractual distinction between slavery and servitude provided a ground for the coerced bargain that brings about a transition from slavery to servitude. Presumably, this transition-stage contract could include gradual manumission among the rights granted to a slave.[35] Consistent with his rather negative assessment of Hobbes's account of coerced servitude, if such contracts are agreed upon in the context of coercion, Locke would have to count them as invalid extensions of slavery.[36]

By reference to the absence of a contractual relationship between masters and servants, both Hobbes and Locke could account for the transformation of a system of servitude into slavery. With regard to the transformation of a system of slavery into servitude, Hobbes would allow slaves to enter a contractual obligation of servitude, whereas Locke spoke in terms of a war captive's forfeiture of her right to life to a just conqueror.[37] Once slaves are acquired through lawful conquest, however, Locke's theory also provided for their manumission:

> For, if once *Compact* enter between them, and make an agreement for a limited Power on the one side, and Obedience on the other, the State of War and *Slavery* ceases, as long as the Compact endures. (*TT*, 2.24:326)[38]

Locke seems to have spoken inconsistently against the validity of coerced contracts when we consider some of the reasons for thinking that a slave's decision to enter a contractual relation of servitude (in exchange for manumission) occurs under coercive conditions.[39]

Locke was apparently inconsistent when he claimed on the one hand that "Captives taken in a just War, are by the Right of Nature subjected to the Absolute Dominion and Arbitrary Power of their Masters" and on the other that "no Body has an absolute Arbitrary Power over himself, or over any other" (*TT*, 2.85:366; 2.135:402). These remarks can be reconciled by taking into account an important modification in Locke's view of natural rights. Just as Hobbes appealed to natural rights to justify conquest and to oppose slavery, in similar fashion Locke appealed to natural rights to justify slavery and to oppose conquest. This similarity is highlighted in the case of defense against an aggressor, a case in which Locke's moral opposition to conquest was tempered:

[H]e who makes an *attempt to enslave me,* thereby puts himself into a State of War with me . . . And therefore it is Lawful for me to treat him, as one who has put *himself into a State of War* with me, i.e. kill him if I can; for to that hazard does he justly expose himself, whoever introduces a State of War, and is *aggressor* in it. (*TT,* 2.17-18:320–21)

By arguing for a potential war captive's right of resistance against an unlawful aggressor Locke moved closer to a Hobbesian view. His granting a right of resistance in this instance, however, conflicts with his general claim that slaves have forfeited all of their rights, for unlawful war captives are nonetheless slaves.[40]

The key to resolving this conflict is to take note of Locke's two competing images of enslavement. When Locke had cases of governmental tyranny in mind, he condemned slavery as inherently evil and, by relying on this image of its immorality, he gave the corresponding argument for the slave's right of resistance.[41] Locke maintained that by right of nature citizens threatened with enslavement to an absolute monarch are entitled to resist being "degraded from the common state of Rational Creatures" (*TT,* 2.91:327). For the most part, slavery was viewed by Locke as an outcome of a war in which there is an aggressor (or unjust conqueror) and a defender against the aggressor (or just conqueror). The war between a just and an unjust conqueror generates two, quite disparate, images of enslaved war captives. Locke conceived the enslaved captives of an unjust conqueror as bearers of rights, whereas he reduced the enslaved captives of the just conqueror to dangerous beasts of prey without rights.[42]

Locke's casting of the aggressor as a "savage ravenous Beast" was in keeping with his justification of slavery (*TT,* 2.181:436). He held that as nonrational creatures whose only means of conflict resolution is to use force and violence, aggressors must be killed or enslaved. He conceived aggressors to be beyond the scope of natural rights, but this move failed to replace entirely Hobbes's less moralized view, according to which even beasts of prey have an inalienable right of resistance.[43] Locke restated Hobbes's idea that the right of nature does not entail any correlative duties in terms of a moral argument to justify both conquest and enslavement of aggressors, as well as resistance to being conquered and enslaved by such aggressors. For Locke, then, the only slave forfeiting her natural rights is an unjust aggressor who is taken as a war captive. The war captive of an unjust aggressor, however, retains a natural right of resistance. In a manner similar to Hobbes, Locke conceived this natural right, which is retained by citizens who are subjected to tyranny, as a right not to be enslaved.

The Overlap of Slavery and Servitude

There is a moral question connected with the definition of slavery that seems to underlie the kind of worry Locke had about Hobbes's endorsement of coerced contracts as a ground on which to justify social and political obligations. Certain differences between their respective concepts of slavery are related to their different views of its injustice. Hobbes used a narrow criterion of corporal liberty to restrict the *definition* of slavery to apply only to those held in physical bondage, while Locke employed a broader criterion of a person being subjected to the arbitrary will of another to restrict the *justification* of slavery to apply only to captives of a just war. With regard to the definition of slavery, Hobbes would only consider the vanquished who are imprisoned, or fettered by chains, as slaves, whereas Locke would include anyone not free from the "Arbitrary power" of another a slave as well (*TT*, 2.222:460). On the morality of slavery, Locke considered slavery justified only if it is restricted to first-generation captives of a just war. Given his view that the slave's right of life is forfeited, Locke's concern with the rights of slaves was only with what is implied by his restricted justification, whereas Hobbes proclaimed a slave's inalienable right of nature, since he saw no justification whatever for slavery. Why then did Hobbes and Locke disagree about whether what each would define as slavery is sometimes justified?

To some extent this disagreement is connected with their respective views of the slave's rights. Although both maintained that a slave remains in the state of nature vis-à-vis her master, only Hobbes saw this as a situation in which a slave retains the inalienable right of resistance. From the perspective of his absolutist theory of obligation, which required that citizens subject their wills to a sovereign, he simply did not view anything other than physical bondage as slavery. Locke, however, preferred to speak of the slave of a just conqueror as someone who has *forfeited* her natural rights. By grounding his justification of slavery on this claim, he masked the inconsistency of his objection to Hobbes's account of coerced servitude.

These differences can be reconciled if we understand each account to be attempting to maintain a distinction between justifiable and unjustifiable forms of domination and servility. The significance of contracts for maintaining this distinction is revealed by considering how each proposed to account for the injustice of slavery by reference to the rights of slaves. Since both used the term "slavery" to refer only to nonconsensual forms of servitude, their theories differ mainly with respect to what each would count as consensual. Locke opposed Hobbes's view that it is morally permissible to coerce an agent into doing something she would otherwise prefer not to do. His disagreement with Hobbes's view of the role of coercion in creating morally binding contracts turns on the contextual ambiguity of assertions regarding an agent's doing something "willingly," signaling an erosion of the ground for employing the notion of a contract to mark a conceptual difference between slavery and servitude.

The difference between their respective concepts of slavery can be represented by a continuum, on which slavery is located at the harsh end and servitude is located at the benign end. On Hobbes's version of the continuum, the overlap of certain forms of benign slavery and certain harsh forms of servitude cannot be represented (see figure 1). This conceptual inaccuracy seems to be corrected on Locke's version of the continuum, where the overlap of slavery and servitude is limited to a small range of cases bordering both sides of the divide between the most benign instances of slavery and the harshest instances of servitude (see figure 2). The accuracy of Locke's view of the overlap can be called in question, however, by considering a graph displaying a different conception (see figure 3). With the same proportion of benign and harsh cases, overlap at both ends of the continuum is acknowledged by representing a greater *spread* of the various forms of servility under both slavery and servitude. Locke's version of the continuum only permits an overlap of benign slavery with the harshest servitude when, in fact, there are

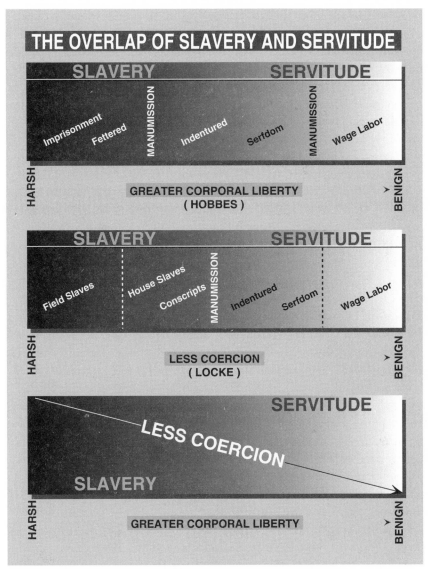

Figure 1 (top): Hobbes's version of the continuum.
Figure 2 (middle): Locke's version of the continuum.
Figure 3 (bottom): The overlap version.
Graphic by Bill Jones.

some forms of harsh servitude that are in certain respects indistinguishable from the harshest slavery. More importantly, on Locke's version, the possibility that some forms of slavery were not as harsh as many forms of servitude is entirely concealed.[44] This graphic distortion has a conceptual counterpart in the idea that slavery is, *by definition,* always harsher than servitude—an idea that has created a conceptual barrier that prevents the application of reasons for condemning slavery to sufficiently similar instances of servitude.

Hobbes's reliance on corporal liberty as a sign of consent renders his account even more vulnerable to this criticism. More than freedom from chains or imprisonment is required in order to transform an involuntary relationship of enslavement into a consensual relationship of servitude. Although coercion was involved in other ways, the perpetuation of the institution of slavery did not always require chains and imprisonment. Many urban American slaves, who were skilled laborers, lived apart from their masters and supported themselves by finding their own work and managing their own affairs.[45] Sometimes they were "hired out" with only an obligation to pay their masters a percentage of their wages. It would be an error, however, to overlook the slave's perspective and conclude from this observation that the harshness of a slave's condition is an indication of whether his relationship with his master is consensual.[46]

Although both Hobbes and Locke acknowledged a distinction between being denied corporal liberty and being coerced such that an agent's having greater corporal liberty does not mean that that agent is therefore less coerced, Locke's distinction between slavery and servitude better accommodates more benign forms of slavery, such as house servants and conscripts, which are excluded from Hobbes's version of the continuum. But even Locke's version of the continuum fails to accommodate other benign cases of managerial (e.g., *oikonomoi*) and elite (e.g., Mamluk) slaves. He rendered the distinction between slavery and servitude in terms of an embattled notion of consent, a notion that obscures the fact that some forms of servitude involved coercion and legal ownership, and some forms of slavery allowed slaves to own slaves themselves.[47]

Perhaps what is essential to the slave's perspective can be salvaged from a contractarian view, such as Hobbes's or Locke's, by focusing on the manner in which their theories aimed to specify a certain *legal* status of slaves by reference to natural rights. Both held that obligations cannot arise except by consent. When a slave is manumitted in exchange for servitude, her contractual relation can be viewed as legally establishing, or restoring, certain rights that are denied to slaves, particularly the right not to be owned by someone and, hence, regarded as merely that person's property. To the extent that manumission is simply a *legal right* of this sort, the war captive paradigm dictates a concept of servants on the model of manumitted slaves who have a right of self-ownership.

The idea that slavery is essentially a legal status of being owned by someone is a widely held view that has been criticized by Orlando Patterson. Patterson noted that this feature is not unique to slavery; hence, it cannot constitute a peculiar injustice.[48] To specify what he considers to be the peculiar injustice of slavery, he instead proposed a definition in terms of a plurality of elements. According to Patterson, the peculiar injustice of slavery is constituted by three principal attributes of powerlessness, natal alienation, and dishonor, although in some of his earlier work he seems to have wanted to place a greater emphasis on natal alienation. By acknowledging that each of these attributes, including natal alienation, is sometimes present in certain forms of servitude, such as coerced serfdom, he postulates that only in the case of slavery do all three ever occur together.[49] Patterson's multiple-attribute definition of slavery has the advantage of allowing natal alienation to be a constitutive element without requiring that it be a unique defining characteristic.

Patterson's move to define slavery in terms of a constellation of attributes, none of which is unique to slavery, virtually ensures overlap once he acknowledges certain forms of servitude and slavery to be indistinguishable. His recognition that each of the three attributes is sometimes present in the case of servitude (e.g., convergent serfdom) required him to treat the notion of slavery as a vague concept with no unique defining characteristics. About ancient slavery he declared, "imperial freedmen and slaves were indeed slaves in the terms in which I have defined the concept."[50] Similarly, with regard to slavery in the Middle Ages he claimed, "European serfdom was, in fact, recombinant slavery."[51] But these remarks only serve to highlight the problem. To admit that slavery and servitude sometimes sufficiently overlap in the sense that certain forms are indistinguishable is to admit that there is no peculiar injustice of slavery. Of course, Patterson would insist on maintaining a distinction in cases of overlap, but it is worth noting that he can do so only by using expressions such as "semislaves" to refer to servants in the overlapping case of convergent serfdom.[52] His insistence that slavery is the only form of servility that has all three attributes seems vacuous insofar as he admits that certain overlapping cases of servitude are indistinguishable.[53] If slavery cannot be defined in terms of a peculiar injustice because of its overlap with certain forms of servitude, can we justifiably condemn slavery as inherently evil, without extending this condemnation to overlapping forms of servitude?

Benign Slavery's Inherent Evil

The debate surrounding the definition of slavery reflects different lines of thought regarding the nature of its injustice. Hobbes and Locke shifted the emphasis either toward or away from Shakespeare's physical bondage model in order to develop political theories that only opposed certain forms of servility. Hobbes's concept excluded non-physical forms of bondage by restricting the application of his definition only to extreme cases of servitude involving a denial of corporal liberty. The inadequacy of drawing this distinction in terms of corporal liberty becomes apparent when we consider whether there can be slaves who are autonomous in this sense.[54] I have already noted that many house slaves were not fettered and had a great deal of freedom of bodily movement. If Hobbes wanted to argue that slavery is evil because it denies this kind of autonomy to slaves, he must concede that the evil of slavery is lessened when slaves are granted a greater measure of it.

Given that within certain categories of slavery there was a wide latitude in this respect, we have some reason to prefer a notion of autonomy that is closer to Locke's view, namely, that one has autonomy to the extent that one is free from the arbitrary will of a master.[55] To what extent, however, does Locke's broader notion of liberty really overcome the difficulty of specifying the autonomy denied to slaves? It is not enough to simply reject the Hobbesian view by acknowledging that some slaves (say, house servants) enjoyed a greater measure of corporal liberty, for the Lockean view must also acknowledge that in some cases slaves who lacked corporal liberty still were not subject to the arbitrary will of their masters. This puzzle arises because there were conscripted slaves, such as Frederick Douglass, who (by his own testimony) had as much corporal liberty as many nonslaves, while at the same time, there were estranged slaves, such as Harriet Jacobs, who (by her own testimony) escaped the arbitrary will of their masters. (Jacobs accomplished this by hiding for an extended period in her grandmother's attic.) Hence, slaves such as Douglass *acquired corporal liberty* in Hobbes's sense and yet *lacked autonomy* in Locke's sense, whereas slaves such as Jacobs *lacked corporal liberty* in Hobbes's sense, and yet *acquired autonomy* in Locke's sense. This puzzle indicates that neither Hobbes nor Locke espoused a notion of liberty that fully accorded with the slaves' view of autonomy.

This shortcoming can be understood by the way Hobbes and Locke sought to reconcile their commitment to natural rights with their respective views of what counts as justifiable forms of domination and servility. As I indicated, a Hobbesian war captive incurs an obligation of servitude in exchange for her release from chains or imprisonment. Locke denounced these extorted contracts as invalid, preferring to speak of a war captive's contract in terms of a restoration of her forfeited rights. What is important for both is that in such cases manumission involved the incurring of an obligation of servitude. We need only consider the harshness of Hobbes's hereditary servitude relative to Locke's nonhereditary slavery to see the problem posed by the overlap of slavery and servitude for this contractual view. It is in cases where more rights are granted under certain forms of slavery than under certain forms of servitude that the problem of specifying a peculiar injustice unique to slavery arises. Indeed, such cases imply that other forms of servility that are as harsh, or more so, are unjust for the same reason that slavery is unjust. Rather than providing a reason to rule out the claim that slavery is inherently evil, the recognition that servitude may sometimes be harsher than slavery indicates instead that a fuller understanding of what is meant by benign slavery is necessary to show that even relatively benign forms are evil.

Hobbes's account of authorization, according to which a con-

119

queror grants a slave manumission in exchange for a servitude contract, was interpreted by Locke as a form of enslavement. Locke's concern with coercion introduces an ambiguity that only becomes apparent when we consider several contrasting cases of slaves entering into such contracts. If we take wage-labor as Locke's paradigm of a voluntary contract, whereby "a Freeman makes himself a Servant to another," we can place contractual manumission at the near end of the gamut of cases that precede it (*TT,* 2.85:365). Beginning at the far end, there are *ransom* cases, such as when enslaved captives were forcibly transported to a distant colony where they were set free with an option to enter "willingly" into a contractual arrangement to work for passage back home.[56] This use of coercion, involving physical force, seems to contrast sharply with the use of contracts as incentives in *legal posting* cases, exemplified by the Latin American practice of "coartacion."[57] In this case, a master is legally required to make public the terms of a slave's manumission, a commonly understood means of establishing the property rights of slaves— including a right to purchase themselves. Each of these is supposed to be radically different from cases of *voluntary contracts,* such as those designed to legally return manumitted slaves to their former status.[58] Yet in all three cases we can speak of a slave "willingly" entering a contract much in the same manner as we speak of a wage laborer "willingly" entering a contract.[59]

The case of the war captive who is manumitted from slavery to servitude was imagined by both Hobbes and Locke to be most like the ransom case because of the use of physical force. But it also shares a similarity with the legal posting case because it may involve a purchase of freedom, and bears a close resemblance to cases of voluntarily contracted slavery, at least to the extent that it constitutes a legal obligation. Although Locke's notion of contractual manumission led him to condone what amounts to voluntarily contracted slavery, so long as it is temporary and limited to specific duties, he gave no reason to suppose that this, or any of the other forms of contracted slavery, is more benign (less coercive). Ironically, Locke critically referred to Hobbes's coerced servitude as slavery, but was particularly concerned that we do not so refer to his version of it.[60] His argument that no one can freely enter a slavery contract, although they can freely enter a contract to drudgery, assumes that even the harshest servitude will always be more benign than any form of slavery.

Barbara Jeanne Fields has railed against the suggestion that the kind of contracted slavery that overlapped free labor in Maryland was benign in some sense that implies that it was any less evil than other forms. She refers to the human suffering resulting primarily from family disruptions as evidence to counter the view that conscript slavery in urban areas such as Baltimore was not as evil as other forms because, by comparison with, say, the harshness of plantation life, it was relatively benign. Although Fields rightfully contests the traditional criteria used to gauge the harshness of slavery, the cogency of her objection to using a notion of benign slavery to refer to conscripts can be undermined by supposing, for the sake of argument, that there had been a special proposal adopted in Maryland to legally require slaveowners to keep slave families intact.[61] If slavery is inherently evil, then to suppose the granting of this right should not weaken the claim that even this more benign form of slavery is evil. Fields rightfully maintains that so-called benign slavery is nonetheless evil, but wrongly concludes from this that it is therefore not benign.

Fields's point that there is no reason to prefer physical bondage as a criterion of slavery's harshness must be well taken. To speak of the slavery Locke justified as "benign" is by virtue of comparing some particular feature of it with a corresponding feature of Hobbes's account of a much harsher form. But what about the fact that, unlike Hobbes, Locke placed a greater significance on the slave's right to property than he placed on her right to life? What criterion do we use to judge whether Locke's stipulation regarding the property and children of slaves is more benign than Hobbes's insistence on the slave's inalienable right of resistance? Similarly, what criterion do we use to rank a male field slave's experience of being fettered and whipped by comparison with a female house slave's experience of being routinely assaulted sexually? The fact that urban, or house, slaves were materially better off than plantation field slaves should not mislead us about the evilness of more benign forms. This point was used by Jacobs to deliver the force of her quite rhetorical description of her childhood experience under a relatively benign form of slavery.

My mother's mistress was the daughter of my grandmother's mistress. She was the foster sister of my mother, they were both nourished at my grandmother's breast. In fact, my mother had been weaned at three months old, that the babe of the mistress might obtain sufficient food. . . . [W]hen they became women, my mother was a most faithful servant to her white foster sister. . . . They all spoke kindly of my dead mother, who had been a slave merely in name. . . . I was told that my home was now to be with her mistress; and I found it a happy one. No toilsome or disagreeable duties were imposed upon me. My mistress was so kind to me that I was always glad to do her bidding, and proud to labor for her as much as my young years would permit.[62]

If we keep Jacobs's abolitionist motives in mind, these remarks can be taken to suggest that slavery remains evil despite the material benefits and other incentives for cooperation provided by its more benign forms. Indeed, from Jacobs's perspective, such benefits are thoroughly contaminated by the *coercive context* of the master's absolute power over the slave's fate.

This point was brought out in a letter to the *New York Tribune* in which Jacobs responded to Julia Tyler's defense of slavery as a benevolent institution. Jacobs was particularly concerned with shedding light on Tyler's claim that slaves were only sold under very peculiar circumstances. She describes what happened when her mother went to her master upon learning of his sexually abusing one of Harriet's sisters.

Nothing could exceed his rage at this, what he called impertinence. My mother was dragged to jail, there remained twenty-five days, with negro traders to come in as they liked to examine her, as she was offered for sale. My sister was told that she must yield, or never expect to see her mother again.[63]

Jacob's reference to her mother's imprisonment and pending sale seems to literally contradict the account she gives in her autobiography of a much less harsh childhood with her mother. This inconsistency can be reconciled if we allow benign practices to manifest some limited amount of incidental, but nonetheless purposeful, harshness. As a function of the absolute power of slaveowners, there is a tandem relation between benign and harsh practices such that benign forms of slavery exist in a context where harsher forms constantly loom in the background as a negative incentive—literally as a physical threat that induces cooperation. It is in this sense that Jacobs's sister's voluntary submission to the master's sexual desires can be understood as a form of conquest that did not require the use of direct force. Conquest of this sort escapes Locke's definition of consent, which was limited to the direct use of force. Locke was clear about his opposition to conquest involving the direct use of force, as in the case of the unjust aggressor, but he was less clear about whether his objection extends to other cases of conquest not involving the direct use of force.[64]

This deficiency in Locke's view of coerced consent can be traced to his notion of liberty. He failed to recognize that the overlap of certain forms of drudgery with certain forms of slavery can be explained in terms of power relations that extend well beyond the master's authority over the slave. The limitations of Locke's focus on the master-slave relationship can be drawn into relief by considering Jacobs's insight regarding her autonomy:

> I and my children are now free! We are as free from the power of slaveholders as are the white people of the north; and though that, according to my ideas, is not saying a great deal, it is a vast improvement in *my* condition.[65]

These remarks display Jacobs's keen understanding that all forms of servility must be questioned. She acknowledged that her escape and eventual manumission from slavery were an improvement, but she also made clear that she did not consider herself free in the sense that, as a servant, she still lacked full autonomy from the *economic* power of a master. This view entails a more radical egalitarian notion of autonomy.

According to this more radical view, a society in which social equality obtains is inconsistent with any of its members occupying a position of domination or servility. Because the natural-rights theories of Hobbes and Locke do not challenge the basic power relations that support and perpetuate a dominant class, their views fall short of what is required for a condemnation of slavery as the institutional-

ization of an inherently evil social relation. The remedy they pre-
scribe for harsh slavery, in lieu of abolition, is to advocate more
benign forms that offer improvement by granting rights to slaves.
Their natural-rights solution of the plight of slaves does not recognize the slave's lack of rights as symptomatic of a deeper social ail-
ment. Once we recognize that servitude is sometimes harsher than
slavery, however, it seems inconsistent to treat as inherently evil a
form of slavery under which slaves have perhaps even more rights
than servants. For both Hobbes and Locke, the distinction between
slavery and servitude is to be understood in wholly legalistic
terms—of whether or not the servant has a contract, perhaps combined with a moralistic concern as to whether coercion, or physical
bondage, was involved, but not in terms of ongoing power relations.
Their emphasis on the moral-legal aspects of enslavement is consistent with the unhappy outcome of systematically granting more
rights to slaves, including manumission, while maintaining a social
arrangement that perpetuates virtually the same power relations of
domination and servility.[66]

Notes

1. John Locke, *Two Treatises of Government*, Peter Laslett, ed., (New York: New
American Library, 1965), *First Treatise*, chap. 1, 175. All references are to this edition. For justifications of benign slavery by contemporary philosophers see, for instance, the two slightly different views maintained by John Rawls in *A Theory of Justice*
(Cambridge: Harvard University Press, 1971), 152 and 248, and Robert Nozick's
defense of voluntary slavery in *Anarchy, State and Utopia* (New York: Basic Books,
1975), 331ff.

2. Paul Edwards, ed., *The Life of Olaudah Equiano, or Gustavus Vassa the African*
(Essex, England: Longman, 1989), 15.

3. This difficulty is faced by some researchers who are reluctant to use the term
slavery in the African context. See, for instance, the use of scare quotes in Igor
Kopytoff and Suzanne Miers, "African 'Slavery' as an Institution of Marginality" in
Slavery in Africa: Historical and Anthropological Perspectives, ed. S. Miers and I. Kopytoff
(Madison: University of Wisconsin Press, 1977). For a useful discussion of the prob-
lem of defining slavery in connection with open and closed systems see James L.
Watson, ed., *Asian & African Systems of Slavery* (Berkeley: University of California
Press, 1980), chap. 1.

4. Compare Rawls, *Theory of Justice*, 158, 167–68, 325–26; R. M. Hare, "What is

Wrong with Slavery," this volume, p. 215. According to Bentham, "If it could be arranged in such a manner that slavery should be so established that there should be only one slave to one master, there might be ground for hesitation in pronouncing before-hand which would have the advantage and which the disadvantage; and it might be possible that, all things considered, the sum of good in this arrangement would be nearly equal to that of evil." John Bowring, ed., *The Works of Jeremy Bentham* (New York: Russell & Russell, 1962), vol. 3, 344.

5. See, for instance, Paul Edwards, ed., *Life of Olaudah Equiano,* 17; Jean Fegan Yellin, ed., *Harriet A. Jacobs, Incidents in the Life of a Slave Girl* (Cambridge: Harvard University Press, 1987), 7; Frederick Douglass, *Narrative of the Life of Frederick Douglass,* in *Frederick Douglass: The Narrative and Selected Writings,* ed. Michael Meyer (New York: Modern Library, 1984), 50; John W. Blassingame, ed., *Slave Testimony* (Baton Rouge: Louisiana State University Press, 1977), 689, 735, 736, and 740.

6. We need only consider the situation of some free blacks who, after purchasing their relatives, inadvertently maintained them as slaves, to understand how the institution of slavery can be evil while certain benign instances are excusable. The problem for utilitarians, however, is not that benign instances are sometimes excused as an evil that must be permitted due to extenuating circumstances, but rather that they are sometimes justified because they are not deemed evil. These cases are presented in Carter G. Woodson, *Free Negro Owners of Slaves in the United States in 1830* (New York: Negro University Press, 1924/68), v–viii.

7. *The Tempest,* Act I, scene ii, pp. 333–34. By contrast, the enslavement of Ariel by Sycorax is represented as an unjustifiably evil act. All references to this work are to William Shakespeare, *The Tempest,* ed. Anne Righter (London: Penguin Books, 1968).

8. *Tempest,* I.ii.344, 362.

9. *Tempest,* I.ii.247.

10. Caliban is permanently *punished* by Prospero for his attempted violation of Miranda's honor, whereas Ariel is temporarily *indebted* to Prospero for releasing him from the tree trunk. Although Prospero has these moral grounds by which to appeal, it is worth noting that Shakespeare does not represent Prospero's claim to a right of dominion as uncontested in either case.

11. See Dean Ebner, "The Tempest: Rebellion and the Ideal State," *Shakespeare Quarterly* 16 (1965): 163; and Stephen J. Greenblatt, "Linguistic Colonialism in *The Tempest*" in *William Shakespeare's "The Tempest,"* ed. Harold Bloom (New York: Chelsea House, 1988), 67. For a discussion of certain nuances that suggest a more ambivalent representation of Caliban, and his relation to the other characters, see Paul Brown, " 'This Thing of Darkness I Acknowledge Mine': The Tempest and the Discourse of Colonialism" in Bloom, 131–51.

12. See R. M. Hare, 212. For a straightforward interpretation of Ariel's status as a slave see Edward Kamau Brathwaite, "Caliban, Ariel, and Unprospero in the Con-

flict of Creolization: A Study of the Slave Revolt in Jamaica in 1831–32," in *Comparative Perspectives on Slavery in New World Plantation Societies,* ed. Vera Rubin and Arthur Tuden (New York: The New York Academy of Sciences, 1977), 43.

13. See, for instance, Frank Kernode, ed., *The Tempest* (Cambridge: Harvard University Press, 1958), xxxviii–xliii and Eric Cheyfitz, *The Poetics of Imperialism: Translation and Colonization from The Tempest to Tarzan* (New York: Oxford University Press, 1991, chap. 7.

14. Aristotle, *Politics,* I.i.

15. *Leviathan,* chap. 15, para. 20, p. 107. All references to *Leviathan* are to *Leviathan,* Thomas Hobbes, ed. Richard Tuck (Cambridge: Cambridge University Press, 1991).

16. *Lev.* 13.4:88 and 15.20:107.

17. *Lev.* "Review and Conclusions," 486.

18. *De Cive,* ed. Howard Warrender (Oxford: Clarendon Press, 1983), chap. 8, sec. 1, p. 117. See also *The Elements of Law,* pt. II, chap. 3, and *Leviathan,* chap. 20. References to *The Elements of Law* are to *The Elements of Law,* ed. Ferdinand Tönnies (New York: Barnes and Noble, 1969) and will be given by title, part number, chapter number, section number, and page number.

19. *EL* 2.4.3:132, *DC* 9.4:123 and *Lev.* 7.7:140.

20. See also *DC* 8.1:117 and *Lev.* 20.15:142.

21. Hobbes claimed that "He that is taken, and put into prison, or chaines, is not Conquered, though Overcome; for he is still an Enemy, and may save himself if hee can." *Lev.* "Review and Conclusions," 484. Hobbes also extended this right to animals. See *EL* 2.4.9:130–31 and *DC* 8.10:120.

22. See *Lev.* 45.12:447 and *DC* 1.12:149.

23. Hobbes draws this contrast in several places. See, for instance, *EL* 2.4.9:134, *DC* 8.1:117 and *Lev.* 18.14:121; 45.12:447.

24. See also *Lev.* 21.22:154.

25. See *DC* 5.8:89 and *DC* 8.7:119. In anticipation of the suggestion that the sovereign's absolute authority implies a loss of liberty for subjects, Hobbes only reiterated his contention that "all *Servants,* and *Subjects* are *free,* who are not fetter'd and imprisoned" (*DC* 9.9:125). He recognized that those subjects who were in a commonwealth established by institution may believe that they are better off than others who were conquered and forced to submit to a sovereign, but he considered this belief to be of little consequence since the authority in both cases is no less absolute.

26. See *EL* 2.3.4:128–29, *EL* 2.4.9:134, *DC* 8.5:119 and *Lev.* 20.13:142.

27. See also *DC* 8.9:119.

28. See *Two Treatises,* preface: 171; 1.1:175; 2.22:324; 2.86:366; 2.149:413; 2.220–22:460.

29. *Two Treatises,* 2.86:366.

30. *Two Treatises*, 2.77:362; 2.85:366; 2.123–24:395.

31. *Two Treatises*, 2.85:366.

32. *Two Treatises*, 2.23:325. For Hobbes's discussion of hereditary servitude, see especially *EL* 2.4.4:133.

33. *Two Treatises*, 2.173:430; 2.174:431; 2.186:439–40; 2.192–96:441–44.

34. *Two Treatises*, 2.186:440.

35. Bentham inconsistently argued this view. After acknowledging "the impossibility of subjecting the authority of a master over his slaves to legal restraint, and of preventing the abuse of his power, if he be disposed to abuse it," he goes on to make the case for the emancipation of slaves by selectively granting them more rights. "Principles of the Civil Code," in *Works*, vol. 3, 346.

36. This seems to be the force of his remarks in the Preface to the *Two Treatises*, but is inconsistent with his statement at 2.24.325–26.

37. *Two Treatises*, 2.181:436. It should be noted that similar remarks regarding a slave's forfeiture of life can be found in Hobbes at *Lev.* 45.12:447.

38. See also *Two Treatises*, 2.172:430.

39. Locke acknowledges the coercive context in the following remarks: "For whenever he finds the hardship of his Slavery outweighs the value of his life, 'tis in his Power, by resisting the Will of his Master, to draw on himself the Death he deserves" (*Two Treatises*, 2.22:325).

40. See *Two Treatises*, 2.23:325; 2.180:435. Locke halfheartedly cashes in Hobbes's inalienable right of resistance, claiming that a person "cannot part with" her liberty except as a substitute for death (2.23:325). Locke's remarks regarding the slave's right to own property are even less clear. He claims that a just conqueror has no right to a war captive's property beyond what is required for reparations. This does not quite fit with his reference to slaves as "those who are stripped of all property," or with his comment "being in the *State of Slavery*, not capable of any Property" (2.173:430; 2.85:366). Locke suggests that the slave's property belongs to his children, who remain free citizens with rights.

41. *Two Treatises*, preface: 171, cited in Richard Ashcraft, *Locke's Two Treatises of Government* (London: Allen & Unwin, 1987), 548.

42. See *Two Treatises*, 2.16:319–20; 2.171:429; 2.181:436. Laslett points out Locke's use of the expression "wild beast, or noxious brute" to refer to kings Locke considered despots, specifically Charles II and James II. See *Two Treatises*, notes, pp. 170 and 429.

43. See Wayne Glausser, "Three Approaches to Locke and the Slave Trade," *Journal of the History of Ideas* 51 (April–June 1990): 214. See above, note 21.

44. Thomas Sowell cites the case of a slave who was a riverboat captain with command over a crew that included whites. John Hebron, "Simon Gray, Riverman: A Slave Who was Almost Free," *Mississippi Valley Historical Review* (December 1962): 472–84, cited in Thomas Sowell, *Markets and Minorities* (New York: Basic Books 1981), 83.

45. See August Meier and Elliott M. Rudwick, *From Plantation to Ghetto* (New York: Hill and Wang, 1969), 65–66; Richard C. Wade, *Slavery in the Cities* (New York: Oxford University Press, 1964), 114; Barbara Jeanne Fields, *Slavery and Freedom on the Middle Ground* (New Haven: Yale University Press, 1985), 40–62.

46. This insight is captured in Frederick Douglass's remarks on his status as a conscript ("hired out"): "Master Hugh seemed to be very much pleased . . . with this arrangement, and well he might be . . . [W]hile he derived all the benefits of slaveholding . . . without its evils, I endured all the evils of being a slave, and yet suffered all the care and anxiety of a responsible freeman." *Frederick Douglass, My Bondage and My Freedom* (New York: Dover Publications, 1969), 328–29, cited in Barbara Jeanne Fields, *Slavery and Freedom*, 49.

47. See Orlando Patterson's discussion of convergent serfdom in his *Freedom* (New York: Basic Books, 1991), chap. 20.

48. See Dale B. Martin, *Slavery as Salvation* (New Haven: Yale University Press, 1990), 5ff.

49. Patterson cites the case of professional athletes. He points out that athletic sales do not count as slavery because nonslaves have a choice in the sale or withdrawal of their services, whereas slaves do not. However, this claim does not fit with Patterson's own discussion of voluntary slavery. Patterson seems inclined to take this case to pose an obvious counterexample, rather than to view it from the athlete's perspective, as a form of benign slavery. *Slavery and Social Death* (Cambridge: Harvard University Press, 1982), 24–26.

50. For instance, in his earlier account Patterson advanced his multi-attribute conception of the slave as "a person without power, natality, and honor," *Social Death*, 27. In a recent discussion of the overlap of slavery and serfdom, however, he admitted that: "The element of slavery that in ancient times had been most constitutive of the relation, natal alienation, was increasingly shared with the bonded person. The only real difference between serfs and slaves pertained to the element of honor, of which slaves had none and serfs some, however small," *Freedom*, 356. Compare these remarks, however, with Patterson's remarks elsewhere regarding the distinction between serfs and slaves. Without mentioning honor he referred to slavery as "the institutionalized alienation from the rights of labor and kinship." "The Structural Origins of Slavery: A Critique of the Nieboer-Domar Hypothesis from A Comparative Perspective" in *Comparative Perspectives on Slavery*, ed. Rubin and Tuden, 15.

51. *Freedom*, 352.

52. *Social Death*, 303.

53. *Freedom*, 351.

54. In his earlier account Patterson refers to "the so-called serfs, most of whom were genuine slaves." *Social Death*, 128. He reiterates this view in his later account: "Freedmen status was so circumscribed, and the continued dependency on the ex-

master, now patron, so similar, that there was little objective socioeconomic difference between the freed tenant and the domiciled slave." *Freedom*, 354.

55. See Gerald Dworkin, *The Theory and Practice of Autonomy* (New York: Cambridge University Press, 1988), 129; James Rachels and William Ruddick, "Lives and Liberty," in *The Inner Citadel*, ed. John Christman (New York: Oxford University Press, 1989), 228ff; Joel Feinberg, "Autonomy, Sovereignty and Privacy," *Notre Dame Law Review* 58 (February 1983): 475.

56. See H. E. Maude, *Slavers in Paradise* (Stanford: Stanford University Press, 1981), chap. 10.

57. See Hubert H. S. Aimes, "Coartados: The Half-Life of Half-Slaves" in *The African in Latin America*, ed. Ann M. Pescatello (New York: Alfred A. Knopf, 1975), 226–29.

58. Barbara Jeanne Fields cites a Maryland law that invited manumitted slaves to renounce their freedom in order to avoid being removed from the state and separated from their enslaved relatives. *Slavery and Freedom*, 28.

59. See Hazel Carby's criticism of John Blassingame's claim that slave women were "literally forced to offer themselves willingly," quoted in her *Reconstructing Womanhood* (New York: Oxford, 1987), 21. Ulrich B. Phillips cites a case in which a slaveowner entered into a contract with his whole group of slaves. *American Negro Slavery* (Baton Rouge: Louisiana State University Press, 1990), 427.

60. See *Two Treatises*, 2.24.326.

61. Bentham suggested this in his remarks regarding family manumission. *Works*, 346.

62. Jacobs, *Incidents in the Life of a Slave Girl*, 7.

63. Harriet A. Jacobs, Letter to *New York Tribune* (22 June, 1853), *BAP*, 4, 164–67; reprinted in *Witness for Freedom*, ed. C. Peter Ripley (Chapel Hill: University of North Carolina Press, 1993), 91.

64. See *Two Treatises*, 2.187.440.

65. Yellin, *Incidents*, 201.

66. This point is emphasized by David Gauthier in the cautionary tale discussed in his *Morals by Agreement* (Oxford: Clarendon Press, 1986), chap. 7.

6

LOCKE AND THE LEGAL
OBLIGATIONS OF BLACK
AMERICANS

Bill E. Lawson

I n the 1960s, the civil rights struggle in America highlighted a
number of challenging and philosophically interesting political
and social questions. One hotly debated issue was the use of
civil disobedience by members of racial minorities acting out of the
claim that they were citizens, but unjustly treated. The conventional
political wisdom was that these activists, as citizens, were obligated
to work through the political system to bring about political and
social change. Thus, much of the debate by philosophers over civil
rights for black Americans centered on the issue of civil disobedience and its role in the civil rights struggle.[1]

Putting the civil disobedience question aside, there is an interesting and quite complex question that I wish to examine: Are there,
in fact, some blacks living in the United States, who because of their
political and social status, can claim exemption from any legal obligation to obey the law, even just laws? That is, are there some blacks
that can justifiably claim that they are in the state of nature and not
genuine citizens of the United States?

As strange as this question may seem, on a recent television talk
show, Robert Brock, president of the Self Determination Committee
of Los Angeles, made the claim that blacks are not legally obligated

to obey the laws of the United States.[2] He argued that (1) blacks had never consented to the United States' Constitution; (2) blacks were made citizens without their consent; (3) blacks were still slaves, just called citizens; and (4) blacks had no legal status as citizens and thus were not legally obligated to obey the laws.[3] On the surface, this argument may appear foolish, if it did not have consequences for our understanding of the legal obligations of politically unprotected citizens. Harvey Natanson realizes the importance of the claim about the legal status of some black Americans and argues that, indeed, some blacks are exempt from all legal obligations.[4] Natanson contends that some blacks have never been in a position to consent to the state.[5] These blacks, he claims, are still in a state of nature and thus are not legally obligated to the state.

Natanson's position draws on what he takes to be a Lockean model of the democratic state, and relies heavily on Locke's notion of government by consent. Natanson thinks that because of Locke's influence on American political thought, it is only natural to use Locke's position to assess the political situation of blacks in America.[6] He labels this Lockean position the "American-traditional" view of legal obligation (135).

Natanson's conclusion is significant for several reasons. First, there have been a number of times in American history that the question of the political status of blacks formed the basis of a national debate. The 1786 Constitutional Convention and the Dred Scott Supreme Court decision (1857) come immediately to mind. But Natanson's position focuses our attention on the period immediately following the end of the Civil War and Reconstruction.[7] It was at this point in American history that the political and philosophical problems regarding the inclusion of persons who had been in slavery into American political life came to the fore. Second, it is important for evaluating the legal status of black Americans and for assessing the role of civil disobedience in the civil rights struggle by blacks in the 1960s. Third, it is also important for our understanding of Locke's political theory.

While the Natanson article was written at the apex of the civil rights struggle, the argument that blacks are not citizens, as noted above, is still articulated in the black community. The position persists primarily because the social and economic status of many blacks has not changed since the 1960s. It is Natanson's argument for the conclusion that some blacks are still in a state of nature that I will analyze.

In what follows, I will argue against Natanson's reading of Locke and show that properly understood, Locke's position, at least in the *Second Treatise,* supports the claim that all black Americans are citizens and, as such, have legal obligations as citizens. There are no blacks in the United States who are in a state of nature. It will be shown that Natanson (a) focuses on the wrong passages in Locke, (b) shows very little insight regarding the political history of black Americans, and (c) neglects the fact that citizenship through birthright is an important aspect of American law. It will also be suggested that Locke's work supports the position that the acts of civil disobedience in the 1960s were, in fact, a justifiable and permissible response to the social and political injustices suffered by those blacks.

I

For his position to stand, Natanson has to give two arguments. First, he must show that at the end of slavery some blacks remained in a state of nature, even after the passage of the Thirteenth and Fourteenth Amendments to the United States Constitution. And second, he must show that there are some present-day blacks who are still in a state of nature. Let us look at his argument for some blacks remaining in the state of nature after emancipation.

Natanson draws on two interrelated arguments from Locke to assess the political status of blacks at the end of the Civil War. He starts with the Lockean proviso: that human beings have inalienable right to life, liberty and estate. This inalienable right existed in the state of nature and should be retained in civil society. Because civil society provides more security, men are therefore quite willing to leave the state of nature and "join in society with others who are already united, or have a mind to unite for the mutual preservation of their lives, liberties and estates" (p. 36).

Natanson does not tell us what he means by protection. And because the right to be protected is remarkably difficult to construe, we know that if a person is to be protected, presumably she is to be protected from something. But what? We can, at least, agree to this:

133

a liberal democratic state must provide protection from such abuses as lynching, assaults, and so forth. In addition, a liberal democratic state must ensure that a citizen be protected from political, legal, and public interference in the exercise of his or her rights as a citizen, when such interference is not grounded on the rights of others.[8]

Drawing on Locke, Natanson thinks that the state must provide the individual with more security than she would have had in the state of nature (p. 36). Otherwise, there is no need to enter into the contract with other individuals.

In the case of many blacks, it is clear that they were not accorded governmental protection, as citizens, while they were slaves. However, blacks, at the end of slavery, believed that they would be accorded the same protection that other genuine citizens received. It was their hope that their life, liberty, and property would be protected in a manner that was not done so before. Unfortunately, their high hopes and the government's actions were not on the same level.[9]

If, at emancipation, a contract was supposed to exist between blacks and the government, the government did not live up to its part of the contract. It is clear, according to Natanson, that some blacks never received the protection of their life, liberty, and property as mandated by contract membership. Because governmental protection was never given, there was no contract to accept. He thinks from this it follows that the Negroes in question are not parties to the contract, for it is the acceptance of the governmental protective services that defines contract membership (p. 37). The government failed to protect some blacks not, as Natanson notes, because these blacks did not want protection, but because the protection was never offered. As a consequence, these blacks remained in the state of nature (p. 39).

II

If the lack of protection were not enough, Natanson thinks that Locke's position on consents, which forms the basis for his second argument, also supports the position that some blacks were still in a state of nature at the end of slavery.

However, Natanson realizes that the political situation in America is very different than that which Locke envisions in the *Second Treatise*. He nevertheless thinks (despite its weakness) that historically the concept of consent has become important in the American political tradition as providing a justification for obedience to the law: the citizen ought to obey the law because he freely chose, by actual acceptance of government protection, to enter into a contract, one that provides him with a superior service that he cannot himself duplicate in a state of nature (p. 38).

Natanson also thinks that when a native-born American joins those who accept the authority of the government, he does not indicate his consent either verbally or in writing, for there are not rites of entry into the social order (p. 37). Is there some evidence that indicates that a native-born American acted by free choice and not coercion to become a willing party to the agreement? Natanson thinks it is by actual acceptance of the most essential service the government can offer him, superior protection of his natural right to life, liberty, and estate (if we reason in line with the basic tenets of the natural rights theory), that the individual expresses his free consent to an agreement or contract between himself and the government. Accepting government protection constitutes consent in its deepest meaning and at the same time is an establishment of contract (p. 37). In other words, to choose to receive the government's protection is to agree to government itself—in essence, it is an acceptance of genuine citizenship with all its benefits and responsibilities (p. 37).

While noting that Locke thinks that it is only through explicit and express consent that a person can become a true citizen, Natanson thinks that this is not applicable to the American scene. In America agreement to the contract is made tacitly, by the act of accepting of governmental protection of one's natural rights. Natanson admits that his version of tacit consent is not at all the type described by Locke. Yet Natanson thinks that his tacit consent is as binding as Locke's expressed consent (p. 38).

It is from this understanding of consent that Natanson wants to assess the political status of freedmen. Locke's position on consent gives rise to the following question: when American citizenship was granted to blacks, were these blacks in a position to give their consent? Natanson believes politically unprotected blacks had not been in a position to dispose of their possessions and persons as they saw fit. Slavery was a condition that severely restricted their personal autonomy. Natanson also seems to think that the historic lack of governmental protection led some people to believe that blacks were unable to be real participants in the social contract. This position draws on the idea that slavery had lowered the intellectual capacity of these blacks, and they were not capable of making a choice.

It appears that when it came to the question of citizenship, blacks were seen as essentially children when it came to knowing the responsibilities of citizenship, and the government of the United States took a paternalistic position regarding citizenship and blacks. Natanson seems to support this position when he states that:

> It seems clear, then that these Negroes have been denied not the freedom to refuse, but rather the freedom to make any choice at all. Such a denial is actually a cancellation of the implicit right of the native-born to be offered contract membership, and in so canceling this right, the government classifies this particular group as basically unable or unworthy to choose. Thus, in their involuntary alienation from the American contract, these Negroes have been considered lacking in the potential for self-determination. (p. 39)

He thinks governmental action supports the position that blacks were unfit to choose whether or not to become citizens.

But if these blacks were capable and yet never offered a choice about citizenship, then it can not be said they freely consented (p. 39). Either way these blacks were made citizens without their consent or input. What then is the political status of these blacks who were made citizens? Natanson wants to claim that these blacks were nonparticipants in the contract, and, as such, were not genuine citizens (p. 39). Why are they nonparticipants? Unprotected blacks were never in a position to acquire the intellectual skills needed to be in a position to know what it meant to consent to the state. The period prior to any talk of contract membership left some blacks unprepared to give real consent. Natanson thinks that the lack of governmental protection in slavery undermined their status as free and independent beings. These blacks could not be real participants, and as such they had a unique status.

In not being able to freely choose whether or not to enter into the contract, since they were never afforded the opportunity of doing so in the first place, they are in a position of never having left their original condition; that is to say, with regard to having a basic relationship with government, they are still in a state of nature. (p. 39)

This idea, according to Natanson, leads to two conclusions. First, they are not genuine citizens and are still in the state of nature. He thinks that it follows from this that they must look to themselves for protection of their inalienable rights because the government cannot be counted upon to honor its part of the contract (p. 39). Second, within the framework of the quid pro quo justice inherent in the American-traditional view of legal obligations, it cannot be held that these excluded Negroes ought to obey the law (p. 39).

III

Let us assume, for the moment, that Natanson is correct and some blacks were not protected and at the emancipation proclamation were not fully cognizant of the responsibilities of citizenship and, further, let us assume that there is no problem with his version of tacit consent. It will also be assumed that his version of consent does bind an individual to the state. First, does it follow that those blacks were left in a state of nature? And second, does it also follow that some present-day blacks are still in a state of nature and not obligated legally to the government of America? The answer to both questions is no.

At the outset, we need to assess Natanson's argument about the legal status of blacks at the end of the Civil War. If his stance is that some blacks were not in a position to give their consent, then we need to know: Were there some blacks at the time of the emancipation proclamation in slavery whose autonomy had been so undermined that they were not in a position to truly consent to the state? Was slavery the ultimate destroyer of autonomy? Did slavery render, as Stanley Elkins claims, the slave incapable of making an informed decision?[10] Did the United States government fail to provide any assistance for newly freed slaves?

To properly evaluate the political status and their legal obligations of those blacks, it is important to remember that blacks gained
American citizenship first under the Civil Rights Act of 1866 and
then under the Fourteenth Amendment to the United States Constitution.[11] This legislation was very important in the political history
of the United States.

> Just how important was seen by Senator Lot M. Morrill of
> Maine. Said Morrill, during debate in the Senate on the legisla-
> tion: "If there is anything with which the American people are
> troubled, and if there is anything with which the American
> statesman is perplexed and vexed, it is what to do with the
> negro, how to define him, what he is in American Law, and
> what rights he is entitled to. What shall we do with the everlast-
> ing, inevitable negro? is the question which puzzles all brains
> and vexes all statesmen. Now, as a definition, this amendment
> [to Section I, to establish the citizenship of the native of Afri-
> can descent] settles it. Hitherto, we have said that he was non-
> descript in our statutes; he had no status; he was ubiquitous; he
> was both man and thing; he was three fifths of a person for the
> representation and he was a thing for commerce and for use.
> In the highest sense, then . . . this bill is important as a defini-
> tion.[12]

While passage of the Civil Rights Acts and the adoption of the Fourteenth Amendment may have settled the question of citizenship for
blacks in the minds of some legal theorists, were blacks in a position
to understand what the passage of these acts and amendments
meant? What actions would show that former slaves had freely consented to the state?

It is possible to draw out one scenario to illustrate what needed
to be done to insure that blacks were informed about what it meant
to be a citizen of the United States. It has been argued that blacks
at the end of the Civil War should have been offered three options:
(a) become citizens of the United States; (b) be allowed to leave the
country; (c) start their own country, either in the United States or
some other country. It would have been the responsibility of the
government to ensure that blacks were informed of their choice and
then to provide the funding necessary for them to carry out their

choices.[13] It must be assumed that, when it is claimed that some blacks did not freely consent, what is meant is that at the enactment of the Fourteenth Amendment some blacks were not in a position to understand what it meant to be citizens or these blacks were not allowed to choose. Natanson, at times, seems to be claiming both of these positions. Either way, their acceptance of the Fourteenth Amendment would not really be consent based.[14]

This position, however, is not supported by a careful reading of African American history, in at least three important ways. First, the debate over the future of blacks in America was not limited to whites. Blacks had discussed the options open to them well before the Emancipation Proclamation. There was much debate over different emigration plans.[15] In the end, the general concerns of blacks were stated in an open letter which Robert Purvis sent to the government emigration agent on 28 August, 1862: "The children of the black man have enriched the soil by their tears, and sweat, and blood. Sir we have [been] born here, and here we choose to remain."[16] Most blacks were committed to becoming United States citizens with all of the rights and responsibilities that come with citizenship.

Second, the view of blacks as hopeless victims has been challenged and shown to be false by Du Bois, Blassingame, Foner, and others. Their research also shows that slavery was not as morally and intellectually damaging for blacks as suggested by Elkins.

While it was true that, for many blacks, emancipation was a period of great sociological and psychological adjustment, it was also a period in which blacks showed that they were capable of citizenship and political responsibility.[17] In South Carolina, for example, there was a generous appraisal of the personnel of a Negro delegation in that they handled the responsibilities of government for the most part with remarkable moderation and dignity. It turns out that many of the state constitutions drawn up in 1867 and 1868 were the most progressive the South had ever known:

> In every state the ballot was extended to all male residents, except for certain classes of Confederates; and it is significant that some Negroes, like Nash of South Carolina and Pinchback of Louisiana, were vigorously opposed to any disqualification of Confederates.[18]

Blacks displayed a political kindness that would not be accorded to them in a few short years.

Third, the federal government did try to help with the adjustment from slavery to freedom. The United States government established the Freedman's Bureau as a government agency to oversee the social and political incorporation of blacks into the system. The bureau was established by an act of the United States Congress on 3 March, 1865. The bureau was to distribute clothing, food, and fuel to the destitute freedmen and oversee "all subjects" relating to their condition in the South. Despite its unprecedented responsibilities and powers, the bureau was clearly envisioned as a temporary expedient, for not only was its life span limited to one year, but, incredibly, no budget was appropriated—it would have to draw funds and staff from the War Department. The bureau was only in existence for a little more than a year.[19]

Still, the Freedman's Bureau did have some impact on the political and educational status of blacks after the Civil War.[20] However, the government failed to protect the legal rights of some blacks by withdrawing federal troops from southern states and doing nothing to prevent the rise of the Ku Klux Klan and the enforcement of Jim Crow laws. Does this failure mean that blacks were no longer citizens? Before we address this question, we can say that what we find is that blacks were cognizant of their choices, chose to accept citizenship, and attempted to make their citizenship real. It turns out that many of the problems that developed around citizenship for blacks followed from governmental inaction.

The governmental inaction was its failure to continue to ensure that the political power of blacks was not usurped by the former slave owners. The government pulled the federal troops out of the South, which allowed the former slave owners to regain political power. This action had the effect of denying to blacks the legal protections they were entitled to, under the provisions of the Fourteenth Amendment, as citizens. As citizens they should have had government protection of their inalienable right to life, liberty, and estate. It is clear that, at least in some southern states, their political power had been usurped and, as a result, blacks were often tyrannized.[21] It is also clear that in many southern states the government officials used race and racism as bases for laws that restricted the political power of blacks, who were citizens. It is at this point that Locke's position on usurpation and dissolution of government becomes crucial to this discussion.

IV

While I do not think Locke's work is totally applicable to the situation of blacks, particularly because Locke is concerned with individual and not group consent and the quasi-historical nature of consent, I do think that this work has historical significance because of the role Locke's view played in the debate about what it meant to be a citizen of the United States. The antislavery advocates in Congress appealed to Locke's concept of natural rights and the role of the government to protect these rights as fundamental. The element that received unvarying emphasis by these writers was once more the protection of the laws and the duty of the government to supply it. They linked this idea to the Lockean premise as to the origin and purpose of government.[22] In this vein, Locke's position can give some insight into the problems of political obligations, civil disobedience, and the status of some black Americans—particularly since blacks were claiming that they were being treated unjustly and saw civil disobedience as a way to address social and political concerns.

Locke, it turns out, does have something to say about the misuse and abuse of political power by the government over citizens and their response to it. In chapters 17–19 of the *Second Treatise,* Locke discusses usurpation of political power, tyranny and the dissolution of the government. He discusses at length the relationship between usurpation and tyranny and concludes that:

> As usurpation is the exercise of power which another has a right to, so tyranny is the exercise of power beyond right, which nobody can have a right to. And this is making use of the power anyone has in his hands, not for the good of those who are under it, but for his own private separate advantage—when the government, however entitled, makes not the law, but his will, the rule and his commands and actions are not directed to the preservation of the properties of his people, but the satisfaction

141

of his own ambition, revenge, covetousness, or any other irregular passion.[23]

Laws enacted under the guise of racism would be an example of irregular passion.[24] For some blacks usurpation came in the form of the denying protection of their legal and political rights, which caused these blacks, who were legally citizens and entitled to protection and the exercise of their rights, to have no say in the political arena. The political power of these blacks had been usurped.

Because it would be futile to attempt to cite all of the ways in which race and racism were used to deny blacks access to the political arena, for the purpose of this paper we can restrict our attention to the plight of blacks with respect to their participation in the political process.

With emancipation, two amendments, the Fourteenth and Fifteenth, were written into the Constitution especially to protect the voting rights of the newly freed slaves. These amendments specifically directed states to guarantee voting rights to black citizens.

Three civil rights acts were enacted between 1866 and 1875 as a way of assuring equality of treatment (including the right to vote) to America's blacks. These acts—the Civil Rights Act of 1866, the Civil Rights Act of 1870, and the Civil Rights Act of 1875—with the constitutional guarantee, served to permit black people in the South to exercise the right to vote with relative ease during the Reconstruction. After the Reconstruction, however, several states adopted so-called grandfather clauses, which restricted registration and voting to persons who had voted prior to emancipation. This practice was finally declared unconstitutional by the Supreme Court in 1915. With this defeat Southerners adopted the "white primary," in which the Democratic party prohibited blacks from participating in primary elections in nine states. When the white primary was outlawed, many southern states resorted to gerrymandering as way of disenfranchising blacks. In a long series of cases, the Supreme Court eventually curbed this practice also.

Besides the above techniques, the poll tax, property, educational, and "character" requirements were used to keep black citizens from voting. Perhaps the most effective means of disenfranchising blacks, however, were those of intimidation and violence. All of these practices invoked against some blacks served not merely to deny them the exercise of a right, but to deny the very right itself: the right to participate in the political process.[25]

The usurpation of political power was tyrannical in the sense that blacks were subject to laws which they could not participate in making and, as free citizens, would not have given their consent to.[26] These blacks were denied both access to political information and the right to exercise their political rights. Many of the laws enacted without the input of these blacks served to lower substantially the overall quality of their social and economic lives.[27] What did this tyrannical use of power do to the political status of blacks? Did this usurpation of political power force blacks back into a state of nature?

Locke makes the distinction between the dissolution of government and the dissolution of society.[28] The usurpation of political power by southern governments did not dissolve society. The southern governments were actually breaking the political trust by their actions. Blacks could have accepted the dictates of these governments and thus legitimated the usurped political power. But they did not, and as Locke notes: "Unless the citizens freely consent to the governmental actions by accepting the new rules, this government is then at war with these citizens."[29] Blacks were still citizens and as such had the right to resist the dictates of the usurpers.[30] Those government officials who used the power they usurped in a tyrannical manner acted contrary to a trust.[31] The society, however, had not dissolved and, thus, blacks were still full members of the state. Certain government officials had put themselves at war with those blacks. Politically unprotected blacks were in a position to morally resist the dictates of that government. They were not, as Natanson claims, in a state of nature. These blacks were citizens under the provisions of the Constitution.[32]

If we take the Fourteenth Amendment to be the beginning of a contract between blacks and the government, then at that moment blacks were citizens and their children's children would be citizens. For some southern blacks, both the federal and state governments failed to uphold their part of the contract. Locke thinks that when this happens the goal of citizens is to get the legislature to act according to the trust.[33] These blacks are to be the judge of what actions to take against the government. Civil disobedience then can be seen as a legitimate method both to make one's plight a matter of public concern and to force the government to uphold its part of the contract.[34] An essential part of that contract is that the government is to provide protection so that these citizens can enjoy their political rights.

At this point the following claims can be made: first, most blacks wanted to be citizens, and when they gained American citizenship showed that they were capable of the responsibilities of citizenship; second, the federal government did make an attempt to help in the adjustment from slavery to freedom; and third, Locke's position on usurpation and dissolution of government does not support the position that blacks were in a state of nature.

V

How do these points affect the claim that present-day blacks are still in a state of nature? Obviously, they cannot still be in a state of nature if, as our reading of Locke and an examination of black political history show, they were not in a state of nature to begin with.

Does it matter, as Natanson claims, that some blacks had never been in a position to exercise their political rights and have never enjoyed the protection of the government? There is to be no logical inconsistency in one not being protected by the government in the American traditional model and being a citizen. It is possible for citizens to have rights on the books, but not be protected against the violation or infringement of these rights by others, even in a liberal democratic state. A political life in a liberal democratic state is compatible with there being laws that are not enforced. It does not follow that these "politically unprotected" individuals are not citizens. It does follow, however, that those citizens who are "politically unprotected" are justified in protesting the lack of protection of their rights, in the American-traditional model.[35]

VI

In the end, if we accept Natanson's position that some blacks are still in a state of nature, we encounter two more difficulties: first, if these individuals are not citizens of the state, their behavior can not be seen as civil disobedience, but as an act of war against the state. It is a war they will lose. They can only claim rights as aliens, not as citizens. They must depend on the goodwill of those individuals who are citizens to try to convince the state to protect them and do whatever is necessary to make their becoming citizens real. However, it is unclear what legal claims they have against the state, as citizens.

Second, to claim that some blacks are not genuine citizens is to deny the two conventional ways of assigning citizenship at birth. Legal scholars

> . . . are generally content to distinguish right of birthplace *(jus soli)* and right of descent *(jus sanguinis)* as the two major alternative principles that states use in assigning citizenship at birth. They describe how different states use one or the other of these principles (or a combination of both) and discuss the problems posed for international order when the laws of different states conflict. They simply assume that people will normally acquire citizenship through birth and that there is nothing problematic about this. (States may permit citizenship to be acquired at a later stage but the very term used for this, "naturalization," suggests that birthright citizenship is the norm.)[36]

In the United States, being born in the country or to parents who are citizens makes one a citizen with all of the rights and responsibilities thereof. To claim that some blacks are still in a state of nature is to claim that even though blacks are born in the United States, they are still not citizens.[37] The position that some blacks, who have never given up their birthright citizenship, are not citizens seems to run counter to our understanding of how we think an individual becomes a citizen of the United States.[38]

VII

Natanson is correct that consent to political protection and the government's protection of members are important aspects of Locke's political theory. But his claim that some blacks are still in a state of nature is not supported by a careful reading of Locke. If what Natanson means by genuine citizen is that a person is a member of the state only if one is protected by the government and accepts that protection, then he seems to have drawn his version of Lockean citizenship much more narrowly than did Locke. Locke's position is more complicated than Natanson has allowed. Natanson placed emphasis on the wrong passages in the *Second Treatise*. If Natanson had focused on chapters 17–19 of the *Second Treatise,* he would see Locke as giving possible support of the use of civil disobedience, as employed by black Americans, in the civil rights struggle. But, more importantly, these chapters, and an insightful reading of black history, support, as do our laws on citizenship, the conclusion that politically unprotected blacks in the United States are citizens, and as such have valid claims to the protection of the state—and also legal obligations to it.[39]

Notes

1. See, for example, Harry Prosch, "Limits to Moral Claim in Civil Disobedience," *Ethics* 75 (January 1965): 103–11; Darnell Rucker, "The Moral Grounds of Civil Disobedience," *Ethics* 76 (January 1966): 142–45; Michael Walzer, "The Obligation to Disobey," *Ethics* 77 (April 1967): 163–67; and Hugo Adam Bedau, *Civil Disobedience: Theory and Practice* (New York: Pegasus, 1969).

2. Robert Brock, *Morton Downey Jr. Show,* August 1988.

3. Brock also argues for reparations for blacks. The question of reparations has been discussed in the philosophical literature. See, for example, Bernard Boxill, "The Morality of Reparations," *Social Theory and Practice* 2 (1972); Howard McGary, "Justice and Reparations" *Philosophical Forum* 9 (Winter-Spring 1977–78); J. W. Nickle, "Should Reparations be to Groups or Individuals," *Analysis* 32 (1972).

4. Harvey Natanson, "Locke and Hume: Bearing on the Legal Obligation of the Negro," *Journal of Value Inquiry* 1 (Winter 1970): 35–43. Parenthetic numerical references are to the pages of this work and will be used throughout.

5. While blacks in the northern part of the United States might have been denied some political protection, for many southern blacks government protection was almost nil. It is these blacks that Natanson must believe are not members of the contract.

6. See, for example, Harry J. Carman and Harold C. Syrett, *A History of the American People* (New York: Alfred A. Knopf, 1957), 114 ff.; J. W. Gough, *John Locke's Political Philosophy* (London: Oxford University Press, 1950), 103; and Alfred H. Kelly and Winfred A. Harbison *The American Constitution* (New York: W. W. Norton, 1963), 90 ff.

7. See, for example, Eric Foner, *Reconstruction: America's Unfinished Revolution 1863–1877* (New York: Harper and Row, 1988).

8. For further discussions of the issues of blacks and governmental protection, see my "African Americans, Crime Victimization, and Political Obligations" in *To Be a Victim,* ed. Diane Shank and David I. Caplan (New York: Plenum, 1991), pp. 141–58. And "Crime, Minorities and the Social Contract" in *Criminal Justice Ethics* 9, 2 (Summer/Fall 1990), pp. 16–24.

9. Reconstruction was a time of hope, the period when the Thirteenth, Fourteenth, and Fifteenth Amendments were adopted, giving Negroes the vote and the promise of equality.

But campaigns of violence and intimidation accompanied these optimistic expressions of a new age, as the Ku Klux Klan and other secret organizations sought to suppress the emergence into society of the new Negro citizens. Major riots occurred in Memphis, Tennessee, where forty-six Negroes were reported killed and seventy-five wounded, and in the Louisiana centers of Colfax and Coushatta, where more than one hundred Negro and white republicans were massacred, *United States Riot Commission Report* (New York: Bantam Books, 1968), 7.

10. Stanley M. Elkins, *Slavery: A Problem in American Institutional and Intellectual Life* (Chicago: The University of Chicago Press, 1959).

11. See, for example, David Donald, *The Politics of Reconstruction* (Baton Rouge: Louisiana State University Press, 1965), and Horace E. Flack, *The Adoption of the Fourteenth Amendment* (Baltimore: Johns Hopkins University Press, 1908).

12. Charles Fairman, *Reconstruction and Reunion 1864–1888,* pt. 1 (New York: Macmillan, 1971), 1181.

13. I. A. Obadele, "The Struggle is For Land," *Pan-Africanism,* ed. Robert Chrisman and Nathan Hare (New York: Bobbs-Merrill, 1974), 175–92.

14. "Concerning the recognition of the Negro as full citizen, Lincoln was of the opinion that with education the Negro would qualify for it, at least on a restricted basis," John Hope Franklin, *From Slavery to Freedom,* 3d ed. (New York: Alfred A. Knopf, 1967), 302.

15. See, for example, Benjamin Quarles, *The Negro in the Civil War* (Boston: Little, Brown and Co., 1953).

16. Quarles, 157.

17. "The freed people's behavior from 1861 onward indicates that damaging as slavery was to the condition and self-esteem of many, the freed man and woman generally maintained a strong self-concept . . . Moreover, freedmen proceeded to reconstruct their communities along lines not entirely preconditioned or dictated by former masters or new allies and guardians from the North. Their design drew upon experiences both in slavery and the old slave quarters and as amended by experiences in the contraband camps, freedmen's villages, and other settlements. They chose institutions that had served antebellum free black communities—the

church, the school, and the mutual-benefit society. They also adopted the political party and the mass meeting and the convention. This particularly emphasizes their adaptability, considering that the masters had denied them access to, and attempted to keep them ignorant of, such democratic American institutions." See Edward Magdol, *A Right to the Land* (Westport, Conn.: Greenwood Press, 1977), 8.

18. Franklin, *Slavery and Freedom*, 317.

19. Charles Sumner had proposed establishing the bureau as a permanent agency with a secretary of Cabinet rank—but such an idea ran counter to the strong inhibitions against long-term guardianship. Indeed, at the last moment, Congress redefined the bureau's responsibilities so as to include southern white refugees as well as freedmen, a vast expansion of its authority that aimed to counteract the impression of preferential treatment for blacks. Foner, *Reconstruction*, 69.

20. See, for example, Horace Mann Bond, *The Education of the Negro in the American Social Order* (New York: Octagon Books, 1966); George R. Bentley, *A History of the Freedmen's Bureau* (Philadelphia: University of Pennsylvania Press, 1955); Donald H. Henderson, *The Negro Freedman* (New York: Henry Schuman, 1952); W. E. B. DuBois, "The Freedmen's Bureau," *Atlantic Monthly* 88 (March 1901); Walter L. Fleming, *Civil War and Reconstruction in Alabama* (New York: Columbia University Press, 1905); Paul S. Pierce, *The Freedmen's Bureau, A Chapter in the History of Reconstruction* (Iowa City: Haskell House Publishers, 1904).

21. William A. Mabry, *Studies in the Disfranchisement of the Negro in the South* (Durham, N.C.: Duke University Press, 1933); William A. Russ, "The Negro and White Disfranchisement during Radical Reconstruction," *Journal of Negro History* 19 (April 1934); C. Vann Woodward, *Reunion and Reaction: The Compromise of 1877 and the End of Reconstruction* (Boston: Little, Brown, 1951).

22. Jacobus Ten Broek, *The Anti-Slavery Origins of the Fourteenth Amendment* (Berkeley: University of California Press, 1951), 66.

23. See sec. 199 of John Locke's *The Second Treatise of Government*, ed. Thomas P. Peardon (New York: Bobbs-Merrill, 1952), 112.

24. Locke, 112, sec. 222.

25. See, for example, Milton D. Morris, *The Politics of Black America* (New York: Harper and Row, 1975).

26. Locke, sec. 198.

27. Sig Synnestvedt, *The White Response to Black Emancipation* (New York: Macmillan, 1972).

28. Locke, 112, sec. 221.

29. Locke, sec. 232.

30. Locke, sec. 233.

31. Locke, 112, sec. 222.

32. For a discussion of the development of national citizenship, see Ten Broek, *Anti-Slavery Origins*.

LOCKE AND THE LEGAL OBLIGATIONS OF BLACK AMERICANS

34. Locke, sec. 233.

35. See John Rawls, *A Theory of Justice* (Cambridge: Harvard University Press, 1971); and Laurence Thomas, "To a Theory of Justice: An Epilogue," *Philosophical Forum* 6 (1975): 46–70.

36. Joseph H. Carens, "Who Belongs? Theoretical and Legal Questions about Birthright Citizenship in the United States," *University of Toronto Law Journal* 37 (1987), 413–35.

37. The question of citizenship for blacks was resolved with the passage of the Fourteenth Amendment. The statement of citizenship for blacks was first issued in the Civil Rights Act of 1866. Its most important part began by declaring "that all persons born in the United States are hereby declared to be citizens of the United States." See Terry Eastland and William J. Bennett, *Counting by Race: Equality from the Founding Fathers to Bakke and Weber* (New York: Basic Books, 1979), 61.

38. Carens notes that, for example, Britain and the United States took different views on the question of whether citizenship acquired at birth entailed perpetual allegiance or could be terminated by voluntary expatriation and subsequent naturalization in a new country. This was an important source of conflict between the two countries for much of the nineteenth century. The most common problems arose from the fact that differences in nationality laws leave some people stateless and others with dual citizenship (which sometimes entail conflicting sets of obligations). See Carens, "Birthright Citizenship," 415.

39. Michael Walzer argues that because blacks in America are oppressed citizens, their legal and political obligations to the state are not the same as fully free and equal members of the state. Michael Walzer, "The Obligations of Oppressed Minorities," in *Obligations* (New York: Clarion Books, 1972).

7

THE MASTER-SLAVE DIALECTIC: HEGEL VS. DOUGLASS

Cynthia Willett

I n the *Phenomenology of Spirit,* Hegel interweaves a modernist locus of the self in the will and its freedom with a classical conception of the self as social. According to Hegel (*Phenomenology,* sec. B, "Self-Consciousness"), the first climactic turn in the constitution of a self takes the form of a "battle for recognition" and yields a dialectic of "master" and "slave."[1] Those who are able to prove that they are not slaves to their own animal-like desires attain the moral status of a person. Those who prove to be weak of will suffer physical bondage and social shame, and, according to Hegel, deservedly so.

While major sociological and historical studies of slavery in America refer to Hegel's analysis to explain the dynamics of master and slave, these same studies, I shall argue, also suggest limitations in Hegel's dialectical methodology. According to this methodology, the consciousness of the slave can reflect nothing more than liminal dimensions of the self-consciousness of the master. The slave is consumed by desires that the master would overcome. The duplicitous symmetries of Hegelian logic conceal, however, what African-American history reveals: The slave is not *in fact* the mirror reversal of the master. Therefore, the experience of the African-American slave demands a second dialectic, one that is irreducible to the Hegelian model of selfhood and freedom.

To discern the crucial elements of a second dialectic, I turn to the slave narratives of Frederick Douglass. Like the *Phenomenology*, these narratives project a nineteenth-century dialectical concept of freedom as recognition rather than an eighteenth-century Enlightenment concept of freedom as individual choice. The Douglass narratives, however, reject what Hegel locates as the stoic underpinnings of the development of freedom in the West. Hegel claims to have uncovered in slavery a necessary condition for freedom when he argues that the slave must overcome the natural proclivity towards sensuality and acquire the discipline of the rational will. He traces the origin of the modern concepts of freedom and reason to the Stoics, who were able to construct an experience of freedom in slavery by severing the inner self from desire and defining their essential self in reason alone. While the philosophy of Stoicism undergoes significant changes in the West, the Western project, as Hegel represents it, perpetuates an asceticism rooted in its Stoic origins.

The Douglass narratives challenge the Stoicism that informs what is called reason in the West and project instead a construct of freedom that develops out of the social eroticism of the self. According to these narratives, while the social self does develop in a "dance of manhood" that bears some resemblance to what Hegel terms the "battle for recognition," the rituals that constitute the self are not, as Hegel claims, "negations of nature." On the contrary, in his autobiographies Douglass acknowledges the social and expressive resources of the fully embodied consciousness and so too deconstructs dualisms between man and his other that propel Western culture.

1: Hegel and a Master Narrative of Freedom

According to Hegel, the human being first becomes conscious of itself as appetite, or in German, *die Begierde*, which emphasizes the predatory, even savage, nature of basic animal desires. Hegel writes: "The simple 'I' is . . . certain of itself only by superseding [*das Aufheben*] this other that presents itself . . . as an independent life" (*PS*, sec. 174:139). Hegel interprets this superseding as the need to destroy the independence of the other (*vernichtet den selbstaendigen*

Gegenstand) (*PS,* sec. 174:139). The self actively sacrifices others not simply for biological satisfaction but also to assert itself as the center of all things.

The centripetal forces of early selfhood, however, do not suffice to organize a fully human self (*die Person*). According to Hegel, the primitive and animal-like self metamorphoses into a fully human self only after realizing the emptiness of an existence defined solely in terms of natural desires. This sense of futility crystallizes with the awareness of death. Man, apparently in distinction to animals, is aware of the possibility of his own death. This awareness motivates man to seek in the self something more than what is circumscribed by the cycles of life and death that define natural existence.

A "person" is defined in terms of its independence in relation to what Hegel calls the "genus of life." Hegel explains that the person is that "for which Life exists as this unity, or as genus" (*PS,* sec. 173). One of the implications of this rather complicated formulation is that those entities (including finally all nonhuman animals) that are not recognized as persons (and Hegel would claim to have located the universal definition of the person) exist only as sacrificial means. Human existence furnishes the meaning and purpose to all other life forms, including those animal or animal-like selves—for Hegel this includes Africans—that fail to fully develop into persons. Hegelian genesis repeats the Biblical bequest of nature and things natural to human domination.

Hegel's aim is to put into practice the Kantian notion that every individual should be treated with respect, not merely as an instrument of another's desire but as an end in his own right. Therefore, Hegel must find some way to make the noumenal side of the person as pure freedom phenomenally accessible. As Hegel writes, each individual must "accomplish the movement of absolute abstraction, of rooting-out all immediate being, and of being merely the purely negative being of self-identical consciousness; in other words, they [must have] . . . exposed themselves to each other as pure being-for-self." (*PS,* sec. 186). Hegel interprets this purely negative being as "the pure negation of its objective mode, or in showing that it is not . . . attached to life" (*PS,* sec. 187). That is, one must manifest his free self in a world where living things appear to be determined solely by their desires, finally the desire for life itself. Therefore, the

153

human being proves he is free only if he can undertake some action that is not motivated by desire, or by any of the interests and satisfactions that define what for Hegel is the animal self and what in contemporary terms is called the "instrumental self." In particular, it is by risking one's life that one proves oneself over the animal and earns the moral status that Hegel terms "recognition."

One cannot grant recognition to oneself. That is, one cannot simply assert or otherwise count oneself as a person and find any reality in this act of self-recognition. Such an act of self-recognition would constitute a total fraud, or worse, a psychological delusion. As Hegel writes, a "[s]elf-consciousness [can] achieve its satisfaction only in another self-consciousness" (*PS*, sec. 175). In particular, according to Hegel, one establishes that one is a person only in a contest that takes place before witnesses. The self that is not publicly performed could be little more than what for Hegel is the animal seeking to satisfy its desires. The self-defined atom of eighteenth-century liberalism lacks a viable construct of freedom and so too a fully human sense of self. The person can seek freedom only through the struggles that earn intersubjective recognition. In other words, personhood (traditionally read as manhood) requires a test of will over desire, and this test must be performed on a public stage.

Hegel also presumes that the self first encounters the Other as a threat. This is because, in a move that is distinctly modernist and arguably masculinist, Hegel measures the reality of the external world in terms of its force of resistance. The alterity of the external world originally appears in the dialectical negation of the self (*PS*, sec. 175). The other person as well as the fully human self first appears on the scene in a contest of wills.

A test of man against nature cannot substitute for a test of wills. As Hegel explains, "on account of the independence of the object [now conceived to be an object that likewise possesses a will], . . . [self-consciousness] can achieve satisfaction only when the object itself effects the negation within itself" (*PS*, sec. 175). Only those objects that possess a will can "negate" themselves, and thereby defer to the will of another. Man seeks in the actions of the Other verification for his own freedom from nature and desire. Only then does he acquire a sense of self. The direct assertion of the self over nature (including such rites of passage into manhood as killing an elephant) retards the human being at the level of the animal. For Hegel, this apparently low level of human existence characterizes cultures that are "primitive."

It is an assumption of Hegel's dialectical methodology that there exists nothing like a purely transcendent experience. The soul does not exist outside of the body. Therefore, a dialectical narrative of history falters if either of the combatants loses his life. Combatants eventually realize that while they are to demonstrate before the Other a willingness to risk their lives, that dare is but a bluff. Or, in more familiar terms, each combatant must play a game of chicken with the Other. The more courageous combatant proves to the Other that he is the real person (or, the real man). At the same time, the loser proves to be less than a person, in fact, a thing to be used, servant to the master.

The relation between master and slave is the most primitive expression of intersubjectivity. It is also, according to Hegel, inherently unstable. Entangled in the very core of the dialectic of master and slave lies a double irony. The first irony is that the master finds himself dependent upon the slave—not simply as chattel or other instrument of desire—but for recognition. The deference of the slave proves the selfhood of the master. This mode of intersubjectivity, asymmetrical as it is, would be no problem except for the second irony. The master finds himself recognized not by another person but by a mere slave, someone who is dependent and not independent of the will of the master, and therefore someone whose recognition does not count. In truth, Hegel argues, the master is no better than the slave upon whom he depends for a sense of self.

That is, the master requires that the slave have a will (in order that the slave may choose freely to recognize the master), and yet at the same time the master reduces the slave (like the animal) to the status of a thing. Therefore, the master can gain only a perverse sense of self in his interactions with the slave. The master finally proves to be the "brute" (to use the language of American slavery) that defines his relation to the slave.

Conversely, it is the slave who, according to Hegel, performs the "labor of the negative," that is, the work that advances history towards its end in universal freedom. More specifically, it is the self-humiliating service and the self-consuming terror of certain death that define the experience of the slave-worker and account for his agency in the liberation of humanity. Through labor for a cause beyond oneself (initially, for the master) and through the certainty that death is "the absolute Lord," the slave develops the potential for understanding himself as "pure being-for-self," or as the freedom that he had apparently lost to the master. As Hegel explains, in the total terror of death, the slave "has been quite unmanned [*Es ist darin innerlich aufgeloest worden*], has trembled in every fiber of its being" but has in this fear achieved what the master achieves through courage, namely, the detachment of the self from its natural existence (*PS*, sec. 194: 148). In other words, in his fear, the slave-worker comes to accept what the animal does not know and what the master believes he has overcome—not just the possibility but the necessity of death. Aware of the finitude of one's own personal life, the individual realizes that as a distinct person disconnected from what turns out to be the larger processes of history, or what Hegel calls Spirit, one ultimately signifies nothing.

Meanwhile, through the discipline of work, the slave creates something that survives the transitions of death and the transitory desires of the individual. By working on the raw materials of nature, the slave transforms the transcendent self that death bares into the materiality of a thing. Therefore, work realizes the personality of the worker as it has been set free from desire by the fear of certain death.

As a worker, the slave contributes to the actualization of freedom in a way that the idle master cannot. By demonstrating that it is the slave and not the leisure class of slaveholders that creates culture, Hegel undermines a key element in the classical concept of the person. Aristotle's leisure class is missing the spirit of contradiction, the awareness of death and the labor of the alienated self, that moves history towards freedom.

If the intertwined concepts of the person and freedom first emerge in the struggle for recognition, these concepts develop in the hands of the laboring slave. The slave, however, does not actualize the concept of freedom without fundamentally altering that concept. The master invokes a *warrior's* concept of freedom. The master is free inasmuch as he proves his courage in a test of wills. The inherent paradox of his position is that he can only prove himself before the eyes of the loser. Therefore, the master's notion of freedom self-destructs.

Hegel's slave transforms the meaning of freedom from the courage of the warrior to asceticism of the *worker*. The problem for the slave is that he must locate a sense of self beyond the alienation of physical existence. According to Hegel, this alienation from materiality is total. The master establishes in the subordination of the slave proof of his own self-mastery. The slave must play the role of what in nineteenth-century American slavery was called the "Sambo," the childlike creature who passively serves the will of another.[2] But the slave also serves the predatory and sexual appetites of the master. Therefore, the slave must represent for the master not only the passive Sambo but also the lustful "brute." The slave, then, while functioning as the castrated servant of the master's desire, nonetheless is at the same time identified with the savage desires that he serves. The slave can be little more, for the Other, than child and/or beast. Given the absolute nature of the slave's alienation from his oppressive existence, the slave can become a person only by severing himself from his body and retreating into a realm of pure thought. The slave-worker finds his freedom in an inner self, beyond the external constraints of an oppressive existence. According to the *Phenomenology, the first philosophy of self-consciousness was the philosophy of slavery, Stoicism.*

Despite the differences, Hegelian master and Hegelian slave have in common a notion of freedom that invokes elements of the European "negation" of nature. For Hegel, the concept of the free self implies an unnatural detachment from the body and its desires. The master proves the force of his will over desire. And the slave severs an inner self from sensuous existence and redefines the will as reason.

Of course, for Hegel, dialectic does not end with Stoic rationality. Eventually, the slaves of Western history acquire freedom by identifying with the higher purposes of community, or Spirit. Hegel's contribution to the Western narrative of freedom is his understanding of the role of intersubjectivity in the development of the self. There is no sense of self apart from the social dynamics of recognition. The sovereign individual cannot gain a sense of self without looking into the eyes of the Other. But then, Hegel's development of freedom as recognition complicates the dominant concept of freedom in America. This concept of freedom as individual autonomy has not fundamentally changed since the period of the Enlightenment. The problem with the eighteenth-century concept is that it cannot address the social dimensions of the self. For example, it cannot account for the limits on freedom posed by social alienation.[3]

2: The African American Experience of Slavery

In a historical and cross-cultural study of the patterns of slavery, sociologist Orlando Patterson confirms what Hegel discerns as the sociopsychological dependency of master on slave. The master depends upon the slave for recognition, or what Patterson analyzes in terms of the timocratic value of honor, and what we also call "deference."[4] Patterson differentiates the liminal social status of the slave from the total outcast who is purged from the community altogether. According to Patterson, the slave, unlike the outcast, "was marginal, neither human nor inhuman, neither man nor beast, neither dead nor alive, the enemy within who was neither member nor true alien" (*SSD*, 48).

Hegel's interpretation of the contorted intersubjectivity between master and slave accounts for the peculiar status of the slave as a liminal person in a social system. The slave must be a person inasmuch as the master seeks to establish his sense of self through his relation with the slave. Without deference, the master's sense of self-worth crumbles. At the same time, the slave is used to satisfy the desires of the master and reflects for the master that animal-like existence. The slave lacks a will and depends upon the master for a sense of purpose. As a consequence of his liminal status, the slave loses not only physical freedom but also suffers social alienation, or what Patterson terms "social death." But unlike the outcast, whose exclusion from the social system is total, the slave exists as a dialectical contradiction and therefore as an impetus towards social change.

However, while Patterson argues that the master could seek to confirm his sense of honor through the slave, Patterson also argues that Hegel fails to allow for the possibility that the master may find recognition among other slaveholders and therefore use the slave solely as an instrument of power.[5] According to Patterson, the master could in theory and did in practice (for example, he argues, in American slavery) preempt the alleged dynamic for social progress by satisfying the need for recognition through other free persons.

Hegel's argument, however, is somewhat stronger. The key to recognition, according to Hegel, is a test of wills. The master wills not the body but specifically the will of the Other. He cannot acquire this recognition from other slaveholders because they have not resisted his will. Therefore, whatever recognition the master might gain from other slaveholders is gratuitous. The master no doubt shares interests with other slaveholders, and in this sense there is common purpose. However, the nineteenth-century notion of honor, as Hegel conceptualizes it, cannot be based on self-interest. On the contrary, one receives recognition for one's honor only by staking one's livelihood in the name of a higher concept of freedom. Therefore, without a contest of wills—a contest that involves the risks of slavery and death—acknowledgment of honor is hollow. Proof of honor requires that the one person challenges another person and proceeds to "negate" (i.e., dominate) that alien will.

In fact, Hegel's claim regarding the *social-psychological,* and not simply economic, dependency of the master on the slave is supported by African American slave narratives. For example, Frederick Douglass often remarks that the gravest of all crimes committed by the slave is not the destruction of property or idleness but sheer impudence.[6] But impudence can threaten the honor of the master only inasmuch as the master depends upon the slave for a sense of self that he cannot find elsewhere.

Because the master depends upon the slave not just for labor but for recognition, slavery—indeed any form of oppression that depends upon persons of liminal social status—proves to be an inherently unstable institution. It is Hegel's understanding of the social pathology of domination and its inherent dynamic towards change that constitutes a decisive advance over classical definitions of slavery.

Nonetheless, Hegel's incomplete familiarity with historical accounts of slavery also blinds him to a fundamental error in dialectical logic. However much the slave may serve as mirror for the master, the master hardly serves as mirror for the slave. As Patterson notes, masters deceive themselves as to the true cleverness of their slaves, not knowing their slaves as well as their slaves know them (*SSD*, 338). For example, while the African American slave might perform the Sambo role of bowing before the master, there is, Patterson argues, historical evidence that slaves played their role as a farce (*SSD*, 96).

Slaveholders obtained slaves through kidnapping or various forms of trading and therefore not through conquest. Nonetheless, the identity of the slaveholder as well as the legitimation of slaveholding would make use of the mythology of heroic conquest. Slaveholders (e.g., Captain Auld or Colonel Lloyd in the Douglass narratives) would adopt for themselves military titles or otherwise perpetuate the image of the plantation as a battlefield where deference was earned.

Moreover, as John Blassingame argues, some American slaves displayed a willingness to stake their lives in order to defend their honor or the honor of other slaves.[7] Not only did slaves refuse to internalize the projections of the slaveholders and turn elsewhere for a sense of self, some slaves also aimed to prove themselves in a contest with their oppressors.

However, if the sense of self invoked by at least some African American slaves exhibits the spiritedness that Hegel discerns in the master-warrior, this expression of self cannot be assimilated into the Hegelian model. The ascetic European tradition defines freedom as the "absolute negation" of desire, and this negation in terms of a cathartic "rooting-out all immediate existence." Hegel preserves this negation even as he sublates it in his conceptualization of universal Spirit. In other words, in European culture, the rational will develops in dialectical opposition to affective and other embodied dimensions of the self. However, the African American brings a culture that does not aim to abstract from but on the contrary can even aim to intensify desire and yet also claim to have reason on its side. For example, Eric Sundquist argues that the "excessive emotionalism" of the rebel leader Nat Turner did express a " 'rational' political intelligence."[8] It is a variation on an ecstatic model of the self (in contrast with the cathartic models that predominate in European cultures) that I shall develop in my examination of Frederick Douglass in part 3.

While the standard Hegelian reading of slavery assumes that the slave lacks the courage (and thus the will) to resist oppression in open struggle and would instead secure freedom through the kind of virtues that are acquired in alienated labor, a different picture emerges from the history of American slavery. As Sundquist documents, "Black antislavery, some time before the advent of Douglass, did not hesitate to invoke violent resistance" (*WN*, 66). While European Christianity attempted to "instill docile passivity" among the slaves, Sundquist observes that "black spirituals were often laden with messages of resistance . . . and that Christ appeared in them less as a forgiving, benevolent savior than as a warrior-leader" (*WN*, 57). Hegel's tale of the history of slavery from Stoicism to the unhappy consciousness of European Christianity and finally to forgiveness in Absolute Spirit appropriates the dualisms of European rationality, or what Nietzsche critiques as European asceticism. Hegel's tale occludes the militant spirituality that defines one significant strand of African American history.

Finally, while European slaves, including the indentured servants who emigrated to America, defined themselves through the discipline of work, blacks, as Paul Gilroy argues, have more likely equated work with slavery, not manhood or freedom, and have defined themselves instead through music or other expressive dimensions of black culture.[9] Those slaves who were forced to devote their lives to labor in the fields did not as did whites separate their work from emotive forms of self-expression but, according to historian Eugene Genovese, measured work by the rhythms of song.[10] Black slaves and ex-slaves resisted demands for regulating their labor in accordance with what social historians term the "industrial morality" of the North. As historian David Roediger demonstrates, white American immigrants internalized ascetic protestantism in accordance with the demands of the white work ethic. These immigrants derived a sense of self by identifying whiteness with worker and in opposition to blackness and slavery.[11] However, slave culture in America did not culminate in the sublation of the enslaved body in the discipline of the worker and the abstract and technical rationality that ensues, but in the expression of the lived black body in the spiritual. Therefore, Hegel's phenomenology of slavery as the Stoic withdrawal from physical existence introduces into his conception of freedom an ideology of Euro-Christian asceticism that does not correspond with resources for self-affirmation that emerge from African American slave culture.

3: Frederick Douglass and a Slave Narrative of Freedom

If Douglass, who claimed a white father and a black mother, does not fully endorse either black separatism or the ecstatic religiosity of black expressive culture, he also does not assimilate a European conception of the free self. Following W. E. B. Du Bois, who portrays a Douglass who stood for "assimilation *through* self-assertion, and on no other terms," I find in the Douglass narratives a universalizing dialectic (not the abstract universal of modernist philosophies, but the mediating universal of dialectic) that speaks to white and black cultures in America but reflects the mulatto origin of its maker.[12]

Most decisive for an understanding of Douglass's conception of the free self is the well-known scene between himself and the slave-breaker, Mr. Covey. This scene defines the climax of the Douglass autobiographies, what Douglass himself terms the "turning-point" in his life as a slave. Moreover, while Douglass clearly subordinates what is often regarded as the second crucial moment in his autobiography, the acquisition of literacy, to his struggle with the slave-breaker, the theme of education interweaves an epistemological strand into the narrative of freedom.

The central elements of the confrontation between Covey and Douglass are condensed in a few paragraphs of the 1845 *Narrative*. The pivotal encounter occurs after Douglass runs off to his owner and appeals for help against what Douglass sees as arbitrary punishment. The owner, who in nineteenth-century ideology was posed as a father, did not respond. Douglass returns to Covey initially intending only to avoid more "punishment." Douglass writes:

> I was called to go and rub, curry, and feed, the horses. I obeyed, and was glad to obey. But whilst thus engaged, . . . Mr. Covey entered the stable with a long rope. . . . Mr. Covey seemed now to think he had me, and could do what he pleased; but at this moment—from whence came the spirit I don't know—I resolved to fight.[13]

After a struggle, Covey backs down. Douglass concludes:

> This battle . . . was the turning-point in my career as a slave. It rekindled the few expiring embers of freedom, and revived within me a sense of my own manhood. . . . The gratification afforded by the triumph was a full compensation for whatever else might follow, even death itself. . . . I resolved that, however long I might remain a slave in form, the day had passed forever when I could be a slave in fact. I did not hesitate to let it be known of me, that the white man who expected to succeed in whipping, must also succeed in killing me. (*N*, 113)

The existential force of triumphant struggle with the oppressor resembles but does not finally accord with the European dialectic of freedom as represented by Hegel. Like Hegel, Douglass does not see the turning point of freedom as residing primarily in the individual and his right to self-ownership but more potently in the recognition that is earned in struggle. In his *Narrative*, Douglass does discuss the sense of self-worth that accrues to one who owns his body and the fruits of his labor. However, in general, Douglass was not especially concerned with the rights of black labor. Not only does he subordinate his discussion of labor issues in his narratives, but he also fails to show much interest in black labor union movements.[14] As Douglass explains, the slave becomes a man when he acquires not power but "the *signs* of power" (*BF*, 152). Without this assertion of self before the Other, the slave might acquire the comforts of property and power. But he still lacks a self. Therefore, for Douglass, freedom would culminate not in the autonomy of the worker but in overcoming what nineteenth-century America terms "social prejudice."

The process by which one overcomes social alienation and earns recognition, however, does not for Douglass subsume the same dualistic notions of self that inform dominant European and European-American traditions. The element of gratification that defines the lived experience of his struggle anticipates not only a break with the ideal of moral purity as promulgated by the Garrisonian Christian abolitionists. The animalistic encounter portrayed through the imagery of fire supersedes the Enlightenment task of grounding the moral self in a rational will detached from body, affect, or desire. So too it diverges from what Hegel recapitulates as the origin of the rational will in European-based philosophies of slavery and free-dom. The philosophical conception of the rational will, which according to the Garrisonians would be accessible through moral suasion unaided by physical and emotive force, traces back from Hegel and Kant to what the *Phenomenology* identifies as the origin of philosophy in Stoicism. The *Phenomenology, and in particular the phenomenology of "Self-Consciousness," thereby subordinates the importance of the philosophy of the slaveholders (Plato and Aristotle) to that of the slaves.* While Hegel's narrative of freedom favors the perspective of the slave over the master, for Hegel this slave must be European. For unlike the "African," the European slave would learn to sever the self from desire, forgive his oppressors in Christian community, and devote himself to a totally concept-based knowledge called Absolute Spirit.

The divergence of the Douglass narratives from the dominant European narratives of freedom is more pronounced in the 1855 *My Bondage and My Freedom.* There Douglass adds the commentary to the critical scene with the slavebreaker: "A man, without force, is without the essential dignity of humanity. Human nature is so constituted, that it cannot *honor* a helpless man, although it can *pity* him; and even this it cannot do long, if the signs of power do not arise." By reconstructing the manhood of the slave through the force of struggle, Douglass decidedly rejects what Hegel argues to be the necessary education of the slave to freedom through the exercises of dutiful labor and abstract reason. At the same time, Douglass rejects the ethics of sentimentality (or in contemporary terms, the care ethic) that developed in opposition to modernist philosophies of rationalism. The rhetoric of sentimentality no less than the Enlightenment and Hegelian project of educating the slaves in European reason could only support nineteenth-century forms of paternalism (among both the slaveholders and the white abolitionists) by reducing the slave to a child. According to this paternalism, the child and the childlike adult would lack the rational will to count as a full moral person. Clearly, Douglass rejects any normative philosophy that would further the humiliation of the slave and embraces instead the more spirited conception of the self as freedom fighter.

If the Douglass narratives reject the dutiful path of the slave towards Christian humility and abstract reason, and therefore also reject Hegel's project for freedom through the discipline of the work ethic, these narratives would seem to invoke the freedom defined by the Hegelian model of warrior-master. Clearly, the subordination of the role of literacy to Douglass's struggle with Covey anchors his conception of the free self in something more akin to the courageous will of Hegel's sovereign master than in the rational will of the Stoic European slave. Indeed, the tendency among the many literary scholars and social theorists who have examined this connection is to locate Douglass's conception of self along these lines. For example, Paul Gilroy argues that Douglass's departure from the pacifism of the white Christian abolitionists "is directly relevant to his critical understanding of modernity. It underscored the complicity of civilization and brutality while emphasizing that the order of authority on which the slave plantation relied cannot be undone without recourse to the counterviolence of the oppressed" (*BA*, 63). Gilroy's own account of the kinship between Douglass and the Hegelian sovereign master overemphasizes the practice of slave suicide (*BA*, 63ff). Both Douglass and Hegel argue that the spirited warrior accepts the risk of death but not the necessity of death. According to Hegel, the certitude of death is experienced only by the slave mentality. Similarly, Douglass indicates his disinterest in suicidal projects by warning against confrontation when the odds are against one. But all the more there seems to be a strong resemblance between the basis for recognition sought by the Hegelian master and that sought by Douglass.

A Douglass biographer, William McFeely, has traced Douglass's exposure to German idealism to his acquaintance with Ottilia Assing, whom he met only after completing his 1855 *My Bondage* (see p. 263). However, the dialectic of manhood that appears in all of Douglass's narratives does not so much assimilate a Romantic European model of freedom as repeat what anthropologists identify as ubiquitous themes of manhood. Near-death experiences and various win-or-lose tests of daring performed on a "public stage" constitute one of the more common rites of passage into manhood across a number of European and non-European cultures.[15] While not all struggles for recognition require physical combat, these struggles do typically involve some threat of force.

Despite the fact that Hegel's narrative distills crucial elements of a large number of historical, literary, and anthropological accounts of manhood, Douglass's rendition of his self-formation differs in significant ways. Central among these differences is that already in the 1845 *Narrative* but even more forcefully in the fictionalized narrative, "The Heroic Slave," and in the 1855 *My Bondage,* Douglass departs from the transcendent and antinatural elements that inform not only the dialectic of the European slave through Stoicism and Christian alienation but also the Hegelian conception of the warrior as developed in the dialectic of master and slave. As Hegel interprets the struggle for recognition, the transformation of the animal in the state of nature into a transcendent human consciousness capable of participating in history cleaves apart animal and human, natural and unnatural.[16]

Douglass's protagonists (including himself) do not appear as "brutes" and yet renaturalize the transcendent self of European lore. For example, Douglass describes his battle with Covey as having "rekindled . . . embers of freedom." The spirit of freedom expressed through the element of fire does not evoke a transcendence of nature but a fervent desire for self. The struggle poses the threat of violence but avoids the predator's lust for the kill. There is a spirit that impels Douglass. This spirit, however, does not transform him from the sensuous animal (or mythic negro) into a transcendent human will. On the contrary, Douglass enters the scene in a position of subordination to animals (specifically to the horses he is ordered to tend). The artificial institution of slavery perpetuates what for Douglass is the unnatural reduction of human being to thing. Douglass emerges from the struggle as a fully embodied will, or as he puts it, a "power on earth." The struggle occurs in the barn with the other animals where slavebreaker and slave are stripped bare of the deceptive pretensions and unnatural perversions that protect slavery and, according to Douglass, destroy the manhood of both enslaver and slave.

The European dichotomy between man and animal never fully disappears from Douglass's narratives. Yet in "The Heroic Slave," Douglass portrays his heroic slave (Madison Washington) as a fearsome warrior and then compares the warrior's courage not only to the spirit of a lion but also to the readiness of the snake to strike.[17]

Moreover, Douglass places Madison's soliloquy on freedom in nature, specifically in the untamed woods, where Madison contrasts his life as a slave to the freedom of the birds (*HS*, 26). As an escaped slave, Madison's first free dwelling is among the bears and wolves (*HS*, 38). Douglass not only comes ever more to question the hypocrisy of the transcendental abolitionists along with the Southern Christian enslavers, both of whom lustily dominate the black body as they proclaim their own transcendence of nature and things natural. More radically, Douglass constructs an image of the free self that traverses the dichotomies between nature and spirit, animal and human, and desire and reason that propel European cultures. The slave who resists his oppressor, as Douglass writes, possesses "animal spirits" (*BE*, 78).

The animal imagery that controls the Douglass narratives of freedom also points towards the irony of the European mythos. The European man is defined through various forms in which he, as Hegel terms it, "negates" nature. As Hegel explains, self-consciousness initially abstracts itself from nature through a primordial struggle for recognition. The irony is that this struggle for transcendence is itself quite natural. It does not so much distinguish man from wolves and other social animals as recall what they have in common. Wolves assert their will in rituals for social status. That animals no less than man do battle for recognition not only renders the European negation of nature problematic but even pathological. The impossible sublations involved in the will to transcendence may account for the excesses of the European fascination with the imagined animality of the black body.

The European enchantment with transcendence, however, does not end with battles for recognition. European cultures, certainly through the nineteenth-century emphasis on literacy, aim finally to transcend the physicality of existence through *logos*. Accordingly, it is the capacity to use what is called language that most completely distinguishes man from animal. Hegel represents this European quest for abstraction in his sublation of the full range of expressive powers that compose the social lives of animals in favor of a totally concept-based knowledge in Absolute Spirit.

While Douglass's autobiographies appropriate the European *logos*, his narrative force goes beyond the dichotomies between impersonal argument and emotive expression. It is not colorless argument but argument embodied in the musical modalities of personal narrative that defines the ultimate import of Douglass's own struggle for recognition. Interestingly, Douglass claims that it was not in a book but through a slave song that he first understood the meaning of freedom (see editor's note in *BF*, 170). As he writes, "the mere hearing of these songs would do more to impress some minds with the horrible character of slavery . . . than the reading of whole volumes of philosophy on the subject could do" (*N*, 57).

Freedom, then, is not a concept, as the Stoics had thought. Freedom is more originally expressed through music. So too an education for freedom must develop not the alienated superstructure of the abstract mind but, more fundamentally, what Douglass identified as the "force" of "manhood" and what we might understand more broadly to include the existential dimensions of the self.

Notes

*I am especially grateful to Robert Bernasconi, Andrew Cutrofello, Lewis Gordon, Frank M. Kirkland, Julie Maybee, and John McCumber for very helpful comments on earlier versions of this essay.

1. G. W. F. Hegel, *Phenomenology of Spirit*, trans. A. V. Miller (Oxford: Oxford University Press, 1977); hereafter cited *PS*. References to the German text are from *Phaenomenologie des Geistes* (Hamburg: Felix Meiner, 1952) and follow references to the English translation.

2. Hegel's analysis here supports in part the analysis of American slavery in Stanley Elkins, *Slavery* (Chicago: University of Chicago Press, 1959), chap. 3.

3. See Howard McGary, "Alienation and the African-American Experience," in *The Philosophical Forum* 24 (Fall-Spring 1992–93): 282–96.

4. Orlando Patterson, *Slavery and Social Death* (Cambridge: Harvard University Press, 1982), 80; hereafter cited *SSD*. Patterson explicitly cites Hegel in order to account for the pathologies of slavery: "As Georg Hegel realized, total personal power taken to its extreme contradicts itself by its very existence, for total domination can become a form of extreme dependence on the object of one's power, and total powerlessness can become the secret path to control of the subject that attempts to exercise power" (*SSD*, 2).

5. Patterson argues against what Kojeve in his reading of Hegel terms the "existential impasse" for the master. Patterson points out that as a matter of historical fact "the master could and usually did achieve the recognition he needed from

other free persons, including other masters" (*SSD*, 99). Compare Allen W. Wood, who uses logical grounds to criticize Hegel on the same point. Wood argues that the master would not logically be dependent upon the slave for recognition but instead could seek recognition from other masters. For Wood's argument, see *Hegel's Ethical Thought* (Cambridge: Cambridge University Press, 1990), 93.

6. Frederick Douglass, *My Bondage and My Freedom*, ed. William L. Andrews (Chicago: University of Illinois Press, 1987), 61; hereafter cited *BF*. Compare Harriet Jacobs, writing as Linda Brent, "Incidents in the Life of a Slave Girl," collected in *The Classic Slave Narratives*, ed. Henry Louis Gates Jr. (New York: Mentor, 1987), 393; see also her observation that even poor whites sought to gain some recognition of their power by torturing or raping blacks (Gates, 408).

7. John Blassingame, *The Slave Community: Plantation Life in the Antebellum South* (New York: Oxford University Press, 1974), 211–12.

8. Eric J. Sundquist, *To Wake the Nations: Race in the Making of American Literature* (Cambridge: Harvard University Press, 1993), 51; hereafter cited *WN*.

9. Paul Gilroy, *The Black Atlantic: Modernity and Double Consciousness* (Cambridge: Harvard University Press, 1993); hereafter cited *BA*.

10. Eugene D. Genovese, *Roll, Jordan, Roll: The World the Slaves Made* (New York: Random House, 1976), 288–324.

11. David Roediger, *The Wages of Whiteness: Race and the Making of the American Working Class* (London and New York: Verso, 1991), 95–96.

12. Frederick Douglass, like W. E. B. Du Bois, accepted the romantic German notion that each culture has its unique gift to contribute to humanity. Douglass also argued for the relative superiority of the hybrid culture produced by the mulattoes over either Eurocentric or Afrocentric cultures. As Waldo E. Martin Jr. explains, mulatto culture represented for Douglass a more perfect revision of the white American ideal of a melting pot. See Martin's *The Mind of Frederick Douglass* (Chapel Hill: University of North Carolina Press, 1984), 222–23. On the "hybrid" aspects of Douglass's reinterpretation of Hegel's dialectic of master and slave, see also Paul Gilroy, *BA*, 61.

My own aim is not to assume with Douglass the cultural superiority of the mulatto, but only to argue that Douglass presents one progressive model of freedom and selfhood.

For the citation from Du Bois, see *The Souls of Black Folk* (New York: Bantam, 1989), 35.

13. Frederick Douglass, *Narrative of the Life of Frederick Douglass, An American Slave*, ed. Houston A. Baker Jr. (New York: Viking Penguin, 1982), 112–13; hereafter cited *N*.

14. William S. McFeely, *Frederick Douglass* (New York: Simon and Schuster, 1991), 271; hereafter cited *FD*.

15. David D. Gilmore, *Manhood in the Making* (New Haven: Yale University Press, 1990), 14.

16. Moreover, while Hegel does not explicitly address the question of gender in his phenomenology of self-consciousness, the assertion of self via a life and death struggle traditionally divides man from woman. At the same time that Douglass's narratives invite the reader to reinterpret the basis for one of the traditional models of manhood, these narratives also complicate the issue of gender difference. Exploration of the issue of gender takes us beyond the limits of the present essay.

17. Frederick Douglass's "The Heroic Slave" in *Three Classic African-American Novels*, William L. Andrews, ed. (New York: Penguin, 1990), 62.

8

SLAVERY AND THE TIES THAT DO NOT BIND

Julius Moravcsik

S lavery might be seen as a bad topic for a philosophy symposium. It is commonly assumed that we know what it is and
that we know that it is wrong. Why, then, discuss it on a
partly theoretical plane? I shall try to show that these initial intuitions are only partly right. I shall then present an analysis of slavery
within a normative theory of communities.[1] I will uncover varieties
of slavery that—if left unanalyzed—might suggest that the notion
has no common conceptual core. I will show, however, that there is
a conceptual core, though not visible on the surface. I will indicate
why judging slavery to be morally wrong is a complex matter. The
approach I take is meant to show also that a moral assessment of
institutions such as slavery can be done more adequately in the
framework of normative communitarianism than within a rights-
based approach. Finally, this essay also exemplifies the claim I made
elsewhere that an adequate analysis of slavery and similar institutions must be done by considering abstract legal structures embodied in ways of life, not merely by viewing it as a system of legal and
moral rules.

Variety and Ingredients

We shall consider briefly three examples to illustrate varieties of slavery. The first is slavery as practiced in ancient Greece. The basis of

this kind of slavery was the outcome of a given war, without anything like the Geneva Conventions. The victor either killed all the men of the losing side, or took them—as well as women and children—as slaves. This basis made the relationship—at least in principle—reversible. The losers of one day could become the victors on another. The arrangement robbed slaves of deliberative powers and choices in their own lives, as well as of their property. It brought with it cruelty in many but not in all cases. In some situations slaves could become tutors or craftsmen. Their influence on society depended on their relationship with their masters. Several of these features look very different when we take as our second example, the galley slaves of the European religious wars. The slaves were Protestant preachers who were chained to benches and made to row in the galleys for the rest of their lives. This relationship was based on religious intolerance, but in fact no attempt was made to destroy the religious lives of the galley slaves. There was extreme restriction on movement, and on property that could be owned. In both cases, there was also an economic interest that considered only what was good for the masters.

These examples should help to set the American experience into perspective. That experience lacks some of the elements of the other cases, but includes new ones. The comparisons should also help us to see that some of the elements that accompanied American slavery are in fact theoretically detachable. Some of these are: racial hatred, kidnapping entire tribes, systematically destroying entire cultures, and systematic sexual abuse. There is a practical value also in seeing this detachability, for it shows that many of these factors might stay with us even after slavery as such is abolished. Furthermore, while economic gain was no doubt a part of the motivation in all three cases, the alleged "basis" differs in each case. This indicates that it is not sufficient to attack the "bases" one by one. We need to see something in the relationship itself that underlies these variations and can be our appropriate target for analysis and moral assessment.

Indeed, we can detect certain underlying ingredients. One of these is *oppression*. This, in turn, has two salient components: The first involves limiting opportunities of living by physical, psychological, or other coercive methods for the oppressed. As we shall see, the notion of limiting opportunities will have to be considered context by context, since there are some limitations on any form of human life, and what should be seen as a limitation in one cultural context might not be seen that way when considering another. For example, the degree of interdependence among humans varies in history and across cultures and thus with it what are desirable or undesirable limitations. Also, while slavery entails oppression, this does not hold the other way around. There are forms of oppression other than slavery. The second component involves the oppressor acting on behalf of others in legal and other social contexts by substituting himself as the agent and considering only the master's interest. Again, some such substitution may be necessary in a complex society, but within contexts we can discern what are extreme and unwarranted substitutions of this sort. This concludes our sketch of the first main ingredient of slavery.

The second main ingredient is *economic exploitation partly using force and considering only the interests of the masters*. For example, there is labor under coercion and without substantial remuneration. Slavery will include this, but again not all forms of economic exploitation entail slavery. Furthermore, we see that for this component, too, we need to talk of inappropriate economic exploitation, with this notion varying in application from context to context. What constitutes inappropriate economic exploitation depends partly on what alternatives were or could have been envisaged within a given situation.

The third ingredient is the *forcible restrictions on deliberative opportunities and choices affecting individual lives* (whom to marry, how to grow up, what to be, etc.). Again, what counts as force here and what restrictions any society might have to invoke under certain circumstances are left to be determined in context. Thus, we need a definition that will include these ingredients that serve as salient necessary conditions and as guidelines for further contextual specifications.

Core Analysis

For the presentation of the core we will utilize the schema for representing lexical meaning that I developed elsewhere.[2] This involves articulating a conceptual core in terms of salient necessary explanatory conditions and using these conditions as guides to specifying

Saptg

appropriate conceptual contexts within which additional conditions yield sufficiency for determining range of application. The proposed core for slavery is: *use of undue force or other pressure for limiting deliberative sphere, choice, opportunities for work, and modes of work and remuneration, designed exclusively with the benefit of the master in mind.*[3] This characterization includes oppression, exploitation, and forced limit on action, as defined in the previous section. At the same time, it forces us to consider from context to context what should count as force, opportunity, and choice over individual life. Arriving at these seminormative conceptual decisions in context involves looking at social and economic structures as embedded in conceptions of individual welfare and qualities of communal life. The "definition" shows that slavery need not be embedded in a legal framework. Thus, abolishing slavery should not mean merely lifting its legal status, but also doing away with the human relationships that it contains. Nor are the efforts to change the relationships aimed solely at removing the involuntary aspects. This pertains especially to our assessment of the relations involved and the particular way in which slaves are treated in a context. Thus, assessing slavery is not merely looking at legal structures, nor simply at intentions or good will (lack of), but at practices and relationships as embedded in communal life. This will involve, among other factors, reflecting on the ties that bind a community within which slavery is practiced.

It follows from our analysis that these ties will include force, other forms of coercion, and acting on the basis of purely one-sided utility considerations. One might want to place oneself voluntarily into such a position, but such a commitment and the ties themselves are indeed fragile. Fragility results because the relation and underlying voluntary commitments rest on a partial ignorance of the human potential or a lack of ability to take on the burden to develop certain areas of human potential. Since the tie also depends on fear and force, and these are easily changeable contingent conditions, the whole fabric is fragile, both practically and psychologically.

To see this more clearly, let us compare these ties with others proposed as binding a healthy, flourishing community.[4] Such ties will involve care, concern for the welfare of others, respect based on certain character traits, and trust. They are much less subject to destruction by external forces, have a deeper psychological root, and hence are a more stable basis for cooperation and mutual sharing of aims. In contrast, slavery in any of its manifestations has built into it as dominant an element of self-centeredness on the part of the master, even when this is covered up on the surface by some form of benevolent paternalism. And even though it was pointed out that cruelty, physical abuse, and the like are not built into the general structure of slavery, the framework is conducive to their emergence.

Still, it should be admitted that, within the constraint of the framework of slavery, there can be respect and fairness. Granted the unequal interactions, a party can still show, relative to that framework, fairness in dealing with others, and respect for achievement and character. Still, some typical manifestations of such attitudes (inviting into the house, eating together, etc.) will be ruled out from the start. Thus, we have at best what one might call "crippled loyalties" and cooperative attitudes. This does not mean that the emotional strength of the loyalty may not be high. But the whole interrelationship with these underlying attitudes is based on a kind of moral blindness; that is, on not seeing other possibilities that because of wider reciprocity, can base communal life on a firmer footing. The cure here seems to be increased self-knowledge, on both communal and individual bases. One might, however, start with a crippled loyalty and gradually transform it into loyalty between equals. (Something like this happens at times as children grow into adulthood and reach the level of their parents.)

This analysis of the conceptual core and how it is used in working out contextual determinations of extension should help to remove stereotypes and so help us get at the more deep underlying issues. The claim of this essay is that these issues can be best addressed by considering conditions of better or worse communities and communal life. But to show this, some reflections on the best known alternative, the rights-based approach, are in order.

Rights and Communal Life

Standard rights-based approaches would say that humans have certain basic inalienable rights. These protect their minimal autonomy. This autonomy is to command a basic respect that would rule out—

175

among other things—slavery, since this is a violation of these rights as a legal or social arrangement. In this section I shall first list some objections to the rights-based approach and then show why I think that the treatment of slavery within normative communitarianism is more adequate.

First, the rights-based approach relies on the notion of autonomy, but this notion is slippery, as used in this moral context. The concept of autonomy was first applied by the Greeks to a community giving laws to itself, as the etiology suggests, and it was applied to human individuals only later, in a derivative way. As applied to communities, we can distinguish different kinds of autonomies, such as cultural or political autonomy. But in the individual case, it seems to constitute a kind of moral and personal independence. This, however, admits of degrees, and in the modern world in which people depend so much on each other, it is difficult to expect that it should be applicable in pure form. If we are, however, discussing individual autonomy in degrees, we might not reconcile this use with the invocation of human rights. Rights come in the form of all or nothing. But can we, in social contexts, talk about independence in this way?[5]

The second objection addresses the fundamentality of these alleged rights. If certain rights are basic and unconditional in our moral system, how will we justify their selection and the need for such rights in general? It is one thing to say that if we were in the position of building up a society from the start, then we could argue that slavery should not be a part of it. But ethical and political theories need to be applied to history in flux. The societies we are considering have historical and cultural contexts. Questions about slavery must be articulated in the context of what the viable alternatives were at that time in the cultural tradition. If the only alternatives that a particular era can conceive of are genocide or slavery, then slavery is preferable. In other cases it may be that an immediate abolition of slavery will result in starvation. It seems that one should address the unacceptability of slavery in the framework of what it will do to communities in general and to a given community in a particular context. Thus, one might want to consider what to do about slavery in terms of the better or worse rather than right or wrong. How would a rights-based approach deal with this? There seems to be a kernel of truth in what the rights-based approach suggests; that is, that slavery should be always a warning signal: this society needs fundamental changes and improvement. But this function of placing slavery in the right moral perspective can be accommodated also by views that are not rights-based.

The rights-based approach places the individual as the main focus of discussion. Is this really correct? Are questions of harm done and suffered, as well as of moral responsibility in the case of slavery, really reducible to laws and individuals? An alternative is to assign responsibility for slavery both to individuals and to communities and to view the harm done also as affecting entities on both levels. It has been said at times that this involves treating communities as persons.[6] This need not be the case. Communities can satisfy the criteria for being agents without having to satisfy the criteria for being personlike. But not only can we take a whole community responsible for slavery, we can also document the harm done to a community, in addition to the harm done to individuals. We tend to focus on the harm done to individual slaves. But we need to look also at the psychological and moral (minimally in terms of character) damage done to the oppressors, and to the damage done to the community, for example, in terms of restricting the kinds of communal activities and ties among people that the society with slavery imposes. Studies of the Holocaust showed also the damage done to the masters and even to their offspring. Again, work by Toni Morrison shows the damage caused by slavery not only to slaves but also to the masters. We can add to this the harm done to the community by adding to it fear of revolt and hence a threat to stability, and the lack of ability to tap all communal resources in the dialogues that a community needs about principles of cooperation to be formulated and ways of implementing these. It has been argued many times over the centuries that people have more respect for communal principles if they had a share in their formulation. Slavery takes away this way of strengthening communal life. A rights-based approach has more difficulties accommodating these points. Using my approach, getting people in a community involved in decision-making is a matter of degrees and depends also on many other factors, such as relations among people and efforts at representing communal interests. The rigidity of the rights-based approach, however, seems inhospitable to such a pragmatic approach.

Let us see briefly how the normative communitarian deals with these issues. First, as our analysis showed, the communitarian approach acknowledged both the varieties and the conceptual common core of slavery. Thus, it will consider certain very general effects of slavery on societies, but then will also suggest guidelines for an additional contextual approach. As we saw, in some cases the benefits of people retaining their own culture in a community need to be stressed; in other cases, the absurdity of religious intolerance leading to total restriction on physical movements must be pointed out. Reflection on what slavery can do to a community should also help us to separate it from other harmful factors that might accompany it. This is clear in the American case. Even if sexual abuse and racial bigotry could be stopped, this might not stop slavery, and—as history shows—things clearly do not work the other way around either. Still, one can point to harm done on the individual and communal levels, arising from what we presented as the conceptual core, and thus suggest that these should be considered in all contexts as we add up good and harmful factors and rank our political/communal options as better or worse. Finally, as we saw above, while the rights-based approach says that slavery is always bad, the normative communitarian will say that the existence of slavery in a society is always a warning signal that legal and human relations need be reconsidered and that on any reasonable criteria we are confronting a crippled community.

Conclusion

Ultimately slavery is bad because it negatively affects basic human potentials. But recently, philosophers such as G. Watson have objected that this kind of ethical stance will have to rely on naturalism, and some appeal to human essence naturalistically defined.[7] But the approach I advocate in this paper is not naturalistic: naturalism must embrace the viability of a sharp fact/value dichotomy in questions concerning human value. But my philosophy follows a line advocated by Plato earlier and Hilary Putnam more recently, according to which there is no purely nonnormative way of delineating a human agent, individual or collective.[8] Being an agent means containing structures encoding priorities, and these cannot be given a purely factual account. Within the confines of this paper I cannot explain in detail the nature of the sort of reflections that result in setting (discovering?) priorities within agents and assessing communal lives. But it might help to note that such discussions mirror in many ways discussions concerning heath. These too cut across the fact/value distinctions.[9]

Finally, a point Royce made already.[10] Communities constitute hierarchies. Thus a sign of a sound community is that it is open to becoming—under certain conditions—part of larger, sound, communities. It is difficult to see how a society within which there is slavery can accommodate itself to this kind of openness. It must live with some fear. But fear, unlike some other conditions mentioned above, is not a tie that we can rely on to bind in the long run.

Overcoming Resentment

Slavery existed in the Western and Mediterranean countries for over 3,000 years. Hence its demise in many of these cultures in the nineteenth century represented a milestone in cultural development. But we should not overestimate what was accomplished, for example, in the United States by the "abolishing" of slavery. That move merely took away the legal status and sanction underlying a certain interpersonal arrangement. The door was left open for a number of oppressive structures flourishing even after the abolition. Hence, it also left behind the enormous question: what to do next? On one level the answer was obvious: there was a need to redefine and reconstruct rights, duties, and opportunities across a number of social and political institutions. But if the main theses of this work are sound, then this "reconstruction" would be affected drastically by underlying conceptions of communal goals, ties, and cooperative ventures. For example, one of the issues that surfaced was the question: under what conditions can a person be said to be a member of a community with consent?

There is a core in the concept of consent that would not be brought into doubt.[11] But this core provides only the guidelines for settling the difficult questions of what counts in which contexts. Legalistic approaches to this issue demand documents and contracts and are too narrow a conception. Such artifacts are often neither

179

available nor to be expected by reasonable people. In some contexts, one could also count as a sign of consent the voluntary joining of cooperative activities aimed at procuring shelter, food, or securing protection. Or perhaps accepting certain services (e.g., education, medicine) counts as consent in joining. Answers to these questions depend partly on conceptions of what binds the community together, what are construed as communal aims and activities, and what actual and potential members of the community take as salient features of human nature (e.g., needing education?). These comments provide evidence for the assertion above that the reconstruction depends partly on underlying attitudes affecting communal and individual ideals.

A variety of attitudes can surface in such context. One of these can be summarized by the nebulous slogan: "Justice has to be done." This slogan can cover a multitude of sins. For example, it can mask a desire for revenge. Such acts are notoriously counterproductive. They create poisonous communal relations, and evoke the next act of "justice" by those harmed in the course of carrying out the first.

Justice can mean also for some "moral bookkeeping." In rough summary: "these people did this, now we have to undo the harm done." This, too, is counterproductive in many contexts. The people to whom the harm was done died; thus, the people who will be made to pay are innocent, and the redress under the new conditions can do more harm than good. This is not to say that redress is never a relevant consideration. But when it cuts across generations, its invocation needs many qualifications.

Quite different problems arise when people call for forgiveness. Such a demand is likely to be unrealistic if it is interpreted so as to ask for wiping clean the emotional slate. It is one thing not to ask for revenge. But we do not control emotions strictly voluntarily. Thus, we cannot simply decide to relate to others who wronged us in the past with only positive feelings.

The approach to be advocated in this section starts by acknowledging that in considering slavery, and many situations analogous to it, representing great upheavals, all parties are likely to be full of resentment. Some resent that their way of life changes, some that what they worked for seems to be lost, even though they did nothing wrong. Others, now that slavery no longer stands as a legal structure, can take a better look at the binds they were in and resent having had that imposed on them. Thus, according to this essay, the main problem is how to overcome resentment. Only in such an atmosphere can meaningful reconstruction take place.

Appeal to self-interest will not solve the problem. What should count as self-interest in this context? For some only economic considerations are relevant; for others this is too narrow. But even if we stick with economics, we get bogged down in choosing parameters. It could be argued that the abolition of slavery was economically bad for the South.[12] Then again, others will argue that this is not true if we take a more long-range point of view. Overcoming resentment cannot be postponed till such issues are settled—if indeed they ever will be. It is better to concentrate on the partly normative issue of whether one takes a narrow or wide notion of self-interest.

Can these questions be thought through clearly during a crisis? Or need we have on the spectacles of hindsight that give us the allegedly 20/20 historical vision? This is most likely not an all-or-nothing matter. It is unfortunate that some of the elements of slave labor were duplicated in industrial labor, coming into its own at that time. The relevant features of slave labor are: (1) complex tasks to be broken up into simple "atomic" ones, (2) simple tasks to be construed so that these could be performed by the uneducated, and (3) a whole operation that could be easily monitored.[13] Though these features might have been seen as contributing to efficiency, their long-term psychological consequences are considerable and raise serious questions. Under these circumstances, the worker is reduced to doing tasks that do not evoke interest. Without complexity the work will lack the possibility of creativity and of alternative ways of executing tasks. Hence, it also deprives the worker of the kind of responsibility that is linked to initiative and a sense of achievement. This mode of working will affect the way workers relate to the task of the community and to the managers. Furthermore, it might be too much to ask that while they work in this manner during most of their time, they adopt quite a different attitude, one needed for membership in a flourishing community, when they participate in communal affairs on various levels.

It requires also detached reflection to separate—as we must in such situations—resentment against individuals from resentment against institutions. Relations between masters and slaves varied greatly. At times slaves were treated well, and at times their jobs were not robotlike.[14] This distinction helps also clarify the issue of paternalism.[15] This notion admits of diverse articulations. But on any reasonable account we must regard only the persons involved as being perhaps paternalistic. This institution itself cannot have this attribute.

We can see this by recalling that according to our analysis, the possibility of using force, without any agreed-upon constraint, lies at the heart of the peculiar mode of oppression we call slavery. This view gains support also from the empirical study of American slavery.[16] The use of force also permeates relationships like that of a family. The family structure cannot be taken for granted by those who wanted it, since the master could separate families by force (rape, sale).

As was pointed out above, both parties were full of resentment. The recognition of this could have provided a basis for facilitating reconciliation. To see this more clearly, we should take a closer conceptual look at the concept of resentment. Resentment is, roughly, the negative feeling we have when we have been treated by individuals, or by humans within an institutional framework, in a way we interpret as causing us undeserved and unnecessary injury, or expressing indifference in contexts in which one would have assumed some concern for others, and seem to be caused by entities that can be expected to be responsible and to be able to detect human feelings and dimensions of self-esteem. Thus, resentment is not the same as wanting revenge, although it may be accompanied by it. Again, its absence does not amount to forgiveness, since it need not involve a total emotional turnabout. Also, resentment need not be accompanied by hatred or a wish to harm. We can resent insult, intrusion, and unfairness without wanting to harm others. Still, resentment leaves us in an uncooperative state of mind, without the willingness to consider sympathetically the state of mind of those who are the object of our resentment.

We shall now turn to a brief sketch of how we can overcome resentment. Philosophers have difficulties dealing with a notion like resentment, since it is not a purely cognitive state, but involves emotional factors.[17] In the type of cases we consider, the problem is exacerbated by the fact that the overcoming must take place after the deed was done and acknowledged as wrong from the legal point of view. We shall restrict ourselves to the topic of overcoming resentment after the legal condemnation of it. We need to sketch briefly both the cognitive and affective factors involved in this task.

Judgments about duty cannot be among the cognitive factors. Because overcoming resentment is partly a matter of feeling, we cannot have an obligation to realize this, only obligations not to express resentment in certain ways. On the other hand, self-interest can enter only in a limited way because its particular interpretation depends on our ethical ideal. So one might as well say that judgments about resentment are at least as fundamental as those about self-interest.

There are, however, three cognitive elements that can contribute to overcoming resentment. One of these is a conception and related judgments concerning the kinds of relations we want with others in our community. A society full of resentful individuals will lack, to a large extent, trust and concern for others and hence will have difficulties with cooperative activities. Furthermore, the emotional satisfaction of remaining resentful is likely to be brief and interferes with other satisfying attitudes. Second, one can have a conception of the human potential that leaves drastic change and reorientation in another individual a live possibility in most cases. Third, one can have a belief that the overcoming of resentment under the circumstances exemplified by the United States after the Civil War would lead to increased freedom and self-control within the individual, thus enabling such a human to embark on further activities deemed to have worth.

Clearly, these cognitive factors are not sufficient for overcoming resentment. One has to want (aspire to, wish for, "desire") the kind of communal existence that resentment hinders, one has to have an interest in human potential, and one has to strive for the kind of character that brings with it the overcoming of resentment. Where would these affective qualities come from? There is one context in human life that is universal, and within which such attitudes can emerge naturally. This is the family. There the view that such attitudes have intrinsic value can develop without much reflection, solely on the basis of immediate emotional give and take. Of course, not every biological family will provide the right background for this. Still, the potential is there. Two other communities can also provide the conditions for developing the attitudes in question. One is that of close friendships and the other that of a cultural community, centered not on political goals but shared poetry, music, carving, architecture, and the like. Indirect evidence comes for this from the fact that, when slave owners wanted to make it difficult for slaves to develop that kind of character, they tried to destroy their cultural identity.[18] Presumably their insecurity led them to such cruelty, in the hope that the slaves become more like mere tools, subject to arbitrary manipulation.

Still, having pointed out these factors, we have given no guarantee that these are sufficient for providing the emotional aspect of the overcoming resentment. For one thing, we need to be able to project these attitudes from the narrow confines mentioned to much wider ranges. Second, even if we can do so, there is no guarantee that these emotional factors will prevail over others counter to them. The ancient Greeks recognized this. Sophocles's play the *Philoctetes* centers on a hero who is justifiably resentful because of the harm that was done to him and who is called upon to overcome his resentment and join his community in what is deemed a necessary cooperative enterprise. This change in attitude is described as "fine," or "noble." But we are given no clues as to how you can get someone to realize it. The dramatist relies on a favorite way out among his contemporaries: divine intervention. This move can be seen as an implicit recognition that we are dealing here with something very basic in human nature, for which there are no recipes.

If we insist on guarantees, then we will end up saying that we have not improved upon Sophocles. But if we are content with sketching a list of relevant factors that facilitate the reorientation, then we can say that the above at least paves the way toward the understanding of a complex phenomenon that is fundamental to healthy social change and is indeed in our world today as much as ever.

Notes

1. J. M. Moravcsik, "Communal Ties," *Proceedings of The American Philosophical Association* 62, supp. (1988): 211–25.

2. J. M. Moravcsik, *Thought and Language* (London: Routledge, 1990).

3. Aristotle's approval of slavery says nothing about "undue force." He did not see this as a necessary part of slavery (*Pol.*, bk. 1, ch. 4, 1254a15–18).

4. J. M. Moravcsik, "Communal Ties."

5. The argument against, for example, Aristotle is that it should be based on fundamental rights, rather than on the dubious psychological thesis that some humans are by nature not capable of autonomy. (*Pol.*, bk. 1, ch. 5, 1254b15–20).

6. Peter French, "The Corporation is a Person," in *The Question of Responsibility*, ed. Peter French (New York: St. Martin's, 1991), 293–334.

7. G. Watson, "Identity, Character, and Morality" in *Identity, Character, and Morality*, Owen Flanagan and Amelie Rorty, eds. (Cambridge: MIT Press, 1990).

8. J. M. Moravcsik, *Plato and Platonism* (Oxford: Blackwell, 1992).

9. J. M. Moravcsik, "Ancient and Modern Conceptions of Health and Medicine," *The Journal of Medicine and Philosophy* 1 (1976): 337–48.

10. See J. Royce, *The Philosophy of Loyalty* (New York: Macmillan, 1916).

11. For discussion, see Howard McGary and Bill Lawson, *Between Slavery and Freedom* (Bloomington: Indiana University Press, 1992), 62.

12. Robert W. Fogel, *Without Consent or Contract: The Rise and Fall of American Slavery* (New York: W. W. Norton, 1989), 388.

13. Fogel, *Without Consent*, 26–27.

14. Fogel, *Without Consent*, 392.

15. McGary and Lawson, *Between Slavery*, 26–28.

16. Fogel, *Without Consent*, 34.

17. For an excellent discussion of resentment see the first essay in P. F. Strawson, *Freedom and Resentment* (London: Methuen, 1974), 5–15.

18. Fogel, *Without Consent*, 395–410.

9

PATERNALISM AND SLAVERY

Howard McGary

H ow should we view those who were the principal actors
during slavery? Were slaves "sambos" who acquiesced in
their own oppression, or were they psychologically whole
people who struggled to end their enslavement? On the other side
of the equation, were slaveholders heartless, money grubbing, evil
people who took delight in the enslavement of Africans, or were
they merely pawns caught up in an evil system? These are complex
questions. Slavery was a multifaceted system. Thus, it is difficult to
give a single description of slavery in the United States that captures
all of its nuances. There has, however, been an intense debate over
how the typical slave and slaveholder should be characterized.

One group of scholars has been reluctant to describe the typical
slaveholder as evil.[1] These commentators argue that slaveholders
had the best interest of the slaves at heart. They describe slaveholders as misguided, ignorant or morally weak. In other words, the typical slaveholder held a set of false beliefs that caused them to act in
what we now can see were clearly morally objectionable ways. Others
have argued that slaveholders appreciated that what they were doing
was wrong, but they did it anyway in order to gain economic power
and social privilege.[2]

This is a complex debate, and I shall not attempt to cover every
facet of it. Instead, I shall focus on one aspect of this debate:

whether or not slavery should be characterized as paternalistic. By a paternalistic explanation of slavery, I mean one that claims that slaveholders held slaves because they believed it was in the slave's best interest or an explanation that claims that slaves viewed their masters in a manner similar to the way children see their guardians. So described, the typical slaveholder was ignorant, but not evil. A case often said to be analogous is the exploitation of women by men. In such cases the behavior of males is objectionable, but the typical male is not thought to be evil. This is not to say that certain males, like certain slaveholders, were not evil, but only that evil does not describe the typical male or slaveholder.

In my view, paternalistic accounts of slavery cannot withstand close scrutiny. This became apparent to me from my reading of the slave narratives, because slaves typically described slavery and their slaveholders in ways that called paternalism into question. In James Pennington's narrative, *The Fugitive Blacksmith*, he writes:

My feelings are always outraged when I hear them speak of "kind masters" . . . "Christian masters," . . . "the mildest form of slavery," . . . "well fed and clothed slaves," as extenuations of slavery; I am satisfied they either mean to pervert the truth, or they do not know what they say. The being of slavery, its soul and body, lives and moves in the chattel principle, the property principle, the bill of sale principle; the cart-whip, starvation, and nakedness, are its consequences to a greater or less extent, warring with the dispositions of men.[3]

Some might say that clearly the description of slavery as a paternalistic institution is false, an attempt to put what is clearly objectionable in a better light. They are correct, but why they are right is much more involved than one might imagine. Paternalistic accounts of slavery support the view that slavery was unjust, but that it was not as bad as some people have thought.

It would be foolish to contend that there were no positive human interactions between slaves and slaveholders, or that slaveholders had no motive for doing things that benefitted slaves. Clearly, after the abolishment of the slave trade in 1808, slaveholders had good self-interested reason for looking out for the welfare of their slaves. Peter Parish, in *Slavery: History and Historians*, notes that a number of historians who defend paternalistic accounts of slavery make use of this fact.[4]

There is, however, a vast difference between providing slaves with the bare necessities to keep them productive and a sincere concern for their welfare. It is doubtful that providing a person with the bare necessities to keep them productive counts as paternalism. The motive for the slaveholder's behavior was his own good, not the good of his slaves. In fact, the slaveholders created the situation that made their alleged paternalism necessary. If I force persons into a situation where I have to meet their needs because it promotes my good, then I am not acting in a paternalistic manner.

I would like to make the strategy of this chapter clear. First, I suggest reasons why scholars have offered paternalistic explanations of slavery. Next, I contend that all paternalistic justifications of slavery are captured by one of the models that I describe below. I then argue that none of these models describes the true relationship between slaves and slaveholders. Finally, I argue that paternalistic explanations of slavery are compatible with our conceptions of what counts as evil. I would also like to make it clear that my aim is not to provide a new justification of paternalism, but to show that, given our present understanding of paternalism, all such defenses of American slavery fail.

Scholars on both sides of the paternalism debate claim that they are only describing or explaining the institution of American slavery, not excusing or justifying it. But, as we know, excuses and justifications are types of explanations, and we evaluate excuses and justifications much the same way as other explanations. Explanations in general answer questions about how or why something happened. Justifications are explanations that put behaviors in the best possible light.

How does the distinction between explanations, excuses, and justifications relate to historical accounts of slavery? I think that, given the intimate connection between explanations, excuses, and justifications, historical explanations can and sometimes do excuse or justify. With excuses, the person thought to be liable is willing to settle for an explanation that puts his behavior in a more favorable light. Imagine the following conversation between A and B:

189

A: Why did slaveholders hold slaves?
B: They did so in order to promote the slave's own good.

B's explanation also counts as an excuse and possibly as a justification for the slaveholder's owning slaves.

Even some scholars who include slave narratives among their sources have claimed that the relationship between the slaveholder and the slave was "paternalistic." For example, the noted historian of slavery, Eugene Genovese, writes:

> For the slaveholders paternalism represented an attempt to overcome the fundamental contradiction in slavery: the impossibility of the slaves' ever becoming the things they were supposed to be. Paternalism defined the involuntary labor of the slaves as legitimate return to their masters for protection and direction. But the masters' need to see their slaves as acquiescent human beings constituted a moral victory for the slaves themselves. Paternalism's insistence upon mutual obligations—duties, responsibilities, and ultimately even rights—implicitly recognized the slave's humanity.[5]

Genovese goes on to say: "whenever paternalism exists, it undermines solidarity among the oppressed by linking them to the oppressors."[6]

Although Genovese clearly condemns the actions of the slaveholders, he still characterizes slavery in paternalistic terms. As the quotation above demonstrates, Genovese sees the paternalism of slavery as a viable explanation for the lack of solidarity among slaves. It is clear to me that Genovese does not intentionally wish to cast the slaveholders and the institution of slavery in a positive light, but some historians have deliberately used the paternalistic explanation to excuse slaveholders and slavery. For example, William K. Scarborough, in his article "Slavery—The White Man's Burden," writes:

> Professor Genovese has elucidated with remarkable perception the paternalistic relationship which bound together masters and slaves in the Old South. My principal quarrel with his interpretation lies in his characterization of the planters, especially in his distressing propensity to assign to them only base and ignoble motives for acts of genuine benevolence.[7]

Genovese rejects Scarborough's position, but in the appendix to his book *Roll, Jordan, Roll* Genovese makes it clear that he does see slavery as a paternalistic institution. He is quick to warn us, however, that "[t]he subordination of one race to another or the people of any country to a welfare state does not constitute a paternalistic order in any historically meaningful sense."[8]

Unfortunately, Genovese never gives us a clear statement of what he means by "paternalism." He does tell us what it is not, for example, the idea that the strong must protect and lead the weak in return for obedience and labor is not paternalistic. But one thing is clear from Genovese's perspective: paternalism requires coercion. He claims that paternalism is incompatible with bourgeois social relations. By this I take him to mean that the idea of individual autonomy is inconsistent with paternalism.

Genovese fails to see that paternalism is not always incompatible with bourgeois social relations. As I shall argue in the final section of this chapter, paternalism has been and continues to be an acceptable and even heralded practice in liberal or bourgeois societies. Given the way that paternalism has been viewed in these societies, such explanations can serve to put what would normally be thought to be reprehensible behavior in a more positive light.

Why Paternalism?

Commentators who have adopted paternalistic accounts of the institution of slavery do so for several reasons. Generally, they believe that such accounts have a great deal of explanatory power. More specifically, some think that these explanations allow us to understand and even justify certain aspects of slave society not justifiable with nonpaternalistic explanations—for example, the apparent devotion that some slaves were said to show towards their masters. Viewing the slaveholder-slave relationship as paternalistic also gives the slave the status of human being, something denied by many whites during slavery. But even if it does, it may come at a great cost. In order for the slave to enjoy the alleged benefits of a paternalistic master, he had to give up all claims to respect as a responsible adult. He had to be a "sambo."[9]

We should be careful to note that to say that slavery was paternalistic could mean several things. One could mean that all or most slave-holders thought that slavery was a good thing for the slaves. In other words, their motives for owning slaves were to promote and protect the slaves' best interest. On the other hand, one could interpret paternalism in such a way that the motives of slaveholders were not the key issue, but rather that slavery was a state of dependency: that the slaves were dependent upon slaveholders for their survival and that the slaves were not capable of being responsible for their own fates. According to the 1850 argument of slavery apologist Dr. Samuel Cartwright of the University of Louisiana, slavery was necessary for the survival of Africans: "The African will starve rather than engage in a regular system of agricultural labor, unless impelled by the stronger will of the white man."[10]

This interpretation as an explanation of slavery would obviously place slavery and the slaveholders in a more positive light. If we accept Cartwright's reasons for holding slaves, then we should view the behavior of slaveholders in less harsh terms, and perhaps we may even excuse it. But clearly one primary reason why slaveholders held slaves was they believed that it was in their best interest to do so.[11] They often gave rationalizations that included concern for the welfare of the slave, but in the overwhelming majority of cases, these explanations were just rationalizations for an oppressive system that worked to the advantage of the slaveholders.

But suppose we say that most slaveholders held slaves because they felt that they had no other viable alternatives. In other words, slaveholders felt that they had to hold slaves because if they didn't, some harsher masters would.[12] They could thus contend that they were holding slaves for the slaves' own good. This argument fails for several reasons. First, it assumes that the profit motive did not play a crucial role in the slaveholder's decision to hold slaves. Second, it assumes that slavery was not a highly coordinated and collective activity.[13] Finally, it assumes that slaveholders felt that slavery was wrong, but nonetheless a kind of necessary evil. I think on any careful reading of the sources all three of these assumptions are false. Therefore any argument that has these assumptions as premises cannot be sound.

Critics might contend that (a) even if during slavery the facts did not support the slaveholder's paternalistic rationalizations of slavery, it does not follow that (b) slavery could not justifiably be given a paternalistic interpretation. If we think that paternalism is a function of an individual's operative beliefs, then (b) does not follow from (a). Suppose many slaveholders just didn't see the facts, even quite obvious ones? Let us say they were in some state that falls on the self-deception continuum. If the slaveholders were self-deceived about the extent to which slaves were capable of living autonomous lives, then (b) is false.

However, it is doubtful that many or most slaveholders believed the false belief that slavery was a beneficent institution. Even though some apologists claimed that slavery was good for slaves, there is little, if any, evidence available to support the strong claim that most or many slaveholders genuinely believed that they were helping blacks by holding them as slaves. No doubt there were some slaveholders who genuinely held such beliefs, but given the lack of evidence for such a belief being epistemically warranted even in the eighteenth and nineteenth centuries, people had to really engage in a strong dose of self-deception in order to convince themselves that their motive for owning slaves was paternalistic.

My reading of the sources, particularly biographies, diaries, and letters of slaveholders, suggests that many of them self-consciously used the paternalistic view of slavery as mere rationalizations when confronted by the critics of slavery.[14] Perhaps the ones who did not were in a state of self-deception fueled by being in a state of "motivated belief." One is in a state of motivated belief in believing that P if (1) one believes that P, and (2) the belief that P is causally sustained by a motive for believing that P. By a "motive" I mean a mental state consisting of certain sorts of beliefs and desires. These beliefs and desires provide the subject with a rationale for doing something—in the case in question for believing that P.

Perhaps I can illustrate what I have in mind here by drawing upon what it means to have a favorable attitude towards someone you like a great deal. Having a pro attitude towards a person, in spite of evidence that would tend to support a negative attitude towards the person, involves what I call being in a state of motivated belief. This state can range from wishful thinking to full blown self-deception. Being in a state of motivated belief directs one's attention away from negative evidence and causes one to exaggerate every small bit of evidence that speaks in the person's favor. When one has a negative disposition then just the opposite is true. For example, when one has a negative attitude it may reveal itself phenomenologically in the agent being irritated or bored when the agent has to evaluate evidence that is of a positive nature about the subject.

There may have been a time in history when a belief that slavery was a beneficent institution was epistemically warranted. This was not true of the antebellum South, however. Even if it were the case that slaveholders genuinely *believed* that slavery was paternalistic, it does not follow that it *was* paternalistic. Historians must separate mere rationalizations and gross self-deception from reality.

But as noted above, some who have explained slavery by using a paternalistic model go beyond making questionable assumptions about the motives of slaveholders; they also present questionable characterizations of slaves. One popular representation of slaves under such models is the slave as a totally dependant being. According to this model, slaves were dependent upon slaveholders because slaves, for a variety of reasons, could not be responsible for defining and promoting their own good. This argument does not rest on the motives of the slaveholders. The contention is that it could be true even if all slaveholders were clearly motivated to hold slaves because they felt it would promote their own good rather than the good of the slaves.

Many of the early supporters of this model blatantly assumed the natural inferiority of slaves. Slaves were thought to be subhuman creatures that could not survive in civilized societies if left to their own devices. But what about the defenders of the paternalistic arguments who denied the natural inferiority of slaves and focused on the so-called lack of autonomy of slaves? Do they fare any better? (This question will be the central issue under discussion in the next section.)

Liberal thinkers in both the human rights and utilitarian traditions have argued that under certain conditions we are justified in making choices for certain agents even when the choices and the actions that result have consequences that primarily affect the actors themselves. Children, women, blacks, and those who have been thought to have arrested development are some of the persons and groups that have been singled out as deserving of paternalistic interference with their liberty. Utilitarians would justify these interferences on the ground that they maximize the greatest utility for society as a whole, while human rights theorists emphasize the importance of protecting human beings from self-inflicted harm.

There can be no denying that there can be praiseworthy motives given for paternalistic interferences. There can also, however, be morally reprehensible ones. For example, paternalistic interferences can be used to justify taking unfair advantage of others under the guise that their actions are protecting the unwilling victims from self-inflicted harm.

I am not the first person to condemn paternalistic explanations or justifications of slavery, and understandably other critics have focused on a controversial premise in paternalistic accounts of slavery: namely, that blacks were in some way(s) incapable of recognizing their own good and that slave masters were in a better position to do so. Usually this premise involves some claims about the natural inferiority of blacks or the claim that blacks were made inferior by their social circumstances. But most of these commentators failed to notice that inferiority is a relative term. The judgment that someone is inferior requires a standard of excellence or normality.

During slavery a common belief held by whites was that blacks were intellectually inferior to whites. Even if this claim were true, however, it would certainly not justify paternalistic explanations and justifications of American chattel slavery. In order for such an account to be viable, it cannot simply be true that blacks were intellectually inferior to whites, but it must further be the case that blacks lacked the mental capacity to understand and promote their own good. So the paternalistic account depends upon blacks failing to reach minimal requirements for autonomous choice. But this claim seems to be clearly false about slaves as a group. Slaves were clearly capable of articulating their conceptions of their good and they fought against incredible odds to put their life plans into action.[15]

What then should we make of these paternalistic accounts? How should they be understood? We should note that not all interference with a person's will or liberty counts as paternalistic. A person who prevents me from unknowingly falling down an open elevator shaft has not treated me in a paternalistic fashion. All forms of paternalism require that the interference be explained or justified by reference to the good of the person who is in some way being interfered with, some inability or lack of knowledge on the part of the person who is treated in a paternalistic fashion, and the judgment on the part of the person doing the interfering that they know what is good for this person. These conditions appear to be clear and straightforward, but when we look at the various models that have been advanced as types of paternalistic explanations for slavery, we discover that they fail to qualify as clear-cut cases of paternalistic interference. In the next section, I shall examine several models of paternalism and show how these models have been used to describe slavery.

Models of Paternalism

There are several models that have been used to illustrate paternalistic behavior. In examining these models, I am not claiming that all interferences that fall under one of these models are justified on grounds of paternalism, but rather that these models have been thought to represent what we have defined above as a paternalistic interference. All the models that I shall examine involve at least two parties. However, it has been argued that people can act paternalistically towards themselves.[16] Such an account eliminates the appearance of a violation of personal autonomy by others. This presents an interesting problem, but it shall not detain us here, for the slaveholder/slave cases involve more than one person. It will, however, be relevant to what I have to say in the next section.

A fairly exhaustive list of popular models of paternalistic interference includes the parent/child model, the mentally competent/incompetent model, the doctor/patient model, the teacher/student model, and the benevolent dictator/citizen model. Can the slaveholder/slave relationship be subsumed under one of the models of paternalistic interferences listed above? I think that the answer is no. Let us turn directly to the question of whether the slaveholder/slave relationship reduces to or is similar in relevant ways to one of these five models.

The parent/child model is the most common model offered as representing a clear example of paternalistic interference.[17] In fact, many paternalistic accounts of slavery often draw upon the parent/child model. In other words, the slaveholder is viewed as the parent and the slave as the child or childlike. The noted historian Kenneth Stampp draws the analogy in the following way:

> The most generous master, so long as he was determined to be a master, could be paternal only toward a fawning dependent; for slavery, by its nature, could never be a relationship between equals. Ideally it was the relationship of parent and child. The slave who had most nearly lost his manhood, who lost confidence in himself, who stood to receive the favors and affection of a patriarch.
>
> The system was in its essence a process of infantilization and the master used the amiable, irresponsible sambos of tradition, who were the most perfect products of the system, to prove that negroes were a childlike race, needing guidance and protection but inviting paternal love as well.[18]

But if we examine carefully the parent/child model advanced by liberal thinkers like Gerald Dworkin, we discover that the analogy between slaveholder/slave and parent/child breaks down.[19] Dworkin tells us that parent's behavior towards their children is thought to be paternalistic because parents force children to do what the parent believes to be in the child's best interest.

The analogy between the parent/child and slaveholder/slave breaks down because the slaves were not all children. But certainly the supporters of this analogy recognize this, so they don't contend that the slaves were children in a chronological sense, but that they were childlike in many important aspects. Many thoughtful historians, however, drawing on various sources including the slaves' own narratives, have concluded that attempts to depict adult slaves as "sambos" or childlike are unfounded. Since slaves were responsible adults who were forced under threat of harm to do the will of another, they cannot accurately be described as children or childlike.

But even if the adult slaves were childlike, the analogy still fails because in the parent/child model, the children will mature and come to see that it was reasonable or unreasonable for their parents to force them, for example, to brush their teeth. The slave as child model keeps the slaves as perpetual children. The slaves never mature and never appreciate the reasonableness of the slaveholders' interferences.

197

If we view the slaves as perpetually childlike, then we move to another model. The competent/incompetent model comes to mind.[20] On this account, slaves are thought to be incapable of determining their own good and choosing the means to achieve it. We should be careful and note that this view does not commit one to the position that slaves were not human beings and thus lacking membership in the moral community. This model includes slaves into the moral community and as Genovese writes, it insists "upon mutual obligations-duties, responsibilities and ultimately rights."[21]

By including slaves into the moral community, however, this model assigns them a moral status—something that was called into question by the very practice of slavery. This account recognizes their humanity or personhood, but what is given with one hand is effectively taken away with the other. Slaves are said to be persons, but they are denied a fundamental feature of personhood; namely, persons should not be used simply as means to the ends of others.

Perhaps I can clarify this point by focusing on how those who are thought to be mentally incompetent have been treated in our society. In brief, the treatment of those who have been characterized as mentally retarded has often been morally reprehensible. Once they were locked away in substandard institutions with little effort being made to see if they could live in mainstream society. Even today far too little is done to determine to what extent these people are capable of shaping and carrying out their own life plans. Very often people designated as retarded were denied what we perceive to be the most basic liberties guaranteed to adult free persons, such as the freedom to enter into sexual relationships. Very often paternalistic reasons were advanced in support of these practices, in spite of the protest of those who were the subjects of these interferences.

What is most interesting about these practices by agents of the state and the medical establishment was that there was often an outright refusal to examine the design of the existing institutions to see if they could be altered or replaced by other institutions that promoted the interests of this group without depriving developmentally disabled citizens of their basic liberties. The tendency was to focus on the individual instead of questioning the existing practices and institutions. The same is true of slavery; it is now clear this social institution could have been abandoned. This would have allowed blacks to enjoy basic liberties. Of course, this would have altered the holdings of those who benefited from the practice of slavery. But should a just society not be willing to do this if it guaranteed basic human liberties to all? The philosopher Rawls thinks so, and I wholeheartedly agree.[22] But how specifically do these remarks relate to the competent/incompetent model as it relates to slavery?

Slaves were not genetically or naturally incompetent. Furthermore, competence is a matter of judgment. It is a socially constructed concept. A person who may be competent in one society may be judged totally incompetent in another. Slaves were made to appear to be incompetent because of the laws, practices, and public opinion in the antebellum South. Slave narratives clearly indicate that even under the most adverse circumstance slaves were able to do the things that we think characterize competent adults. The competent/incompetent model does not apply to slavery.

The teacher/student model may seem to be identical to the competent/incompetent model, but it is not. The student is thought to be uneducated, not incompetent. In the liberal tradition, students are coerced to do things that will enhance their learning because it is felt that doing so promotes their own good. Is the teacher/student model analogous to the slaveholder/slave relationship? I think not.

Some slaveholders did contend that slaves in their natural state were heathens, that it was their duty to educate them in Christian ways, and that slavery was necessary in order to do this. The crucial term here is the necessity of slavery to educate slaves. Clearly there were less coercive and morally acceptable means for converting slaves to Christianity. But let us suppose that there were not more appropriate means available for educating newly acquired adult slaves. This still would not justify the American chattel-slavery practice of keeping the children of slaves and their children enslaved.

What about the doctor/patient model?[23] Can the slaveholder be thought of as the doctor or professional and the slave as his patient or client? I think not? What is crucial in this model is the idea that the patient has chosen to be treated by the doctor. The idea of explicit consent, implied consent, or tacit consent by the patient is thought to justify the doctor substituting her judgment for the judgment of her patient. The question then becomes: has the slave given her consent in one of these ways for the slaveholder to substitute his judgment for the slave's on matters of great importance in the slave's life?

It is clear that the relationship between slave and slaveholder was not voluntary. But not all doctor/patient relationships are clearly voluntary. What about emergency situations where doctors care for patients without their consent? Is the slaveholder/slave relationship like these cases? I think not. In these cases doctors proceed because consent cannot be given. The patient is either unconscious or in some unconsciouslike state. But when the patient regains consciousness, she certainly has the right to elect to change doctors and in some cases to even refuse medical attention. But again, the slaveholder/slave situation is not like these cases. The slave was never given the opportunity to sever the relationship with the slaveholder.

The doctor/patient relationship that results from emergency situations comes about because there are no other viable alternatives. The slaveholder could claim that if he didn't care for the slaves by substituting his judgment for theirs, the slaves would experience death or great misfortune. But if this were so, it was true only because of the institution of slavery (an institution slaveholders created and controlled) and not because of some physical or mental incapacity of the slaves. The slaveholder, unlike the doctor, had other viable alternatives.

What about the final variation: the benevolent dictator/citizen model? Is the slaveholder/slave relationship analogous to this? Let me say first that in my mind there is real doubt about whether such a model should be thought of as paternalistic. In order to make the benevolent dictator/citizen model paternalistic, we must note that the dictator's motive for mandating the policies and laws that he does is the promotion of the good of his citizens. It is not done for personal gain, although personal gain could be a consequence of the dictator's action. We must further add that there is some reason to think that the citizens are not able to recognize and promote their own good. The most controversial assumption, however, is that the dictatorship is preferable on utilitarian grounds to other forms of government, including democracy. In adding this condition, we assume that the liberty to decide who will govern and how is not so weighty that it will override the advantages gained by being subjected to the will of the benevolent dictator.

The model, explained in this way, is paternalistic because it judges the good of the citizens in strict utilitarian terms. I think there is real room for doubt about whether this case is paternalistic. It seems not to be paternalistic because it minimizes the importance of personal autonomy. The benevolent dictator model might be likened to Plato's *Republic.* But on my reading of *The Republic,* it would be wrong to characterize the philosopher-king as forcing the citizens against their wills to promote their own good. The citizens of Plato's *Republic* did not conceive of themselves in individualistic terms. They did not separate their individual good from the common or communal good. If autonomy is not weighty or important, then paternalism is not much of an issue. But the major voices in the paternalistic debate, Mill, Dworkin, and Feinberg, think that autonomy is the issue.

Of course, if we say that what is at stake in paternalistic explanations is not personal autonomy, then this case can count as paternalistic and so could slavery. But since I think that what is at stake in describing something as paternalistic is an imposition upon the autonomy of others, I would not label either relationship paternalistic. Thus, if what I have argued above is true, we have no good reasons for defining slavery as a paternalistic institution.

Slavery, Paternalism, and Liberalism

Paternalistic explanations have been frequently advanced to support despicable practices in societies that have an allegiance to such things as individual liberty and human rights. These societies also have a strong commitment to a conception of justice that gives priority to the right over the good. The commitment to these things in liberal societies is not merely verbal. There is a long tradition in Western societies of appealing to these ideas to condemn or justify certain practices. Given that this has been and still is the case, why have paternalistic explanations been so pervasive when it comes to explaining or evaluating the condition of oppressed groups, particularly racial groups?

In an interesting essay, Robert J. Cottrol, a law professor and legal historian, claims that "the contradiction of slavery in liberal America helped to fashion the South's paternalistic ideology.[24] By this he means that the South faced a dilemma: how to embrace the liberal view that all men should be equal before the law and yet condone slavery. He believes that this was an especially acute problem in nineteenth-century America because in this century there was an extension of suffrage to the nonpropertied, the opening of public schools, and the abolition of imprisonment for debt. All of these liberal reforms contributed to an expansion of freedom for white men and a formal egalitarianism in America, including the South.

This attitude of liberalism fueled abolitionist movements; the proslavery response denied the humanity of blacks and created the paternalistic justification for slavery. By the nineteenth century, the eighteenth-century rationalizations that slavery must be preserved until some more prudent new social order could be arranged was rejected and replaced by arguments claiming that slavery was beneficial to the slaveholders as well as the slaves.[25] Why was this so?

I contend that a large part of the answer lies in the fact that paternalistic explanations allow people who benefit from the exploitation of others to mask the contradictions in liberal society. They can use and exploit some members of their society without having to admit that these people are being sacrificed or used strictly as means to support the ends of the dominant group.

The utilitarian principle, which could justify these practices, sticks in the throats of liberals as I have defined them. The utilitarian principle conflicts in a fundamental way with notions that liberals hold dear. Remember, utilitarianism gives priority to the good over the right and this is hard to swallow for liberals who believe that people should be allowed to define and pursue their own accounts of the good constrained by the right.

The problem for these liberals who are either the powerful majority or a strong minority, then, is to explain how they can continue to enjoy the fruits that result from the exploitation of certain groups and still hold on to the beliefs that I have designated as being central to their liberal ideology. They do not want to deny the personhood or humanity of the exploited, nor do they wish to endorse the idea that certain human beings can be used solely as a means for the ends of others. So, for these liberals, paternalism is a way of achieving what they want without having to commit themselves to positions that they find unacceptable. When you add to this the difficulty of saying what counts as paternalism and the cultural and ideological bases for judging competence, then the move to paternalism as a way of masking exploitation is a quite effective strategy for rationalizing the status quo.

My critique of liberalism, as it has related to slavery, raises an apparent paradox. As I define liberalism, the ideology gives considerable weight to personal autonomy. But when faced with tough choices as it relates to their own real or perceived self-interest, liberals often readily embrace paternalism. Of course, this apparent paradox could be explained as merely a failure of will. However, I think the matter is much more complex.

It is safe to say that both John Rawls and Robert Nozick are both liberals even though they clearly disagree over what the state has the right to do when it comes to interfering in the affairs of its citizens.[26] Nozick, for example, contends that the just state has no right to tax its citizens to fund programs to care for needy orphans. While Rawls, on the other hand, thinks that not only are such programs permissible, they are required by correct principles of justice. Both Rawls and Nozick give priority to the right over the good. In other words, they both claim that they are not imposing a conception of the good upon citizens. But both Rawls and Nozick appeal to a conception of "morality" or a conception of the good based upon an assumed definition of personhood. This is something that is characteristic of all liberals who give priority to right.

It follows that deciding who is a person or a rightholder is crucial for the liberal. Unfortunately, giving necessary and sufficient conditions for personhood is no simple matter. We only have to turn to the heated debate over abortion to attest to this fact. Liberals must contend with two questions: "Who are full-fledged persons?" and "Are all full-fledged persons entitled to decide their own fates even at the cost of lowering their own individual life prospects or social utility?" Few liberals have been able to maintain consistency in answering these tough but crucial questions.

Above, I have argued that American chattel slavery was not paternalistic. If one is still unconvinced by my argument, then perhaps the following example will drive the conclusion home. When slavery and its impact on slaves is discussed, the focus is typically on black males. But what about black females? Didn't their experiences form an important part of the American slavery experience?

Clearly, the answer is yes, and critical studies of the role of black women held as slaves attest to this fact. Important works by Angela Davis, Elizabeth Fox-Genovese, Paula Giddings, Darlene Clark Hines, and Deborah White help us understand American chattel slavery and its aftermath by providing us with insightful journeys into the world of female slaves.[27] Since the female experience was no minor part of the overall slave experience, one would expect that any paternalistic argument would cover their experiences as well. I think the experiences of female slaves cast serious doubt on paternalistic explanations of slavery.

As a number of historians have shown, black women were typically coerced to bear children. These children were frequently taken away and sold to other slaveholders. The consequence of this practice, as slave narratives graphically reveal, were horrendous. Consider the plight of the slave mother Eliza and her children, Emily and Randall. Their story is told in Solomon Northup's narrative *Twelve Years a Slave*. Northup describes the scene in which Emily and Randall are sold away from their mother:

> I have seen mothers kissing for the last time the faces of their dead offspring; I have seen them looking down into the grave, as the earth fell with a dull sound upon their coffins, hiding them from their eyes forever; but never have I seen such an exhibition of intense, unmeasured, and unbound grief, as when Eliza was parted from her child. She broke from her place in the line of women, rushing down where Emily was standing, caught her in her arms. The child, sensible of some impending danger, instinctively fastened her hands around her mother's neck, and nestled her little head upon her bosom. Freeman sternly ordered her to be quiet, but she did not heed him. He caught her by the arm and pulled her rudely, but she only clung closer to the child. Then, with a volley of great oaths, he struck her such a heartless blow, that she staggered backwards, and was like to fall. Oh! how piteously then did she beseech and beg and pray that they might not be separated. Why could they not be purchased together? Why not let her have one of her dear children. "Mercy, mercy, master!" she cried, falling on her knees. "Please, master, buy Emily. I can never work any if she is taken from me: I will die."[28]

Northup notes that Eliza never saw or heard of her children again, but she never forgot them.

What explanation could be provided for saying that such a practice was done for the good of female slaves, or for that matter, slaves in general? One could, I suppose, put forth the transparent argument that slave children would be better off because they could not be cared for properly by their natural mothers. But such a reason is obviously unacceptable. The children were sold to other plantations where they were cared for by female slaves. In fact, if this reason were true, this would be a strong reason for not coercing females to bear children. It is not a reason to have them bear children and then have them sold away.

There is a real danger in going to such lengths to put the above behavior in a better light by describing it as paternalism. Of course, it is good to be sympathetic in interpreting a complex institution like slavery, but there is also a difference between sympathy and distortion. Even allowing individuals of good will to have too much freedom to rationalize inhumane actions has negative consequences. We find this today with people who attempt to minimize the horrors of the Holocaust by maintaining that Nazis were self-deceived, and as such, not evil persons. In a similar manner, people who claim that slaveholders were holding slaves because it promoted the interest of slaves are undermining our common understanding of what counts as an evil act or an evil person.

Perhaps we can all agree that a person who knowingly violates the rights of innocent human beings simply for the sake of doing so is evil. But what about those persons who violate the rights of others in order to gain or profit? In other words, they don't act this way for its own sake, they do so only because it is a means to what they need or desire. Should such people be described as bad or evil? I think so. If the end they seek can be obtained by a means that does not violate the rights of others, then they can be described as evil for not choosing one of these means. In the case of slavery, the evidence shows that slaveholders were aware that there were other ways to make a living. Nonetheless, they chose to enslave Africans because they wanted a higher standard of living without extending the toil that would have made such a way of life possible.

But the supporters of paternalistic explanations of slavery might object that my analysis fails to appreciate that slaveholders, because of the racism of their times, did not "know" that blacks were deserving of the same protections as whites. They might argue that each generation has moral blind spots. Fifty years from now we may come to deplore things that we now accept as perfectly permissible. The blind spots argument seems to be most compelling in cases where the society at large is blind to certain things because of a lack of information about alternative ways of thinking. This was not the case about the issue of slavery. During the nineteenth century, slaveholders were well aware that there were arguments against slavery and that there were forceful arguments against the belief that blacks were not persons. But what about those who argue that during the nineteenth century there was still enough uncertainty about the moral status of blacks to warrant slaveholders acting as if blacks had no moral rights? Even if this claim is empirically accurate, it would not justify slavery as a paternalistic institution. If there is uncertainty about the moral status of a being, then it does not follow that one should act as if the being has no moral status.

In my view, to ignore the evidence and to continue to describe slavery as paternalistic jeopardizes our understanding of what it means to describe behavior as bad or evil. If we employ the rationalizations that are used to describe slavery as paternalistic, we can use these same rationalizations to put in a better light behavior that most, if not all, would consider to be reprehensible. We can justify slavery as paternalistic only at the expense of undermining any realistic account of a public morality.

Notes

1. Ulrich B. Phillips, *American Negro Slavery* (New York: D. Appleton, 1918; reprint, Baton Rouge: Louisiana State University Press, 1996); William K. Scarborough, "Slavery: A White Man's Burden," in Harry P. Owens, ed., *Perspectives and Irony in American Slavery* (Jackson: University of Mississippi Press, 1976), 103–36; and Robert Fogel and Stanley Engerman, *Time on the Cross: The Economics of American Negro Slavery* (Boston: Little, Brown and Co., 1974).

2. Kenneth Stampp, *The Peculiar Institution: Slavery in the Antebellum South* (New York: Alfred A. Knopf, 1956) and John Blassingame, *The Slave Community* (New York: Oxford University Press, 1972).

3. James W. C. Pennington, *The Fugitive Blacksmith or Events in the History of James W. C. Pennington,* 2d edition (London: Charles Gilpin, 1849), iv.

4. Peter Parish, *Slavery: History and Historians* (New York: Harper and Row, 1989), 124–25.

5. Eugene Genovese, *Roll, Jordan, Roll* (New York: Pantheon Books, 1974), 5.

6. Genovese, 5.

7. Scarborough, "Slavery: A White Man's Burden," 108–109.

8. Genovese, *Roll, Jordan, Roll,* 661.

9. For a good description of the sambo personality see Stanley M. Elkins, *Slavery* (Chicago: University of Chicago Press, 1976), 82.

10. Quoted in William Loren Katz, ed., *Five Slave Narratives: A Compendium* (New York: Arno Press, 1968), vi.

11. Stampp, *The Peculiar Institution,* 5.

12. I thank Felmon Davis for this possible line of argument.

13. See Howard McGary and Bill E. Lawson, *Between Slavery and Freedom* (Bloomington: Indiana University Press, 1992), chap. 1.

14. See, for example, George Fitzhugh, *Cannibals All! or Slaves Without Masters* (Cambridge: Harvard University Press, 1960), especially chap. 19.

15. See Blassingame, *The Slave Community.*

16. Douglass Husak, "Paternalism and Autonomy," *Philosophy and Public Affairs* 10 (1981): 43–46.

17. See Joel Feinberg's, "Legal Paternalism," 3, and Gerald Dworkin's, "Paternalism," in Rolf Sartorius, *Paternalism* (Minneapolis: University of Minnesota Press, 1983), 28.

18. Stampp, *The Peculiar Institution,* 327.

19. Dworkin, "Paternalism."

20. For a good account of this debate see Rolf Sartorius, "Paternalistic Grounds for Involuntary Civil Commitment: A Utilitarian Perspective," in Sartorius, *Paternalism,* 95–102.

21. Genovese, *Roll, Jordan, Roll,* 5.

22. John Rawls, *A Theory of Justice* (Cambridge: Harvard University Press, 1971), 3–4.

23. For a discussion of the medical model, see Allen E. Buchanan, "Medical Paternalism," in Sartorius, *Paternalism,* 61–73.

24. Robert J. Cottrol, "Liberalism and Paternalism: Ideology, Economic Interest and the Business of Slavery," *The American Journal of Legal History* 31 (1987): 368.

25. Cottrol, 364, and G. M. Frederickson, *The Black Image in the White Mind: The Debate on Afro-American Character and Destiny, 1817–1914* (New York: Harper and Row, 1971), 68–78.

26. John Rawls, *A Theory of Justice,* and Robert Nozick, *Anarchy, State, and Utopia* (New York: Basic Books, 1974).

27. Darlene Clark Hine, "Lifting the Veil, Shattering the Silence: Black Women's History in Slavery and Freedom" in Darlene Clark Hine, ed., *The State of Afro-American History* (Baton Rouge: Louisiana State University Press, 1986); Angela Davis, *Women, Race, and Class* (New York: Vintage Books, 1983); Gerder Lerner, ed., *Black*

Women in White America: A Documentary History (New York: Pantheon Books, 1972); Deborah Gray White, *Ar'n't I a Woman? Female Slaves in the Plantation South* (New York: W. W. Norton, 1985); and Paula Giddings, *When and Where I Enter: The Impact of Black Women on Race and Sex in America* (New York: Bantam Books, 1988).

28. Solomon Northup, *Twelve Years a Slave* (New York: Dover Publications, 1970), 85–86.

10

WHAT IS WRONG WITH SLAVERY

R. M. Hare

N early everybody would agree that slavery is wrong; and I can say this perhaps with greater feeling than most, having in a manner of speaking *been* a slave. However, there are dangers in just taking for granted that something is wrong; for we may then assume that it is obvious that it is wrong and indeed obvious why it is wrong; and this leads to a prevalence of very bad arguments with quite silly conclusions, all based on the so-called absolute value of human freedom. If we could see more clearly what *is* valuable about freedom, and why it is valuable, then we might be protected against the rhetoric of those who, the moment anything happens that is disadvantageous or distasteful to them, start complaining loudly about some supposed infringement of their liberty, without telling us why it is wrong that they should be prevented from doing what they would like to do. It may well *be* wrong in many such cases; but until we have some way of judging when it is and when it is not, we shall be at the mercy of every kind of demagogy.

This is but one example of the widespread abuse of the appeal to human rights. We may even be tempted to think that our politics would be more healthy if rights had never been heard of; but that would be going too far. It is the unthinking appeal to ill-defined rights, unsupported by argument, that does the harm. There is no doubt that arguments justifying some of these appeals are possible;

but since the forms of such arguments are seldom understood even by philosophers, it is not surprising that many quite unjustified claims of this sort go unquestioned, and thus in the end bring any sort of appeal to human rights into disrepute. It is a tragedy that this happens, because there really are rights that ought to be defended with all the devotion we can command. Things are being done the world over which can be properly condemned as infringements of human rights; but so long as rights are used so loosely as an all-purpose political weapon, often in support of very questionable causes, our protests against such infringements will be deprived of most of their force.

Another hazard of the appeal to rights is that it is seldom that such an appeal by one side cannot be countered with an appeal to some conflicting right by the opposite side. The controversies which led finally to the abolition of slavery provide an excellent example of this, with one side appealing to rights of liberty and the other to rights of property. But we do not have to go so far back in history to find examples of this sort of thing. We have only to think of the disputes about distributive justice between the defenders of equality and of individual liberty; or of similar arguments about education. I have written about both these disputes elsewhere, in the attempt to substitute for intuitions some more solid basis for argument.[1] I have the same general motive in raising the topic of slavery, and also a more particular motive. Being a utilitarian, I need to be able to answer the following attack frequently advanced by opponents of utilitarianism. It is often said that utilitarianism must be an objectionable creed because it could in certain circumstances condone or even commend slavery, given that circumstances can be envisaged in which utility would be maximized by preserving a slave-owning society and not abolishing slavery. The objectors thus seek to smear utilitarians with the taint of all the atrocious things that were done by slave traders and slave owners. The objection, as I hope to show, does not stand up; but in order to see through this rhetoric we shall have to achieve a quite deep understanding of some rather difficult issues in moral philosophy; and this, too, adds up to the importance and interest of the topic.

First, we have to ask what this thing, slavery, is, about whose wrongness we are arguing. As soon as we ask this question we see at once, if we have any knowledge of history, that it is, in common use, an extremely ill-defined concept. Even if we leave out of account such admittedly extended uses as "wage slave" in the writings of Marxists, it is clear that the word "slave" and its near-equivalents such as *"sersus"* and *"doulos"* have meant slightly different things in different cultures; for slavery is, primarily, a *legal* status, defined by the disabilities or the liabilities which are imposed by the law on those called slaves; and obviously these may vary from one jurisdiction to another. Familiar logical difficulties arise about how we are to decide, of a word in a foreign language, that it means the same as the English word "slave." Do the relevant laws in the country where the language is spoken have to be identical with those which held in English-speaking countries before slavery was abolished? Obviously not; because it would be impossible for them to be identical with the laws of all such countries at all periods, since these did not remain the same. Probably we have a rough idea of the kind of laws which have to hold in a country before we can say that that country has an institution properly called 'slavery'; but it is pretty rough.

It would be possible to pursue at some length, with the aid of legal, historical, and anthropological books on slavery in different cultures and jurisdictions, the different shades of meaning of the word "slave." But since my purpose is philosophical, I shall limit myself to asking what is essential to the notion of slavery in common use. The essential features are, I think, to be divided under two heads: slavery is, first, a *status* in society, and second, a *relation* to a master. The slave is so called first of all because he occupies a certain place in society, lacking certain rights and privileges secured by the law to others, and subject to certain liabilities from which others are free. And second, he is the slave *of* another person or body (which might be the state itself). The first head is not enough to distinguish slavery from other legal disabilities; for example the lowest castes in some societies are as lacking in legal rights as slaves in some others, or more so, but are not called slaves because they are not the slaves *of anybody.*

The *status* of a slave was defined quite early by the Greeks in terms of four freedoms which the slave lacks. These are: a legally recognized position in the community, conferring a right of access to the courts; protection from illegal seizure and detention and other

211

personal violence; the privilege of going where he wants to go; and that of working as he pleases. The first three of these features are present in a manumission document from Macedonia dated about 235 B.C.; the last is added in the series of manumission documents from Delphi which begins about thirty years later.[2] The state could to some extent regulate by law the treatment of slaves without making us want to stop calling them slaves, so that the last three features are a bit wobbly at the edges. But we are seeking only a rough characterization of slavery, and shall have to put up with this indefiniteness of the concept.

The *relation* of the slave to a master is also to some extent indefinite. It might seem that we could tie it up tight by saying that a slave has to be the *property* of an *owner;* but a moment's reflection will show what unsafe ground this is. So-called property owners do not need to be reminded that legal restrictions upon the use and enjoyment of property can become so onerous as to make it almost a joke to call it property at all. I am referring not only to such recent inventions as zoning and other planning laws (though actually they are not so recent, having been anticipated even in ancient times), and to rent acts, building regulations, clean air acts, and the like, but also to the ancient restrictions placed by the common law on uses of one's property which might be offensive to one's neighbors. In relation to slavery, it is also instructive to think of the cruelty-to-animals legislation which now rightly forbids one to do what one likes to one's own dog or cow which one has legally purchased. Legislation of just this kind was passed in the days before abolition, and was even to some extent enforced, though not always effectively. The laws forbidding the slave trade were, of course, the outstanding example of such legislation preventing people from doing what they wanted with their own property.

However, as before, we are seeking only a general and rough characterization of slavery, and shall therefore have to put up with the open texture of the concept of property. This, like slavery itself, is defined by the particular rights and obligations which are conferred or imposed by a particular legal system, and these may vary from one such system to another. It will be enough to have a general idea of what would stop us calling a person the slave of another—how far the law would have to go in assigning rights to slaves before we stopped using that word of them. I have gone into these difficulties in such detail as space has allowed only because I am now going on to describe, for the purposes of our moral discussion, certain conditions of life about which I shall invite the reader's judgement, and I do not want anybody to say that what I am describing is not really slavery. The case I shall sketch is admittedly to some extent fantastic; and this, as we shall later see, is very important when we come to assess the philosophical arguments that have been based on similar cases. But although it is extremely unlikely that what I describe should actually occur, I wish to maintain that if it occurred, we should still call it slavery, so that if imaginary cases are allowed to be brought into the arguments, this case will have to be admitted.

It may be helpful if, before leaving the question of what slavery is, I list a few conditions of life which have to be *distinguished* from slavery proper. The first of these is *serfdom* (a term which, like "slavery" itself, has a wide range of meaning). A serf is normally tied, not directly to a master, but to a certain area of land; the rights to his services pass with the land if it changes hands. This very distinction, however, separates the English villein in gross, who approximates to a slave although enjoying certain legal rights, from the villein regardant, whose serfdom arises through his feudal tenure of land. Those who unsuccessfully tried to persuade Lord Mansfield in Sommersett's case that slavery could exist in England attempted to show that the defendant was a villein in gross.[3] Second, one is not a slave merely because one belongs to a *caste* which has an inferior legal status, even if it has pretty well no rights; as I have said, the slave has to be the slave *of* some owner. Third, slavery has to be distinguished from *indenture,* which is a form of contract. Apprentices in former times, and football players even now, are bound by contract, entered into by themselves or, in the case of children, by their parents, to serve employers for a fixed term under fixed conditions, which were in some cases extremely harsh (so that the actual sufferings of indentured people could be as bad as those of slaves).[4] The difference lies in the voluntariness of the contract and in its fixed term. We must note however that in some societies (Athens before Solon for example) one could *choose* to become a slave by selling one's person to escape debt, and it might be possible to sell one's children as well, as the Greeks sometimes did, so that even the heritability of the slave status does not serve to make definite the rather fuzzy boundary between slavery and indenture.[5]

We ought perhaps to notice two other conditions which approximate to slavery but are not called slavery. The first is compulsory *military* or *naval service* and, indeed, other forced labor. The impressed sailors of Nelson's navy no doubt endured conditions as bad as many slaves; Dr. Johnson remarked that nobody would choose to be a sailor if he had the alternative of being put in prison.[6] But they were not called slaves, because their status as free men was only in abeyance and returned to them on discharge. By contrast, the galley slaves of the Mediterranean powers in earlier times really were slaves. Second, although the term "penal servitude" was once in use, *imprisonment* for crime is not usually called slavery. This is another fuzzy boundary, because in ancient times it was possible for a person to lose his rights as a citizen and become a slave by sentence of a court for some crime, and in prerevolutionary France one could be sentenced to the galleys, though when something very like this happened recently in South Africa, it was not *called* slavery, officially.[7] Again, prisoners of war and other captives and bondsmen are not always called slaves, however grim their conditions, although in ancient times capture in war was a way of becoming a slave, if one was not fortunate enough to be ransomed.[8] I have myself, as a prisoner of war, worked on the Burma railway in conditions not *at the time* distinguishable from slavery; but because my status was temporary I can claim to have been a slave only "in a manner of speaking."

I shall put my philosophical argument, to which we have now come, in terms of an imaginary example, to which I shall give as much verisimilitude as I can. It will be seen, however, that quite unreal assumptions have to be made in order to get the example going—and this is very important for the argument between the utilitarians and their opponents. It must also be noted that to play its role in the argument the example will have to meet certain requirements. It is intended as a fleshed-out substitute for the rather jejune examples often to be found in antiutilitarian writers. To serve its purpose it will have to be a case in which to abolish slavery really and clearly would diminish utility. This means, first, that the slavery to be abolished must really be slavery, and, second, that it must have a total utility, clearly but not enormously greater than the total utility of the kind of regime which would be, in that situation, a practical alternative to slavery.

If it were not *clearly* greater, utilitarians could argue that, since all judgements of this sort are only probable, caution would require them to stick to a well-tried principle favoring liberty, the principle itself being justified on utilitarian grounds (see below); and thus the example would cease to divide them from their opponents, and would become inapposite.

If, on the other hand, the utility of slavery were *enormously* greater, anti-utilitarians might complain that their own view was being made too strong; for many antiutilitarians are pluralists and hold that among the principles of morality a principle requiring beneficence is to be included. Therefore, if the advantages of retaining slavery are made sufficiently great, a nonutilitarian with a principle of beneficence in his repertory could agree that it ought to be retained— that is, that *in this case* the principle of beneficence has greater weight than that favoring liberty. Thus there would again be no difference, in this case, between the verdicts of the utilitarians and their opponents, and the example would be inapposite.

There is also another dimension in which the example has to be carefully placed. An antiutilitarian might claim that the example I shall give makes the difference too small between the conditions of the slaves and those of the free in the supposed society, and the number of slaves too great. If, he might claim, I had made the number of slaves small and the difference between the miseries of the slaves and the pleasures of the slave owners much greater, then the society might have the same total utility as mine (that is, greater than that of the free society with which I compare it), but it would be less plausible for me to maintain that if such a comparison had to be made in real life, we ought to follow the utilitarians and prefer the slave society. I deal with this objection only so far as it concerns slavery such as might occur in the world as we know it. *Brave New World* situations, in which people are conditioned from birth to be obedient slaves and given disagreeable or dangerous tasks, require separate treatment which is beyond the scope of this paper, though antiutilitarian arguments based on them meet the same defence, namely the requirement to assess realistically what the consequences of such practices would actually be.

I cannot yet answer this objection without anticipating my argument; I shall merely indicate briefly how I would answer it. The answer is that the objection rests on an appeal to our ordinary intuitions; but that these are designed to deal with ordinary cases. They give no reliable guide to what we ought to say in highly unusual cases. But, further, the case desiderated is never likely to occur. How could it come about that the existence of a small number of slaves was necessary in order to preserve the happiness of the rest? I find it impossible to think of any technological factors (say, in agriculture or in transport by land or sea) which would make the preservation of slavery for a small class necessary to satisfy the interests of the majority. It is quite true that in the past there have been *large* slave populations supporting the higher standard of living of *small* minorities. But in that case it is hard to argue that slavery has more utility than its abolition, if the difference in happiness between slaves and slave owners is great. Yet if, in order to produce a case in which the retention of slavery really would be optimal, we reduce the number of slaves relative to slave owners, it becomes hard to say how the existence of this relatively small number of slaves is necessary for the happiness of the large number of free men. What on earth are the slaves doing that could not be more efficiently done by paid labor? And is not the abolition (perhaps not too abrupt) of slavery likely to promote those very technical changes which are necessary to enable the society to do without it?

The crux of the matter, as we shall see, is that in order to use an appeal to our ordinary intuitions as an argument, the opponents of utilitarianism have to produce cases which are not too far removed from the sort of cases with which our intuitions are designed to deal, namely the ordinary run of cases. If the cases they use fall outside this class, then the fact that our common intuitions give a different verdict from utilitarianism has no bearing on the argument; our intuitions could well be wrong about such cases, and be none the worse for that, because they will never have to deal with them in practice.

We may also notice, while we are sifting possible examples, that cases of *individual* slave owners who are kind to their slaves will not do. The issue is one of whether slavery as an institution protected by law should be preserved; and if it is preserved, though there may be individuals who do not take advantage of it to maltreat their slaves, there will no doubt be many others who do.

Let us imagine, then, that the battle of Waterloo, that "damned nice thing, the neatest run thing you ever saw in your life," as Wellington called it, went differently from the way it actually did go, in two respects.[9] The first was that the British and Prussians lost the battle; the last attack of the French Guard proved too much for them, the Guard's morale having been restored by Napoleon who in person led the advance instead of handing it over to Ney. But secondly, having exposed himself to fire as Wellington habitually did, but lacking Wellington's amazing good fortune, Napoleon was struck by a cannon ball and killed instantly. This so disorganized the French, who had no other commanders of such ability, that Wellington was able to rally his forces and conduct one of those holding operations at which he was so adept, basing himself on the Channel ports and their intricate surrounding waterways; the result was a cross between the Lines of Torres Vedras and the trench warfare of the First World War. After a year or two of this, with Napoleon out of the way and the war party discredited in England, liberal (that is, neither revolutionary nor reactionary) regimes came into power in both countries, and the Congress of Vienna reconvened in a very different spirit, with the French represented on equal terms.

We have to consider these events only as they affected two adjacent islands in the Caribbean which I am going to call Juba and Camaica. I need not relate what happened in the rest of the world, because the combined European powers could at that time command absolute supremacy at sea, and the Caribbean could therefore be effectively isolated from world politics by the agreement which they reached to take that area out of the imperial war game. All naval and other forces were withdrawn from it except for a couple of bases on small islands for the suppression of the slave trade, which, in keeping with their liberal principles, the parties agreed to prohibit (those that had not already done so). The islands were declared independent and their white inhabitants, very naturally, all departed in a hurry, leaving the government in the hands of local black leaders, some of whom were of the calibre of Toussaint l'Ouverture and others of whom were very much the reverse.

On Juba, a former Spanish colony, at the end of the colonial period there had been formed, under pressure of military need, a militia composed of slaves under white officers, with conditions of service much preferable to those of the plantation slaves, and forming a kind of elite. The senior sergeant-major of this force found himself, after the white officers fled, in a position of unassailable power, and, being a man of great political intelligence and ability, shaped the new regime in a way that made Juba the envy of its neighbors.

What he did was to retain the institution of slavery but to remedy its evils. The plantations were split up into smaller units, still under overseers, responsible to the state instead of to the former owners. The slaves were given rights to improved conditions of work; the wage they had already received as a concession in colonial times was secured to them and increased; all cruel punishments were prohibited. However, it is still right to call them slaves, because the state retained the power to direct their labor and their place of residence and to enforce these directions by sanctions no more severe than are customary in countries without slavery, such as fines and imprisonment. The Juban government, influenced by early communist ideas (though Marx had not yet come on the scene) kept the plantations in its own hands; but private persons were also allowed to own a limited number of slaves under conditions at least as protective to the slaves as on the state-owned plantations.

The island became very prosperous, and the slaves in it enjoyed a life far preferable in every way to that of the free inhabitants of the neighboring island of Camaica. In Camaica there had been no such focus of power in the early days. The slaves threw off their bonds and each seized what land he could get hold of. Though law and order were restored after a fashion, and democracy of a sort prevailed, the economy was chaotic, and this, coupled with a population explosion, led to widespread starvation and misery. Camaica lacked what Juba had: a government with the will *and the instrument, in the shape of the institution of slavery,* to control the economy and the population, and so make its slave-citizens, as I said, the envy of their neighbors. The flood of people in fishing boats seeking to emigrate from free Camaica and insinuate themselves as slaves into the plantations of Juba became so great that the Juban government had to employ large numbers of coast guards (slaves of course) to stop it.

That, perhaps, will do for our imaginary example. Now for the philosophical argument. It is commonly alleged that utilitarianism could condone or commend slavery. In the situation described, utility would have been lessened and not increased if the Juban government had abolished slavery and if as a result the economy of Juba had deteriorated to the level of that of Camaica. So, it might be argued, a utilitarian would have had to oppose the abolition. But everyone agrees, it might be held, that slavery is wrong; so the utilitarians are convicted of maintaining a thesis which has consequences repugnant to universally accepted moral convictions.

What could they reply to this attack? There are, basically, two lines they could take. These lines are not incompatible but complementary; indeed, the defence of utilitarianism could be put in the form of a dilemma. Either the defender of utilitarianism is allowed to question the imagined facts of the example, or he is not. First let us suppose that he is not. He might then try, as a first move, saying that in the situation *as portrayed* it would indeed be wrong to abolish slavery. If the argument descends to details, the antiutilitarians may be permitted to insert any amount of extra details (barring the actual abolition of slavery itself) in order to make sure that its retention really does maximize utility. But then the utilitarian sticks to his guns and maintains that in that case it *would* be wrong to abolish slavery, and that, further, most ordinary people, if they could be got to consider the case on its merits and not allow their judgement to be confused by association with more detestable forms of slavery, would agree with this verdict. The principle of liberty which forbids slavery is a prima facie principle of admitting exceptions, and this imaginary case is one of the exceptions. If the utilitarians could sustain this line of defence, they would win the case; but perhaps not everyone would agree that it is sustainable.

So let us allow the utilitarian another slightly more sophisticated move, still staying, however, perched on the first horn of the dilemma. He might admit that not everyone would agree on the merits of this case, but explain this by pointing to the fantastic and unusual nature of the case, which, he might claim, would be unlikely to occur in real life. *If* he is not allowed to question the facts of the case, he has to admit that abolition would be wrong; but ordinary people, he might say, cannot see this because the principles of political and social morality which we have all of us *now* absorbed (as contrasted with our eighteenth-century ancestors), and with which we are deeply imbued, prevent us from considering the case on its merits. The principles are framed to cope with the cases of slavery which actually occur (all of which are to a greater or lesser degree harmful). Though they are the best principles for us to have when confronting the actual world, they give the wrong answer when presented with this fantastic case. But all the same, the world being as it is, we should be morally worse people if we did not have these principles; for then we might be tempted, whether through ignorance or by self-interest, to condone slavery in cases in which, though actually harmful, it could be colorably represented as being beneficial. Suppose, it might be argued, that an example of this sort had been used in antiabolitionist writings in, say, 1830 or thereabouts. Might it not have persuaded many people that slavery *could* be an admirable thing, and thus have secured their votes against abolition; and would this not have been very harmful? For the miseries caused by the *actual* institution of slavery in the Caribbean and elsewhere were so great that it was desirable from a utilitarian point of view that people should hold and act on moral convictions which condemned slavery as such and without qualification, because this would lead them to vote for its abolition.

If utilitarians take this slightly more sophisticated line, they are left saying at one and the same time that it would have been wrong to abolish slavery in the imagined circumstances, *and* that it is a good thing that nearly everyone, if asked about it, would say that it was right. Is this paradoxical? Not, I think, to anybody who understands the realities of the human situation. What resolves the paradox is that the example *is* imaginary and that therefore people are not going to have to pronounce, as a practical issue, on what the laws of Juba are to be. In deciding what principles it is good that people have, it is not necessary or even desirable to take into account such imaginary cases. It does not really matter, from a practical point of view, what judgements people reach about imaginary cases, provided that this does not have an adverse effect upon their judgements about real cases. From a practical point of view, the principles which it is best for them to have are those which will lead them to make the highest proportion of right decisions in actual cases where their decisions make a difference to what happens— weighted, of course, for the importance of the cases, that is, the amount of difference the decisions make to the resulting good or harm.

It is therefore perfectly acceptable that we should at one and the same time feel a strong moral conviction that even the Juban slave system, however beneficial, is wrong, *and* confess, when we reflect on the features of this imagined system, that we cannot see anything specifically wrong about it, but rather a great deal to commend. This is bound to be the experience of anybody who has acquired the sort of moral convictions that one ought to acquire, and at the same time is able to reflect rationally on the features of some unusual imagined situation. I have myself constantly had this experience when confronted with the sort of antiutilitarian examples which are the stock-in-trade of philosophers like Bernard Williams. One is led to think, on reflection, that *if* such cases were to occur, one ought to do what is for the best in the circumstances, as even Williams himself appears to contemplate in one of his cases; but one is bound also to find this conclusion repugnant to one's deepest convictions; if it is not, one's convictions are not the best convictions one could have.[10]

Against this, it might be objected that if one's deep moral convictions yield the wrong answer even in imaginary or unusual cases, they are *not* the best one could have. Could we not succeed, it might be asked, in inculcating into ourselves convictions of a more accommodating sort? Could we not, that is to say, absorb principles which had written into them either exceptions to deal with awkward cases like that in my example, or even provision for writing in exceptions *ad hoc* when the awkward case arose? Up to a point this is a sensible suggestion; but beyond that point (a point which will vary with the temperament of the person whose principles they are to be) it becomes psychologically unsound. There are some simple souls, no doubt, who really cannot keep themselves in the straight and narrow way unless they cling fanatically and in the face of what most of us would call reason to extremely simple and narrow principles. And there are others who manage to have very complicated principles with many exceptions written into them (only "written" is the wrong word, because the principles of such people defy formulation). Most

221

of us come somewhere in between. It is also possible to have fairly simple principles but to attach to them a rubric which allows us to depart from them, either when one conflicts with another in a particular case, or where the case is such an unusual one that we find ourselves doubting whether the principles were designed to deal with it. In these cases we may apply utilitarian reasoning directly; but it is most unwise to do this in more normal cases, for those are precisely the cases (the great majority) which our principles *are* designed to deal with, since they were chosen to give the best results in the general run of cases. In normal cases, therefore, we are more likely to achieve the right decision (even from the utilitarian point of view) by sticking to these principles than by engaging in utilitarian reasoning about the particular case, with all its temptations to special pleading.

I have dealt with these issues at length elsewhere.[11] Here all I need to say is that there is a psychological limit to the complexity and to the flexibility of the moral principles that we can wisely seek to build deeply, as moral convictions, into our character; and the person who tries to go beyond this limit will end up as (what he will be called) an unprincipled person, and will not in fact do the best he could with his life, even by the test of utility. This may explain why I would always vote for the abolition of slavery, even though I can admit that cases could be *imagined* in which slavery would do more good than harm, and even though I am a utilitarian.

So much, then, for the first horn of the dilemma. Before we come to the second horn, on which the utilitarian is allowed to object to his opponents' argument on the ground that their example would not in the actual world be realized, I wish to make a methodological remark which may help us to find our bearings in this rather complex dispute. Utilitarianism, like any other theory of moral reasoning that gets anywhere near adequacy, consists of two parts, one formal and one substantial. The formal part is no more than a rephrasing of the requirement that moral prescriptions be universalizable; this has the consequence that equal interests of all are to be given equal weight in our reasoning: everybody to count for one and nobody for more than one. One should not expect such a formal requirement to generate, by itself, any substantial conclusions even about the actual world, let alone about all logically possible worlds.

But there is also a substantial element in the theory. This is contributed by factual beliefs about what interests people in the real world actually have (which depends on what they actually want or like or dislike, and on what they would want or like or dislike under given conditions); and also about the actual effects on these interests of different actions in the real world. Given the truth of these beliefs, we can reason morally and shall come to certain moral conclusions. but the conclusions are not generated by the formal part of the theory alone.

Utilitarianism therefore, unlike some other theories, is *exposed* to the facts. The utilitarian cannot reason a priori that *whatever* the facts about the world and human nature, slavery is wrong. He has to show that it is wrong by showing, through a study of history and other factual observation, that slavery does have the effects (namely the production of misery) which make it wrong. This, though it may at first sight appear a weakness in the doctrine, is in fact its strength. A doctrine, like some kinds of intuitionism, according to which we can think up examples as fantastic as we please and the doctrine will still come up with the same old answers, is really showing that it has lost contact with the actual world with which the intuitions it relies on were designed to cope. Intuitionists think they can face the world armed with nothing but their inbred intuitions; utilitarians know that they have to look at what actually goes on in the world and see if the intuitions are really the best ones to have in that sort of world.

I come now to the second horn of the dilemma, on which the utilitarian is allowed to say, "Your example won't do: it would never happen that way." He may admit that Waterloo and the Congress of Vienna could have turned out differently—after all it was a damned nice thing, and high commanders were in those days often killed on the battlefield (it was really a miracle that Wellington was not), and there were liberal movements in both countries. But when we come to the Caribbean, things begin to look shakier. Is it really likely that there would have been such a contrast between the economies of Juba and Camaica? I do not believe that the influence of particular national leaders is ever so powerful, or that such perfectly wise leaders are ever forthcoming. And I do not believe that in the Caribbean or anywhere else a system of nationalized slavery could be made to run so smoothly. I should, rather, expect the system to deteriorate very rapidly. I base these expectations on general beliefs about human nature, and in particular upon the belief that people in the power of other people will be exploited, whatever the good intentions of those who founded the system.

Alternatively, if there really had been leaders of such amazing statesmanship, could they not have done better by abolishing slavery and substituting a free but disciplined society? In the example, they gave the slaves some legal rights; what was to prevent them giving others, such as the right to change residences and jobs, subject of course to an overall system of land-use and economic planning such as exists in many free countries? Did the retention of *slavery* in particular contribute very much to the prosperity of Juba that could not have been achieved by other means? And likewise, need the government of Camaica have been so incompetent? Could it not, without reintroducing slavery, have kept the economy on the rails by such controls as are compatible with a free society? In short, did not the optimum solution lie somewhere *between* the systems adopted in Juba and Camaica, but on the free side of the boundary between slavery and liberty?

These factual speculations, however, are rather more superficial than I can be content with. The facts that it is really important to draw attention to are rather deep facts about human nature which must always, or nearly always, make slavery an intolerable condition.[12] I have mentioned already a fact about slave ownership: that ordinary, even good, human beings will nearly always exploit those over whom they have absolute power. We have only to read the actual history of slavery in all centuries and cultures to see that. There is also the effect on the characters of the exploiters themselves. I had this brought home to me recently when, staying in Jamaica, I happened to pick up a history book written there at the very beginning of the nineteenth century, before abolition, whose writer had added at the end an appendix giving his views on the abolition controversy, which was then at its height.[13] Although obviously a kindly man with liberal leanings, he argues against abolition; and one of his arguments struck me very forcibly. He argues that although slavery can be a cruel fate, things are much better in Jamaica now: there is actually a law that a slave on a plantation may not be given more than thirty-six lashes by the foreman without running him up in front of the overseer. The contrast between the niceness of the man and what he says here does perhaps more than any philosophical argument to make the point that our moral principles have to be designed for human nature as it is.

The most fundamental point is one about the human nature of the slave which makes ownership by another more intolerable for him than for, say, a horse (not that we should condone cruelty to horses). Men are different from other animals in that they can look a long way ahead, and therefore can become an object of deterrent punishment. Other animals, we may suppose, can only be the object of Skinnerian reinforcement and Pavlovian conditioning. These methods carry with them, no doubt, their own possibilities of cruelty; but they fall short of the peculiar cruelty of human slavery. One can utter to a man threats of punishment in the quite distant future which he can understand. A piece of human property, therefore, unlike a piece of inanimate property or even a brute animal in a man's possession, can be subjected to a sort of terror from which other kinds of property are immune; and, human owners being what they are, many will inevitably take advantage of this fact. That is the reason for the atrocious punishments that have usually been inflicted on slaves; there would have been no point in inflicting them on animals. A slave is the only being that is *both* able to be held responsible in this way, *and* has no escape from, or even redress against, the power that this ability to threaten confers upon his oppressor. If he were a free citizen, he would have rights which would restrain the exercise of the threat; if he were a horse or a piece of furniture, the threat would be valueless to his owner because it would not be understood. By being subjected to the threat of legal and other punishment, but at the same time deprived of legal defences against its abuse (since he has no say in what the laws are to be, nor much ability to avail himself of such laws as there are) the slave becomes, or is likely to become if his master is an ordinary human, the most miserable of all creatures.

No doubt there are other facts I could have adduced. But I will end by reiterating the general point I have been trying to illustrate. The wrongness of slavery, like the wrongness of anything else, has to be shown in the world as it actually is. We can do this by first reaching an understanding of the meaning of this and the other moral words, which brings with it certain rules of moral reasoning, as I have tried to show in other places.[14] One of the most important of these rules is a formal requirement reflected in the Golden Rule: the requirement that what we say we ought to do to others we have to be able to say ought to be done to ourselves were we in precisely their situation with their interests. And this leads to a way of moral reasoning (utilitarianism) which treats the equal interest of all as having equal weight. Then we have to apply this reasoning to the world as it actually is, which will mean ascertaining what will actually be the result of adopting certain principles and policies, and how this will actually impinge upon the interests of ourselves and others. Only so can we achieve a morality suited for use in real life; and nobody who goes through this reasoning in real life will adopt principles which permit slavery, because of the miseries which in real life it causes. Utilitarianism can thus show what is wrong with slavery; and so far as I can see it is the kind of moral reasoning best able to show this, as opposed to merely *protesting* that slavery is wrong.

Notes

1. See R. M. Hare, *Essays on Political Morality* (Oxford: Clarendon Press, 1989), 122; and R. M. Hare, "Opportunity for What?: Some Remarks on Current Disputes about Equality in Education," *Oxford Review of Education* 3 (1977).

2. W. L. Westermann, *The Slave Systems of Greek and Roman Antiquity* (American Philosophical Society, 1955), 35.

3. Lord Mansfield, Judgment in Sommersett's case, King's Bench, 12 Geo.III, reprinted in *Howells State Trials* 20, pp. 1ff. See also summing up for defense.

4. Orlando Patterson, *The Sociology of Slavery* (MacGibbon and Kee, 1967), 74; A. Sampson, *Drum* (Collins, 1956), chap. 3.

5. Westermann, *Slave Systems*, 4.

6. J. Boswell, *Life of Johnson*; references are to the edition of G. B. Hill and L. F. Powell (Oxford: Oxford University Press, 1934), 348.

7. Westermann, *Slave Systems*, 81; Sampson, *Drum*, 241.

8. Westermann, *Slave Systems*, 2, 5–7, 29.

9. E. Longford, *Wellington: The Years of the Sword* (New York: Weidenfeld and Nicholson, 1969), 489.

10. B. A. O. Williams, "A Critique of Utilitarianism" in *Utilitarianism For and Against*, J. J. C. Smart and B. A. O. Williams, eds. (Cambridge: Cambridge University Press, 1973), 99.

11. R. M. Hare, "Ethical Theory and Utilitarianism" in *Contemporary British Philosophy* 4, H. D. Lewis, ed. (London: Allen and Unwin, 1976). Reprinted in *Utilitarianism and Beyond*, A. K. Sen and B. A. O. Williams, eds. (Cambridge: Cambridge University Press, 1982), and in R. M. Hare, *Essays in Ethical Theory* (Oxford: Oxford University Press, 1989).

12. Patterson, *Sociology of Slavery*; Stanley M. Elkins, *Slavery* (Chicago: University of Chicago Press, 1959).

13. R. C. Dallas, *The History of the Maroons* (London: Longman, 1803; reprinted Cass, 1968).

14. Hare, "Ethical Theory"; R. M. Hare, *Moral Thinking: Its Levels, Method, and Point* (Oxford: Oxford University Press, 1981).

11

SLAVERY AND SURROGACY

Anita L. Allen

Introduction

S ince the 1980s, surrogate parenting has been one of the most widely discussed solutions to the problem of childlessness caused by female sterility, infertility, and disability.[1] Surrogacy is also discussed as a possible option for able-bodied, fertile women who simply do not wish to undergo pregnancy. The practice of surrogacy raises a host of legal and ethical questions. Critics object that it treats babies like commodities and exploits women.

Of interest here, surrogate parenting has been compared to slavery. Some argue that it is a form of slavery.[2] Critics characterize surrogacy as "baby selling"—commercial trafficking in human beings. They often argue that because surrogacy agreements precede the child's conception, they are ethically and legally distinguishable from traditional adoption agreements. "Baby selling" is not the only aspect of surrogacy that some view as analogous to slavery. The "womb renting" and "autonomy sharing" aspects of surrogacy contracts arguably make the surrogate mother, like the child she bears, a victim, a kind of slave.

If surrogacy is a form of slavery, then African American women who contract to become surrogate mothers are complicit in a novel form of enslavement. With this startling possibility in view, I will consider—but reject—the notion that surrogacy is equivalent to slavery. Having rejected the slavery/surrogacy equation, I will show that the experience of black slavery is nonetheless an illuminating backdrop for grappling with issues raised by surrogate parenting and by black women's participation in a particular form of surrogacy sometimes called "gestational" surrogacy. Alice Walker has written that surrogacy by black women puts a new face on an old problem: other people owning black women's wombs.[3] Toward a fuller understanding of an important perspective she shares with others, I assess *Johnson v. Calvert*, an important California case brought by a black surrogate mother against the couple that hired her to bear a child.[4] The court in *Johnson v. Calvert* held that gestational surrogates are not natural mothers and have no parental rights whatsoever in their offspring. Although the California Supreme Court expressly rejected the argument that gestational surrogacy runs afoul of prohibitions against slavery, *Johnson v. Calvert* sparked a new wave of concern that surrogate motherhood turns women into "commercial slaves 24 hours a day for 270 days."[5] The *Johnson* case highlights a troubling truth underlying the rhetoric that contemporary surrogacy is slavery. Affluent and white women's infertility, sterility, preferences, and power threaten to turn poor and black women, already understood to be a servant class, into a surrogate class.

There are obvious risks inherent in surrogacy arrangements. These risks centrally include the emotional devastation experienced by surrogates who are compelled to give up the children that they have agreed to bear for others. Parental rights deemed inalienable prior to childbirth could perhaps reduce the emotional risk of commercial surrogacy to white genetic and gestational surrogates. But in light of widespread prejudice, racism and racial segregation, such a right would be of doubtful practical value to black gestators who bear white children. Without a per se ban on commercial surrogacy, it is not clear that poor and black women can be protected from the risks of surrogacy arrangements.

Surrogacy Is Not Slavery

The characteristic feature of slaves is that they lack self-ownership. Slave owners sell, use, and dominate. Although there are a few who would argue that slavery is not inherently immoral, Joel Feinberg, Gerald Dworkin, and other philosophers have commonly used slavery as the paradigm case of a socioeconomic practice that is profoundly and patently immoral. Slavery, they say, is plainly wrong; thus, anything that looks a lot like slavery is also wrong.

Lawyers use slavery as a paradigm case, too, but of a practice that is illegal under the Constitution and unacceptable public policy. Hence, the normative advice given by both ethicists and lawyers to policy-makers is the same: to wit, avoid practices that have too many traits in common with slavery. Labeling surrogacy "slavery" is thus moral and policy condemnation. It is to imply that well-meaning surrogates and consumers and facilitators of surrogacy are immoral, or complicit in immorality. For example, it is to imply that well-meaning lawyers and judges who have facilitated surrogacy agreements are parties to immorality.

It is unhelpful to equate surrogacy with slavery in an attempt to "prove" surrogacy immoral. Surrogacy is not slavery. To treat it as such is to gloss over the enormous scope of the historical slave owner's control that is quite lacking in surrogacy arrangements. Surrogacy is not slavery, yet the experience of American Negro slavery can illuminate some aspects of the moral and legal policy debates about surrogacy, and why many people find the practice of commercial surrogate parenting disturbing. Before the American Civil War, virtually all southern black mothers were, in a sense, surrogate mothers. Slave women knowingly gave birth to children on the understanding that those children would be owned by others.

One such woman brought and prevailed in two remarkable lawsuits, one for her own freedom and a second to obtain custody of her teenage daughter.[6] Polly Crocket's successful custody battle against her child's white owners is reminiscent of Mary Beth Whitehead Gould's battle against the Sterns in the *Baby M* case.[7]

Polly's Story

Polly's tale is a little known true story from the annals of American legal history.[8] In the early 1800s a happy little girl by the name of Polly Crocket was living in Illinois. One dismal autumn night Polly was kidnapped and sold into slavery in Missouri. Her first owner was a poor farmer; the second, a wealthy gentleman named Taylor Berry whose wife trained Polly as a seamstress. Polly grew up and was permitted to marry another Berry slave, Apollo. Polly and Apollo managed to have two children, Lucy and Nancy, before Apollo was sold to a distant owner "way down South."[9]

The years passed. With deaths and marriages, the ownership of Polly and her daughters was passed in and out of the Berry family. Encouraged by Polly, daughter Nancy escaped to freedom in Canada. Desperate to join her, Polly attempted to escape, and made it all the way to Chicago. Because the Fugitive Slaves Laws were in effect, however, "negro-catchers" were permitted to arrest her and return her to her owner in Missouri.[10]

Upon return to Missouri, Polly took the bold step of finding a good lawyer. She successfully sued for her freedom on the theory that she was not a slave, but a free woman who'd been wrongfully sold into slavery. Now a free woman anxious to have her family together again, Polly decided to buy her daughter Lucy out of slavery. But Lucy was not for sale. Lucy was owned by a Mr. Mitchell. Mitchell wanted to keep Lucy to please his wife. Polly filed a lawsuit against Mitchell on 8 September 1842, for the possession of her daughter, Lucy. During the seventeen-month pendency of her mother's civil suit, poor Lucy was locked away in jail.

Polly's suit ended in victory, and she was awarded possession of Lucy. On the final day of the trial, Polly's lawyer, the slaveholding jurist, Edward Bates, summed up his case to the jury:

> Gentleman of the jury, I am a slave-holder myself, but thanks to Almighty God I am above the base principle of holding anybody a slave that has a right to her freedom as this girl has been proven to have; she was free before she was born; her mother was free but kidnapped in her youth, and sacrificed to the greed of negro-traders, and no free woman can give birth to a slave child, as it is in direct violation of the laws of God and man.[11]

This poignant story vividly illustrates the sense in which the legal concept of ownership completely lacks inherent moral content and can work like a two-edged sword. Polly legally owned herself, yet she lived most of her life as a slave. Once she proved in court that the master who possessed her did not lawfully own her, she became capable of lawfully owning her own daughter, Lucy. But Lucy was precious putative property, not for sale. Properly law could not compel Mitchell to sell, so Polly used slave law to prove unlawful possession.

In the end, mother and daughter owned themselves. But the institution of slavery was still intact, and Mr. Mitchell was out the price of a housemaid. Notice that, under black slavery, all mothers were surrogate mothers. Master X or Mistress Y owned their children. These women gave birth to children with the understanding that those children would be owned by others.

What is to be learned from Polly's case? First, Polly's case reminds us that well-meaning people, including business people, lawyers, and judges sometimes participate in unjust, immoral practices. Most people would agree with this proposition in the abstract, but are reluctant to confront it in concrete cases. To declare that a controversial practice, engaged in by well-meaning citizens, is immoral is to appear intolerant and presumptuous: who are you to judge? what gives you the right to say? As sometimes interpreted, liberalism treats all moral judgment as moralism, and all public moral inquiry as privacy invasion. Morality is mum, relegated to secrecy. This is bad news, because, sometimes, we have to be willing to criticize public officials and even our friends and neighbors. That's how we got rid of slavery.

Polly's case brings to mind a subtler point. The fact that the law is receptive to the claims of some individuals wronged by a practice does not vindicate the practice. Polly's daughter was returned to her because of an earlier injustice. Something had gone wrong. But the practice of slavery, of owning mothers and their daughters, of denying daughters to mothers, continued. That Polly was able to get justice did not mean that the practice of slavery was all right. That Mary Beth Whitehead Gould got her day in court when things went wrong does not mean others should be permitted to carry on with the practice of surrogacy. The fact that child custody arrangements can be made when agreements break down does not mean we are without reasons to halt the practice. Polly's case suggests a third point. Even in social contexts where the expectations of motherhood do not exist—where one understands that one is a member of a slave race without meaningful claims to one's own children, the desire to parent and enjoy the companionship of one's children can be strong. One can imagine that Mary Beth Whitehead Gould's anguish at losing her daughter was not unlike Polly's.[12] Both women's

233

senses of security—responsibility and identity—were deeply tied up in children they supposedly had no right to parent.

A fourth and final message to be drawn from Polly's case is this. The law can easily accommodate the commercialization of human life. So we have to be careful. As the legal positivists John Chipman Gray and Hans Kelsen made plain, in principle, anything can have a right to anything.[13] In our jurisprudence, the conceptual vocabulary is in place to make alienable property of women, of children, of kidneys, of hearts, of spleens, and even of Mr. Moore's cell line.[14] The concepts of property and ownership are elastic enough to let us buy and sell anything we want. We cannot look to the language of law to draw the lines. We have to draw the lines and make the lines we want a matter of law.

Anna's Story

Many state courts and legislatures have opted to permit contract parenting.[15] The commercialization of reproduction may not amount to slavery, but it represents special risks for the ancestors of America's former slave class. Black surrogate mothers are not slaves and are not complicit in slavery, any more than white surrogate mothers; but the practice of gestational surrogacy may expose black women to harms beyond those experienced by white surrogates. It is now possible for a surrogate to give birth to a child to whom she is not genetically related. Black women will never be permitted to own infants who are the genetic property of whites, in spite of the labors of gestation that have traditionally accorded women the legal title "natural mother."

On 19 September 1990, in Orange County, California, a twenty-nine-year-old black woman named Anna L. Johnson gave birth to a six-pound, ten-ounce baby boy.[16] A casual observer visiting the maternity ward at St. Joseph's Hospital would have found nothing unusual in the sight of Anna Johnson breastfeeding the tiny newborn. However, as the journalists who swarmed into the hospital to report the birth knew, Johnson and the infant she delivered had an unusual relationship. They were not genetically related. They were not even of the same race. For the first time in history, an African American woman had given birth to a child exclusively of European and Asian ancestry.[17]

Anna Johnson's pregnancy was the result of *in vitro* fertilization and pre-embryo transplant.[18] Physicians had surgically implanted into Johnson's uterus a preembryo formed *in vitro* from donated gametes. Already the single mother of a preschool-aged daughter named Erica, Johnson underwent the procedure as a service to Mark and Crispina Calvert. Mark Calvert was a thirty-four-year-old insurance adjuster and Crispina Calvert, who had lost her uterus to cancer, was a thirty-six-year-old registered nurse.[19] Crispina Calvert worked at the hospital where Anna Johnson worked as a licensed vocational nurse.[20] The Calverts promised to pay Johnson $10,000 for her trouble.[21]

Anna Johnson was a new kind of "surrogate mother," a surrogate gestational mother. But the human interest in Anna Johnson's miracle was not just that she was a surrogate gestational mother; Anna Johnson was, in addition, a surrogate gestator who had changed her mind about giving up a child to whom she was not genetically related.[22] Commercial surrogate mothers had been known to change their minds before, but this was the first publicized instance in which a "surrogate carrier, gestator, womb mother, or placental mother" had done so.[23]

Johnson filed a lawsuit on 13 August 1990, when she was seven-and-a-half months pregnant. Alleging that the Calverts had neglected her during the pregnancy and failed to make payments, and that she had developed a bond with the unborn child, Johnson sued for parental rights and child custody. The Calverts answered that the baby was theirs alone: "He looks like an oriental baby with my husband's nose," Crispina Calvert said.[24] Although Johnson was willing to accept a court-ordered joint custody arrangement, the Calverts were not. They announced to the news media that they would rather see the baby they would name "Christopher" in a foster home than share parenting with their hand-picked gestator. Johnson's lawyer, Richard C. Gilbert, countered that he could not comprehend the Calverts' belief that it would be "in the baby's best interest to be taken from the breasts of its birth mother."[25]

In September 1990, Orange County Superior Court Judge Richard N. Parslow Jr. awarded temporary custody to the Calverts and granted Johnson visitation rights. In an October hearing, the court heard legal argument and expert testimony on the question of permanent custody.[26] Some expert testimony favored the Calverts. However, medical and psychological experts testified on behalf of Anna Johnson's claim to be the "true" mother.[27] Johnson also had other authority on her side. A California statute expressly provided that birth mothers are the natural and legal parents of their offspring.[28] In addition, a 1989 U. S. Supreme Court case had denied parental rights to a sperm donor claiming only a genetic link to a child.[29]

Anna Johnson testified at the October hearing that she did not initially plan to keep the child. Johnson said that she first changed her mind when Mark Calvert refused to take her to the hospital. She was forced to take a cab for what proved to be false labor pains. While Johnson was a patient, Crispina Calvert, who worked in the same hospital, refused to visit. Even after she began to want the child, Johnson said that she was "in a state of denial," and she kept "trying to tell myself that I am not supposed to have any emotion toward my child, but there is no way that you can prevent those emotions from taking over, and those instincts came out naturally."[30] Describing her state of mind at the time as confused, anxious and desperate, Johnson admitted sending the Calverts a letter on 23 July 1990, threatening to withhold the baby unless they paid her $5,000 immediately.[31] She also acknowledged that the Calverts had sent her two periodic payments early.

After her testimony, Johnson told reporters she was confident of obtaining at least joint custody and visitation rights: "I know he's there . . . I know he won't forget me."[32] However, on 2 October 1990, Judge Parslow ruled that Anna Johnson had no parental rights whatsoever in the child she bore. By way of consolation, the judge offered that Crispina Calvert might elect to provide Anna Johnson with "a picture now and then, a note as to how this child is doing in life."[33] Unwilling to settle for a picture and a note, Anna Johnson appealed her case to the California Supreme Court. She lost there, too.

Anna's "Mistakes and Weaknesses"

Public reaction to the superior court decision in the *Johnson* case was mixed.[34] It is unclear that the outcome of Anna Johnson's case was a bad outcome on the merits. There was too little information in the court transcript and in newspaper accounts to meaningfully assess the relative strengths of the parties and various alternate child custody options. However, one can argue that presiding Judge Parslow's highly revealing attempts to rationalize his decision fell short.

Judge Parslow delivered a thirty-five-minute statement from the bench to a packed courtroom.[35] He did not announce his decision right away, nor did he need to. Judge Parslow's opening remarks made obvious his ultimate ruling. He declared that the case before him was "not an adoption relinquishment case, . . . not a baby selling case, . . . not a *Baby M*-type case where we had natural parents on two sides of a situation competing."[36] To say that the *Johnson* case was unlike *Baby M* was already to conclude that a surrogate gestator who received a donated pre-embryo is not a "natural" mother on par with a surrogate gestator who supplies her own ovum. Yet any gestator's relationship to the child she delivers is undeniably biological; in that sense it is also "natural."

As soon as Johnson's suit became public, legal policy analysts discussed *Johnson* v. *Calvert* as the next chapter in the history of a reproductive revolution of which *Baby M* was but a dramatic early scene. Many observers viewed the cases as closely analogous. In both cases women became pregnant for a cash payment of $10,000 and out of a desire to help a childless married couple have a child of their own. In both cases the surrogate said she had developed a bond during pregnancy that made it difficult to part with the newborn as agreed. In both cases the contract to exchange reproductive services for cash raised concerns about gender inequality and "baby selling." In both cases the presumption that a woman who gives birth to a child is its legal mother seemed to implicate adoption policies. Yet, contrary to these views, Judge Parslow tried to rapidly distinguish the case before him from *Baby M*. Judge Parslow's sense of the case was that neither adoption laws, proscriptions against commercial trafficking in human beings, gender inequality, nor the developing law of genetic surrogate motherhood was relevant to his decision. He asserted in his opening statement that awarding the child to two mothers was not in the boy's emotional best interest.[37] Therefore, he would award only one of the two female parties custody over the child. Once the judge refused to view the case as involving a surrogate mother or adoption agreement, his rejection of a "three parent/two mother" model could have meant only one thing: he would select Crispina Calvert, not Anna Johnson, as the child's sole, rightful mother. Theoretically, Judge Parslow might have rejected both Johnson and the Calverts in favor of a neutral third-party caregiver, such as a foster mother. But Judge Parslow ruled out third-party alternatives. He understood his role as Solomonic: unable to divide the baby in half, the judge would choose between the genetic and gestational mothers.[38]

The race issue, Anna Johnson's race, also made Judge Parslow's ultimate decision predictable.[39] Throughout history, black women and mulatto women have been hired or enslaved to play a number of important de facto "mothering" roles in American families.[40] Moreover, black women who marry white men have sometimes wound up "mothering" white stepchildren. However, I suspect that few regard black women as the appropriate legal mothers of children who are not at least part black. Blacks are not supposed to have white children. Blacks are not supposed to want to have white children of their own—not in the adoption context and not, therefore, in the surrogacy context.[41]

For better or for worse, race is a factor in adoption, and it will also be a factor in surrogate gestation. Against this background, it was unimaginable that Anna Johnson would win custody of the child she bore from the Calverts' genetic material. Arguably, a lawsuit against the Calverts brought by a white or Asian surrogate gestator would have the same outcome. A judge deciding such a case would foresee the possibility that a black or brown or yellow gestator might someday wind up with a white couple's genetic child unless it set a firm precedent favoring genetic parents.

Judge Parslow very briefly recited the facts of the case as follows:[42] The parties met and discussed a gestation arrangement in the winter of 1989–90. They entered into a formal agreement on 15 January 1990. Against the scientific odds, a successful pre-embryo transplant took place just four days later on 19 January 1990. Johnson agreed orally and in writing to "relinquish the child to the Calverts and make no claim for parental rights."[43]

The court had little to say about Anna Johnson's pregnancy. Judge Parslow spoke of Johnson's role in the passive voice: "A baby boy was delivered from Anna Johnson on 19 September 1990."[44] Test results "showed that Anna has no genetic relationship to the child, and that there is a 99.999 percent probability that the Calverts are the genetic parents of the child."[45] On the basis of the genetic tests, the judge found "beyond a reasonable doubt that Crispina Calvert is the genetic, biological and natural mother . . . and that Mark Calvert is the genetic, biological and natural father of the child."[46] If future courts followed Judge Parslow, genes alone would establish natural and biological motherhood. In the state supreme court case, genes were not the whole story, but close to it. The court concluded that the Calverts alone should have parental rights since the Calverts initiated the surrogacy agreement that led to the child's existence and the parties to the agreement intended that the Calverts would parent the child.

Judge Parslow employed two analogies that are indicative of how courts may come to characterize the unique role of the surrogate gestator. He analogized Johnson to a "foster parent providing care, protection and nurture during the period of time that the natural mother, Crispina Calvert, was unable to care for the child."[47] Judge Parslow admitted that "there is [sic] a lot of differences" between a gestator and foster parent, but concluded that "there is [sic] a lot of similarities."[48]

His second analogy compared surrogate gestators to "wet-nurses."[49] As recently as the last century, it was common for affluent European and American families to pay women to breastfeed and tend their infants and small children. Judge Parslow thought it was plain enough that wet-nurses lacked parental rights: "I'm not sure anyone would argue that the person that nursed the child . . . from seven pounds to thirty pounds got parental rights and became the mother."[50] In the judge's view, surrogate gestators are just as plainly without parental rights. One might have expected the court to resist an analogy to the medically and socially discredited practice of wet-nursing. If surrogate gestation is like wet-nursing, perhaps it, too, should be relegated to history.

To counter the impression that he endorsed the use of surrogacy by women who are neither infertile nor sterile, Judge Parslow under-scored the Calverts' medical need. "This is not a vanity situation, somebody looking to avoid stretch marks," he said.[51] For medical reasons, Crispina Calvert "has no place to carry the child."[52] The question of vanity versus medical need may be a different, deeper matter for the courts to consider in the future. It is for "medical" reasons that couples often cannot reproduce on their own. But it was not for medical reasons alone that Crispina Calvert possessed a pre-embryo in need of a gestator. It was also for psychological and social reasons. Crispina Calvert wanted a child, and she valued genetic parentage over other options such as adoption. It was not for medical reasons alone that researchers learned to create pre-embryos in petri dishes and test tubes. It was also for the sake of satisfying the public preference for genetic parentage.[53] What courts must confront is whether the satisfaction of the strong desire to have one's own genetically related children is worth the social price of surrogacy arrangements.

These rationales raise serious questions. Why does a person who is like a foster mother or a wet-nurse have no parental rights? Why does a surrogate gestator have no parental rights against those who seek out her services for "medical" reasons? To answer these questions, Judge Parslow focused on what gestators and genetic parents provide their offspring. The genes we get from our genetic parents determine "who we are, what we become."[54] By comparison to what we get through our genes, we get little in the uterine environment, not even a clear-cut reciprocal bond with our gestators.[55] The limited comparative impact of the gestator on the child's future self, and Judge Parslow's doubt of the reality for a mother-child bond during pregnancy, were the core of a larger set of arguments he offered against parental rights for gestators.

Writing about the *Baby M* case, I stressed the importance of the genetic ties that Mary Beth Whitehead Gould had to her child.[56] I argued that the parity of the surrogate's genetic ties with the biological father's was one reason to accord her equal parental rights.[57] But to say that genetic heritage is a factor to consider in surrogate mother cases involving disputes between genetic parents is not to say that in a battle between genetic and gestational parents, genetic parents should always win out. Like the knowledge of genetic linkage, the experiences of pregnancy and childbirth can also have an important role in shaping women's sense of their identities and responsibilities.

Introducing additional concerns, Judge Parslow argued that both the emotional well-being of the child and policies against custody disputes or extortion militate against awarding parental rights to a "gestational carrier." Interestingly, the judge did not mention the race issue in his decision on the case. The closest he came was to allude to the potential "identity problems" a child raised by two mothers might have. Racial identity is one kind of identity individuals in our society normally develop, along with their gender, ethnic, religious, regional, and other forms of identity. Also weighing against the gestator, in Judge Parslow's view, is the desirability of a judicial policy favoring "surrogacy contracts in the *in vitro* fertilization cases."[58] There is, he said, "a tremendous demand longing [sic] out there for genetic children of people that are not able to have children."[59] Surrogacy contracts are neither "void nor against public policy," ruled Judge Parslow, and are "enforceable by . . . specific performance, [or] arguably even by habeas corpus, if necessary."[60] This is precisely contrary to the ruling of New Jersey Supreme Court Chief Judge Wilenz in the *Baby M* case, who held that surrogacy contracts are void, against public policy, and not specifically enforceable.[61]

The main thrust of Judge Parslow's argument for enforcement of the surrogacy contract was that opportunistic, dishonest Anna Johnson had signed the contract voluntarily. The judge doubted the sincerity of Johnson's statements that she believed the child was hers and that she had bonded with the child. He intimated that Anna Johnson's lawsuit was opportunistic since such statements were first made shortly before the lawsuit was filed. Yet Johnson cannot fairly be blamed for the timing of her action. It would have been in the later stages of pregnancy that she would have been likely to experience the keenest maternal feelings. Bringing a lawsuit promptly at that point to clarify her legal rights and duties was a responsible course.

Judge Parslow also intimated that Anna Johnson was dishonest. He said she omitted unspecified facts about the difficulty of her first pregnancy and misrepresented her feelings and intentions in this case. As for the contract itself, Judge Parslow concluded that Anna Johnson knew what she was doing. Johnson was "29 years old, educated, a licensed professional, . . . [who had spent two or three years

241

in the Marine Corps]."[62] She "sounded . . . articulate and intelligent."[63] Judge Parslow said he couldn't "remember having seen a cooler witness testifying in court."[64] His words hinted that Anna Johnson was perhaps too cool for the occasion. Although "sometimes there is a problem there where a flat effect . . . is presented by a witness," he said, "I don't think she had any problems with the lawyers at all."[65]

The large constitutional questions of family and reproductive privacy that occupied the trial and state supreme court in *Baby M* barely surfaced in the Johnson case, until the case reached the state supreme court. Judge Parslow seemingly danced over the whole tapestry of constitutional concerns in a sentence.[66] He was sure that the "genetic" mother, and not the "carrying person," has whatever procreative rights the U.S. Supreme Court has established as fundamental.[67] It is far from clear that he was right about this. After all, in this context, the surrogate undergoes the greatest physical burdens of procreation, embryo transplant and pregnancy. Moreover, the thrust of the fundamental privacy rights established in *Roe v. Wade* would seem to be that a range of contractual limitations on pregnancy termination and prenatal conduct would be void, notwithstanding the procreative interests of infertile couples.[68] The extensive literature in the field makes plain that these matters of constitutionally protected rights are much more complicated than even the questions suggested in light of *Roe v. Wade*.[69]

The judge was more attentive when stating recommendations for state law. Judge Parslow's central recommendation was that the California legislature enact a surrogate gestator statute. His ruling effectively brushed off as irrelevant California Civil Code Section 7003.82. He nonetheless called for legislation clarifying the statute "given the technology that we can have a different natural mother than the person from whom the child emerges."[70]

Given his remarks about Johnson's competence and voluntary action, the tenor of the judge's specific recommendations for legislative policy are puzzling. Although he emphasized that Johnson acted intentionally and intelligently, he recommended strenuous surrogate screening procedures by disinterested agencies to determine "how they [potential surrogates] feel about various aspects in these situations."[71]

Judge Parslow mentioned that enforcing surrogacy agreements was a way to avoid patronizing women, yet several of his recommendations appear to contradict this intent. As institutionalized support for backsliders, he recommended a twenty-four-hour "hotline" to reinforce surrogates' resolve to give up the children they carry. This recommendation seemed to imply that surrogates will not, on the whole, be fully committed to their undertaking and that second thoughts about surrogacy are a predictable "crisis" requiring intervention measures. Further, he recommended a requirement that only women unable to bear children for "medical" reasons be permitted to employ surrogates. No vanity uses of surrogacy would be allowed. Finally, Judge Parslow recommended a legal requirement that surrogates be experienced natural mothers: "I think they know what it's like, they know what their feelings are, and it would assist them in their decision-making process."[72] The value of this recommendation is questionable given that the two most famous surrogate mothers in the United States to date, Anna Johnson and Mary Beth Whitehead Gould, already had one or more children when they reneged on their surrogacy agreements.

The baby boy Anna Johnson carried in her womb and delivered was awarded categorically to the Calverts. The court denied the request of Johnson's attorney for a continuation of visitation rights pending appeal. His reason was simple. At the age of five weeks "things [such as bonding] are happening psychologically."[73] To Anna Johnson the court awarded a philosophy of self-blame attributed to the Greek philosopher Democritus: "Everywhere man blames nature and fate, yet his fate is mostly but the echo of his character and passions, his mistakes and weaknesses."[74] Her fate, too.

Beyond Anna's Story

What norms should govern modern procreative arrangements and parental status? Professor Marjorie Shultz defends a principle of intent as the optimal norm.[75] The California Supreme Court cited her work with approval in its opinion in *Johnson* v. *Calvert* and relied heavily on an intent standard.

Shultz urged that the inevitable disputes that arise in the context of collaborative procreation made increasingly possible through new reproductive technologies should be resolved, in the first instance, by reference to the intentions of the parties. The standard of intent presumably respects the autonomous plans and expectations created through voluntary exchanges. It assumes women's competence. It avoids judicial paternalism by giving effect to women's efforts to make choices concerning the use of their reproductive capacities. It assures men secure, responsible roles in procreation. The norm of intent entails legal respect for individual autonomy, including female autonomy, and legal minimalization of the impact of knowing or purposeful harm.[76] Yet the norm of intent is problematic. It is inconsistently applied, and it is based on an assumption of greater equality of opportunity than actually exists.

On the surface, the standard of intent appears morally well founded. Its "morality" justifies the pain it causes those who change their minds and renege on prior agreements. Courts that enforce surrogacy agreements of the sort at issue in *Baby M* and *Johnson* inflict pain on the losing surrogate. A losing surrogate not only suffers grievous emotional loss, but she must also confront a fate she once chose in ignorance of its true character but no longer chooses. From the point of view embraced when the standard of intent is accepted, the evils that the losing surrogate suffers are not evils at all; they are voluntary choices. Or, if they are evils, they are justly imposed.

One problem with the standard of intent is that it is and would be inconsistently applied. Already it is not applied across the board in cases involving non-traditional parenting arrangements, such as homosexual relationships.[77] Moreover, if courts can justify enforcing surrogacy contracts by appeal to intent, they can, by the same token, justify enforcing betrothals, marital vows, and other personal undertakings. Yet, the latter contracts are no longer enforced. I believe surrogacy arrangements should be treated in the same manner as other personal agreements, that is, as unenforceable commitments, rather than as enforceable commercial contracts.[78] In those instances where custody battles arise out of failed surrogacy agreements, courts should be ready to intervene in the "best interest of the child," just as they currently intervene when custody battles arise out of failed marriages or love affairs.

In practice, the "best interest of the child" interventions might still turn out to favor genetic parents more often than gestators. But the explicit reason would not be the backward-looking reason that parties once intended that result. It would be the forward-looking reason that the court is persuaded of the genetic parents' superior abilities to provide a home for the child. Conceivably, genetic parents would always win under a "best interest of the child" analysis when they were white or more affluent that the child's minority gestator.

Another problem with the standard of intent is that it presupposes a backdrop of greater social equality and equality of economic opportunity than presently exists. *Ceteris paribus*, a woman with practical nursing skills has more opportunity and a wider foundation for self-determination than a woman without skills and no high school diploma. Yet, opportunity is a matter of degree. The United States has a recent history of legally enforced race and gender inequality. Economic and social pressures over which individuals have little control significantly dictate their "voluntary" choices. A 1989 study showed that 43.2 percent of all black women with children under the age of eighteen in the United States lived below the poverty level.[79] Habitually low social expectations concerning appropriate vocations for white women and certain minority groups limit the horizons of individuals in these groups faced with "free" choices. Moreover, some forms of liberty and contractual voluntarism impinge upon other, equally important values. If liberty must be tempered by fairness, equality, and dignity, it is doubtful that the standard of intent can do all of the normative work that must be done in the wide field of procreative arrangements and parental status.

New Face, Old Problem

For four hundred years he ruled over the Black woman's womb. . . . It was he who placed our children on the auction block. . . . We see him . . . make the Black mother, who must sell her body to feed her children, go down on her knees to him.[80]

Minority women increasingly will be sought to serve as "mother machines" for embryos of middle and upper-class clients. It's a new, virulent form of racial and class discrimination. Within a decade, thousands of poor and minority women will likely be used as a "breeder class" for those who can afford $30,000 to $40,000 to avoid the inconvenience and danger of pregnancy.[81]

It has been said many times before, but it bears repeating: tolerating practices that convert women's wombs and children into valuable market commodities threatens to deny them respect as equals. Commercial surrogacy encourages society to think of economically and socially vulnerable women as at its disposal for a price. Segments of the public will draw the obvious parallels to slavery and prostitution.[82] Their reaction may seem melodramatic. But it is a telling reminder of social attitudes and history. Genetic heritage, while a factor, should not be dispositive in a battle between genetic and gestational parents. The experience of pregnancy and childbirth, like the knowledge of genetic linkage, can play an important role in shaping women's senses of themselves and their responsibilities.

I believe that policy-makers should discourage surrogacy, chiefly by (1) refusing to legally enforce commercial surrogacy agreements; (2) ascribing to surrogates parental rights that they may voluntarily relinquish only after the birth of a child they are paid to carry; and by (3) making no distinction between genetic and gestational surrogates when it comes to the assignment of parental rights.[83] Legislation shaped around points (1) and (3) would increase the risks of entering into surrogacy arrangements for the economically more powerful parties (the consumers and brokers of surrogacy) and decrease the risk of surrogacy arrangements for the less economically powerful (the surrogates).

Black gestators would remain vulnerable to emotional devastation even if surrogacy policies were in line with all three points, and if race were not a factor for the court in awarding child custody under the "best interest" standard. A black gestator who wanted to keep her white offspring, as Anna Johnson did, would likely be pressured by family, friends, and experts to do otherwise. She would know that racism could add special stresses on individual members of her multiracial family, leading to acrimony and rejection.[84]

Limitations on the alienability of parent rights, point (2) above, can greatly benefit some surrogate mothers. Inalienable postdelivery parental rights as limitations on surrogacy would clearly benefit white surrogates who, like Mary Beth Whitehead Gould, want to keep their genetically related children. The benefit of point (2) to gestational surrogates, especially black gestational surrogates, is less clear. First, genetic ties have special meaning in American culture. In deciding child custody under the "best interest of the child" standard, I predict courts would be reluctant to award children to gestational, as opposed to similarly situated genetic, parents. Second, since genetic parents will probably be better educated and more affluent than gestational surrogates, courts are likely to view them as better equipped to provide good homes. Third, most consumers of surrogacy are whites who want white children. Although black women's infertility and sterility rate is higher than white women's, few black women utilize surrogate mothers.[85] Adoption is a realistic, inexpensive option for many black women. It follows that most blacks who are surrogates will be surrogate-gestators for whites. The children born to black gestational surrogates will be of another race. Racial difference between mother and child may incline courts against awarding custody to the black surrogate gestator.

The number of black gestators who could master their rational fears and overcome judicial resistance to go with their hearts would likely be small compared to the number who, with tragic emotional consequences, would feel compelled to give up their offspring. We can only imagine what Anna Johnson's life would have been like had she prevailed in her custody bid. Perhaps her own biracial heritage steeled her for the battles she would have faced as head of a multiracial family. Her willingness to fight to parent her gestational child was virtually as remarkable as the biotechnology that made it possible. Like Polly, the slave who sued for her own freedom and then for the right to own her own child, Anna Johnson was exceptionally courageous.

Conclusion

Surrogate parenting is not, strictly speaking, slavery. Surrogate mothers and the children they bear are not properly analogized to slaves. Still, surrogacy is a potentially exploitative and demoralizing

ANITA L. ALLEN

business, especially for black women who contract to serve as surrogate gestators. American law will not support black surrogates who change their minds and desire to keep gestational children. Courts might award a black child to a black women, but it is virtually inconceivable that a court would award a black surrogate mother her white offspring. Black women wishing to own their own lives and fully possess the fruits of their reproductive labors must understand that contract pregnancy easily devolves into servitude. As an ironic consequence, black gestators could be the safest surrogate mothers for white women who want white children.[86] The *Johnson* case may force the conclusion on behalf of black women that a per se ban on commercial surrogacy is the wisest course.

Notes

*This essay incorporates two previously published essays: Anita L. Allen, "Surrogacy, Slavery and the Ownership of Life," *Harvard Journal of Law and Public Policy* 13 (Winter 1990): 139–49, and Anita L. Allen, "The Black Surrogate Mother," *Harvard Blackletter Journal* 8 (Spring 1991), 17–31.

1. "Surrogate" parenting can be defined as a practice by which a woman ("surrogate mother") bears a child intended for rearing by another woman, man, or couple. In commercial settings, before conception, and for a fee, a surrogate mother agrees to become pregnant (e.g., via intercourse, artificial insemination, or embryo transplant) and later to terminate parental rights and surrender custody of the resulting child. Surrogate mothers are sometimes called "contract" mothers.

Gestational surrogacy is a process whereby a pre-embryo is created from the egg of a woman and the gametes of a man (spouse or donor) through *in vitro* fertilization. The pre-embryo is implanted into the uterus of a second woman, who becomes pregnant and carries the child to term. As will be discussed later, this practice has currently been used only in cases where the woman who supplied the egg was medically unable to become pregnant. There are, however, no rules that require a preexisting medical condition before making use of a gestational surrogate.

2. In the essay, "Surrogacy, Slavery and Ownership of Life" (hereinafter "Surrogacy, Slavery"), I considered—and rejected—the "slavery equation argument" against surrogate motherhood. The argument that slavery and surrogacy are morally equivalent ignores the virtually total control of the slave owner over the slave that is absent from surrogacy arrangements. On the other hand, American slavery was analogous to a de facto system of surrogacy. Slave owners were recognized not

only as the owners of the slaves but they were also owners of the natural children to which the slaves gave birth. These ownership rights allowed the children to be bought or sold to third parties, regardless of the wishes of the natural mother.

3. Alice Walker, "What Can the White Man Say to the Black Woman," *The Nation* 691 (1989): 248.

4. *Johnson* v. *Calvert*, 5 Cal. 4th 84, 851 P.2d 776 (1993). The transcript of the superior court proceeding in the case is also of great interest. See *Reporter's Transcript, Johnson* v. *Calvert* (no. X 63 31 90 consolidated with AD 57638) (Cal Super. Ct., Oct. 22, 1990), hereinafter *Transcript.*

5. Andrew Kimbrell, "Put A Stop To Surrogate Parenting Now," *USA Today*, final edition, 20 August 1990, sec. A, 8. In its final decision the California Supreme Court declared that "We see no potential for that evil [involuntary servitude] in the [gestational surrogacy] contract at issue here, and extrinsic evidence of coercion or duress is utterly lacking." 5 Cal. 4th 84 at 96.

Economic disparities between the races fuel concerns about creating a servant class of surrogates. According to figures published by the U.S. Department of Labor, Bureau of Labor Statistics in 1989, about the time the Calverts and Anna Johnson struck a deal, black females were underrepresented in the highly paid, largely female occupations of sales, professionals, managerial, and administrative support. They were overrepresented in the low-paid, less prestigious occupations of service workers, operators, and household workers. David Swinton, "The Economic Status of African Americans: 'Permanent' Poverty and Inequality," in *The State of Black America 1991*, J. Dewart, ed. (1991), 63. In addition 43 percent of all black women with children under eighteen lived in poverty in 1989. See Dewart, 43. It is predicted that if current trends continue "we can expect to see an increasing inequality gap between black and white women." Dewart, 53.

6. Polly Crocket's story is told in Lucy Delaney, *Struggles for Freedom*, in *Six Women's Slave Narratives*, ed. Henry Louis Gates Jr. (New York: Oxford University Press, 1988), 9.

7. In re *Baby M*, 217 N.J. Super. 313, 525 A. 2d 1128 (Ch. Div. 1987), affirmed in part, reviewed in part, remanded 109 N.J. 396, 537 A. 2d 1227 (1988). See generally Phyllis Chesler, *Sacred Bond: The Legacy of Baby M* (New York: Times Books, 1988). In my essay, "Privacy, Surrogacy and the *Baby M* Case," I rejected the privacy argument for specific enforcement of surrogacy agreements and defended the plausibility of an inalienable constitutional right of surrogate mothers to a postnatal opportunity to change their minds about relinquishing parental rights. See Anita Allen, "Privacy, Surrogacy and the *Baby M* Case," *Georgetown Law Journal* 76 (1988): 1759 (hereinafter "Privacy, Surrogacy").

8. Delaney, "Struggles for Freedom."

9. Delaney, "Struggles for Freedom," 14.

10. Delaney, "Struggles for Freedom," 23.

ANITA L. ALLEN

11. Delaney, "Struggles for Freedom," 42.

12. See Allen, "Privacy, Surrogacy," 1790.

13. John C. Gray, *The Nature and Sources of the Law* (New York: Columbia University Press, 1909), 28–63; H. Kelsen, *General Theory of Law and the State* (Cambridge: Harvard University Press, 1945), 93–109.

14. See *Moore* v. *Regents of University of California*, 202 Cal. App., 3d 1230, 249 Cal. Rtr. 494 (1988).

15. In the *Johnson* case, the California Supreme Court declined to follow the New Jersey high court, which has declared all surrogacy contracts void as against public policy.

16. "Custody Battle Begins Over Surrogate's Baby," *Los Angeles Times*, Orange County edition, 21 September 1990, Sec. A, 1, col. 3 (hereinafter "Custody Battle").

17. This was the first case in which a surrogate mother without genetic links to the child sought custody of the child. See Mardi Kasindorf, "Birth Mother is True Parent, Doctor Testifies," *Newsday*, 10 October 1990, news, 15 (hereinafter "Birth Mother"). Anna Johnson, described in the media as black or as an African American, described herself at the evidentiary hearing in her case as "half-white." See Mardi Kasindorf, "Overwhelming Maternal Instincts; Surrogate Mom Explains Decision," *Newsday*, 11 October 1990, 15 (hereinafter "Overwhelming Maternal Instincts"). Mark Calvert, the father, was described as Caucasian. Crispina Calvert, the genetic mother, was described in news reports both as a "Filipina" and as of "mixed Asian ancestry." See Charles Bremner, "Surrogate Mother Loses Claim to Baby," *The Times*, overseas edition, 23 October 1990, 11, col. 4.

18. See *Ethics Committee of the American Fertility Society* 46, "Ethical Considerations of the New Reproductive Technologies" (supp. 1, 1986), 58S (hereinafter "Ethical Considerations").

19. See Kasindorf, "Overwhelming Maternal Instincts."

20. Kasindorf, "Overwhelming Maternal Instincts." See also Kasindorf, "Birth Mother."

21. Kasindorf, "Birth Mother."

22. Kasindorf, "Birth Mother."

23. The first reported childbirth by a surrogate gestational mother occurred in April 1986 in Cleveland, Ohio. The genetic mother, like Crispina Calvert, had had a hysterectomy. Physicians at the Mt. Sinai Clinic created a pre-embryo *in vitro*, using an egg harvested from the genetic mother's ovaries and her husband's sperm. The pre-embryo was implanted into the uterus of a second woman. The second woman, like Anna Johnson, became pregnant and carried the child to term. See "Ethical Considerations," 58S. After Anna Johnson's case, California courts heard other disputes involving gestational contract pregnancies. These cases show that it is not always the surrogate mother who changes her mind. One of the parties who

250

hired her may have a change of heart, with extraordinary consequences. See *Jaycee B.* v. *Superior Court of Orange County*, 42 Cal. App. 4th 718 (1996); In re: the *Marriage of Cynthia J. and Robert P. Moschetta*, 25 Cal. App. 4th 1218 (1994).

24. "Custody Battle."

25. "Custody Battle."

26. See "Who's Mommy? Without a Law It's Hard to Know," *Newsday*, Nassau and Suffolk edition, 24 September 1990, 48. See also "Genetic Parents Given Sole Custody of Child," *Los Angeles Times*, 23 October 1990, sec. A, 1, col. 2 (hereinafter "Genetic Parents").

27. Kasindorf, "Birth Mother."

28. *California Civil Code Sec. 7003* (1983) reads in part:

§ 7003 Method of establishment: The parent and child relationship may be established as follows: (1) Between a child and the natural mother it may be established by proof of her giving birth to the child, or under this part . . .

See also a related statute, *California Civil Code Section 7001* (1983):

§ 7001. Parent and child relationship; defined

As used in this part, "parent and child relationship" means the legal relationship between a child and his natural or adoptive parents incident to which the law confers or imposes rights, privileges, duties, and obligations. it includes the mother and child relationship and the father and child relationship.

29. *Michael H. and Victoria D.* v. *Gerald D.*, 491 U.S.110 (1989).

30. Kasindorf, "Overwhelming Maternal Instincts."

31. In the transcript of a tape-recorded conversation between Mary Beth Whitehead Gould and William Stern, Gould threatened to kill herself and Baby M. Nonetheless, she was eventually awarded parental rights.

32. See "Genetic Parents." Johnson's confidence proved to have been misplaced.

33. See *Transcript*, 20.

34. Sonni Efron and Kevin Johnson, "Decision Hailed as Proper, Criticized as Outrageous," *Los Angeles Times*, Orange County edition, 23 October 1990, Sec. A, 1, col. 5. See also "Voices," *Los Angeles Times*, Orange County edition, 23 October 1990, sec. A, 12, col. 1.

35. No formal opinion was issued in *Johnson* v. *Calvert* at the time of the superior court ruling against Anna Johnson. The court reporter's official transcript memorialized the judge's, at times, awkward explanation of his difficult decision. See *Transcript*.

36. *Transcript*, 3.

37. *Transcript*, 3.

38. *Transcript*, 3.

39. The Calverts' attorney raised the issue of race in what one reporter described as an "emotional" courtroom, asking Johnson whether she had ever told anyone

she had always wanted a white baby. Johnson said no, "considering I'm half-white myself." See Kasindorf, "Overwhelming Maternal Instincts."
40. See Walker, "What Can the White Man Say to the Black Woman."
41. Official bans on transracial adoptions have been held unconstitutional. See, for example, *Compos* v. *McKeithen*, 341 F. Supp. 264 (E. D. La. 1972) (three-judge court) (invalidating Louisiana statute prohibiting interracial adoption as a violation of the Equal Protection Clause). However, while whites are sometimes permitted to adopt black or bi-racial children, it is virtually unheard of for an adoption agency to offer a healthy, able-bodied white child to black parents for adoption. Compare Patricia Ballard, "Racial Matching and the Adoption Dilemma," *Journal of Family Law* 17 (1978–79): 333; Susan Grossman "A Child of a Different Color," *Buffalo Law Review* 17 (1968): 303; Shari O'Brien, "Race in Adoption Proceedings," *Tulsa Law Journal* 21 (1986): 485. Compare Richard Posner, "The Regulation of the Market in Adoptions," *Boston University Law Review* 67 (1987): 59.
42. *Transcript*, 3–4.
43. *Transcript*, 3–4.
44. *Transcript*, 4.
45. *Transcript*, 4.
46. *Transcript*, 4–5.
47. *Transcript*, 5.
48. *Transcript*, 6.
49. *Transcript*, 17.
50. *Transcript*, 17.
51. *Transcript*, 6.
52. *Transcript*, 6.
53. See "California Surrogacy Case Raises New Questions About Parenthood," *Christian Science Monitor*, 25 September 1990, 2, col. 1.
54. *Transcript*, 8.
55. *Transcript*, 8.
56. See Allen, "Privacy, Surrogacy," 1790.
57. Allen, "Privacy, Surrogacy," 1764.
58. *Transcript*, 11.
59. *Transcript*, 11.
60. *Transcript*, 11.
61. 109 N.J. 396, 537 A.2d 1227 (1988).
62. *Transcript*, 11. See also "Genetic Parents."
63. *Transcript*, 12–13.
64. *Transcript*, 13.
65. *Transcript*, 15 ("I think, probably, as I see it, there are some constitutional problems with trying to outlaw them [i.e., surrogacy agreements] all together.").
66. *Transcript*, 15–16.

67. Court enforcement of any abortion or other prenatal conduct constraints which parties may incorporate into surrogacy contracts appear to be in tension with the spirit of *Roe* v. *Wade*, which prohibits state diminution of the right to procreative choice in the absence of a compelling state interest. See *Roe* v. *Wade*, 410 U.S. 113 (1973).

68. See, for example, Richard Posner, "The Ethics and Economics of Enforcing Contracts of Surrogate Motherhood," and Walter J. Wadlington, "*Baby M:* Catalyst for Reform?" *Journal of Contemporary Health Law & Policy* 5 (1989): 1; Allen, "Privacy, Surrogacy," supra note 2; Katharine Bartlett, "Re-Expressing Parenthood," *Yale Law Journal* 98 (1988): 293; James Flaherty, "Enforcement of Surrogate Mother Contracts: Case Law, the Uniform Acts and State and Federal Legislation," *Cleveland State Law Review* 36 (1988): 223; Thomas W. Mayo, "Medical Decision-Making During a Surrogate Pregnancy," *Houston Law Review* 25 (1988): 599; Steven Miller, "Surrogate Parenthood and Adoption Statutes: Can a Square Peg Fit in a Round Hole?," *Family Law Quarterly* 22 (1988): 199; E. De Marco, "The Conflict Between Reason and Will in the Legislation of Surrogate Motherhood," 1987 *American Journal of Jurisprudence* 23 (1987); Note, "Rumpelstiltskin Revisited: The Inalienable Rights of Surrogate Mothers," *Harvard Law Review* 99 (1986): 1936, 1950; "Note, Surrogate Motherhood: The Outer Limits of Protected Conduct," *Detroit College of Law Review* 4 (1986): 1131, 1141; Lizabeth Bitner, "Womb for Rent: A Call for Pennsylvania Legislation Legalizing and Regulating Surrogate Parenting Agreements," *Dickenson Law Review* 90 (1985): 227, 236–37; Barbara Cohen, "Surrogate Mothers: Whose Baby Is It?," *American Journal of Law and Medicine* 10 (1985): 243, 256; Note, "Developing a Concept of the Modern 'Family': A Proposed Uniform Surrogate Parenthood Act," *Georgia Law Journal* 73 (1985): 1283–1284 n. 5; George Smith and Roberto Iraola, "Sexuality, Privacy and the New Biology," *Marquette Law Review* 67 (1984): 263, 285; John A. Robertson, "Procreative Liberty and the Control of Conception, Pregnancy and Childbirth," *Virginia Law Review* 69 (1983): 405, 420; Phyllis Coleman, "Surrogate Motherhood: Analysis of the Problems and Suggestions for Solutions," *Tennessee Law Review* 50 (1982): 71, 82. See generally Martha A. Field, *Surrogate Motherhood* (Cambridge: Harvard University Press, 1988).

69. *Transcript*, 18.

70. *Transcript*, 16–17.

71. *Transcript*, 15.

72. *Transcript*, 15.

73. *Transcript*, 24.

74. *Transcript*, 24.

75. Marjorie Shultz, "Reproductive Technology and Intent-Based Parenthood: An Opportunity for Gender Neutrality," *Wisconsin Law Review* (1990): 297, 302 (hereinafter "Reproductive Technology and Intent-Based Parenthood").

76. Shultz, "Reproductive Technology and Intent-Based Parenthood."

77. In a case involving a lesbian couple who had intentionally utilized artificial insemination to become the parents of two children, the court refused to endorse either woman's proposed child-custody plan, and denied parental and visitation rights. The court deemed the intentions of the lesbian parents irrelevant. See "Lesbian is Denied Custody After Breakup," *New York Times*, 24 March 1991, 22, col. 1.

78. See Allen, "Surrogacy, Slavery," 147. ("Surrogacy arrangements are best viewed as unenforceable personal commitments or vows between unmarried individuals.") Compare Allen, "Privacy, Surrogacy and the *Baby M* Case."

79. See *U.S. Department of Labor, Bureau of Labor Statistics*, supra note 13 and accompanying text.

80. Walker, "What Can the White Man Say to the Black Woman."

81. Jeremy Rifkin and Andrew Kimbrell, "Put a Stop to Surrogate Parenting Now," *USA Today*, 20 August 1990, sec. A at 8.

82. Ruth Baum, Letter to the editor, *San Francisco Chronicle*, 6 November 1990, sec. A, 20. "I've got just one question concerning the Anna Johnson surrogate mother case: If a woman can legally rent her uterus for nine months, why should the law prevent her from renting her vagina for an hour or two?. . . [Prostitution and surrogacy involve] commercial use of one's body for someone else's convenience or pleasure." See Allen, "Privacy, Surrogacy," supra note 2.

83. For example, a black gestator could foresee that her multiracial family could attract curiosity and prejudice.

84. Laurie Nsiah-Jefferson, "Reproductive Laws, Women of Color, and Low-Income Women," in *Reproductive Laws for the 1990's*, Sherrill Colhen and Nadine Taub, eds. (Clifton, N.J.: Humana Press, 1989), 23.

85. Nsiah-Jefferson, "Reproductive Laws," 23.

86. Compare "California Surrogacy Case Raises New Questions About Parenthood," *Christian Science Monitor*, 25 September 1990, 2, col. 1. Presents the argument that there is a potential for racial discrimination since a "couple may be more inclined to hire a minority woman to carry the child, either for financial or other reasons."

12

AMERICAN SLAVERY AND
THE HOLOCAUST: THEIR
IDEOLOGIES COMPARED

Laurence Thomas

When I was young, I never understood how the shape of a table, say, could be so important in the Vietnam War negotiations. "What does the shape of a table have to do with ending the war?" I would intone. But I think I understand better now, as I have discovered that the order in which one mentions the two institutions under discussion is taken as a political statement of some sort: it is assumed that implicit in the order mentioned is a difference in the importance that one attaches to them, with the first mentioned being the most important. Although the events are listed chronologically in the title, I do not adhere to that order throughout the essay.

I can only speak in a somewhat informed way to the pain, moral and otherwise of blacks and Jews. However, I wish to record my awareness of the suffering of other peoples: specifically, in this instance, Armenians and Native Americans. Between 1915 and 1923, nearly one and a half million Armenians were killed by the Turks; and to varying degrees the attitude of the Turks towards the Armenians was not unlike the attitude of the Nazis towards the Jews. Native Americans, of course, have experienced their share of dehumanization, deception, and marginalization at the hands of Christian whites. While acknowledging the suffering of others is, to be sure, no substitute for understanding their suffering, I should very much hope that acknowledgment is a gesture in the right direction.[1]

American slavery and the Holocaust were fundamentally different from one another. They were such radically dissimilar institutions that no sense whatsoever can be made of the view that one was more evil than the other.[2] I shall begin by discussing the two institutions from the standpoint of coercion: the Holocaust was coercive in a way that slavery was not. Then I take up natal alienation, which has to do with not having any historical moorings: American slavery was natally alienating, whereas the Holocaust was not. And, finally, I shall offer an account of the conception which each institution had of its victims: the Jew was considered irredeemably evil, whereas the black was not.

From the outset, however, a caveat is in order. So very often discussions about the Holocaust, where at least six million Jews were killed, and American slavery, as a result of which approximately twenty million blacks lost their lives, take on the air of a contest in which evil is matched for evil—especially in light of the heightened tension between Jews and blacks nowadays. But if, as I believe, we have two radically different forms of evil here, then there will be evils in the Holocaust which have no parallel in slavery, and conversely. And this truth does not make either any less a horrendous form of evil. It is most unfortunate that our endeavor to understand the Holocaust and American slavery should be clouded by what is surely a most pernicious form of competitive ideology of which no good can possibly come, namely the view that the evil that one group has suffered is somehow diminished unless the evil visited upon it can be shown to be equal or parallel in all respects to the evil visited upon the other group. An institution need not be evil in any and all ways in order to be profoundly evil. American slavery and the Holocaust were each profoundly evil in their own ways.

The person left a paraplegic by a drunken driver and the person left whole but without family by the same drunken driver have both suffered in such radically different ways that it would be foolish, pointless, and just plain wrong for either to insist upon having suffered the most, as if this judgment were indispensable to recognizing the depth of the suffering of either. It is in this spirit that I write about both the Holocaust and American slavery.

A final comment: The account that follows is not meant to be an indictment of every German or white who lived under either Nazi Germany or American slavery. It is manifestly false that every such German or American white viewed Jews and blacks, respectively, in any or all of the ways indicated below. Further, in some instances, at least, there was undoubtedly ambivalence on the part of those whose behavior was quite morally reproachable. I hardly wish to deny any of this. Rather, I am interested in capturing the kinds of considerations which were a part of the horrendous moral climate of the two oppressive institutions under discussion, although these considerations—as is the case with any moral climate—were embraced to varying degrees by the members of the societies in question.

The Coercive Factor

In *The Concept of Law*, H. L. A. Hart conclusively demonstrated that, contra John Austin (*The Province of Jurisprudence Determined*), a legal system does not reduce to simply a set of commands backed up by threats.[3] He distinguished between the external point of view and the internal point of view, and maintained that essential to the existence of any legal system is that a substantial number of its constituents have the internal point of view towards it: that is, they obey the laws of the legal system because they see such laws as rightly binding upon them. If a substantial number of constituents fail to have the internal point of view, but have only the external point of view, then on Hart's view what we have instead is an extraordinarily coercive system. There can be no doubt that Nazi Germany and American slavery were both coercive institutions. Even so, on this score we have a most important difference between them.

It is wildly implausible to suppose that Jews during the Holocaust had anything remotely resembling the internal point of view towards the extremely anti-Semitic laws of Nazi Germany calling for the death of the Jews. The Nazis were never under the illusion, nor was it ever remotely their hope, that the Jews would come to see the genocide which the Nazi state was imposing upon them as something to which they should rightly submit. And, of course, the Jews did not come to see the genocide imposed upon them in this way. More generally, there is no respect in which Jews can be said to have extolled the "virtues" of the Holocaust. To be sure, it seems evident that some Jews regarded the Holocaust as in some way a profound judgment of God upon the Jews. But to so view the Holocaust is not at all to look favorably upon any aspect of it—for even the wicked can be pawns in the hands of God—but rather to understand its significance and the possibility of its occurrence in a certain light.

The Holocaust was an entirely coercive institution. And it was seen as such by the Jews. The genocide of the Jews was the aim of the Holocaust; and this evil institution was designed to succeed in the complete absence of any cooperation with and trusting of Nazis by the Jews. The moral climate of the Holocaust was intended to insure compliance by destroying the very will of its victims to resist their deaths.

Needless to say, among Jews who had converted to Christianity there were some who saw the Holocaust as giving Jews their just desert. The remarks in the preceding paragraph, however, are meant to refer to individuals of Jewish birth who identified with being Jewish, and not to those so born who explicitly and completely rejected their Jewish origins by converting to Christianity.

Now, while American slavery was indisputably a coercive institution, slavery, being what it is, was not entirely so; on the contrary, slavery works best—that is, it is most stable as an institution— precisely when slaves believe, at least to some extent, that they are rightly subordinate to the will of slavemasters. There was cooperation and trust between blacks and whites, as well as feelings of affection, good will, and loyalty. What is more, significant numbers of slaves believed that there were right and wrong—good and bad— ways for slavemasters to treat blacks as slaves.[4] That is, normative assessments of the role of the slavemaster were made from the internal point of view of the institution of slavery—or, at any rate, what was very nearly that. Indeed, slaves were even able to see themselves as deserving of some instances of punishment. The sentiments just mentioned, which to varying degrees obtained on the part of blacks and whites towards one another, could have done so only if not only whites viewed slavery from the internal point of view but to some extent at least blacks did as well—which, of course, is not to maintain that every slave viewed slavery from the internal point of view.

Consider, for instance, the role of the black nanny. This role simply cannot be understood from an entirely coercive point of view. No role could be more incompatible with pure coercion. One wants the person who cares for one's children to do so with concern for the well-being of one's children and, indeed, with affection for them. One wants the person to take a measure of pride in the flourishing of one's children. It must be assumed that things were no different with slaveholders. And there is the simple truth that these favorable attitudes cannot be produced by coercion. Of course, slaveholders no doubt wanted slaves to perform all of their tasks with such favorable attitudes toward them. But these attitudes are not thought to be an essential ingredient in the production of such finished products as a well-kept field or floor, say; whereas these attitudes are thought to be part and parcel of what proper child care involves. The role of nanny could not have existed had some blacks not been trustworthy caretakers of the children of whites; and this blacks could not have been in the absence of their having the internal point of view toward the role of nanny.

Obviously, none of this is an all-or-nothing matter. Needless to say, many slaves were not viewed as trustworthy. Nor do I claim that black women who were nannies were completely content with their role, or that they never harbored any ill will towards their owners. And so on. And while I do not for a moment want to suggest that black women took such delight in caring for white children that they gave no thought to the conditions of slavery, it is important to realize that such besottedness is not required in order to allow that black women experienced feelings of affection, and so forth, for the white children in their charge. After all, black slaves did not subscribe to a conception of whites which would have been cognitively incompatible with their experiencing feelings of affection for white children that naturally arise in warm adult-child interactions. My claim is simply that the role of the nanny is incompatible with pure coercion, because it is most unreasonable to suppose that slave owners would have allowed their children to be cared for by black women they did not trust at all. The considerations just adduced are part of the explanation for why black women could be trusted as nannies.

Not surprisingly, the Holocaust had nothing analogous to the role of the black nanny. More generally, Jews did not play an intimate role in the family lives of the Nazis to the extent that black slaves did in the family lives of white slaveholders. Or, to put a finer touch on the point, there were no institutional practices, informal or otherwise, which were definitive or characteristic of the Holocaust where Jews played this role in the family lives of Nazis, whereas slavery had many such institutional practices where black slaves played an inti-

259

mate role in the lives of whites.[5] There were the black confidante and the black cook. And while it may seem that the latter role did not involve trust, a moment's reflection should suffice to reveal that it surely did. One is very loath to eat food prepared by one whom one believes is chafing at the bit to poison one. And while a cook's poisoning of the family would surely have brought down the wrath of other whites, this could hardly have given a white family much comfort. For one thing, an avenged death is no substitute for living. For another, and much more importantly, the threat of death would carry little weight with slaves who would rather run the risk of death than endure the injustices of slavery; and there was no formal way slaveholders could rule out the possibility that the slaves who cooked for them were of this mind-set. In the absence of some degree of trust, it would have been most imprudent for slaveholders to have slaves cooks for them. And in the context of slavery, trusting blacks in this regard makes sense only if the blacks trusted have, to some extent, the internal point of view toward the institution of slavery, as presumably some did; for in the eyes of the slaveholder, there were "good" and "bad" blacks, the former being more trustworthy. In general, it was possible for slaves to play an important role in affirming the self-worth of slave owners. And this would not have been possible if some slaves did not adopt the internal point of view towards the institution of slavery. Jews simply did not play an affirming role in the lives of the Nazis. Quite the contrary.

The idea that victims of oppression may unwittingly contribute to or participate in their own oppression by accepting, to varying degrees, the very norms of the institutional practices which oppress them is not a new one.[6] And the point being made here is that one fundamentally important difference between the Holocaust and American slavery is simply this: Jews most certainly did not come to accept the norms of the Holocaust—that is, the view that they were vermin worthy only of death at the hands of the Nazis. There were, of course, Jews who committed suicide during the Holocaust, but certainly not because they believed that the Nazis were right in holding that Jews did not deserve to live, and so wanted to contribute in their own way to the realization of that end. By contrast, the conclusion that backs to varying degrees accepted some of the norms of the institutional practices of slavery, and so had an internal point of view towards slavery, seems very nearly inescapable.[7]

There is, for instance, the notion of an Uncle Tom, namely a servile black who is unduly solicitous of the approval of whites. From the standpoint of slaveholders, an Uncle Tom is a "good black" because he knows his place, and his sense of worth is to a significant degree tied to measuring up to the roles as defined for him by the institutional practices of slavery itself or, after slavery, those practices which embodied the belief that blacks are rightly subordinate to whites. One aspect of the evil of slavery lies in the fact that it defined a set of roles to which the self-esteem of blacks could be tied, although such roles were part of an institution that was manifestly oppressive of blacks. As one female slave remarked:

I hope and prays to git to hebben. Whether I's white or black when I git dere, I'll be satisfied to see my Savior dat my old marster worshipped and my husband preached 'bout. I wants to be in hebben wid all my white folks, just to wait on them and love them and serve them, sorta lak I did in slavery time. Dat will be 'nough hebben for Adeline.[8]

Another slave remarked:

When us was slaves Marster tell us what to do. He say, "Henri, do dis, do dat." And us done it. Den us didn't have to think where de next meal comin' from, or de next pair of shoes or pants. De grug and clothes gives was better'n I ever gets now.[9]

But all and all, white folks, den were de really happy days for us niggers. Course we didn't habe de 'vantages dat we has now, but dere was sump'n back dere dat we ain't got now, an' dat secu'aty. Yassuh, we had somebody to go to when we was in trouble. We had a Massa dat would fight fo' us an' help us an' laugh wid us an' cry wid us. We had a Mistus dat would nuss us when we was sick, an' comfort us when we hadda be punished.[10]

By contrast, one aspect of the evil of the Holocaust is that it embodied so undesirable a conception of Jews—namely, the Jew as irredeemably evil, so I shall argue presently—as to preclude the very possibility of there being roles to which the self-esteem of Jews could be tied. This gives us a sharp conceptual difference between the Holocaust and American slavery: During the Holocaust, the only good Jew was a dead Jew; whereas during American slavery, it is simply false that the only good black was a dead black. Blacks, while not considered intrinsically useful, were certainly considered useful, whereas Jews were considered intrinsically detrimental. This difference lies at the heart of the explanation for why Jews did not come to have the internal point of view towards the Holocaust, whereas numbers of blacks did, to varying degrees, come to have this point of view towards slavery. The psychological makeup of human beings is such that people cannot adopt an internal point of view towards a practice if it is impossible for their self-esteem to be in any way enhanced by acting in accordance with the practice. And, of course, the sheer physical brutality of the Holocaust made it irrational for any Jew to see the Holocaust as in any way affirming. The Holocaust could not have been described as a form of mass martyrdom.

Before moving on, perhaps the most important single piece of evidence available showing that blacks to some degree came to have the internal point of view towards slavery is to be found in the linguistic practices of blacks. If the word "nigger" was a derogatory term adopted by whites in referring to blacks, one cannot help but be struck by the extent to which blacks used the term in referring to themselves both negatively and positively.

> Dere wuz a lot'ta mean "Niggers" in dem days too. Some "Niggers" so mean dat white fo'ks didn't bodder'em much."[11]
>
> So white fo'ks have deir service in de mornin' an' "Niggers" have deirs in de evenin'. . . . Ya'see "Niggers" lack'ta shout a whole lot an' wid de white fo'ks al'round'em, dey couldn't shout jes'lack dey wan to. . . . "Nigger" preachers in dem times wuz might-nigh free. . . ."[12]

Even after slavery—until very recently in fact, the term "nigger" continued to have considerable currency in black speech practices. A black could be a good, sweet, or mean "nigger," all admitting of positive connotations. The Holocaust did not yield an analogous linguistic practice amongst Jews. But this should come as no surprise if, as I have claimed, one difference between the Holocaust and slavery is that Jews did not at all come to have the internal point of view towards the Holocaust, given its sheer coercive nature, whereas in significant ways blacks did towards slavery.[13]

The Issue of Natal Alienation

The concept of natal alienation sheds further light on why blacks came to have the internal point of view towards slavery, whereas Jews did not come to have this attitude towards the Holocaust.[14] We have natal alienation in the lives of an ethnic group when the social practices of the society in which they are born serve to prevent most of the individuals from fully participating in, and thus having a secure knowledge of, their historical-cultural traditions. Natal alienation is not an all-or-nothing matter; and, if stopped early enough, it is the sort of thing that can be arrested and, in some cases, reversed.

A factor most relevant to whether the harm of natal alienation occurs and the extent to which it does is time: the longer the members of an ethnic group are exposed to oppressive institutions which are natally alienating the more likely it is that they will become natally alienated. This is because substantial natal alienation of an ethnic group requires several generations. The first generation of an ethnic group subjected to natally alienating institutions will have first-hand knowledge of their historical-cultural traditions, since prior to the subjugation this generation will have fully (that is, actively and directly) participated in the historical-cultural traditions of their people—and, let us assume, in an environment which affirms their doing so. Accordingly, individuals belonging to this generation will have a vividness as to who they are historically and culturally that can only come in the wake of direct participation in one's historical-cultural traditions. For these reasons, the lives of those belonging to the first generation will bear a full imprimatur, let us say, of their historical-cultural traditions; and the significance of this imprimatur in their lives cannot be eradicated by being subjugated to natally alienating institutions, although the individuals are no longer able to participate fully in their historical-cultural traditions. By contrast, the lives of those in the very next, and thus first, generation born into natally alienating institutions will not—indeed, cannot—have a full imprimatur of the cultural-historical traditions which belong to their people. At best, they will have firsthand reports from those with a full imprimatur. By the fourth and fifth generations, however, it is clear that not only will no one among the subjugated people be fully participating in the historical-cultural traditions of their people, but worse yet there will be few, if any, first-hand reports from those who did. By the seventh generation, of course, there will be no surviving members bearing a full imprimatur of their historical-cultural traditions.

After seven generations of having been subjugated to very natally alienating institutions, an ethnic group's historical-cultural traditions can no longer be seriously defined in terms of the historical cultural traditions which were theirs prior to the oppression. Or, at any rate, we have two different historical-cultural traditions, even if the latter is an offshoot of the former. For historical-cultural traditions survive only insofar as individuals can fully participate in the practices that define them; and precisely what natally alienating institutions do is make such participation impossible by ensuring that the practices definitive of the historical-cultural traditions simply do not survive.

By the 1650s, slavery was well underway in the United States. By 1750, there were more slaves in the United States who had been born here than had been forcibly brought here. And by 1860 virtually all slaves in the United States had been born here, since the slave trade ended around 1808. Taking a generation to be twenty years, the natal alienation of blacks ranged over ten generations, and became especially efficacious from 1750 onwards, and even more so by 1808; since from 1750 onwards, we have five generations where both the numbers and the circumstances of birth increasingly favored the natally alienating institutions of slavery, and dramatically so after 1808.

Now, the concept of natal alienation gives us yet another important insight into the difference between the Holocaust and American slavery. The evil of the former lay in the painfully many deaths of Jews it brutally brought about in the attempt to exterminate the entire Jewish people; the evil of the latter lay in the painful degree of natal alienation it brought about through the enslavement of blacks. Now, it might be tempting to think that these two forms of evil are on a continuum, with death being the worse of the two. But this line of thought should be resisted. One does not wish to offend with too imaginative an example, but the truth of the matter is that by the present criteria by which a person is deemed a Jew—being born of a Jewish woman or conversion, complete natal alienation alone is as much of a threat to the existence of Jews as is genocide. If over seven generations none of the rituals of Judaism were allowed to be practiced—if there were no circumcisions, no Bat or Bar Mitzvahs, no synagogues, and no conversions; and if over seven generations, Jewish women had fewer and fewer children because as a result of social indoctrination their sense of worth became ever more tied to caring for the children of others rather than bearing children, and if children born of Jewish women were separated from their families at birth and raised as non-Jews, if all these things happened over seven generations, it is not clear if anyone could say with any confidence that the Jews as an ethnic group still existed—at least not if the criteria stated above were used. By then it would be well nigh impossible for anyone to know who had been born of a Jewish woman, although this would perhaps be true of some individuals.

It goes without saying that no ethnic group can survive mass murder. However, it does not follow that an ethnic group will survive just because its members are not victims of this sort of evil. For if participating in certain practices is definitive of who the group is, and, moreover, there are no phenotypical features which could be deemed decisive in this regard, then the elimination of those practices from the lives of the group over seven generations would suffice to eliminate the group itself; since by then it would no longer be possible to determine with any assurance who belonged to the group by reference to ancestry, which is the only criterion that would be available to one. There is a difference between individual survival and group survival; and while it is certainly true, as a matter of logic, that a group will not continue to exist if none of the individuals belonging to it survives, it is nonetheless false that if those belonging to the group survive, then, as a matter of logic, the group itself will continue to exist.

Individuals who survive successive generations survive as an identifiable group only if there is some criterion by which it is possible to distinguish them as a group. And from the fact that a people are not murdered, or do not have their deaths hastened in other coercive ways, it does not thereby follow that a criterion for distinguishing them as a group obtains. Hitler was concerned to bring about the end of a *people*—not just people. And while extermination is a most efficient means of achieving this end, it is not the only means. Of course, given Hitler's conception of the Jews as irredeemably evil, no doubt nothing short of their extermination would have recommended itself to him.

However, because skin color is often taken as decisive when it comes to determining ethnic identification, and by that measure it is clear that people of African descent survived slavery, it is easy for the profoundly fatally alienating character of slavery to go unappreciated. If it is obvious that people of African descent survived slavery, what is anything but obvious is exactly what they survived as. Only if one trivializes the practices which were definitive of the historical-cultural traditions of Africans prior to their enslavement can one possibly think it obvious what blacks survived as.

Now, in claiming that slavery was natally alienating, what I am not claiming is that nothing from Africa survives in the culture of black America. It is generally held that Africa left its influence upon the music and, especially, the religious practices preferred by a great many black Americans, such as the spiritual "shout" in church.[15] While I should not want to trivialize this influence, I think it is a mistake to regard this influence as the centerpiece of the historical-cultural traditions which blacks inherited from Africa. This is because what is being referred to here is primarily style, form, and mode of (self-) expression, and not narrative content; and without a narrative a people cannot maintain a sense of their history. Indeed, they are without an interpretation of the very practices said to inform their identity.[16]

Before moving on, we might try the following thought experiment. An oppressor says to a victim "choose—choose, that is, between the physical death of your people or the complete and total natal alienation of your people, as a result of which the ethnic identity of your people is forever lost." The only thing I would like to say here is that I do not see how anyone could rationally choose. People do die for what they believe in. And death can be preferable to certain forms of degradation. So it is not at all obvious that it is better to live as something than to die, if that something is radically at odds with how one presently and profoundly identifies with oneself. If death were indisputably the worse of these two evils, then the choice should be obvious. It is surely not, however. And this suggests that it is a mistake to suppose that these two are on a continuum with death being indisputably the worse of the two.

I have said that what distinguishes the Holocaust from American slavery is that the Holocaust was not natally alienating. Needless to say, this in no way diminishes the evil of the Holocaust, any more than the truth that slavery was not about genocide diminishes the evil of slavery. Ironically, the Holocaust was not natally alienating precisely because the genocide of the Jews was its very aim; for (as we shall see below) the official doctrine of Nazi Germany held Jews to be irredeemably evil and thus was incompatible with wanting Jews to survive in any way; and the natal alienation of a people can occur only if they are not killed off.[17] Further, the brutal events of the Holocaust took place over a single generation. This is not enough time for significant natal alienation to occur, which is hardly to deny that the Holocaust had grave deleterious psychological effects upon Jews. But not every grave psychological harm constitutes a form of natal alienation. So, although the Holocaust made it extremely difficult for Jews to participate in the practices definitive of their historical-cultural traditions, and although very many Jewish families were separated, the time-frame in which these events occurred was short enough that neither the historical-cultural traditions of Jews nor the practices definitive of these traditions were lost. The pain of the Holocaust was, of course, extraordinary. But that pain was not about a people desperately in search of some thread of their historical-cultural traditions, groping to identify or to relearn the practices definitive of these traditions. Quite the contrary, it was the pain of a people desperately seeking to reconcile their commitment to their historical-cultural traditions in the face of the extraordinary suffering they had undergone. Had, in fact, the Holocaust been natally alienating, this very profound pain could not have been experienced.[18]

The Conception of the Victims

No oppression of a people can be fully articulated without an account of the way in which the victims were conceived of by those

267

who oppressed them.[19] Here, again, we get a most important difference between the Holocaust and American slavery. Although both institutions considered their respective victims to be morally inferior, they did so in quite different ways. With the Holocaust the only good Jew was a dead Jew—not a subservient Jew but a dead Jew; whereas with American slavery, a good black was indeed a properly subservient black. Slavery's "official" view of blacks is that they were by natural constitution moral simpletons, if you will—creatures not capable of excelling at the high moral and intellectual virtues on account of having diminished moral and intellectual capacities. I do not claim that this view was consistent with all the ways in which slavemasters (and whites, generally) interacted with blacks. It clearly was not. However, this view is consistent with many of the severe forms of treatment which blacks received for not behaving as desired. Assuming a kind of Skinnerian stimulus-response model, one can treat a creature severely in the hopes of eliciting the right behavior from it without attributing high moral and intellectual powers to the creature. What is more, we sometimes think that creatures incapable of either virtue or vice, strictly speaking, can nonetheless mimic such moral behavior. And on some occasions, their doing so can result in our having genuine moral feelings appropriate to the behavior in question, as if it were in fact characteristic of a virtue or a vice. Observe that whereas one can become outraged at one's dog for having just ruined one's garden, one does not become outraged at one's tree for having just lost a branch which fell upon the top of one's car and damaged it. Trees are not capable of enough agency to make conceptual sense of rage towards them. Dogs are—or so we seem to believe. I have drawn attention to this point about behavior and displays of moral attitudes because it is important to realize that the slavery conception of blacks as moral simpletons is not discredited by pointing to the truth that some of the slave owner's attitudes and behavior towards blacks can only be described as moral in character.

On the other hand, Nazi Germany's "official" view of Jews was that they were irredeemably evil—although capable of moral agency, they were so constituted by their very nature that extreme vice was necessarily the dominant expression of their moral agency.

As Nazi doctor Fritz Klein responded when asked how he could reconcile killing Jews with the Hippocratic oath:

> Of course I am a doctor and I want to preserve life. And out of respect for human life, I would remove a gangrenous appendix from the diseased body. The Jew is the gangrenous appendix in the body of mankind.[20]

Jewish infants were deemed no less possessing of this nature than Jewish adults. This nature of vice was not thought to be one that could be diffused if only one got to it early enough. Accordingly, the Nazis viewed Jewish infants with as much disfavor and disdain as they viewed Jewish adults. No social interaction between any Jew of any age and any non-Jew of any age met with approval. This is in sharp contrast to slavery, where it was not at all out of the ordinary for the children of slave owners and the children of slaves to play together. Slave owners were not merely chafing at the bit waiting for black children to become old enough to perform the tasks of slaves. The play between black and white children was often greeted with approval.

It is most rare for young children (seven and under) to bear the full brunt of hostility directed against the ethnic group to which they belong. As I have indicated, what most distinguished white and black children during times of slavery, at least often enough, was the difference in what the future held for them—not the amount of suffering that black children experienced in comparison to white children. No such claim can be made concerning Jewish and non-Jewish children during the Holocaust. Absolutely not. This difference underscores the moral significance of the difference in the way that each of these two institutions conceived of its victims. If a people are held to be irredeemably evil, then the only appropriate moral and psychological attitude to have towards them is one of complete and utter dissociation from them. There could be no reason to approve of any form of social interaction with them, as the very existence of any of them, at whatever stage of life, would represent that which one should oppose at all costs.[21] On this view, children could not be the exception to the rule. And indeed they were not. If, on the other hand, a people are held to be moral simpletons, this is not, in and of itself, a reason to oppose their very existence, let alone to do so at all costs. Quite the contrary, one can even have a caring and protective attitude toward moral simpletons. So, a fortiori, one can have such an attitude toward the children of such a people. Not only that, since children generally do not exhibit great moral and intellectual maturity, the psychological attitude towards the children of a people with truncated moral capacities would not be substantially different from the psychological attitude towards children of people without truncated moral capacities, except insofar as the future would bear upon matters.

The following observations bring into sharper relief the importance of the difference between the ways in which the American slavery and the Holocaust each conceived of its victims. The belief that a people are moral simpletons is perfectly compatible with having norms of benevolence towards them—with believing that there are good and bad, appropriate and inappropriate ways of treating them. This is so even if one does not believe that the people fall under the scope of justice itself. After all, the norms of benevolence operate nowadays with respect to animals, although few are inclined to think that animals fall within the purview of justice. And as the case of animals shows, the norms of benevolence may be anchored in deep moral considerations, and thus not stand as optional claims upon our behavior.

On the other hand, if a people are held to be irredeemably evil, then surely norms of benevolence towards them would be out of place. This characterization of a people simply does not support any sustained benevolent psychological attitudes towards them. Indeed, it is not clear what an appropriate practice of kindness towards the irredeemably evil would be. The virtue of forgiveness might come naturally to mind here.[22] I am not even confident of this, though. I believe that the psychology of forgiveness is such that it is extraordinarily difficult to forgive those whom we believe are constitutionally committed to doing wrong, who have a deep and unshakable preference for doing that which is wrong. While I should like to stop short of saying that this is impossible for any individual to do, I doubt that forgiving the irredeemably evil could be a norm among people, for a norm refers to a stable practice, and I do not see that forgiving the redeemably evil could ever be a stable practice. For an irredeemably evil person is too much of an affront to the very act of forgiving.

Now, while American slavery was undoubtedly a nefarious institution, it must nonetheless be conceded that in individual slave households there were norms of benevolence towards slaves, which is what one would expect given the view of the black as a moral simpleton. Although there were vicious slavemasters, to be sure, there were also slavemasters who felt it their moral duty, in virtue of their role as slavemaster, to treat their slaves with kindness. And it is precisely because there were such slavemasters against the backdrop of an otherwise evil institution that we can make sense of the various instances of strong loyalty which slaves had toward their slavemasters. For there is no better way to occasion gratitude on the part of individuals among an oppressed people, and feelings of loyalty too, than to treat them less harshly than one has a right to treat them, according to prevailing institutional practices, and so less harshly than many others actually treat them. It is not necessary that the individuals be treated as they rightly should be treated; it suffices that they can count upon being treated by those having power over them better than other similarly situated oppressed individuals can.

This is an extraordinarily deep and important feature of the psychology of persons. We are understandably grateful to another for whatever relief from evil or suffering that other offers us, even if that person still contributes to our oppression in other ways. If we can be extremely grateful for an isolated instance of relief, then it stands to reason that sustained relief may go beyond just generating increasingly deeper feelings of gratitude. The most natural other feeling to have towards another as a result of sustained feelings of gratitude is loyalty owing to a debt of gratitude.

As one might imagine, norms of benevolence during the Holocaust on the part of Nazis towards Jews were virtually nonexistent, which is what one expects, given the view of the Jew as irredeemably evil. There were no Nazis who thought it incumbent upon them, in virtue of their role as Nazis, to treat Jews with kindness. And it was with rare exception that Jews could count upon any Nazi to treat them with leniency. With slavery, there can be no denying that some slave owners were touched by the humanity of the slaves. With the

Holocaust, what is astounding is that so few Nazis were touched by the humanity of the Jews.

Although there were no norms of benevolence, some Nazis were more humane in their treatment of Jews than others. The most outstanding case in this regard was a Dr. Ernst B., a Nazi doctor at Auschwitz.[23]

> Former prisoner doctors, in both their written and their oral accounts, constantly described Dr. B. as having been a unique Nazi doctor in Auschwitz: a man who treated inmates (especially prisoner doctors) as human beings and who saved many of their lives; who had refused to do selections in Auschwitz; *who had been so appreciated by prisoner doctors that, when tried after the war, their testimony on his behalf brought about his acquittal;* who was *"a human being in an SS uniform."*[24]

I have italicized the point in this passage to which I wish to draw attention. The point is echoed by the second passage below.

One barely has conceptual space for the idea of Jewish survivors of Auschwitz being so grateful to a committed Nazi doctor in Auschwitz as to rally to win his acquittal at Nuremberg—and Dr. B. was a committed Nazi. But against the backdrop of Nazi evil, and in comparison to the way in which other Nazi doctors at Auschwitz treated prisoners, Dr. B. consistently offered a humaneness in his treatment of prisoners that no one in the concentration camps could ever have had reason to hope for. So upon reflection we can see that there is nothing strange in the enormous gratitude which Auschwitz survivors had for Dr. B. For in general, we are very grateful to those who do more than they have to by way of helping us, as determined by expectations anchored in prevailing institutional practices. Dr. B., as it turns out, did considerably more by doing considerably less. The prevailing norm in concentration camps was brutal mercilessness on the part of Nazi doctors. Dr. B.'s behavior fell considerably short of that norm. As one Holocaust survivor so poignantly put it:

> [Dr. B.'s] very first visit to the lab of Block 10 . . . was an extraordinary rise for us. He came into the lab without force unlike the other SS, without a dog (Weber always came with a dog),

272

locked the doors behind him [so that his behavior could not be observed by other SS], said "Good day" and introduced himself, . . . offering his hand to my colleagues and me. . . . We were . . . long unused to anyone from among the camp authorities treating us as people equal to himself.[25]

I remarked earlier that regarding a being as a moral simpleton is quite compatible with having strong norms of benevolence towards it, whereas this is obviously not so if a being is regarded as irredeemably evil. One could easily, in the absence of any great imaginative feats, believe that it was ordained by God that one should treat moral simpletons with benevolence in a systematic way, whereas it does require quite a feat of imagination to believe that it has been ordained by God that one should so treat the irredeemably evil. What makes Dr. B.'s humane treatment of numerous Jews most incredible is that he so treated Jews without ever rejecting—at least not entirely—Nazi ideology, as he did not condemn Nazi practices, including the selection of Jews for the gas chambers, although he himself did not perform any selections.

We see here how the ideological conception of a victim makes such a phenomenal difference in terms of social practice. As a slave owner, one could be good to slaves in a systematic way without at all condemning, or calling into question, the practice of slavery itself.[26] This is because the very conception of the victim, although quite compatible with being cruel towards it, is equally compatible with being kind towards it; hence, kind behavior did not require any great psychological feats of reconciliation or compartmentalization. A kind slavemaster, for instance, in order to make sense of his acceptance of the practice of slavery, was not forced to play down either his own kindness toward slaves or the cruelty of other slavemasters towards slaves; for he could perfectly well acknowledge that some (he among them) were better slavemasters than others, without calling into question the practice, just as it is acknowledged that some parents are better than others without calling into question the practice of parenting. Thus, being a kind slavemaster did not require psychologically blocking out or down-playing the cruelty of other slavemasters, any more than being a kind parent does vis-à-vis other parents.

Finally, the practice of slavery was not something that a slave owner had to continue participating in or supporting. It happened often enough that slaves were willed free upon the death of their slavemasters.[27] The logic, if you will, and ideology of slavery is perfectly compatible with granting slaves freedom.

Things were quite different with the Holocaust, however. To be kind towards Jews was to call into question the very conception of the Jew as pronounced by Nazi ideology. Thus, Nazi doctors who did not want to participate in the selection of Jews for the gas chambers had to claim psychological inability on their part rather than voice their objection to the practice itself—if, that is, they wished to avoid punishment.[28] Nazism itself allowed no room for a good Nazi to be kind towards Jews. And Nazi doctors who were consistently or frequently kind did so at great psychic costs. They could not allow themselves to appreciate the implications of their own deeds of kindness. Their being kind was viewed by themselves and others as more like something that *happened* to them rather than a profound expression of their recognition of the humanity in Jews. In this way, the doctors could manage to avoid seeing that their being kind to Jews was a moral condemnation of Nazi ideology. Whereas a slave-master could regard his being kind to slaves as a virtue, a Nazi doctor could do no such thing. The Nazi regime was relentless in its demand that its practices meet with public approval.

Perhaps nothing brings out the difference between the way the Holocaust and American slavery each conceived of its victims than the difference in sexual attitudes towards them. Of course, black women were raped during American slavery, and Jewish women were raped during the Holocaust.[29] But the raping of Jewish women and, more generally, sexual relations between Jews and non-Jews, were forbidden, the official reason being that Jews were too low a form of human life, in terms of evilness of character, for there to be such interaction between a Jew and a non-Jew even just for mere sexual pleasure. The having of sexual relations with a Jew by a Nazi citizen was viewed as a form of grave moral contamination of the citizen. Recall Klein's remark that "The Jew is the gangrenous appendix in the body of mankind." This is exactly what one would expect, given the conception of the Jew as irredeemably evil. By contrast, while sexual relations between white slave owners and black slaves were not officially sanctioned by marriage, such relations were certainly common. Indeed, some were long-lasting and exceedingly rich in character. Miscegenation was common enough that schools were set up for children of "mixed" blood to attend. The conception of the black under slavery was that of a moral simpleton; given this conception of black people, one would not expect the kind of hostility on the part of whites towards sexual relations with blacks that Nazi Germany exhibited towards Jews.

I should like to conclude this section by focusing on a similarity between U.S. slavery and the Holocaust which is nonetheless owing to an important difference. There can be no denying that both blacks and Jews were victims of extreme injustice. But even here ideology makes a difference. Blacks were deemed not deserving of justice in the way that things or animals are deemed not deserving of justice. A thing or an animal belongs to the wrong category to be deserving of justice. This is not, however, because animals and things have a morally depraved character, but because they lack the requisite moral complexity. Jews were deemed not deserving of justice, not because they were thought to belong to the category of things lacking the requisite moral complexity, but because they were held to be so morally depraved and thus evil that the restraints of justice no longer applied to the treatment of them.[30] Thus, from the standpoint of the official doctrine of the Holocaust and American slavery, Jews and blacks turn out not to be deserving of justice for radically different reasons. And radically different forms of injustice were meted out.

Conclusion

On the one hand, we have the horror of brutal genocide; on the other hand, we have the horror of brutal natal alienation. Each horror stands in its own right in that neither is the logical predecessor or successor to the other. Neither horror could have given rise to the other without being radically different. And if this is so, then there are no clear criteria by which one institution could be deemed more evil than the other. I do not see that there are any considerations by which it would be rational for one group to prefer the suffering of the other to its own, on the grounds that the other group experienced less evil.

I believe that by endeavoring to understand more fully the ways in which the Holocaust and American slavery differ, we can leave aside the invidious comparison of numbers. True enough, the magnitude of an evil institution is a function of the number of people harmed, but that is not the only determining factor. Equally relevant is the very character, as revealed by its practices, of the evil institution itself. To lose sight of this truth is to embrace a very narrow-minded view of the nature of evil. And to do this with piety and self-righteousness is to aid and abet evil, if only unwittingly.[31]

Notes

1. For an important discussion of the difference between the case of the Armenians and the Jews, see Berl Lang, *Act and Idea in the Nazi Genocide* (Chicago: University of Chicago Press, 1990), 7–8.

2. *Contra*, Richard L. Rubenstein, *The Cunning of History* (New York: Harper and Row, 1975), chap. 3. He writes: "Slavery in North America was thus an imperfectly rationalized institution of nearly total domination under conditions of *a shortage of productive labor.* The death camp was a fully rationalized institution of total domination under conditions of a *population surplus*" (p. 41, emphasis in original)— Rubenstein's point being that as bad as slavery was, the Holocaust was significantly worse.

3. Oxford University Press, 1961.

4. Frederick Douglass, a former slave who symbolizes the ideal of a self-determining black and who did not hold back his criticisms of slavery, nonetheless wrote: "I had resided but a short time in Baltimore before I observed a marked difference, in the treatment of slaves, from that which I had witnessed in the country. A city slave is almost a freeman, compared with a slave on the plantation. . . . Few [slaveholders] are willing to incur the odium attaching to the reputation of being a cruel master and above all things, they would not be known as not giving a slave enough to eat. Every city slaveholder is anxious to have it known of him, that he feeds his slaves well. . . ." Taken from *Narrative of the Life of Frederick Douglass: An American Slave Written by Himself,* ed. Benjamin Quarles (Cambridge: Harvard University Press, 1988), 59–60. All further references to Douglass are to this edition.

5. The remarks about trust in the text presuppose a sharp distinction between trust and prediction. While trust entails prediction, the converse does not hold. I have attempted a more complete analysis of trust, as it differs from prediction, in

"Trust, Affirmation, and Moral Character: A Critique of Kantian Ethics," in *Identity, Character, and Morality: Essays in Moral Psychology,* ed. Owen Flanagan and Amelie Rorty (Cambridge: MIT Press, 1990).

6. Compare Herbert Marcuse, *An Essay on Liberation* (Boston: Beacon Press, 1969). Consider, for instance, the internalization of sexist attitudes on the part of women. I have discussed this in my "Sexism and Racism: Some Conceptual Differences," *Ethics,* vol. 90 (1980).

7. Douglass tells of slaves of different masters quarreling, whenever they got together, over which master was richer or smarter. He went on to write: "They seemed to think that the greatness of their masters was transferable to themselves. It was considered as being bad enough to be a slave; but to be a poor man's slave was deemed a disgrace indeed!" *Narrative,* 44.

8. Quoted from Eugene Genovese, *Roll, Jordan, Roll* (New York: Basic Books, 1972), 355. Needless to say, I do not mean to suggest here that there were no slave testimonies disparaging slavery. There most certainly were, as Howard McGary has forcibly reminded me. The point, rather, is to bring out the kinds of favorable attitudes that slaves were capable of having regarding the interpersonal relationships between themselves and the slavemasters.

9. Quoted from Genovese, *Roll, Jordan, Roll,* 126.

10. Quoted from Genovese, *Roll, Jordan, Roll,* 119–20.

11. Quoted from John W. Blassingame, ed., *Slave Testimony* (Baton Rouge: Louisiana State University Press, 1977), 641–42.

12. Blassingame, *Slave Testimony,* 643.

13. Sterling Stuckey, *Slave Culture: Nationalist Theory and the Foundations of Black America* (Oxford: Oxford University Press, 1987), who is concerned to show that American black culture is basically African at its roots, nonetheless admits that the term "nigger" is evidence of some assimilation on the part of blacks: "The peculiar mixture of Africanity and assimilationism, the latter symbolized by the word nigger, does not hide the fact that the values are African throughout."

14. I borrow the idea of natal alienation from Orlando Patterson, *Slavery and Social Death* (Cambridge: Harvard University Press, 1982).

15. Stuckey, in chap. 1, pp. 3–97, *Slave Culture,* argues this. On the significance of the "shout," see 86–90.

16. In *Slave Culture* Stuckey suggests that the "shout" had great meaning in African contexts (88). This I hardly deny; however, I do not see that the "shout" retained that significance in black worship; and if it did not, then the self-identity of black Americans is not as informed by the "shout" from Africa as Stuckey would have us believe.

17. On this way of understanding how Jews were conceived of during the Holocaust, I am indebted to Richard L. Rubenstein and John K. Roth, *Approaches to Auschwitz: The Holocaust and Its Legacy* (New York: John Knox Press, 1987), chap. 2.

18. For an important implication regarding natal alienation, see my essays "Liberalism and the Holocaust: An Essay on Trust and Black-Jewish Relationship," in *Echoes from the Holocaust: Philosophical Reflections on a Dark Time*, eds. Alan Rosenberg and Gerald E. Myers (Philadelphia: Temple University Press, 1988); and "Jews, Blacks, and Group Autonomy," *Social Theory and Practice* 14 (1988). I argue in these essays that Jews have more group autonomy than blacks, a claim which does not revolve around invidious comparisons.

19. The failure to be clear about the proper characterization of the way in which Jews were conceived of by the Nazis presents a difficulty for Berl Lang's otherwise very illuminating discussion of the contributory role of the Enlightenment to the occurrence of the Holocaust (chap. 7). See my "Characterizing and Responding to Nazi Genocide," *Modern Judaism* (1991).

20. Quoted from Robert Jay Lifton, *Nazi Doctors: Medical Killing and the Psychology of Genocide* (New York: Basic Books, 1986), 16. Nazi doctors were affiliated with certain concentration camps. Not all had terminal medical degrees or had completed genuine medical training.

21. For a masterful discussion in this regard, see Berl Lang, chap. 1, sect. 2, p. 39. The Nazis were determined to exterminate the Jews even at the risk of losing the wider war they were fighting. Lang writes: "Up until the last days of the war, in May 1945, the extermination of the Jews continued, with the diversion that this entailed of material resources (trains, supplies) and of personnel."

22. Recently, Howard McGary, "Forgiveness," *American Philosophical Quarterly* 26 (1989), has suggested that there could be self-interested reasons for forgiving others. But for reasons mentioned in the text, I do not see that such reasons can operate with respect to the irredeemably evil.

23. For the account of Ernst B. offered, see Robert Jay Lifton, *Nazi Doctors*, chap. 16, "A Human Being in an SS Uniform: Ernst B."

24. Lifton, 303. Former prisoner doctors also rallied behind Dr. B. with impressive testimony on his behalf. See Lifton, 326.

25. Lifton, 303.

26. Of his own slavery in Baltimore, Douglass wrote ". . . few slaves could boast of a kinder master and mistress than myself." *Narrative*, 75.

27. Blassingame, *Slave Testimony*, 480, n.22, points out that Jefferson provided for the manumission of some of his slaves. Of course, as Blassingame observes (363–64), wills which manumitted slaves were sometimes set aside. But needless to say, this hardly vitiates the point being made in the text.

28. Lifton, 109, n. 198.

29. As bell hooks so forcibly reminds us in *Ain't I a Woman* (Boston: Beacon Press, 1982).

30. Whether from a conceptual point a person can be so evil that the restraints of justice no longer apply, I do not know. What I do know, though, is that a person

can be deemed so evil that decent people no longer feel bound by the dictates of justice in their treatment of the individual. Presumably, Hitler comes readily to mind here.

31. It has been suggested to me that the practice of segregation in the Old South, which was absent during slavery, would indicate that blacks came to be regarded as irredeemably evil by whites. Not so, however. The segregated South unquestionably had a place for blacks. Blacks could work (indeed, prepare the food) in a restaurant in which they could not eat; and they could clean in a neighborhood in which they could not live. Jews did not play a like role in Nazi Germany.

A version of this paper was read at the New York Society for Philosophy and Public Affairs to a most responsive audience. Thanks are also owed to Steven Kepnes, who has listened most patiently to and commented most thoughtfully upon the ideas in this essay; to Alan Berger who wrote extensive comments, not all of which I have been able to accommodate; to Claudia Card who offered much helpful advice; and to Susan Shapiro, who was extremely encouraging from the start. A special word of thanks goes to Howard McGary, who has so fruitfully disagreed with me. Likewise for Bill E. Lawson. Michael Stocker has been an everpresent sounding board and source of encouragement. Finally, I am delighted to acknowledge the helpful comments of Joshua Cohen, Thomas Digby, Samuel Gorovitz, and Richard Wilkens. A version was given as the 1990 Martin Luther King Jr. Lecture at Eastern Michigan University. This essay is part of a larger work: *Vessels of Evil: The Psychology of American Slavery and the Holocaust* (Philadelphia: Temple University Press, 1992).

13

THE ARC OF THE MORAL
UNIVERSE

Joshua Cohen

> Through all the sorrow of the Sorrow Songs there breathes a hope—a
> faith in the ultimate justice of things. The minor cadences of despair
> change often to triumph and calm confidence. Sometimes it is faith in
> life, sometimes a faith in death, sometimes assurance of boundless jus-
> tice in some fair world beyond. But whichever it is, the meaning is
> always clear: that sometime, somewhere, men will judge men by their
> souls and not by their skins. Is such a hope justified? Do the Sorrow
> Songs sing true?
>
> —W. E. B. Du Bois, "The Sorrow Songs"[1]

I. Ethical Explanation

William Williams was born into slavery in Salisbury, North
Carolina. He escaped to Canada in 1849, where he was
later interviewed by the American abolitionist Samuel
Gridley Howe. It was two years into the American Civil War, and
Williams said: "I think the North will whip the South, because I
believe they are in the right."[2]

Williams's remark provides a striking example of an *ethical explanation*. Generally speaking, ethical explanations cite ethical norms—
for example, norms of justice—in explaining why some specified
social facts obtain, or, as in Williams's case, can be expected to obtain. The norms are offered in *explanations* of social facts, not only
in appraisals of them: Williams expects the North to win *because* they
are right.[3] Similarly, the great abolitionist minister Theodore Parker

predicted defeat for the "slave power" *because* it was wrong: Speaking to the New England Anti-Slavery Convention in 1858, he said of the slave power: "Its Nature of wickedness is its manifest Destiny of Ruin."[4]

Philosophers, historians, and social scientists often recoil from ethical explanations: How *could* the injustice of slavery contribute to explaining its demise? Or the justice of sexual subordination to explaining the instability of systems that subordinate women? Or the injustice of exclusion from the suffrage to explaining twentieth-century suffrage extension? Such explanations seem both too relaxed about distinctions between fact and value and too Panglossian: Does right really make might? Still, ethical explanations play an important role in certain common-sense schemes of social and historical understanding: they are elements of certain folk moralities, so to speak. Martin Luther King said that "the arc of the moral universe is long but it bends toward justice."[5] If there is an arc, King is right about its length. But is there one that bends toward justice? Do the "Sorrow Songs" sing true? More immediately, do ethical explanations withstand reflective examination, or are they simply collages of empirical rumination and reified hope, pasted together with rhetorical flourish?

I think that some ethical explanations—for example, about slavery, sexual subordination, and suffrage extension—have force. That force derives from the general claim that the injustice of a social arrangement limits its viability. This general claim rests in turn on the role played by the notion of a voluntary system of social cooperation in plausible accounts of both justice and the long-term viability of social forms. Social arrangements better able to elicit voluntary cooperation have both moral and practical advantages over their more coercive counterparts.[6]

This theme lies at the basis of Enlightenment theories of history: Adam Smith's account of the pressures that encourage the emergence of a system of natural liberty,[7] Hegel's account of the instabilities of social systems that enable only incomplete forms of human self-consciousness,[8] and Marx's thesis that exploitative social relations ultimately give way because of the constraints they impose on the free development of human powers.[9] Enlightenment historical sociology was too sanguine about the importance of the connection between justice and viability in accounting for historical change, insufficiently attentive to the grim side of such change, and of course unaware of (and unprepared for) this century's carnage. Nevertheless, there may be something to the connection.

To argue the case that there is, I will sketch, in very spare terms, an argument for a thesis that is broader than William Williams's claim about the outcome of the American Civil War, but not quite so sweeping as the general claim about the connections between justice and viability: that the injustice of slavery contributed to its demise. I will defend this claim by arguing for the following four:

Thesis One: *The basic structure of slavery as a system of power stands in sharp conflict with fundamental slave interests in material well-being, autonomy, and dignity.*

Thesis Two: *Slavery is unjust because the relative powerlessness of slaves, reflected in the conflict between slavery and slave interests, implies that it could not be the object of a free, reasonable, and informed agreement.*

Thesis Three: *The conflict between slavery and the interests of slaves is an important source of the limited viability of slavery.*

Thesis Four: *Characterizing slavery as unjust conveys information relevant to explaining the demise of slavery that is not conveyed simply by noting that slavery conflicts with the interests of slaves.*

I will start by setting out some background claims about the nature of slavery and the bases of its reproduction as a system (section 2). I then present a defense of the ethical explanation by presenting some considerations in support of these four theses (section 3). The presentation throughout is relatively bloodless and highly abstract: I am largely inattentive to the sheer murderousness of slavery, the gruesome slave trade, and the infinite variety of forms of slavery. These qualities are dictated in part by the problem of squeezing a large claim into a small space, but they also reflect the content of my principal thesis, which requires that I work with a very general characterization of slavery. I know that such abstractness has costs, but the remarks of Williams, Parker, King, and Du Bois persuade me that the claim is sufficiently important to outweigh those costs.

283

Before getting to the argument, though, I want to clarify its aims by distinguishing my concerns from those in two related debates, one in history, the other in philosophy. First, my focus here is on the role (if any) played by the injustice of slavery in explaining the ultimate demise of slavery. Slavery is unjust—as Lincoln said, "If slavery is not wrong, then nothing is wrong"—and it has been abolished.[10] But did its wrongness contribute to its demise? Historians continue to debate the role of moral convictions about the injustice of slavery—held, for example, by Quakers—in accounting for the abolition of slavery.[11] I do not doubt the causal importance of these convictions, much less their sincerity. Indeed, I will eventually make them part of the story about *how* the injustice of slavery contributed to its demise. But my topic is different. I am not concerned principally with the causal importance of moral convictions in the decline of slavery but the importance of the *injustice itself* in accounting for that demise. In short, I am concerned with the consequences of slavery's injustice—whether "Its Nature of wickedness is its manifest Destiny of Ruin"—and not simply the consequences of the fact that some people came to think of it as wrong.

Second, some philosophers—they might be called "scientific moral realists"—have argued that the objectivity of moral discourse depends on there being substantial moral facts and that establishing the existence of such facts requires that we show a role for them in the causal explanation of human behavior, moral beliefs, social evolution, or some other nonmoral facts about the world.[12] Scientific moral realism seems to me a mistaken view about moral facts, truth, and objectivity. But I will not argue this claim here because my concerns are more or less orthogonal to the debate about its merits. I am not aiming to defend morality, show that slavery was immoral, or argue for any particular philosophical theory about morality or moral objectivity. Instead, I begin, from within morality, premise slavery's injustice, note the practice of ethical explanation, and ask whether there is anything to a particular instance of that practice: the claim—made by Williams and Parker, among others—that slavery's injustice contributed to its demise. What is at stake is not the appropriate moral attitude toward slavery or philosophical outlook on morality, but the appropriate attitude toward the social world. How accommodating is the social world to injustice? Is it reasonable, from a moral point of view, to hate the world?

284

Having drawn this distinction, however, I need to supplement it with two observations—one about the assumptions of my argument, one about its implications—that do bear on debates about moral realism. First, a defense of ethical explanations is not *necessary* to showing that some moral claims are true, or, correspondingly, that there are moral facts. So when I assume that some moral claims are true—in particular, that "slavery is unjust" states a truth and expresses a fact—I am not begging any questions against the critic of ethical explanations. Second, the ethical explanation I will defend is consistent with a minimalist outlook in morality, according to which moral claims can be assessed as true or false, and true moral claims correspond, as a matter of platitude, to moral facts. No more substantial commitment to moral realism is required, nor is any implied.[13] Thus, a defense of ethical explanations is neither necessary for moral truth, nor *sufficient* for establishing a robust form of moral realism.

II. Slavery

My argument that the injustice of slavery contributed to its demise depends on several background ideas about slavery and slave interests. Briefly summarized, I propose that slavery is a distinctive distribution of de facto *power*, that this distribution was reproduced through both force and "consent," and that patterns in the use of force and strategies for inducing consent provide a basis for attributing to slaves basic interests in material well-being, autonomy, and dignity. Though these ideas are not uncontroversial, I am unable here to defend them properly. But I need to say something about them—about slavery as a framework and slaves as agents—both to explain the terms of the argument, and to make it plausible.

Power

Slavery is best understood, I suggest, in terms of the notion of *de facto power*, rather than, for example, in terms of familiar cultural or legal representations of slaves—as extensions of the will of masters, or as property.[14] To be specific: a slave is, in the first instance, someone largely lacking in the power to dispose of his/her physical and mental powers, including both the capacity to produce and control of the body generally (extending to sexuality and reproduction); the power to dispose of the means of production; the power to select a place a residence; the power to associate with others and establish stable bonds; the power to decide on the manner in which one's children will be raised; and the (political) power to fix the rules governing the affairs of the states in which one resides. Slaves are distinguished from other groups—helots, serfs, sharecroppers, poor but propertied peasants, and propertyless proletarians—by the combination of the breadth and the depth of the limits on their powers. The limits extend over all aspects of life, the restrictions cut deeply into each aspect, and there is a corresponding breadth and depth to the powers that others have over them.

When I say that these powers of slaves were greatly confined, I mean to indicate that there was a wide range of activities (including those using the powers just enumerated) that slaves were required to engage in if the master sought to require them (e.g., sexual intercourse), or de facto prevented from pursuing at all if their master wanted to prevent them; or if they had some possibility of pursuing activities against the will of their master (e.g., selecting a place of residence by running away, withdrawing labor power by feigning illness, fixing the rules of association by establishing an independent "maroon" community, selecting a sexual partner by saying "no"), then the likelihood of success was small and the costs of failure (public humiliation, corporal punishment, death) were very great.

But slaves were not entirely powerless—mere extensions and instruments of another's will.[15] To be sure, their power was highly confined, dangerous to exercise, and nearly always insufficient to overturn slavery itself. But slaves did not, as a general matter, lack all forms of power, and sometimes asserted it to improve their conditions and shape the terms of order within the framework of slavery. As an ex-slave and blacksmith named J. W. Lindsay put it in an 1863 interview with the Freedman's Inquiry Commission, "Of course, they treated me pretty well, for the reason that I would not allow them to treat me in any other way. If they attempted to use any barbarity, I would walk off before their faces."[16] Though Lindsay's remark is almost certainly an exaggeration, and certainly not a plausible generalization, it captures a truth that was put more subtly by Harriet Jacobs who said, "My master had power and law on his side; I had a determined will. There is might in each."[17]

The power of slaves was most clearly in evidence in the range of activities that are commonly grouped together as "slave resistance":[18]

First, a variety of forms of resistance could be pursued individually and were not threatening to slavery, including: "Taking" from masters (what slaves called "taking" the masters called "stealing"[19]), lying, feigning illness, slowing down the pace of work, damaging tools and animals, self-mutilation, suicide, infanticide, abortion, arson, murdering the master, and running away. Running away was particularly important as a display of power, both because it showed the costs that slaves could impose on masters (masters lost a considerable capital investment and needed to increase their investment in enforcement), and because running away could be a collective enterprise, sometimes indistinguishable in its effects on the sustainability of slavery from rebellions, as in the case of the massive exoduses of slaves (especially plantation slaves) in French West Africa beginning in 1895,[20] or in the massive fleeing of so-called "contraband" slaves during the American Civil War, or in the flight of more than twenty thousand slaves from Deceleia in the final decade of the Peloponnesian War.

A second form of resistance—less frequent, but also more collective and threatening—was the widespread phenomenon of "maroon" communities.[21] Established by runaway slaves, some maroon communities were quite small—the Hanglip community near Cape Town; the watoro communities on the Swahili coast; the various Western African cases of maroon activity in the eighteenth and nineteenth centuries; and the many maroon colonies in the southern United States (particularly in the eighteenth century), some based on Indian-black alliances. Others were large-scale and long-standing—including the Jamaican communities established in the 1650s, consolidated through the first Maroon War of 1725–1740, and recognized by a treaty with the British in 1738; and several of the Brazilian *quilombos*, in particular the *quilombo* of Palmares—an African state in Pernambuco and Alagoas, which lasted for nearly a century (from c.1605 to 1695), included (on some estimates) as many as twenty to thirty thousand slaves, and fought off some eighteen Dutch and Portuguese expeditions over a period of more than fifty years.

Finally, most dramatically, there are slave revolts: three major rebellions in Italy and Sicily between 140 and 70 B.C., the first of which involved some two hundred thousand rebels, and the last (led by Spartacus in 73–71 B.C.) involving as many as one hundred fifty thousand rebels; the 14-year war of the Zanj against the Abassid Empire in the mid-ninth century; the one significant slave rebellion per decade in the Guineas in the eighteenth and early nineteenth centuries (one of which involved some ten to twenty thousand slaves); and the revolution in Saint Dominique stimulated by the French Revolution.[22]

These examples underscore the limits of the extension-of-will and ownership conceptions of slavery: To appreciate the power of slaves we must distinguish real from legal disabilities, and from the public interpretation of those disabilities. Slaves of course suffered from legal disabilities, which both codified and contributed to their lack of power. But their general lack of legally codified or publicly acknowledged rights also exaggerated their real situation. Thus the slaves were commonly able to do what the law denied them the right to do.

For example, slave "marriages" were not recognized at law, but more or less stable unions were part of the practice of virtually all slave societies.[23] And while slaves had no legal right to control the pace of their work, they had, as a general matter, some power—highly qualified, limited, and always dangerous to exercise—to help to shape it through various forms of resistance and threats of resistance. While, then, the actual terms of association among slaves themselves and between slaves and masters reflected the need to find a stable accommodation between agents with vastly different powers, the legal and moral representation of those relations denied that need, emphasizing instead the unilateral dictation of terms and conditions by masters, and the absence of a capacity for independent action by slaves.

Force and Consent

Premising this conception of slavery as a distinctive form of power, we come now to the question: How was this form reproduced?

First, through force. Force plays a central role in the initial enslavement of individuals and groups. Voluntary enslavement is quite rare in the history of slavery. War and kidnapping, in contrast, are among the most familiar means for initially enslaving nonslave populations, though most slaves were born into it.[24] Furthermore, masters themselves, or their agents (drivers, overseers, etc.), commonly deployed force—in particular, the force of the lash[25]—directly against slaves. Throughout antiquity, slaves alone were subject to corporal punishment, and were permitted to give evidence only under torture.[26] Greek and Roman slave owners had the right to punish and torture their own slaves for offenses committed against the master and on his property.[27] And Orlando Patterson estimates that in 75 percent of slave societies, masters received either negligible or mild punishment for killing slaves.[28]

But the use of force against slaves was not simply a common feature of slavery. According to a seventeenth-century Brazilian saying, "Whoever wants to profit from his Blacks must maintain them, make them work well, and beat them even better; without this there will be no service or gain."[29] Force, that is, was an essential feature whose role can be explained in terms of the basic properties of slavery.

To see how, let us distinguish symbolic, distributive, and productive uses of force. Force is used symbolically when masters use it to exemplify or express the public understanding of slaves as fully subordinate to them, on analogy with the practice of giving slaves new names, or requiring them to wear special forms of clothing. I will put this symbolic use to the side here, principally because we are not able to understand the central role of violence in slave systems, or the patterns in the use of violence against slaves, in terms of its role as a symbol of domination and emblem of servitude.

Force is used distributively when it is deployed to ensure a favorable distribution of the benefits of social order—to ensure, that is, a greater share of the benefits than one would be able to secure through bargaining on equal terms. The importance of the distributive use of force can be underscored by noting that slavery commonly emerges under conditions of labor scarcity.[30] With labor relatively scarce, owners of land and other nonhuman resources would face a relatively unfavorable bargaining position, if they had to bargain. As a Dr. Collins, a planter in the West Indies, wrote in an 1811 treatise, "the sugar colonies, *in their present state of slender population* [emphasis added], can only be wrought by slaves, or by persons so much at our command, as to be obliged to labor whether they will or not." Drawing the natural consequence about the use of force as a way to ensure that slaves fulfill their obligations, he says that, "Where slavery is established, and the proportion of slaves outnumbers their masters ten to one, terror must operate to keep them in subjection, and terror can only be produced by occasional examples of severity."[31]

But the distributive use, too, does not explain the patterns in the use of force in different slave systems, in particular the especially high levels of force used against slaves involved in plantation agriculture and mining. This pattern suggests that force did not serve simply to symbolize or preserve inequalities of power, but also was deployed as a means of eliciting effort. I refer to this as "the productive use of force." Force is used productively, then, when it is employed to provide incentives to increase the level of output (for example, by increasing labor intensity), rather than simply to ensure a favorable distribution of a fixed output.

The productive use has a familiar economic rationale. Limited in their power, slaves drew limited benefits from social cooperation, and, since they did not have to sell their labor to gain their subsistence, such benefits as they did get were importantly independent from their activity. So masters faced problems in motivating slaves to work. Force was *one* solution (we will come to the others). As Adam Smith put it, "A person who can acquire no property, can have no other interest but to eat as much, and to labor as little as possible. Whatever work he does beyond what is sufficient to purchase his own maintenance, can be squeezed out of him by violence only, and not by any interest of his own."[32] Smith's contention about "violence only" is overstated, in ways that will become clear when I discuss the use of positive incentives. But it captures an important problem for masters, and provides a good characterization of the basis of the productive use of force.

Appreciating the scope and limits of the productive use of force requires attention to the costs (to masters) of using force as distinct from other incentives.[33] It might require a staff of overseers, or some other diversion of resources from more productive uses, and might damage the human beings one is seeking to "motivate." Those costs would be worth incurring, however, if they were low relative to the benefits generated by the use of force.

Two conditions help to produce such a violence-generating cost-benefit structure. First, the costs of enforcement depend in part on the nature of the activities being enforced. And the costs of using force are likely to be relatively low when—as in important areas of agriculture and mining—performance is easy to monitor (the tasks are straightforward, can be performed in groups or gangs, and performance is easily measurable), and the work sufficiently distasteful that considerable material incentives would be required to motivate its performance.

The benefit side depends on the responsiveness of slaves to force as against compensation. Thus, force will be encouraged if slaves have a "target" income beyond which they are relatively unresponsive to further material incentives, and if the tasks they are expected to perform require intensive effort, rather than high levels of skill and attention. The reason for this is that intensive effort can plausibly be motivated by threats of pain rather than promises of reward.

This cost-benefit structure is characteristic of work in agriculture and mining. And, as I indicated, we do see force playing an especially central role in slavery when slaves are integrated into the economy, more particularly when they work in mines and on plantations (more so with cotton than tobacco), and, in the case of sugar, more in planting and harvesting cane than in milling it.[34] Under such circumstances, as Dr. Collins put it, "a system of remuneration alone is inadequate, for the reward must ever be incommensurate to the service, where labour is misery, and rest, happiness."[35] In contrast, we find other means of eliciting effort from slaves who were more skilled, or located in urban settings.

The maintenance of slavery could not, then, proceed through force alone.[36] Masters wanted to elicit greater effort, slaves typically faced impossible odds if they sought their own emancipation, and the result was superficially more consensual forms of servitude. Abstracting from endless varieties of compromise and accommodation, varying across time and place, we can distinguish two broad ways to make servitude (superficially) more voluntary: First, masters deployed positive incentives—what Dockès has called the "paraphernalia of 'voluntary' servitude"[37]—including material reward, authority, autonomy, family security, and manumission. The importance of the strategic use of incentives is a common theme in ancient and modern treatises on slave management. Genovese quotes an overseer making the strategic case for permitting slaves to pursue private cultivation: "Every means are used to encourage them, and impress on their minds the advantage of holding property, and the disgrace attached to idleness. Surely, if industrious for themselves, they will be so for their masters, and no Negro, with a well-stocked poultry house, a small crop advancing, a canoe partly finished, or a few tubs unsold, all of which he calculates soon to enjoy, will ever run away. In ten years I have lost by absconding, forty-seven days, out of nearly six hundred Negroes."[38] Similarly, a Brazilian advice book instructs planters in Rio de Janeiro that: "Their gardens and what they produce in them cause them to acquire a certain love of country, distract them a bit from slavery, and delude them into believing they have a small right to property. . . . Extreme discomfort dries up their hearts, hardens them, and inclines them to evil."[39] Autonomy, in the form of time free from labor, for example, was distributed with similar aims. A West Indian planter summarized this strategy:

[T]he best way of rewarding them . . . is to assign them a task, regulated by [a] given quantity, and to require as much from them every day, leaving them to effect it at what hours they please, and *let them enjoy to their own use, whatever time they do it in less*. This will encourage every negro to make his utmost exertion, in consequence of which, the work of twelve hours will be dispatched in ten, and with much more satisfaction to themselves.[40]

According to Frederick Douglass, holidays were among the "most effective means in the hands of the slaveholder in keeping down the spirit of insurrection. . . . The holidays serve as conductors or safety valves, to carry off the rebellious spirit of enslaved humanity." Emphasizing the role of holidays as an incentive, he says that they are "part and parcel of the gross fraud, wrong, and inhumanity of slavery. They are professedly a custom established by the benevolence of the slaveholders; but I undertake to say that, it is the result of selfishness. . . . They do not give the slaves this time because they would not like to have their work during its continuance, but because they know it would be unsafe to deprive them of it."[41]

A majority of slave systems relied as well on practices of manumission through which slaves were individually emancipated by their masters, though rates of manumission varied greatly across different slave systems.[42] The practice might take the form of self-purchase, with the slave using his or her *peculium* to pay for freedom (the Cuban *coartacion* and Islamic *murgu* both involved gradual self-purchase). Other standard processes included freeing of concubines, emancipating the children of concubines, and manumitting slaves as displays of piety in Islamic societies. A central motivating idea behind the practice of manumission is stated clearly in a Peripatetic treatise on economics: "It is essential that each slave should have a clearly defined goal (*telos*). It is both just and advantageous to offer freedom as a prize—when the prize and the period of time in which it can be attained, are clearly defined, this will *make them work willingly*."[43] Aristotle, too, notes in the *Politics*, that "it is expedient that liberty should always be held out to [slaves] as the reward of their services."[44]

In light of Aristotle's official views about slavery, the proposed rationale for this strategy is puzzling. According to Book 1 of his *Politics*, some human beings are naturally slaves—those lacking the capacity for deliberation—and so are appropriately subordinated to those possessed of adequate deliberative powers. More particularly, natural masters have the capacity to foresee by the exercise of mind, whereas natural slaves have only the power to implement such foresight with their bodies. But to say that slaves will work willingly when they have a goal and can see how their present actions connect to the achievement of that goal, suggests that slaves have greater powers of deliberation and foresight than this justification permits. Here we see a characteristic tension between the public justifications for slavery and features of the practice of slavery, tensions I will emphasize in my later discussion of slave interests and the injustice of slavery.

Alongside force and positive incentives, cultural representations of slavery as reasonable—religious and ethical representations justifying slavery—also figure in explaining compliance.

Rousseau's *Social Contract* emphasizes what has come to be a commonplace of modern social theory: that the "strongest is never strong enough to be master all the time, unless he transforms force into right and obedience into duty."[45] The thought is that existing power is made more powerful by public ideas that represent it as a necessity, make a virtue of such necessity, and thereby suggest that the terms of order are an object of common consent and that subjects willingly comply. It seems indisputable that slavery was sustained in part by the acceptance on the part of slaves of religious and ethical views that present their status as suitable for them, and by the more willing compliance resulting from such acceptance: though vast inequalities of power typically excluded determined resistance, the phenomenology of compliance appears not to have been exhausted by strategic accommodation to those inequalities. But three qualifications are equally important.

First, slaves typically did not simply embrace the dominant religious and ethical interpretations of their nature and condition. More commonly, they either developed syncretic religious views, combining religious conceptions and practices formed prior to enslavement with distinctive interpretations of the dominant religious tradition—as in the case of Afro-Baptist conceptions of the soul,[46] or in the reported case of a religious confraternity in Salvador, Brazil, called "Confraternity of our Lady of the Good Death"[47]—or pursued dual systems of religious belief and practice, as with the simultaneous embrace by Brazilian slaves of Bantu and Yoruban cults as well as Christianity. Syncretism and dualism provided frameworks for incorporating themes favorable to the interests of slaves into slave religions.[48]

American Afro-Baptism, for example, rejected doctrines of original sin and predestination, and emphasized Old Testament themes of earthly deliverance, comparing the situation and prospects of slaves with the deliverance of the Jews from bondage in Egypt.[49] Thus, the "Freedman's Hymn": "Shout the glad tidings o'er Egypt's Dark Sea; Jehovah has triumphed, his people are free." Similarly, the religious views characteristic of East African coastal slaves blended hinterland beliefs and practices with a distinctive form of Islam, which rejected the dominant conception of sharp divisions within God's creation in favor of an emphasis on the importance of love for the Prophet and the possibility of attaining religious purity through that love.[50]

Second, even when slave understandings served as a basis for an accommodation to slavery, the fact that they were not fully accom-

modations turned them into potential sources of "internal normative criticism" and resistance. By "internal normative criticism"
(sometimes called "restorationist" or "traditionalist" criticism) I
mean the criticism of practices by appeal to understandings, norms,
and values that are, at some level of generality, widely shared.

So, for example, we find cases in which slaves appear to embrace
the language and moral ideals of a dominant paternalistic conception of the relations between masters and slaves, thus describing and
evaluating their own position on the model of relations between
parents and children.[51] The practical correlates of this paternalism—what gave it experiential resonance—were the various positive
incentives I just discussed. But while masters would characterize
their paternalist "obligations" to provide such incentives and the
various actions undertaken in fulfillment of those obligations as expressions of their own benevolence, and the benefits they conferred
on slaves as grants of *privilege* revocable at will, slaves appear to have
interpreted them in terms of masters' obligations and/or slaves'
rights.

Such slave interpretations served in turn as bases for resisting unilateral shifts in the traditional terms of relation between masters and
slaves—for example, in Confederate states during the Civil War, or
in areas of French West Africa, Coastal Guinea, and the East African
coast that experienced large-scale slave exoduses in the late nineteenth and early twentieth centuries.[52] While masters might have
taken such shifts to be legitimate revocations of privilege, the slaves
took them to be infringements of obligations and violations of enti-
tlements. Similarly, we find slave resistance in the mid- and late nineteenth century in the Sokoto Caliphate in the western Sudan
organized around millennial interpretations of dominant Islamic
ideals, ideals that had served earlier in the century to mobilize slaves
to join in the *jihad* that had established the caliphate.[53]

Finally, no sharp and useful distinction can be drawn between the
use of internal norms to criticize practices and more radical forms
of criticism that reject those norms in favor of other norms. And the
views of some slaves—how many we will never know—seem most
plausibly characterized as continuing internal normative criticism to
the point where it passes into external criticism.

Consider a few examples. Frederick Douglass tells the story of bringing his weekly wages of six dollars to his master, and sometimes being given six cents to "encourage" him. But, Douglass says, this "had the opposite effect. I regarded it as a sort of admission of my right to the whole. The fact that he gave me any part of my wages was proof, to my mind, that he believed me entitled to the whole of them."[54] Or consider what is sometimes referred to as the "antinomianism" of American slaves, reflected for example in the willingness of slaves to endorse theft from masters—they referred to such "theft" as "taking," not "stealing"—while acknowledging the wrong of theft from other slaves.[55] Commenting on this willingness, Thomas Jefferson observes:

> That disposition to theft, with which [slaves] have been branded, must be ascribed to their situation, and not to any depravity of the moral sense. The man in whose favor no laws of property exist, probably feels himself less bound to respect those made in favor of others. When arguing for ourselves, we lay it down as fundamental, that laws, to be just, must give reciprocation of right; that without this, they are mere arbitrary rules, founded in force, and not in conscience, and it is a problem which I give the master to solve, whether the religious precepts against the violation of property were not framed for him as well as his slave? and whether the slave may not justifiably take a little from one who has taken all from him, as he may slay one who would slay him?[56]

Similarly, Brazilian slaves are reported to have sung these words:

> The white man says: the black man steals
> The black man steals for good reason.
> Mister white man also steals
> When he makes us slave.[57]

Are these cases in which slaves embrace such plausibly widespread internal norms, as that people may legitimately take back what has been stolen from them, steal in cases of extreme need, or own what they make? Or does the application of these norms to themselves show that slaves are advancing a divergent interpretation of widely accepted norms? What seems most plausible is that the very idea that these norms apply to slaves as well as nonslaves, and the attendant suggestion of the moral equality of masters and slaves, is such a departure from dominant understandings—such a distinctive interpretation of the moral community covered by the norms—that we have now passed from internal to external criticism. At the same time, this expansion of the moral community and the associated passage from internal to external criticism is arguably anticipated when the internal norms are presented to slaves as considerations they should recognize as binding, and by appeals to reciprocity in justifications of slavery.[58] In any case, it seems clear that no crisp line can be drawn between different forms of normative criticism, and that the pursuit of one may often lead to the pursuit of the other.

Whereas the claim that moral acceptance leads to compliance has some force, then, that force is limited. Its limits are not to be found (at least not exclusively) in the rejection by slaves of moral ideas, or their failure to take moral notions seriously. To the contrary, they are marked by the fact that regnant norms and alternative interpretations of those norms can themselves serve as bases for moral criticism of social arrangements, and by the fact that internal criticism can pass over into more radical forms of moral criticism that appeal to a distinctive set of moral ideals. But to understand better the critical use of norms, the development of alternative interpretations of norms, the uses slaves made of their power, and the importance and prevalence of positive incentives, we need an account of slave interests.

Interests

Slaves had interests in material well-being, autonomy, and dignity. Perhaps that goes without saying. But the enterprise of attributing interests to people seems to some arbitrary, and attributions of these interests to slaves may strike others as anachronistic, romantic, ideologically blinded, or simply ignorant. These interests, however, play two roles in my argument: the case for both the injustice of slavery and its limited viability turns on the claim that slavery conflicts with the legitimate interests of slaves in material well-being, autonomy, and dignity. So I need to say enough about them to explain why that later appeal is plausible.

As a general matter, then, a course of action or state of affairs is in a person's interests just in case that course or state is the best way to realize an end that he or she would affirm on reflection—considering his or her life as a whole, conflicts between and among current aims, the strength of various desires, and the conditions that may have engendered current ends—given full information and full imaginative powers.[59] In practice, however, we base attributions of interests on a person's actual ends (abjuring the hypothetical aims that figure in the definition) because we in effect assume that reflection would not produce changes in the relevant ends. The burden of proof falls on challengers to attributions based on actual ends; they must provide a reason for thinking that those ends would shift on reflection. Applying these general observations to my comments here, I will sketch some evidence that slaves cared substantially about material well-being, autonomy, and dignity, leaving it to those who doubt the attributions of interests to show that reflection would have dissolved these concerns.

First, then, the phenomena of resistance and revolt support the view that at least some slaves cared greatly about autonomy—enough to accept significant risks, for example, the risks taken by the six thousand crucified slaves who lined the road from Capua to Rome after the defeat of the rebellion led by Spartacus (one hundred thousand slaves were killed in this revolt).[60] This willingness to accept risks for autonomy is clearest in the case of individual runaways, maroons, and rebels.

Furthermore, this aspiration to autonomy appears to be quite general. Referring to the phenomenon of mass departures by slaves in, for example, Northern Nigeria, Guinea, and the French Sudan between 1895 and 1910, Lovejoy claims that this "exodus was so large that it represents one of the most significant slave revolts in history."[61] But even the less determined forms of resistance indicate a desire for greater control by slaves over the circumstances of their lives.

Second, the provision of material incentives and manumission, and the various other paraphernalia of voluntary servitude, indicate that slaves wanted material improvement and autonomy, and that masters, aware of those wants, sought to elicit more cooperative behavior by promising to reward such behavior by satisfying those wants. Earlier I mentioned the passages in the Peripatetic treatise addressing manumission. We find closely parallel arguments in the Roman agricultural treatises of Cato, Varro, and Columella, the last of which mentions the importance of "decent living conditions, of time off from work, the fostering of family life among slaves," and above all the prospect of manumission in encouraging cooperative behavior.[62]

Third, evidence for the desire for autonomy is provided by American slave narratives, and the interviews conducted by both the Freedman's Inquiry Commission and the Works Progress Administration. They provide substantial testimony on the aspiration to autonomy; indeed, the slave narratives are organized around that aspiration. And they commonly return to the theme suggested by the phenomenon of manumission: that the desire for autonomy is not simply in service of material improvement.

Mary Prince, for example, writes that: "All slaves want to be free—to be free is very sweet. I have been a slave myself—and I know what slaves feel—I can tell by myself what other slaves feel, and by what they have told me. The man that says slaves be quite happy in slavery—that they don't want to be free—that man is either ignorant or a lying person."[63] Writing some eighteen hundred years earlier, the ex-slave Phaedrus suggested that the classical Roman fable of the dog, who is well-fed and has a place to live but who is kept in chains during the day, and the wolf, who is hungry and homeless but free, expresses the slaves' sense of how sweet liberty is.[64]

Returning to the narratives, my claim that they are organized around the aspiration to freedom is best captured by a passage near the end of Linda Brent's *Incidents in the Life of a Slave Girl*, where she says: "Reader, my story ends with freedom; not in the usual way, with marriage. I and my children are now free! We are as free from the power of slaveholders as are the white people of the north; and though that, according to my ideas, is not saying a great deal, it is a vast improvement in *my* condition."[65]

Fourth, the central role of force in establishing and sustaining slave systems also argues for the presence of interests in material well-being and autonomy. The fact that slave "recruitment" typically involved force indicates that slavery was rarely chosen by slaves—and then only under difficult circumstances—and that observing the conditions of others who had been enslaved did not encourage self-enslavement.[66] Further, the fact that force and threats of force were regular features of the lives of slaves indicates that masters thought that slaves themselves would not consent to the continuation of slavery, given an alternative.

Finally, this claim about interests receives support from the combination of ambiguous acceptance and rejection of the regnant justifications of slavery. The fact that slaves did not fully internalize regnant justifications for slavery, together with the fact that an acceptance of the justifications would have put them at disadvantage in pursuing material well-being and autonomy, provides indirect support for the claim that they had these fundamental interests. Since full acceptance might have disarmed slaves even when the balance of forces turned in their favor, they were led away from it. Lacking the resources to forge wholly independent and distinctive ideals, they developed variants of the dominant views with an affinity to their interests, or embraced alternatives to those dominant ideas. The interests of slaves are, in short, reflected in the content and interpretation of the dominant norms and ideals themselves.

Coming now to dignity: the central feature of dignity for our purposes is its social aspect—that it involves a desire for public recognition of one's worth. Though a person can sustain a sense of self-worth in the face of repeated insults, still, public recognition is related to dignity in two ways: first, persons with a sense of their own worth regard such recognition as an appropriate acknowledgment of that worth; and, second, recognition provides psychological support for that sense, making it easier to sustain. In particular, having a sense of dignity, we want others to recognize that we have aims and aspirations and to acknowledge the worth of those aims and aspirations by, inter alia, providing conditions (opportunities and resources) that enable us to pursue them.

Several considerations support the attribution to slaves of an interest in conditions that support and are appropriate to a sense of dignity. First, when we consider the few oral and written records left by slaves, from the fables collected by Phaedrus to American slave narratives, what we find are repeated assertions of their sense of self-worth, and the ways that their conditions violate that sense.[67]

Second, as I already indicated, the normative understandings of slavery held by slaves press the worth of the slaves into focus. This sense of worth is suggested both by the content of those views—for example, by the slave interpretations of dominant norms—and by the very concern that there be a justification for the slave condition. For example, I mentioned earlier the claim that benefits conferred by masters are matters of right, not privilege. A particularly striking statement of this is provided by an ex-slave named Benjamin Miller. In a Freedman's Inquiry Commission interview, Miller says: "I was in bondage in Missouri, too. I can't say that my treatment was bad. In one respect I say it was not bad, but in another I consider it was as bad as could be. I was a slave. That covers it all. I had not the rights of a man."[68]

Third, the desire for dignity is closely linked to a desire for social conditions that support autonomy and decent material circumstances. For such conditions provide support for a sense of dignity, both because of the obvious difficulties in maintaining a sense of self-worth without resources, and because having a decent level of resources (or at least a substantial opportunity to secure them) is itself an index of respect.[69] This connection between material welfare, autonomy, and dignity suggests that the pursuit of welfare and autonomy may in part be animated by a desire for the public affirmation and recognition ingredient in conditions that enable people to secure their autonomy and material welfare.

Taking these remarks about the different interests together, I will hereafter use the term "fundamental interests" as shorthand for the three interests I have just discussed.

III. Injustice and the Limits of Slavery

Slavery, I have proposed, is best understood as a particular form of power; that form was reproduced through force, strategic incentives, and moral-religious norms; and slave interests in material improvement, autonomy, and dignity are revealed in the practices that reproduce slavery. With these claims as background, I come to the main argument about the injustice of slavery and its viability, which I will pursue by taking up, in turn, the four theses stated earlier.

Slavery and Slave Interests

Thesis One: *The basic structure of slavery as a system of power stands in sharp conflict with fundamental slave interests in material well-being, autonomy, and dignity.*

Consider, first, the interest in material well-being. The intuitive argument for this aspect of Thesis One is that being a slave is materially undesirable because slaves are relatively powerless. Limited power means limited capacity to bargain for advantage, which means limited capacity to protect basic material interests in nourishment and health. So it seems plausible that it is materially better not to be a slave, even if one is a serf or poor peasant. Given the breadth and depth of the limits that define the condition of slave, one can expect to have more power if one is not a slave and to be able to turn that power to material advantage.

Against this intuitive argument, it has been said—most famously in Fogel and Engerman's *Time on the Cross*—that the relative powerlessness of slaves can work to their material advantage: Because of the limits on their power, they can be subjected to the productive use of force.[70] If they are, output per worker increases, enabling slaves themselves to live a materially better life than if they were emancipated. The intuitive idea is straightforward. Suppose two modes of production are in operation: peasant farms worked by family labor and plantations worked by slave gangs. Suppose, too, that output per worker is greater on the plantations than on the family farms. Greater output per head in the plantation system permits owners to provide a higher standard of living to slaves than is available to the family farmers. But why couldn't families in the small-holding sector pool their resources to form larger units and reap the benefits of the scale economies? Or if the costs of pooling are too high, why couldn't the small holders offer their labor to plantation owners for a wage in excess of what they can earn on their own farms? Why is being enslaved essential to reaping the benefits?

The answer lies in the fact that increased output per worker on large plantations is not generated by increasing returns to scale, but by high intensity, continuous work imposed by masters in the plantation sector on slaves: Fogel estimates that slaves on medium and large plantations worked 76 percent more intensely per hour than free Southern farmers or slaves on small plantations.[71] Because of the nonpecuniary costs of such intense and continuous labor, no one would perform it willingly without substantial pecuniary compensation. Because slaves were relatively powerless, they could be forced to do it. And when they were forced, output per person increased, and slaves themselves ended up consuming more than they would have been able to consume if they were not slaves. As Fogel and Engerman put it, "it was only by applying force that it was possible to get blacks to accept gang labor without having to pay a premium that was in excess of the gains from economies of scale."[72] Why, then, isn't relative powerlessness in the slave's material interest?

Two considerations suggest doubts about the force of this argument. First, the argument about material well-being assumes that we can assess the material welfare of a group simply by considering its level of compensation. But what about the interest in not performing intense, undesirable labor? And what about the fact that increased consumption may fail to compensate for the greater expenditures of energy required by such labor? To be materially well off is in part a matter of being well nourished. But nourishment is not a function simply of food consumption levels.[73] The same basket of food can produce widely different levels of nourishment depending on such factors as metabolic rates, body size, sex, activity levels, and access to medical services. But the argument I have been considering assumes that the level of output per person was increased by imposing conditions of intense labor and pain that presumably decrease the level of nourishment resulting from a fixed quantity of food consumption.[74] To argue, under these conditions, that slavery improves material welfare by enabling an increased level of food consumption is, then, a form of fetishism.[75]

Put otherwise, in the passage I cited earlier, Fogel and Engerman refer to "economies of scale" associated with gang labor. But their argument about the material benefits of powerlessness is, as I have indicated, not really about scale economies, but about the forcible extraction of more intense and continuous labor.[76] Thus, Fogel estimates that gang-system plantations in the South had a 39 percent advantage in total factor productivity over free farms, but that this advantage was due to "the greater intensity of labor per hour" imposed by the gang system.[77] Acknowledging this, we need to consider whether the added income made available by forced high labor intensity sufficed to compensate for its burdens. Fogel notes some suggestive evidence: while slaves "earned 15 percent more income per clock-time hour . . . their income per equal-efficiency hour was 33 percent less than that of free farmers."[78]

Second, the argument requires both that slavery generate increased output per head, and that slaves reap some of the gains. But in determining whether slavery is materially beneficial for slaves, we cannot include a specified level of compensation in the characterization of the slave condition. I have not included such specification in the characterization of slavery as a form of power. More substantively, because slaves were relatively powerless—not merely subordinate at work, but relatively powerless across the board—they would not have the power to enforce a specified share of the potential gains, or perhaps even bargain for more than a bare minimum. Even, then, if relative powerlessness helps produce potential material gains, such powerlessness makes it unreasonable to expect to benefit in the distribution of those gains. So, the position of slave will, as a general matter, be the most materially disadvantageous social position.

The conflict between slavery and the autonomy interests of slaves is more straightforward. Autonomy is a matter of being able to set and to pursue one's aspirations. To be in the relatively powerless position of slave is on the whole to lack just such power, or to have it as a result of conditions that are more fortuitous in the lives of slaves than they are even in the lives of other socially subordinate groups. This is clear not just in the arena of work, but (particularly for women slaves) with respect to sexuality as well.[79]

The case of dignity seems equally clear. A characteristic feature of slave systems is that both the organization of power and the symbolic understandings of that organization—especially the pervasive symbolism of social death—deny that slaves command public respect.[80] Thus the organization of power largely deprived slaves of the powers required for advancing their interests; and the symbolic expression of that organization represented slaves as extensions of the wills of their masters or as their property, as having no legitimate social place, and as legitimately denied the powers required for protecting and advancing their interests.

In his opinion in *Dred Scott*, Chief Justice Taney said that when the Constitution was written, blacks had "for more than a century been regarded as beings of an inferior order . . . so far inferior that they had no rights which the white man was bound to respect."[81] Because the interest in dignity carries with it an interest in such respect and recognition—both as appropriate to and as supportive of the sense of dignity—both the structure of slavery and the forms of public culture that grow up around it are more sharply at odds with the interests of slaves than alternative systems are with the interests of their members. Emphasizing the concern for dignity, its independent standing, and the hostility of slavery to it, an unidentified former slave said: "We knowed freedom was on us, but we didn't know what was to come with it. We thought we was going to get rich like the white folks. We thought we was going to be richer than the white folks, 'cause we was stronger and knowed how to work, and the whites didn't, and we didn't have to work for them any more. But it didn't turn out that way. We soon found out that freedom could make folks proud, but it didn't make 'em rich."[82]

Injustice

Thesis Two: *Slavery is unjust because the relative powerlessness of slaves, reflected in the conflict between slavery and slave interests, implies that it could not be the object of a free, reasonable, and informed agreement.*

In stating this second thesis, I introduce a particular account of justice, based on an idealized notion of consensus—a free, reasonable, and informed agreement.[83] I will not defend this account of justice here, nor does the argument depend on its details. What does matter are the intuitive ideas that the ideal consensus view articulates: that a just arrangement gives due consideration to the interests of all its members, and that we give due consideration when we treat people as equals, taking their good fully into account in our social arrangements. The ideal consensus view articulates this requirement of treating people as equals by asking what arrangements people themselves would agree to, if they looked for arrangements acceptable to all, understood as equals. By a *free* agreement, then, I mean an agreement reached under conditions in which there are no bargaining advantages. An agreement is *reasonable* only if it is reached on the basis of interests that can be advanced consistent with the aim of arriving at a free agreement. I will hereafter call such interests "legitimate interests." An *informed* agreement is one in which the parties correctly understand the consequences of the agreement.

According to this ideal consensus view of justice, then, slavery is unjust because it could not be the object of a free and reasonable agreement. Why not? What features of slavery preclude it from being the object of such an agreement? Given the relative powerlessness that defines the condition of slavery, the force essential to sustaining it, and the public interpretation of slaves that is encouraged by that distribution of power, it is reasonable for slaves to have very low expectations about the satisfaction of their fundamental interests, lower even than in alternative systems of direct social subordination. Given this low expectation, slaves could only "consent" to their condition if the relations of power between masters and slaves determined the rational course of their conduct. But such power is excluded by the requirement of a free agreement.

This rejection is reasonable because the fundamental slave interests that lie at its foundation are legitimate. Advancing them was consistent with acknowledging that everyone has the fundamental interests, and the structure of the social order ought to accommodate those interests. While a material gain for slaves may well have involved reduced expectations at dominant social positions—I am not assuming that the elimination of slavery must represent a Pareto-improvement over a status quo with slavery—those expectations would still have been considerably greater than the expectations of slaves under slavery. Moreover, a gain in dignity for slaves need imply no loss in dignity for masters. The rejection of slavery would have been reasonable, then, because the elimination of slavery would have improved the conditions of slaves with respect to their fundamental interests; but that improvement need not have imposed on any group a burden at all comparable to that borne by slaves under slavery.[84]

Consider, by contrast, the interest in having slaves—which I suppose at least some masters to have had. This was not a morally legitimate interest, since it could not be advanced as a basis for an agreement consistent with the aim of reaching a free agreement on terms of cooperation. Slavery was in the sharpest conflict with the fundamental interests of slaves. Given that slaves had these interests, masters could only propose slavery if they were not aiming to find mutually acceptable terms of social order, but instead seeking to advance their particular interests. And masters could not reasonably expect slaves to agree to terms that conflict with their interests simply because such an agreement would be advantageous to masters—not as part of a free agreement.

This rejection of slavery would have been an *informed* rejection in that it turns on the general features of slavery that I sketched earlier: that slaves are relatively powerless; because they are relatively powerless their legitimate interests in material well-being and autonomy are at best marginally and insecurely protected; such protection as they in fact receive results either from the whims of masters or from a precarious and shifting balance of power between masters and slaves; and since their interests are typically not recognized as significant either in the organization of power or in the dominant conceptions of slaves and their social standing, slavery is an insult to their dignity. This argument does not turn on identifying slavery with its most murderous forms or slaves as utterly powerless, nor does it assume that slaves are always and everywhere "worked like animals . . . [and] housed like animals," living lives of joyless degradation. Relative powerlessness itself suffices.[85]

Limited Viability

Thesis Three: *The conflict between slavery and the interests of slaves is an important source of the limited viability of slavery.*

Slavery is unjust, then, because it conflicts with certain interests of slaves—interests that are identified as morally legitimate by the ideal consensus view (and no doubt by other views). Does this injustice-making conflict help to account for the demise of slavery? And where, if at all, does the injustice itself enter in? As a first step to answering these questions, I defend the third thesis by sketching two sources of the limited viability of slavery—two lines of argument that figure as important strands in plausible accounts of abolition.

The first source emphasizes the *recognition of injustice*. The idea is that slavery is undermined in part because it was unjust, because that injustice was recognized, and that recognition motivated opposition. Here the injustice of slavery plays an explanatory role, roughly, by virtue of its being cognized and then serving to motivate moral opposition.

Let's separate the contention that recognition of injustice is relevant to explaining the demise of slavery into three components: some consequential opposition to slavery was motivated by moral conviction; the content of those moral convictions can reasonably be represented by the ideal consensus conception of justice that I have presented here; and those moral convictions are themselves explained in part by the injustice of slavery. Without this third point, it would not be the injustice itself that helps to explain the demise, but only the belief that slavery is wrong. I will consider the first two points here, and return later to the third.

First, then, it seems clear that moral opposition motivated at least some eighteenth- and nineteenth-century abolitionist opponents of slavery who fought against the slave trade and for the abolition of slavery, who objected to slavery on grounds of principle, whose interests are not sufficient to explain their opposition—Quakers being only the most familiar case—and whose opposition was important to abolition.[86] Fogel, who emphasizes the economic success and viability of American slavery, puts the case especially strongly: "[Slavery's] death was an act of 'econocide,' a political execution of an immoral system at its peak of economic success, incited by men ablaze with moral fervor."[87] Moral conviction also provides an explanation of some of the motivations of slaves, particularly those who were animated by external moral criticisms of slavery.

Concerning the second point: Slaves, I have suggested, were motivated to oppose slavery in part by indignation and outrage, and not only by their interests. But this does not suffice to show that they were motivated by a recognition of the injustice of slavery as I have characterized the notion of injustice here. Sometimes—in the case of internal moral criticism—their indignation could be explained by the fact that masters had violated traditional norms and customary understandings. But as I suggested in my earlier discussion of external criticism, the continuity between internal and external criticism, and the expanded conception of the moral community associated with such criticism, not all slave opposition can be explained in those terms. Among the forms of opposition that cannot be are the views advanced in the course of the Haitian revolution, in slave petitions in the United States, in Jamaica's 1831 Christmas rebellion, and in the views that animated the participation of ex-slaves in the fight against the Confederacy. In all these cases, opposition was shaped in part by the notions of due consideration and treating people as equals that provide the intuitive foundation of the ideal consensus conception.[88]

More generally, the conception of slavery—and not merely the slaves' own individual enslavement or the violations by masters of customary expectations—as unjust helps to explain the late eighteenth-century shift that Genovese has described from restorationist rebellions to revolutionary opposition to slavery.[89] Furthermore, this opposition (particularly the revolution in Ste. Dominque) was consequential, and contributed to the end of slavery by, among other things, helping to limit the expansion of slavery and contributing strength to movements to end the slave trade.

The case for the first two aspects of the recognition-of-injustice view seems plausible. Still, we have not yet arrived fully at the recognition of injustice; for that we must also vindicate the claim that there is an explanatory connection between the injustice of slavery and moral beliefs about it. I will discuss this issue later on, and respond in particular to the objection that all that matters here are beliefs about injustice, and that talk about "recognition" is misplaced.

The second view is what I call the *conflicting interests* account. This view locates viability problems in slavery directly in the conflict between slavery and the fundamental slave interests, without the mediation of moral beliefs. The contention is that these conflicts are a key source of pressure to move from slave to nonslave systems, because they are a source of conflict within slave systems and of disadvantages that slave systems face when they compete economically and conflict militarily with nonslave systems.

To bring out the content of this view, I want to note that it helps to explain the force and limits of classical economic arguments about the limits of slavery. Those arguments emphasize the costliness of slave labor, deriving from high enforcement costs, constrained productivity, and difficulties of securing a biologically reproductive slave population.[90] Adam Smith, for example, thought that slave labor was the most costly, and was imposed because of false pride and a desire to dominate, not for sound economic reasons.[91] The conflicting interests view argues that these liabilities of slavery result principally from difficulties in inducing the willing cooperation of slaves, and that those problems of motivation in turn reflect the underlying conflict of interests.

If that explanation is right then we should expect problems deriving from the conflicting interests to have noneconomic manifestations as well—for example, relative military weakness, overt slave resistance, and a loss of political confidence by owners.

Consider the military issue. Wars present two problems for slave systems. First, in a wide range of systems, slaves were either not trusted to fight, or otherwise excluded from fighting. With a segment of the population thus excluded, military potential is diminished. For example, the constraints slavery imposed on military potential became an important issue in the Confederacy in 1863–64. General Patrick Cleburne said that "slavery, from being one of our chief sources of strength at the commencement of the war, has now become, from a military point of view, one of our chief sources of weakness." To remedy this weakness, he proposed to recruit an army of slaves, and in return to guarantee freedom "within a reasonable time to every slave in the South who shall remain true to the Confederacy." But the slave-owning class resisted, and the Confederate Congress did not authorize black enlistment until March 1865. As a Mississippi congressman put it, "Victory itself would be robbed of its glory if shared with slaves." A Georgian made the even more telling observation that "The day you make soldiers of them is the beginning of the end of the revolution. If slaves will make good soldiers our whole theory of slavery is wrong."[92]

A second, closely related point is that slave societies are constantly threatened by "two-front wars," a problem that Aristotle counted among the chief considerations that make slavery a troublesome affair, thinking of the problems that the Thessalians faced from the Penestae, and that the helots gave to the Spartans, "for whose misfortunes they are always lying in wait."[93] In such cases, the slaves either rebel or fight for the other side while the society is under attack.[94]

Because of these problems of limited military potential and two-front wars, military conflicts—including conflicts surrounding Islamic *jihads*—served as one of the principal historical stimuli to emancipation.[95] The Emancipation Proclamation in 1863 is only the most familiar example of military manumission, and the failure of the Confederacy to enlist or manumit is, so to speak, the exception that proves the rule. In explaining his decision to issue the Emancipation Proclamation, Lincoln said in July 1862 that he had concluded that emancipation was "a military necessity, absolutely essential to the preservation of the Union. We must free the slaves or ourselves be subdued. The slaves were undeniably an element of strength to those who had their service, and we must decide that element should be with us or against us."[96] Bolivar and San Martin also used military manumissions as a fundamental strategy in the Independence Wars in Spanish America, giving the fight for independence an anti-slavery cast.[97] And a Roman imperial code compiled in A.D. 438 states that:

> Of course we believe that free-born persons are motivated by patriotism; nevertheless we exhort slaves too, by the authority of this edict, to offer themselves for the exertions of war as soon as possible, and if they take up arms as men fit for military service, they are to obtain the reward of freedom.[98]

In general, then, the conflicting-interests view contends that the demise of slavery results in part from the *practical advantages* in competition and conflict available to systems less sharply in conflict with the interests of their members than slavery is—advantages expressed through mechanisms akin to natural selection.

A problem for the conflicting interests theory is that it may appear to explain "too much." While conflicts between slavery and slave interests have been fundamental and persistent, slavery was not in permanent crisis. But the conflicting interests account does not imply that it would be. That account is not intended to provide a comprehensive explanation of the evolution and demise of slavery, but rather to characterize one important, destabilizing determinant

311

of that evolution. The importance and effects of conflicts between slave interests and slavery, manifest in internal opposition and in disadvantages in economic competition and military conflict, vary widely across systems of slavery and across social environments. More particularly, the pressures away from slavery produced by conflicts of interest are greatest in periods of military conflict or when slaves are used as productive laborers in a system that produces for external markets, as distinct from cases in which slaves are "accumulated" as luxury goods or as outward displays of status, or when the ratio of slave to free is high, slaves are relatively homogeneous (ethnically and linguistically), and regularly brought into contact with other slaves, thus reducing the barriers to collective action.

The importance and effects of conflicts between slave interests and slavery vary widely, then, across systems of slavery and across external environments. Absent the kinds of "environmental" factors I just mentioned, the problems rooted in conflicting interests will be less pressing. Despite such variations, however, slave systems do face viability problems resulting from forces internal to slavery, and those problems are important in understanding what happens in "unfavorable" environments.

Justice and Viability

Thesis Four: *Characterizing slavery as unjust conveys information relevant to explaining the demise of slavery that is not conveyed simply by noting that slavery conflicts with the interests of slaves.*

Suppose, then, that the conflict between slave interests and slavery limits the viability of slavery. What, then, does injustice have to do with limited viability? Why would the same limits not exist even if slave interests were not legitimate? What force is added to the explanation by noting that slave interests are morally weighty?

I suggest two ways that our understanding of the limits of slavery is aided by noting that moral weight. The first is provided by considerations about the recognition of injustice. Recall where we left the discussion of that recognition: I indicated that moral convictions motivated some consequential opposition to slavery, and that the content of those moral convictions could reasonably be characterized by the ideal consensus conception of justice. Still, the injustice of slavery is not perhaps evident in this argument. How does the injustice itself shape the moral motivations of opponents? It might be said that simple beliefs on the part of abolitionists and slaves that slavery is unjust suffice to motivate opposition, quite apart from the actual injustice of slavery.

The objection seems to me not to have much force since it is natural to want an explanation of the moral beliefs as well. And part of the explanation for the moral beliefs is that slaves have interests in material well-being, autonomy, and dignity, and are recognized as having them; that slavery sharply conflicts with those interests, and is recognized as so conflicting; and that those interests are legitimate, and recognized as such. And why is this sequence of points not naturally captured by saying that people believe slavery to be unjust in part because it is unjust? To see why this rendering is appropriate, consider the force of the "because" in "because it is unjust." We can interpret it as follows: Suppose people reason morally about the rightness or wrongness of slavery, and pursue that reasoning in light of an understanding of certain facts about slave interests and the conflict between slavery and those interests. Because the reasoning is moral, it is guided by the thought that the interests of slaves need to be given due consideration, as they are, for example, in the requirement of free agreement. Pursuing that reasoning, they will be driven to the conclusion that slavery is wrong: they do not see how slavery could result from a free agreement. (It is not that difficult to see how this might go: after all, we do something like this now when we ask whether slavery is wrong.)

What is essential is to acknowledge that slaves have legitimate interests. And the key to that acknowledgment is to see that slaves have the properties—for example, the interests and the capacity for deliberate action—that others have (masters, or other members of the free population) in virtue of which people are prepared to attribute legitimate interests to those others. (Recall the remark I cited earlier: "The day you make soldiers of them is the beginning of the end of the revolution. If slaves will make good soldiers our whole theory of slavery is wrong.") But this recognition is available to anyone who reflects on the practices that help to sustain slavery, in particular on the practice of providing the incentives I mentioned earlier. For those incentives are in effect the homage paid by a scheme of domination to fundamental human aspirations; to provide them is in effect to acknowledge that slaves have the relevant interests and capacities.[99]

Recall, for example, my earlier discussion of the tension between the Aristotelian view that slaves lack a substantial capacity to deliberate and the argument that slaves will be made more cooperative by providing them with the prize of freedom. To offer freedom as a goal is to assume that slaves do have powers of foresight and self-control; otherwise an offer of distant freedom would not be expected to shape current action. But this suggests the recognition that slaves have the powers that are relevant to their membership in the moral community, and so are bearers of legitimate interests. Or, to take a more prosaic example, consider the remark of a Wisconsin cavalry officer, made in light of the performance of the largely ex-slave black soldiers in the Civil War: "I never believed in niggers before, but by Jasus they are hell in fighting."[100]

Suppose, then, that one comes to understand certain facts, all of which can be recognized independent from the procedures of moral reasoning: that slaves share the natural properties that are sufficient for being subjects of legitimate interests, that they have the fundamental interests, and that slavery sharply conflicts with those interests. Moral reasoning about slavery, proceeding in light of these facts, and giving due consideration to the interests of slaves, is bound to recognize the interests as legitimate and to condemn slavery as unjust. To say, then, that the wrongness of slavery explains the moral belief is to note the following: that moral reasoning mandates the conclusion that slavery is unjust; and that the moral belief is produced in part by that kind of reasoning. And once the injustice is recognized, it is reasonable to expect that that recognition plays some role in motivation, that it contributes to the antagonism of slaves to slavery, that it adds nonslave opponents to the slave opponents, and that, once slavery is abolished, it helps to explain why there are not strong movements to bring it back.

The moral weight also figures implicitly in the conflicting interests view. To see how, keep in mind that an explanation of the demise of slavery is not simply an account of opposition to slavery, or of shifts away from slavery—an account of the evolution of institutional variation—but also an account of the eventual retention of nonslave arrangements, of the absence of "wandering" from slave to non-slave and then back. The competitive disadvantages of slave systems are important to understanding this retention. The conflict of slavery with legitimate slave interests, and the fact that masters' interests in preserving slavery are not legitimate, plausibly helps to "tip the balance" in favor of stable departures from slavery.

To see how, consider a remark from a nineteen-year-old black soldier and ex-slave, who, after the Battle of Nashville, used his furlough to pay a visit to his former mistress. She asked him: "You remember when you were sick and I had to bring you to the house and nurse you?" When he replied that he did remember, she responded: "And now you are now fighting me." To which the soldier said: "No'm, I ain't fighting you. I'm fighting to get free."[101] To appreciate the bearing of this remark on the issue here, recall that the rejection of slavery was reasonable and slave interests legitimate because the fundamental interests of slaves could be advanced consistent with the aim of reaching a free agreement. The fundamental interests that provide the basis for a reasonable rejection of slavery are shared by masters, and slavery imposes great hardship on slaves while alternatives to slavery do not impose a hardship on any other group comparable to the hardship imposed on slaves by slavery. Alternatives to slavery accommodate the interests of subordinate groups better than slavery does. Moreover, they provide substantial protections of the fundamental interests at the superordinate positions. By contrast, the slaveowner interest in maintaining slavery was not shared by slaves. Because slaves and masters shared the fundamental interests, slaves could reject slavery consistent with extending to masters the same standing that they desired for themselves. But masters could not have advanced their interest in maintaining slavery except by failing to extend to slaves the same recognition that masters desired for themselves. These facts about common and conflicting interests are the basis for the moral condemnation of slavery.

Suppose slave interests were not legitimate. Slaves might still have resisted just as much. But the economic and military disadvantages of slavery, the abolition of slavery, and the apparent stability of that abolition, would be more surprising. Suppose in particular that the fundamental interests were not capable of mutual satisfaction. Then we would expect dissatisfaction with abolition leading to struggles for slavery's reimposition. We would also not expect any particular practical advantage to be conferred by the absence of slavery if those other systems conflicted with the interests of some of their members as sharply as slavery does with some of its members. For if the conflicts were as sharp, then they would have the same difficulties as slavery in eliciting cooperation. Of course, other systems of social subordination are also unjust. But slavery is on the extreme end of powerlessness; alternatives to it permit greater space for material improvement, increased scope for autonomy, and do not rest on an enslaving denial of dignity. So the sources of conflict and instability in the alternatives to slavery do not tend to produce returns to slavery. And the fact that those replacements are improvements with respect to justice makes the stability of the shift away from slavery less surprising.

Thus, the fact that there is not wandering back and forth between slavery and abolition reflects the fact that the fundamental slave interests were shared and so could serve as the basis of an agreement.[102] Stating that slavery is unjust and that slave interests are legitimate interests conveys all these relevant facts about the conflict between slavery and the interests of slaves. It represents a second, distinct reason for citing the injustice in an explanation of the end of slavery. We cite the injustice itself, first, then, to indicate that moral reasoning mandates a certain conclusion, that people arrived at the conclusion because they reasoned, and were motivated to act. And we cite it, second, to convey information about the features of the system and of the alternatives to it in virtue of which the moral reasoning condemns it as unjust, and to claim that those very features are a source of instability. I do not deny that there are other ways of conveying those features. One could simply state the properties of slavery—the conflict between slavery and slave interests—and of the alternatives, without taking a position on whether those properties indeed are what makes slavery unjust; in short (and putting the issue of recognition to the side), the fact that the properties are injustice-making is not itself a part of my argument. Still, they are, and can unobjectionably be presented via the moral classification. Moreover, that mode of presentation is morally important. For the world looks different if we think that injustice-making features limit the viability of systems that have them.

In sum, then, we have no reason to correct William Williams or Theodore Parker. Ethical explanations have some force, given certain plausible background beliefs about the connections between the satisfaction of fundamental interests and the justice of social forms, about the tendency of people to act on their interests, and about the relationship between the satisfaction of those interests and the viability of social arrangements (especially when those arrangements operate under conditions of competition and conflict). To be sure, an explanation of the demise of slavery might proceed without embracing the ethical account of that explanation, simply by citing the injustice-making properties—the properties moral reasoning singles out in condemning slavery. Injustice, in short, is not indispensable to the explanation.

But this observation is no objection because my aim has not been to argue that slavery is really wrong, nor to demonstrate the objectivity of moral norms by indicating their indispensability to explanation, nor even to persuade people who do not give ethical explanations that they ought to start. Instead, starting from within morality and its concern about the relationship of moral norms to the social world, and premising that we (or some us) give ethical explanations, I have asked whether more reflective forms of historical and social inquiry condemn that practice, and its relaxed attitude to the distinction between fact and value.

My answer is a qualified: No.

Scaffold and Throne

Appeals to the injustice of slavery can play a role in explaining the demise of slavery. But that role is limited, no greater than the advantages conferred by moral improvements. Those limits in turn underscore the length of the arc of the moral universe. King often coupled his reference to that arc with a stanza from James Russell Lowell:

Truth forever on the scaffold,
Wrong forever on the throne;
Yet that scaffold sways the future,
And behind the dim unknown

317

JOSHUA COHEN

Standeth God within the shadow
Keeping watch above His own.

Many of us do not share Lowell's faith—or King's—in a God who
keeps watch above his own. But even if we do not, we can find some
support for the hopefulness of Lowell, King, and William Williams
in the human aspirations and powers that shape the arc of our part
of the moral universe.

Notes

This essay first appeared in *Philosophy and Public Affairs* 26 (Spring 1997): 91–
134. I wrote the first draft for a 1986 symposium on "Moral Realism" at the annual
meeting of the American Political Science Association, and presented subsequent
versions to philosophy colloquia at Carnegie-Mellon University and Columbia Uni-
versity, the Western Canadian Philosophical Association, the Harvard Government
Department's political theory colloquium, New York University Law School, the
Pacific Division meetings of the American Philosophical Association, the Bay Area
Group on Philosophy and Political Economy, the Society for Ethical and Legal
Philosophy, the Olin Conference on Political Economy at Stanford University, the
A. E. Havens Center for the Study of Social Structure and Social Change at the
University of Wisconsin, Madison, and the Universidade Federal Fluminens. I am
grateful to audiences at each of these occasions for their comments and criticisms.
I especially wish to thank Robert Brenner, David Brink, Robert Cooter, Michael
Hardimon, Paul Horwich, Frances Kamm, George Kateb, Ira Katznelson, Harvey
Mansfield, Amelie Rorty, Charles Sabel, Michael Sandel, T. M. Scanlon, Samuel
Scheffler, Anne-Marie Smith, Laura Stoker, and Erik Olin Wright for helpful sug-
gestions. Karen Jacobsen, Anne-Marie Smith, and Katia Vania provided invaluable
research assistance. I received research support from a National Endowment for
the Humanities summer fellowship, and Massachusetts Institute of Technology's
Levitan Prize in the Humanities, generously supported by James and Ruth Levitan.

1. *The Souls of Black Folk* (New York: Vintage, 1990), 188.

2. Cited in John W. Blassingame, ed., *Slave Testimony* (Baton Rouge: Louisiana
State University Press, 1977), 437.

3. For philosophical endorsement of ethical explanations, see Plato, *Republic*,
trans. Allan Bloom (New York: Basic Books, 1968), 509B; G. W. F. Hegel, *Lesser
Logic*, trans. William Wallace (Oxford: Oxford University Press, 1892), paragraph
234. Contemporary philosophical discussion of ethical explanations is set within
the context of debates about moral realism and moral objectivity. See, among much
else, Gilbert Harman, *The Nature of Morality* (Oxford: Oxford University Press,

1977), esp. chap. 1; Nicholas Sturgeon, "Moral Explanations," in David Copp and David Zimmerman, eds., *Morality, Reason, and Truth: New Essays on the Foundations of Ethics* (Totowa: Rowman and Allanheld, 1985), 49–78; Peter Railton, "Moral Realism," *Philosophical Review* 95 (April 1986): 163–207; Warren Quinn, "Truth and Explanation in Ethics," *Ethics* 96 (April 1986): 522–44; Thomas Nagel, *The View From Nowhere* (Oxford: Oxford University Press, 1986), 144ff.; David Brink, *Moral Realism and the Foundations of Ethics* (Cambridge: Cambridge University Press, 1989); Crispin Wright, *Truth and Objectivity* (Cambridge: Harvard University Press, 1992), chap. 5; Judith Jarvis Thomson, "Moral Objectivity," in Gilbert Harman and Judith Jarvis Thomson, *Moral Relativism and Moral Objectivity* (Cambridge: Blackwell, 1996). I comment on the connections of my argument with this debate in the text at pp. 285–86.

4. Theodore Parker, *The Relation of Slavery to a Republican Form of Government* (Boston: William Kent and Company, 1858), 20. Strictly speaking, Williams and Parker make ethical predictions: they predict a change in a world, and base the predictions on norms of rightness. No doubt that they would have embraced the claim that the North won because it was in the right.

5. The phrase "arc of the moral universe" or variants on it occur throughout King's writing and speeches. See Martin Luther King, *A Testament of Hope: The Essential Writings of Martin Luther King, Jr.*, ed. James Washington (San Francisco: Harper and Row, 1986), 141, 207, 230, 277, 438. According to Taylor Branch, the phrase comes from Theodore Parker. See *Parting the Waters: America in the King Years 1954–63* (New York: Simon and Schuster, 1988), 197n.

6. For suggestive discussion, see Jürgen Habermas, *Legitimation Crisis*, trans. Thomas McCarthy (Boston: Beacon Press, 1975), Part 3; and Jürgen Habermas, *Communication and the Evolution of Society*, trans. Thomas McCarthy (Boston: Beacon Press, 1979).

7. Adam Smith, *Wealth of Nations* (New York: Random House, 1965), Book 3.

8. G. W. F. Hegel, *Philosophy of History*, trans. J. Sibree (New York: Dover, 1900).

9. Karl Marx, "Preface" to *A Contribution to the Critique of Political Economy*, and Karl Marx and Frederick Engels, *German Ideology*, in Robert Tucker, ed., *Marx-Engels Reader*, 2d ed. (New York: W. W. Norton, 1978), 4–5, 146–200.

10. Quoted in David Potter, *The Impending Crisis: 1848–1861*, completed and edited by Don E. Fehrenbacher (New York: Harper and Row, 1976), 342. The passage comes from Lincoln's letter to Albert G. Hodges (4 April 1864).

11. For criticism of explanations of the decline of ancient slavery in which religious morality plays a central role, see Keith Bradley, *Slavery and Society at Rome* (Cambridge: Cambridge University Press, 1994), chap. 8; Pierre Dockès, *Medieval Slavery and Liberation*, trans. Arthur Goldhammer (Chicago: University of Chicago Press, 1982), 145–49; G. E. M. de Ste. Croix, *The Class Struggle in the Ancient Greek World* (London: Duckworth, 1981). For recent debate on the complexities of assess-

JOSHUA COHEN

ing the contribution of moral convictions to modern abolitionism, see the debate
between John Ashworth, David Brion Davis, and Thomas Haskell, in *The Antislavery
Debate: Capitalism and Abolitionism as a Problem in Historical Interpretation*, ed. Thomas
Bender (Berkeley: University of California Press, 1992).

12. On scientific moral realism, see Sturgeon, "Moral Explanations," Brink,
Moral Realism; and especially Railton's excellent, "Moral Realism."

13. Here I follow Crispin Wright's discussion of moral explanations and mini-
malism in *Truth and Objectivity*, chap. 5.

14. For general discussions of the nature of slavery see Ste. Croix, *Class Struggle,*
esp. p. 135, where he discusses the definition of slavery in the 1926 Slavery Convention organized by the League of Nations; H. J. Nieboer, *Slavery as an Industrial
System*, 2d ed. (New York: Burt Franklin, 1910; reprint, 1971), part I, chap. 1; Orlando Patterson, *Slavery and Social Death*, chaps. 1–3; Dockès, *Medieval Slavery*, 4–8;
Moses Finley, *Ancient Slavery and Modern Ideology* (Harmondsworth: Penguin, 1980),
chap. 2; Moses Finley, *Economy and Society in Ancient Greece* (Harmondsworth: Pen-
guin, 1983), chaps. 6–9; Igor Kopytoff and Suzanne Miers, "African Slavery as an
Institution of Marginality," in Suzanne Miers and Igor Kopytoff, eds., *Slavery in
Africa: Historical and Anthropological Perspectives* (Madison: University of Wisconsin
Press, 1977), 3–81; "Slavery as an Institution: Open and Closed Systems," in James
Watson, ed., *Asian and African Systems of Slavery* (Berkeley: University of California
Press, 1980); Paul Lovejoy, *Transformations in Slavery: A History of Slavery in Africa*
(Cambridge: Cambridge University Press, 1983), chap. 1; James Oakes, *Slavery and
Freedom: An Interpretation of the Old South* (New York: Alfred A. Knopf, 1990), chap.
1. The conception of slavery I present in the text draws as well on the discussion of
"property relations" in G. A. Cohen, *Karl Marx's Theory of History: A Defense*
(Princeton: Princeton University Press, 1978), 219–22.

15. Bradley says that "To live in slavery . . . was to be utterly disempowered." But
he backs this assertion with observations about the absence of slave rights and master obligations, thus running together the relations of power with legal-cultural
representations. See Bradley, *Slavery and Society*, 27.

16. Blassingame, *Slave Testimony*, 397.

17. Cited in Elizabeth Fox-Genovese, *Within the Plantation Household: Black and
White Women of the Old South* (Chapel Hill: University of North Carolina Press, 1988),
290.

18. For discussion, see Keith R. Bradley, *Slavery and Rebellion in the Roman World
140 B.C.–70 B.C.* (Bloomington: Indiana University Press, 1989); Pierre Dockès,
Medieval Slavery (see n. 11), 210–11; Orlando Patterson, *The Sociology of Slavery: An
Analysis of the Origins, Development and Structure of Negro Slave Society in Jamaica* (London: MacGibbon and Kee, 1967), chap. 9; Raymond A. Bauer and Alice H. Bauer,
"Day to Day Resistance to Slavery," *Journal of Negro History* 27 (October 1942): 388–
419; Eugene D. Genovese, *Roll, Jordan, Roll* (New York: Pantheon 1974), book 4;

Eugene D. Genovese, *From Rebellion to Revolution: Afro-American Slave Revolts in the Making of the New World* (New York: Vintage, 1979); Mary Karasch, *Slave Life in Rio de Janeiro 1808–1850* (Princeton: Princeton University Press, 1987), chap. 10; Barbara Bush, *Slave Women in Caribbean Society 1650–1838* (Kingston: Heineman Publishers, 1990), chap. 5; Isaac Mendelsohn, *Slavery in the Ancient Near East* (New York: Oxford University Press, 1949), 66, 121; Ruth Mazo Karra, *Slavery and Society in Medieval Scandinavia* (New Haven: Yale University Press, 1988), 123–27; Frederick Cooper, *Plantation Slavery on the East Coast of Africa* (New Haven: Yale University Press, 1977), 200–10; Richard Roberts and Martin A. Klein, "The Banamba Slave Exodus of 1905 and the Decline of Slavery in the Western Sudan," *Journal of African History* 21 (1980): 375–94; Paul Lovejoy, *Transformations in Slavery: A History of Slavery in Africa* (Cambridge: Cambridge University Press, 1983), chap. 11; Paul Lovejoy, ed., *Africans in Bondage: Studies in Slavery and the Slave Trade* (Madison: University of Wisconsin Press, 1986); Suzanne Miers and Richard Roberts, eds., *The End of Slavery in Africa* (Madison: University of Wisconsin Press, 1988), chaps. 3, 6, 9, 13. For some skeptical remarks, see Finley, *Ancient Slavery*, 111–16.

19. On stealing and resistance, see Genovese, *Roll, Jordan, Roll*, 599–612.

20. See Roberts and Klein, "Banamba Slave Exodus," and Lovejoy, *Transformations*, 266ff. For doubts about the extent of desertions in the period of African abolition, see Richard Roberts and Suzanne Miers, "The End of Slavery in Africa," in Miers and Roberts, eds., *End of Slavery in Africa*, 27–33.

21. On maroon activity, see Patterson, *Sociology of Slavery*, 266–73; Cooper, *Plantation Slavery*, 200–10; Allan G. B. Fisher and Humphrey J. Fisher, *Slavery and Muslim Society in Africa: The Institution in Saharan and Sudanic Africa and the Trans-Saharan Trade* (London: C. Hurt and Co., 1971), 94; and Genovese, *From Rebellion to Revolution*, chap. 2.

22. For discussions of these and other slave rebellions see C. L. R. James, *The Black Jacobins: Toussaint L'Ouverture and the San Domingo Revolution* (New York: Random House, 1963); Genovese, *Roll, Jordan, Roll*, 587–98; Genovese, *From Rebellion to Revolution*; John W. Blassingame, *The Slave Community: Plantation Life in the Antebellum South*, 2d ed. (New York: Oxford University Press, 1979), 125–31; David Brion Davis, *Slavery and Human Progress* (Oxford: Oxford University Press, 1984), 5–8; Moses Finley, *The Ancient Economy* (Berkeley: University of California Press, 1973), 89, 92; P. A. Brunt, *Social Conflicts in the Roman Republic* (New York: W. W. Norton, 1971), 114–15; Dockès, *Medieval Slavery*, chap. 4; Patterson, *Sociology of Slavery*, 266–73; Bradley, *Slavery and Rebellion*. For references on and discussion of African cases, see Cooper, *Plantation Slavery*, 202–3; Frederick Cooper, "Review Article: The Problem of Slavery in African Studies, *Journal of African History* 20, no. 1 (1979): 103–25; Roberts and Klein, "Banamba Slave Exodus"; Lovejoy, *Transformations in Slavery*.

23. See Patterson, *Slavery and Social Death*, 186: "In 97 percent of the societies

falling in the sample of world cultures, masters recognized the unions of slaves. In not a single case, however, did such recognition imply custodial powers over children." On the U.S. case, see Genovese, *Roll, Jordan, Roll*, 433–535; Herbert Gutman, *The Black Family in Slavery and Freedom, 1750–1925* (New York: Vintage, 1977).

24. See Patterson, *Slavery and Social Death*, chaps. 4, 5, for discussion of the frequency of different forms of enslavement.

25. Thus Patterson claims that "there is no known slaveholding society where the whip was not considered an indispensable instrument." *Slavery and Social Death*, 4. For some vivid details, see Bradley, *Slavery and Society*, 165–73, and Karasch, *Slave Life in Rio de Janeiro*, 113–25.

26. Finley, *Ancient Slavery*, 93–94; Thomas Wiedemann, *Greek and Roman Slavery* (Baltimore: Johns Hopkins University Press, 1981), 74, 166–69.

27. Edward Peters, *Torture* (Oxford: Basil Blackwell, 1985), 18ff.

28. Patterson, *Slavery and Social Death*, 193.

29. Cited in Stuart B. Schwartz, *Sugar Plantations in the Formation of Brazilian Society: Bahia, 1550–1835* (Cambridge: Cambridge University Press, 1985), 133.

30. For discussion of this "Nieboer-Domar hypothesis," see Evsey D. Domar, "The Causes of Slavery or Serfdom: A Hypothesis," *Journal of Economic History* 30 (March 1970): 18–32.

31. Dr. Collins, *Practical Rules for the Management and Medical Treatment of Negro Slaves in the Sugar Colonies* (London: J. Barfield, 1811), 33, 36.

32. Smith, *Wealth of Nations*, 365.

33. The discussion that follows draws on Stefano Fenoaltea, "Slavery and Supervision in Comparative Perspective: A Model," *Journal of Economic History* 44 (September 1984): 635–68.

34. Writing about Bahian sugar plantations, for example, Schwartz claims that none of the "commentators on the engenho operations speaks of drivers or the whip being used inside the fabrica." See *Sugar Plantations*, 154, and the subsequent discussion of the need for incentives, 155–59.

35. Collins, *Practical Rules*, 170.

36. For a valuable summary of the evolving literature on this issue in the case of American slavery, see Robert W. Fogel, *Without Consent or Contract: The Rise and Fall of American Slavery* (New York: W. W. Norton, 1989), chap. 6.

37. Dockès, *Medieval Slavery*, 208.

38. Genovese, *Roll, Jordan, Roll*, 539. On private cultivation as an incentive in other settings, see Rebecca Scott, *Slave Emancipation in Cuba: The Transition to Free Labor, 1860–1899* (Princeton: Princeton University Press), 15; John Edwin Mason, "Fortunate Slaves and Artful Masters: Labor Relations in the Rural Cape Colony During the Era of Emancipation, ca. 1825–1838," in *Slavery in South Africa: Captive Labor on the Dutch Frontier*, ed. Elizabeth A. Eldredge and Fred Morton (Boulder, Colo.: Westview Press, 1994), 67–91.

39. Cited in Robert Conrad, *Children of God's Fire: A Documentary History of Black Slavery in Brazil* (Princeton: Princeton University Press, 1983), 78.

40. Collins, *Practical Rules*, 152.

41. Frederick Douglass, *Narrative of the Life of Frederick Douglass, An American Slave*, in Henry Louis Gates, ed., *The Classic Slave Narratives* (New York: Signet, 1987), 300.

42. See Patterson, *Slavery and Social Death*, chaps. 8–10; Keith Hopkins, *Conquerors and Slaves* (Cambridge: Cambridge University Press, 1978), 117–18, 126, 128, 131, 147; Cooper, *Plantation Slavery*, 242–52; Frederick Cooper, "Islam and Cultural Hegemony," in *The Ideology of Slavery in Africa*, ed. Paul Lovejoy (Beverly Hills: Sage, 1981), 287–88.

43. *Oeconomica*, trans. Benjamin Jowett, in *The Works of Aristotle*, ed. W. D. Ross, vol. 10 (Oxford: Oxford University Press, 1921), 1344b12–22.

44. *Politics*, 1330a33ff.

45. Jean-Jacques Rousseau, *Social Contract*, ed. Roger D. Masters and trans. Judith R. Masters (New York: St. Martin's Press, 1978), 48. The literature on the subject is vast. For an especially illuminating discussion, see James C. Scott, *Domination and the Arts of Resistance: Hidden Transcripts* (New Haven: Yale University Press, 1990), especially chaps. 3 and 4.

46. Mechal Sobel, *Trabelin' On: The Slave Journey to an Afro-Baptist Faith* (Princeton: Princeton University Press, 1988), 105.

47. Katia M. deQueiros Mattoso, *To Be A Slave In Brazil: 1550–1888*, trans. Arthur Goldhammer (New Brunswick: Rutgers University Press, 1986).

48. For an alternative view in the case of Cariocan slave religion—as essentially a continuation of flexible Central African traditions, rather than as syncretic or dualistic—see Karasch, *Slave Life*, chap. 9.

49. Genovese, *Roll, Jordan, Roll*, 232–55; for qualifications, see Patterson, *Slavery and Social Death*, 73–76. On the importance of deliverance in slave spirituals, see Blassingame, *Slave Community*, 141–45.

50. Cooper, *Plantation Slavery*, 236–42, and "Islam and Cultural Hegemony," 291–93.

51. Genovese, *Roll, Jordan, Roll*.

52. See Leon F. Litwack, *Been in the Storm So Long: The Aftermath of Slavery* (New York: Vintage, 1979), 5–6; Martin A. Klein, "Slave Resistance and Slave Emancipation in Coastal Guinea," in Miers and Roberts, eds., *The End of Slavery in Africa*, 203–19.

53. For detailed discussion of this important range of issues and cases, see Genovese, *Roll, Jordan, Roll;* Cooper, "Islam and Cultural Hegemony"; Richard Roberts, "Ideology, Slavery, and Social Formation: The Evolution of Maraka Slavery in the Middle Niger Valley," in Lovejoy, *Ideology of Slavery;* Dockès, *Medieval Slavery*, 212–15; Lovejoy, "Problems of Slave Control in the Sokoto Caliphate," in *Africans in Bondage: Studies in Slavery and the Slave Trade*, ed. Paul Lovejoy (Madison: University of Wisconsin Press, 1986), 262–64.

54. Douglass, *Narrative*, 317.

55. Blassingame, *Slave Testimony*, 374. For a detailed discussion of theft and its implications for the moral rejection of slavery and the development of a "counter-morality," see Alex Lichtenstein, "'That Disposition to Theft, With Which They Have Been Branded': Moral Economy, Slave Management, and the Law," *Journal of Social History* 21 (1988): 413–40.

56. Quoted in Alex Lichtenstein, "That Disposition to Theft," 413.

57. Mattoso, *To Be A Slave*, 137.

58. See the suggestive remarks on unanimity, in Scott, *Domination*, 55–58; on the importance of reciprocity in shaping public justifications of power, see Barrington Moore, *Injustice: The Social Bases of Obedience and Revolt* (White Plains, N.Y.: M. E. Sharpe, 1987).

59. The account of interests draws on the discussion of deliberative rationality in Rawls, *Theory of Justice*, sec. 64; Albert O. Hirschman, *The Passions and the Interests: Political Arguments for Capitalism Before its Triumph* (Princeton: Princeton University Press, 1977); Railton, "Moral Realism"; Raymond Geuss, *The Idea of a Critical Theory: Habermas and the Frankfurt School* (Cambridge: Cambridge University Press, 1981), chap. 2; and William Connolly, *The Terms of Political Discourse*, 2d ed. (Princeton: Princeton University Press, 1983), chap. 2.

60. Finley, *Ancient Slavery*, 98; Wiedemann, *Greek and Roman Slavery*, 222, citing a passage from Appian's *Roman Civil Wars;* Bradley, *Slavery and Rebellion.*

61. Lovejoy, *Transformations in Slavery*, 267. He adds that "some scholars have argued that African servility depended on attitudes quite unrelated to the concept of 'freedom.' African thought, they claim, did not consider freedom a desirable or possible status. There can be no mistake about this matter. The massive desertions by slaves throughout the nineteenth century and especially at the end of the century when European conquest was well underway, demonstrates that the views of these scholars are incorrect." For an alternative view, see Igor Kopytoff, "The Cultural Context of African Abolition," in Miers and Roberts, eds., *The End of Slavery in Africa*, 485–503, especially the illuminating remarks about demarginalization, social dependence, and social belonging, 494–502

62. Bradley, *Slaves and Masters in the Roman Empire: A Study in Social Control* (New York: Oxford University Press), 25.

63. Mary Prince, *History of Mary Prince, A West Indian Slave*, in Gates, *Classic Slave Narratives*, 214.

64. For discussion of the fables, see Bradley, *Slaves and Masters*, 150–53.

65. Linda Brent, *Incidents in the Life of a Slave Girl*, ed. L. Marian Child, in Gates, ed., *Classic Slave Narratives*, 513. Or see Lucy A. Delaney, *From the Darkness Cometh the Light or Struggles for Freedom*, in *Six Women's Slave Narratives* (New York: Oxford University Press, 1988), 58.

66. On self-enslavement, see Patterson, *Slavery and Social Death*, 130–31.

67. "There is," according to Patterson, "absolutely no evidence from the long and dismal annals of slavery to suggest that any group of slaves ever internalized the conception of degradation held by their masters." Patterson, *Slavery and Social Death*, 97.

68. Blassingame, *Slave Testimony*, 439.

69. See Rawls's discussion of the social bases of self-respect in *Theory of Justice*, 179, 440–42.

70. Robert W. Fogel and Stanley L. Engerman, *Time on the Cross*, 2 vols. (Boston: Little, Brown, and Co., 1974).

71. Robert W. Fogel *Without Consent or Contract: The Rise and Fall of American Slavery* (New York: W. W. Norton, 1989), 78–79.

72. Fogel and Engerman, *Time on the Cross*, vol. 1, 237.

73. For a discussion and exploration of implications, see Amartya Sen, "Well-Being, Agency, and Freedom," *Journal of Philosophy* 82 (April 1985), 195–200.

74. Paul David and Peter Temin, "Slavery: The Progressive Institution," in Paul David et al., eds., *Reckoning with Slavery* (New York: Oxford University Press, 1976), 178–86; Yoram Barzel, "An Economic Analysis of Slavery," *Journal of Law and Economics* 21 (April 1977): 95.

75. I have focused on implications for consumption and nourishment. On health, see Joseph C. Miller, *Way of Death: Merchant Capitalism and the Angolan Slave Trade 1730–1830* (Madison: University of Wisconsin Press, 1988), chaps. 9, 10; Karasch, *Slave Life in Rio de Janeiro*, chap. 5; Richard Steckel, "A Dreadful Childhood: The Excess Mortality of American Slaves," *Social Science History* 10 (Winter 1986): 427–65; Fogel, *Without Consent or Contract*, chap. 5.

76. Robert Brenner has emphasized this point in several discussions.

77. Fogel, *Without Consent or Contract*, 78; see also Stefano Fenoaltea, "The Slavery Debate: A Note From the Sidelines," *Explorations in Economic History* 18 (1981): 304–8.

78. Fogel, *Without Consent or Contract*, 79.

79. See, for example, Bush, *Slave Women*, 110–18; Karasch, *Slave Life*, 205–10.

80. Patterson, *Slavery and Social Death*.

81. *Dred Scott v. Sanford*, 60 U.S. 393.

82. Cited in Gutman, *Black Family in Slavery and Freedom*, 361.

83. I draw, as will be evident, on Rawls, *A Theory of Justice*, T. M. Scanlon, "Contractualism and Utilitarianism," in Amartya Sen and Bernard Williams, eds., *Utilitarianism and Beyond* (Cambridge: Cambridge University Press, 1982).

84. I focus here on the injury of slavery to slaves, not on claims about the general benefits of abolition. For an especially eloquent statement of those benefits, see Joaquim Nabuco, *Abolitionism: The Brazilian Antislavery Struggle*, trans. Robert Conrad (Urbana: University of Illinois Press, 1977), especially 83.

85. James, *Black Jocobins*, 10.

86. On the complex background and implications of moral opposition, see David Brion Davis, *The Problem of Slavery in the Age of Revolution, 1770–1823* (Ithaca: Cornell University Press, 1975); Jean R. Soderlund, *Quakers and Slavery: A Divided Spirit* (Princeton: Princeton University Press, 1985).

87. Fogel, *Without Consent or Contract*, 410.

88. Davis, *Problem of Slavery*, 137–51, 276; Genovese, *Rebellion to Revolution*. On the interaction between metropolitan abolitionism and slave resistance, see Seymour Drescher, *Capitalism and Antislavery: British Mobilization in Comparative Perspective* (London: Macmillan, 1986), 100–103.

89. Genovese, *Rebellion to Revolution*.

90. See, for example, Smith, *Wealth of Nations*, 363–67; Karl Marx, *Capital*, vol. 1, trans. Ben Fowkes (Harmondsworth: Penguin, 1976), 303–4 n.18. On the problem of biological reproduction, see Max Weber's essay on "Social Causes of the Decline of Ancient Civilization," reprinted in Max Weber, *The Agrarian Sociology of Ancient Civilizations*, trans. R. I. Frank (London: New Left Books, 1976); Gavin Wright, "The Efficiency of Slavery: Another Interpretation," *American Economic Review* 69 (March 1979): 219–26; Ste. Croix, *Class Struggle*, 229–37. For criticism of the economic arguments, see Fogel, *Without Consent or Contract*, chaps. 3, 4. For criticisms of Ste. Croix's argument about conflicts between biological reproduction and full economic exploitation, see Keith R. Bradley, "Wet-Nursing At Rome: A Study In Social Relations," in Beryl Rawson, ed., *The Family in Ancient Rome: New Perspectives* (Ithaca: Cornell University Press, 1986), 211–12.

91. Smith, *Wealth of Nations*, 365.

92. Cited in James McPherson, *Battle Cry of Freedom: The Civil War Era* (New York: Oxford University Press, 1988), 832–35.

93. Aristotle, *Politics*, 1268b38. Lovejoy, "Problems of Slave Control," 247, discusses an early nineteenth-century example from the Oyo kingdom in the Sudan.

94. On the two-front war in the Confederate case, see Ira Berlin, Barbara J. Fields, Steven F. Miller, Joseph P. Reidy, and Leslie S. Rowland, "The Destruction of Slavery," in *Slaves No More: Three Essays on Emancipation and the Civil War* (Cambridge: Cambridge University Press, 1992), 3–76.

95. Patterson, *Slavery and Social Death*, 287–93; Wiedemann, *Greek and Roman Slavery*, 64–68; Lovejoy, "Problems of Slave Control," 246–49. Analogously, military conflict has played an important role in democratization. See Dietrich Rueschemeyer, Evelyne Huber Stephens, and John D. Stephens, *Capitalist Development and Democracy* (Chicago: University of Chicago Press, 1992), 70–71, 279.

96. McPherson, *Battle Cry*, 504, and more generally, 354, 490–510.

97. Robin Blackburn, *The Overthrow of Colonial Slavery 1776–1848* (London: Verso, 1988), chap. 9.

98. Wiedemann, *Greek and Roman Slavery*, 67–68.

99. The incentives represent what is sometimes described as the "inherent con-

tradiction" of slavery: its treatment of human beings as though they were mere things. See G. W. F. Hegel, *The Phenomenology of Spirit*, trans. A. V. Miller (Oxford: Oxford University Press, 1977), 111–19; Karl Marx, *Grundrisse*, trans. Martin Nicolaus (New York: Random House, 1973), 463; David Brion Davis, *The Problem of Slavery in Western Culture* (Ithaca: Cornell University Press, 1966), 25–27, 58–62.

100. Litwack, *Been in the Storm So Long*, 101.

101. Cited in Litwack, *Been in the Storm So Long*, 97.

102. It might be objected that the decline of slavery with the end of the Roman Empire, and its reemergence with New World plantation slavery represent precisely such abolition and reimposition. But see William D. Phillips, *Slavery From Roman Times to the Early Transatlantic Trade* (Minneapolis: University of Minnesota Press, 1985); Robin Blackburn, *The Making of New World Slavery: From the Baroque to the Modern 1492–1800* (London: Verso, 1997), chap. 1.

Bibliography

Adams, Francis. *Three Black Writers in Eighteenth Century England*. Belmont: Wadsworth, 1971.

Allen, Anita L. "The Black Surrogate Mother." *Harvard BlackLetter Journal* 8 (Spring 1991): 17–31.

———. "Privacy, Surrogacy and the *Baby M* Case." *Georgetown Law Journal* 76 (1988).

———. "Surrogacy, Slavery and the Ownership of Life." *Harvard Journal of Law and Public Policy* 139 (Winter 1990): 139–49.

Anstey, Roger. *The Atlantic Slave Trade and British Abolition 1760–1810*. Atlantic Highlands, N.J.: Humanities Press, 1975.

Aristotle. *The Politics*, trans. Carnes Lord. Chicago: University of Chicago Press, 1984.

Ashcraft, Richard. *Revolutionary Politics and Locke's Two Treatises of Civil Government*. Princeton: Princeton University Press, 1986.

Ballard, Patricia. "Racial Matching and the Adoption Dilemma." *Journal of Family Law* 17 (1978–79).

Barzel, Yoram. "An Economic Analysis of Slavery." *The Journal of Law and Economics* 21 (April 1977).

Bauer, Raymond A., and Alice H. Bauer. "Day to Day Resistance to Slavery." *Journal of Negro History* 27 (October 1942): 388–419.

Bayliss, John F. *Black Slave Narratives*. New York: Macmillan, 1970.

Becker, Carl. *The Declaration of Independence*. New York: Random House, 1970.

Bender, Thomas, ed. *The Antislavery Debate: Capitalism and Abolitionism as a Problem in Historical Interpretation*. Berkeley: University of California Press, 1992.

Benezet, Anthony. *Some Historical Account of Guinea*. London, 1788.

Blackburn, Robin. *The Making of New World Slavery: From the Baroque to the Modern 1492–1800*. London: Verso, 1997.

———. *The Overthrow of Colonial Slavery 1776–1848*. London: Verso, 1988.

Blassingame, John W. *The Slave Community: Plantation Life in the Antebellum South*. New York: Oxford University Press, 1974.

———. ed. *Slave Testimony*. Baton Rouge: Louisiana State University Press, 1977.

Bracken, H. M. "Essence, Accident and Race." *Hermathena* 116 (Winter 1973), 81–96.

———. "Philosophy and Racism." *Philosophia* (Israel) 8 (November 1978): 241–60.

Bradley, Keith R. *Slavery and Rebellion in the Roman World 140 B.C.–70 B.C.* Bloomington and Indianapolis: Indiana University Press, 1989.

———. *Slavery and Society at Rome.* Cambridge: Cambridge University Press, 1994.

———. *Slaves and Masters in the Roman Empire: A Study in Social Control.* New York: Oxford University Press.

Brathwaite, Edward Kamau. "Caliban, Ariel, and Unprospero in the Conflict of Creolization: A Study of the Slave Revolt in Jamaica in 1831–32." In *Comparative Perspectives on Slavery in New World Plantation Societies,* ed. Vera Rubin and Arthur Tuden. New York: The New York Academy of Sciences, 1977.

Brunt, P. A. *Social Conflicts in the Roman Republic.* New York: Norton, 1971.

Bush, Barbara. *Slave Women in Caribbean Society 1650–1838.* Kingston, N.Y.: Heinemann, 1990.

Carby, Hazel. *Reconstructing Womanhood.* New York: Oxford University Press, 1987.

Chesler, Phyllis. *The Sacred Bond: The Legacy of Baby M.* New York: Times Books, 1988.

Clarkson, Thomas. *An Essay on the Slavery and Commerce of the Human Species.* London: Phillips, 1786; 2d ed., 1788.

Cohen, G. A. *Karl Marx's Theory of History: A Defense.* Princeton: Princeton University Press, 1978.

Collins, Dr. *Practical Rules for the Management and Medical Treatment of Negro Slaves in the Sugar Colonies.* London: J. Barfield, 1811.

Conrad, Robert. *Children of God's Fire: A Documentary History of Black Slavery in Brazil.* Princeton: Princeton University Press, 1983.

Cooper, Frederick. "Islam and Cultural Hegemony." In *The Ideology of Slavery in Africa,* ed. Paul Lovejoy. Beverly Hills: Sage, 1981.

———. *Plantation Slavery on the East Coast of Africa.* New Haven: Yale University Press, 1977.

———. "Review Article: The Problem of Slavery in African Studies." *Journal of African History* 20 (1979): 103–25.

Costanzo, Angelo. *Surprising Narrative: Olaudah Equiano and the Beginnings of Black Autobiography.* New York: Greenwood Press, 1987.

Cottrol, Robert J. "Liberalism and Paternalism: Ideology, Economic Interest and the Business of Slavery." *The American Journal of Legal History* 31 (1987).

Curtin, Philip D. *The Image of Africa: British Idea and Action 1780–1850.* Madison: University of Wisconsin Press, 1964.

Dallas, R. C. *The History of the Maroons.* New York: Longman 1803; repr. Cass 1968.

David, Paul, and Peter Temin. "Slavery: The Progressive Institution." In *Reckoning With Slavery,* ed. Paul David, et al. New York: Oxford University Press, 1976.

Davies, K. G. *The Royal Africa Company*. New York: Atheneum, 1970.

Davis, Angela. *Women, Race, and Class*. New York: Vintage Books, 1983.

Davis, David Brion. *The Problem of Slavery in the Age of Revolution, 1770–1823*. Ithaca: Cornell University Press, 1975.

———. *The Problem of Slavery in Western Culture*. Ithaca: Cornell University Press, 1966.

———. *Slavery and Human Progress*. Oxford: Oxford University Press, 1984.

Delaney, Lucy A. *From the Darkness Cometh the Light or Struggles for Freedom*. In *Six Women's Slave Narratives*. New York: Oxford University Press, 1988.

Dockès, Pierre. *Medieval Slavery and Liberation*, trans. Arthur Goldhammer. Chicago: University of Chicago Press, 1982.

Domar, Evsey D. "The Causes of Slavery or Serfdom: A Hypothesis." *Journal of Economic History* 30 (March 1970): 18–32.

Douglass, Frederick. *The Life and Times of Frederick Douglass*. New York: Collier Books, 1962.

———. *The Life and Writings of Frederick Douglass*, 6 vols., ed. Philip S. Foner. New York: International Publishers, 1975.

———. *My Bondage and My Freedom*. New York: Dover Publications, 1969.

Drescher, Seymour. *Capitalism and Antislavery: British Mobilization in Comparative Perspective*. London: Macmillan, 1986.

Dunn, John. "The Politics of Locke in England and America." In *John Locke: Problems and Perspectives*, ed. John Yolton. Cambridge: Cambridge University Press, 1969.

Dworkin, Gerald. "Paternalism." In *Paternalism*, ed. Rolf Sartorius. Minneapolis: University of Minnesota Press, 1983.

Edwards, Paul, ed. *Cugoano's Thoughts and Sentiments on the Evils of Slavery*. London: n.p., 1787. Reprinted, London: Dawson, 1969.

———, ed. *Equiano's Travels*. Oxford: Heinemann, 1989.

Edwards, Paul, and Rosalind Shaw. "The Invisible Chi in Equiano's *Interesting Narrative*." *Journal of Religion in Africa* 19 (1989): 146–56.

Elkins, Stanley M. *Slavery: A Problem in American Institutional and Intellectual Life*. Chicago: University of Chicago Press, 1959.

Falconbridge, Alexander. *An Account of the Slave Trade on the Coast of Africa*. London: n.p., 1788.

Farr, James. " 'So Vile and Miserable an Estate,' The Problem of Slavery in Locke's Political Thought." *Political Theory* 14 (May 1986).

Feinberg, Joel. "Autonomy, Sovereignty and Privacy." *Notre Dame Law Review* 58 (February, 1983).

———. "Legal Paternalism." In *Paternalism*, Rolf Sartorius, ed. Minneapolis: University of Minnesota Press, 1983.

Fenoaltea, Stefano. "Slavery and Supervision in Comparative Perspective: A Model." *Journal of Economic History* 44 (September 1984): 635–68.

331

———. "The Slavery Debate: A Note From the Sidelines." *Explorations in Economic History* 18 (1981): 304–8.

Fields, Barbara Jeanne. *Slavery and Freedom on the Middle Ground.* New Haven: Yale University Press, 1985.

Finley, Moses. *The Ancient Economy.* Berkeley: University of California Press, 1973.

———. *Ancient Slavery and Modern Ideology.* Harmondsworth: Penguin, 1980.

———. *Economy and Society in Ancient Greece.* Harmondsworth: Penguin, 1983.

Fisher, Allan G. B., and Humphrey J. Fisher. *Slavery and Muslim Society in Africa: The Institution in Saharan and Sudanic Africa and the Trans-Saharan Trade.* London: C. Hurt and Co., 1971.

Fitzhugh, George. *Cannibals All! or Slaves Without Masters.* Cambridge: Harvard University Press, 1960.

Fogel, Robert W. *Without Consent or Contract: The Rise and Fall of American Slavery.* New York: W. W. Norton, 1989.

Fogel, Robert, and Stanley Engerman. *Time on the Cross: The Economics of American Negro Slavery.* Boston: Little, Brown, 1974.

Fortenbaugh, W. "Aristotle on Slaves and Women." In *Articles on Aristotle,* vol. 2, ed. J. Barnes, M. Schofield, and R. Sorabji. London: Duckworth, 1977.

Fox-Genovese, Elizabeth. *Within the Plantation Household: Black and White Women of the Old South.* Chapel Hill: University of North Carolina Press, 1988.

Franklin, John Hope. *From Slavery to Freedom,* 3d ed. New York: Alfred A. Knopf, 1967.

Frederickson, G. M. *The Black Image in the White Mind: The Debate on Afro-American Character and Destiny, 1817–1914.* New York: Harper and Row, 1971.

Gauthier, David. *Morals by Agreement.* Oxford: Clarendon Press, 1986.

Genovese, Eugene D. *From Rebellion to Revolution: Afro-American Slave Revolts in the Making of the New World.* Baton Rouge: Louisiana State University Press, 1979.

———. *Roll, Jordan, Roll: The World the Slaves Made.* New York: Pantheon, 1974.

Giddings, Paula. *When and Where I Enter: The Impact of Black Women on Race and Sex in America.* New York: Bantam Books, 1988.

Gilroy, Paul. *The Black Atlantic: Modernity and Double Consciousness.* Cambridge: Harvard University Press, 1993.

Glausser, Wayne. "Three Approaches to Locke and the Slave Trade." *Journal of the History of Ideas* 51 (April–June 1990).

Gould, Stephen Jay. *The Mismeasure of Man.* New York: W. W. Norton, 1981.

Grant, Ruth W. *John Locke's Liberalism.* Chicago: University of Chicago Press, 1987.

Greenblatt, Stephen J. "Linguistic Colonialism in *The Tempest.*" In *William Shakespeare's The Tempest,* ed. Harold Bloom. New York: Chelsea House, 1988.

Hare, R. M. *Essays in Ethical Theory.* Oxford: Oxford University Press, 1989.

———. *Essays on Political Morality.* Oxford: Clarendon Press, 1989.

———. "Ethical Theory and Utilitarianism." In *Contemporary British Philosophy* 4, ed. H. D. Lewis. London: Allen and Unwin, 1976.

————. *Moral Thinking: Its Levels, Method, and Point*. Oxford: Oxford University Press, 1981.

Hegel, G. W. F. *Phenomenology of Spirit*, trans. A.V. Miller. Oxford: Oxford University Press, 1977.

————. *Philosophy of History*, trans. J. Sibree. New York: Dover, 1900.

Hobbes, Thomas. *Leviathan*, ed. Richard Tuck. Cambridge: Cambridge University Press, 1991.

Hogg, Peter. *Slavery*. British Library booklets, 1979.

Hopkins, Keith. *Conquerors and Slaves*. Cambridge: Cambridge University Press, 1978.

Husak, Douglass. "Paternalism and Autonomy." *Philosophy and Public Affairs* 10 (1981): 43–46.

James, C. L. R. *The Black Jacobins: Toussaint L'Ouverture and the San Domingo Revolution*. New York: Random House, 1963.

Jordan, Winthrop D. *White Over Black*. Baltimore: Penguin Books, 1968.

Karasch, Mary. *Slave Life in Rio de Janeiro 1808–1850*. Princeton: Princeton University Press, 1987.

Karra, Ruth Mazo. *Slavery and Society in Medieval Scandinavia*. New Haven: Yale University Press, 1988.

Katz, William Loren, ed. *Five Slave Narratives: A Compendium*. New York: Arno Press, 1968.

King, Martin Luther. *A Testament of Hope: The Essential Writings of Martin Luther King Jr.*, ed. James Washington. San Francisco: Harper and Row, 1986.

Kopytoff, Igor, and Suzanne Miers, "African Slavery as an Institution of Marginality." In *Slavery in Africa: Historical and Anthropological Perspectives*, ed. Suzanne Miers and Igor Kopytoff. Madison: University of Wisconsin Press, 1977, 3–81.

————. "Slavery as an Institution: Open and Closed Systems." In *Asian and African Systems of Slavery*, ed. James Watson. Berkeley: University of California Press, 1980.

Lang, Berl. *Act and Idea in the Nazi Genocide*. Chicago: University of Chicago Press, 1990.

Lerner, Gerder, ed. *Black Women in White America: A Documentary History*. New York: Pantheon Books, 1972.

Lichtenstein, Alex. " 'That Disposition to Theft, with Which They Have Been Branded': Moral Economy, Slave Management, and the Law." *Journal of Social History* 21 (1988): 413–40.

Litwack, Leon F. *Been in the Storm So Long: The Aftermath of Slavery*. New York: Vintage, 1979.

Locke, John. *An Essay Concerning Human Understanding*, ed. Peter H. Nidditch. Oxford: Clarendon Press, 1975.

————. *Some Thoughts Concerning Education*, ed. John W. Youlton and Jean S. Youlton. Oxford: Oxford University Press, 1989.

———. *Two Treatises of Government*, ed. Peter Laslett. Cambridge: Cambridge University Press, 1988.

Long, Edward. *A History of Jamaica*. London: n.p. 1774.

Lorde, Audre. "The Master's Tools Will Never Dismantle the Master's House." In *This Bridge Called My Back*, ed. Cherrie Moraga and Gloria Anzaldua. New York: Kitchen Table: Women of Color Press, 1983.

Lovejoy, Paul. "Problems of Slave Control in the Sokoto Caliphate." In *Africans in Bondage: Studies in Slavery and the Slave Trade*, ed. Paul Lovejoy. Madison: University of Wisconsin Press, 1986.

———. *Transformations in Slavery: A History of Slavery in Africa*. Cambridge: Cambridge University Press, 1983.

———, ed. *Africans in Bondage: Studies in Slavery and the Slave Trade*. Madison: University of Wisconsin Press, 1986.

Martin, Dale B. *Slavery as Salvation*. New Haven: Yale University Press, 1990.

Martin, Waldo E. Jr. *The Mind of Frederick Douglass*. Chapel Hill and London: University of North Carolina Press, 1984.

Marx, Karl. *Capital*, vol. 1, trans. Ben Fowkes. Harmondsworth: Penguin, 1976.

———. *Grundrisse*, trans. Martin Nicolaus. New York: Random House, 1973.

Mason, John Edwin. "Fortunate Slaves and Artful Masters: Labor Relations in the Rural Cape Colony During the Era of Emancipation, ca. 1825–1838." In *Slavery in South Africa: Captive Labor on the Dutch Frontier*, ed. Elizabeth A. Eldredge and Fred Morton. Boulder: Westview Press, 1994.

Mattoso, Katia M. de Queiros. *To Be A Slave In Brazil: 1550–1888*, trans. Arthur Goldhammer. New Brunswick: Rutgers University Press, 1986.

McFeely, William S. *Frederick Douglass*. New York: Simon and Schuster, 1991.

McGary, Howard, and Bill Lawson. *Between Slavery and Freedom*. Bloomington: Indiana University Press, 1992.

Mendelsohn, Isaac. *Slavery in the Ancient Near East*. New York: Oxford University Press, 1949.

Miers, Suzanne, and Richard Roberts, eds. *The End of Slavery in Africa*. Madison: University of Wisconsin Press, 1988.

Miller, Joseph C. *Way of Death: Merchant Capitalism and the Angolan Slave Trade 1730–1830*. Madison: University of Wisconsin Press, 1988.

Moore, Barrington. *Injustice: The Social Bases of Obedience and Revolt*. White Plains, N.Y.: M.E. Sharpe, 1987.

Moore, Jane. "Sex, Slavery and Rights in Mary Wollstonecraft's Vindications." In *The Discourse of Slavery: Aphra Behn to Toni Morrison*, ed. Carl Plasa and Betty Ring. London and New York: Routledge, 1994.

Moravcsik, J. M. "Ancient and Modern Conceptions of Health and Medicine." *The Journal of Medicine and Philosophy* 1 (1976): 337–48.

———. "Communal Ties." *Proceedings of The American Philosophical Association*. 62, suppl. (1988): 211–25.

————. *Plato and Platonism.* Oxford: Blackwell, 1992.

————. *Thought and Language.* London: Routledge, 1990.

Nabuco, Joaquim. *Abolitionism: The Brazilian Antislavery Struggle,* trans. Robert Conrad. Urbana: University of Illinois Press, 1977.

Natanson, Harvey. "Locke and Hume: Bearing on the Legal Obligation of the Negro." *Journal of Value Inquiry* 1 (Winter 1970): 35–43.

Nieboer, H. J. *Slavery as an Industrial System,* 2d ed. New York: Burt Franklin, 1910. Reprint 1971.

Northup, Solomon. *Twelve Years A Slave.* New York: Dover Publications, 1970.

Oakes, James. *Slavery and Freedom: An Interpretation of the Old South.* New York: Alfred A. Knopf, 1990.

Parish, Peter. *Slavery: History and Historians.* New York: Harper and Row, 1989.

Patterson, Orlando. *Freedom.* New York: Basic Books, 1991.

————. *Slavery and Social Death.* Cambridge: Harvard University Press, 1982.

————. *The Sociology of Slavery: An Analysis of the Origins, Development and Structure of Negro Slave Society in Jamaica.* London: MacGibbon and Kee, 1967.

Pennington, James W. C. *The Fugitive Blacksmith or Events in the History of James W. C. Pennington,* 2d ed. London: Charles Gilpin, 1849.

Phillips, Ulrich B. *American Negro Slavery.* New York: D. Appleton, 1918. Reprinted Baton Rouge: Louisiana State University Press, 1996.

Phillips, William D. *Slavery From Roman Times to the Early Transatlantic Trade.* Minneapolis: University of Minnesota Press, 1985.

Popkin, Richard. "The Philosophical Bases of Modern Racism." *The High Road to Pyrrhonism.* San Diego: Austin Hill Press, 1980.

Ramsay, James. *An Address on the Proposed Bill for the Abolition of the Slave Trade.* London, n.p., 1788.

————. *Essays on the Treatment and Conversion of African Slaves in the British Sugar Colonies.* London, n.p., 1784.

————. *An Inquiry into the Effects of Putting a Stop to the African Slave Trade.* London: n.p., 1784.

Rawls, John. *A Theory of Justice.* Cambridge: Harvard University Press, 1971.

Ripley, C. Peter, ed. *Witness for Freedom.* Chapel Hill: University of North Carolina Press, 1993.

Roberts, Richard, and Martin A. Klein. "The Banamba Slave Exodus of 1905 and the Decline of Slavery in the Western Sudan." *Journal of African History* 21 (1980): 375–94.

Roediger, David. *The Wages of Whiteness: Race and the Making of the American Working Class.* London and New York: Verso, 1991.

Rousseau, Jean-Jacques. *On the Social Contract,* ed. Roger D. Masters and trans. Judith R. Masters. New York: St. Martin's Press, 1978.

Rubenstein, Richard L., and John K. Roth. *Approaches to Auschwitz: The Holocaust and Its Legacy.* New York: John Knox Press, 1987.

Scarborough, William K. "Slavery: A White Man's Burden." In *Perspectives and Irony in American Slavery*, ed. Harry P. Owens. Jackson: University of Mississippi Press, 1976.

Schwartz, Stuart B. *Sugar Plantations in the Formation of Brazilian Society: Bahia, 1550–1835.* Cambridge: Cambridge University Press, 1985.

Scott, James C. *Domination and the Arts of Resistance: Hidden Transcripts.* New Haven: Yale University Press, 1990.

Scott, Rebecca. *Slave Emancipation in Cuba: The Transition to Free Labor, 1860–1899.* Princeton: Princeton University Press, 1986.

Seliger, M. "Locke, Liberalism and Nationalism." In *John Locke: Problems and Perspectives*, ed. J. Yolton. Cambridge: Cambridge University Press, 1969.

Sen, A. K., and B. A. O. Williams, eds. *Utilitarianism and Beyond.* Cambridge: Cambridge University Press, 1982.

Sen, Amartya. "Well-Being, Agency, and Freedom." *Journal of Philosophy* 82 (April 1985): 195–200.

Shakespeare, William. *The Tempest*, ed. Anne Righter. London: Penguin Books, 1968.

Sharp, Granville. *Tracts on Slavery and Liberty.* London: n.p. 1776; Reprint, Westport, Conn.: Negro University Press, 1969.

Smart, J. J. C., and B. A. O. Williams, eds. *Utilitarianism For and Against.* Cambridge: Cambridge University Press, 1973.

Smith, Adam. *Wealth of Nations.* New York: Random House, 1965.

Smith, Nicholas D. "Aristotle's Theory of Natural Slavery." *Phoenix* 37 (1983).

Sobel, Mechal. *Trabelin' On: The Slave Journey to an Afro-Baptist Faith.* Princeton: Princeton University Press, 1988.

Soderlund, Jean R. *Quakers and Slavery: A Divided Spirit.* Princeton: Princeton University Press, 1985.

Stampp, Kenneth. *The Peculiar Institution: Slavery in the Antebellum South.* New York: Alfred A. Knopf, 1956.

Ste. Croix, G. E. M. de. *The Class Struggle in the Ancient Greek World.* London: Duckworth, 1981.

———. "Slavery and Other Forms of Unfree Labour." In *Slavery and Other Forms of Unfree Labour*, ed. Léonie Archer. London: Routledge, 1988.

Steckel, Richard. "A Dreadful Childhood: The Excess Mortality of American Slaves." *Social Science History* 10 (Winter 1986): 427–65.

Strawson, P. F. *Freedom and Resentment.* London: Methuen, 1974.

Stuckey, Sterling. *Slave Culture: Nationalist Theory and the Foundations of Black America.* Oxford: Oxford University Press, 1987.

Sundquist, Eric J. *To Wake the Nations: Race in the Making of American Literature.* Cambridge: Harvard University Press, 1993.

Tully, James. "Rediscovering America: The *Two Treatises* and Aboriginal Rights."

In *An Approach to Political Philosophy: Locke in Context*. Cambridge: Cambridge University Press, 1993.

Watson, James L., ed. *Asian and African Systems of Slavery*. Berkeley: University of California Press, 1980.

Weber, Max. "Social Causes of the Decline of Ancient Civilization." Reprinted in Max Weber, *The Agrarian Sociology of Ancient Civilizations*, trans. R. I. Frank. London: New Left Books, 1976.

Westermann, William L. *The Slave Systems of Greek and Roman Antiquity*. Philadelphia: American Philosophical Society, 1955.

White, Charles. *Regular Gradation in Man*. London: C. Dilly, 1790.

White, Deborah Gray. *Ar'n't I a Woman? Female Slaves in the Plantation South*. New York: W. W. Norton, 1985.

Wiedemann, Thomas. *Greek and Roman Slavery*. Baltimore: Johns Hopkins University Press, 1981.

Williams, Eric. *Capitalism and Slavery*. Chapel Hill: University of North Carolina Press, 1994.

Woodson, Carter G. *Free Negro Owners of Slaves in the United States in 1830*. New York: Negro University Press, 1924/68.

Wright, Gavin. "The Efficiency of Slavery: Another Interpretation." *American Economic Review* 69 (March 1979): 219–26.

Yellin, Jean Fagan, ed. *Harriet A. Jacobs, Incidents in the Life of a Slave Girl*. Cambridge: Harvard University Press, 1987.

INDEX

66, 168n5, 172–75, 177, 182, 188,
190–92, 195, 197, 204, 211–13, 225,
232, 247, 258, 268, 271, 273–74,
276n4, 277n7, 278n26, 285–93, 295–
98, 300–302, 304, 306–9, 313, 315,
320n15, 322n23, 325n67
master/slave, xv; relationship, xvi, 103,
111, 122
McFeely, William, 165
McGary, Howard, 277n8, 278n22
Messenian Oration of Alcidamas, 6
metaphysical, xiv, 81, 84
metic, 5, 55
military, 160, 214, 218, 310, 312, 315,
326n95; conquest, 3; service, 4, 311
mining, 4, 290–91
miscegenation, 275
misogynist, 14
modernity, 21, 165
Molyneaux, William, 63–64, 66, 68, 76
monogenetic theory, 86
moral: basis, xv; epistemology, xiii–xiv,
37–38, 40; ideals, xix, 295, 297; objectivity, xix, 284, 318n3; realism, xii,
xix, 284–85, 318n3; self-evident
propositions, xiii; thought, xix
morality, xvii–xviii, 29–30, 38, 112–13,
161, 203, 206, 215, 220, 226, 231,
244, 284–85, 317, 319, 324; truths of,
xiv, 36
mulatto, 169n12
mythology, 16, 160

Natason, Harvey, 139, 144–45
Native Americans, 86, 255
natural: law. See law, natural; rights. See
rights, natural; slave. See slave, natural; tendencies, 9
naturalism, 178
naturalistic fallacy, 31
nature, xiii, xv, 1, 6, 9, 12, 20–21, 28, 38,
42, 45, 58, 64, 77, 82–84, 87–90, 97,
112, 117, 141, 152–54, 156–57, 164,
167, 179, 185, 194, 197, 219, 243,
263, 268–69, 276, 282–84, 291, 294,

320; human, xiv, 32–35, 37, 39–40,
61–62, 81, 180, 184, 223–25; slavish,
11; state of, xv, 52, 56–57, 59, 61, 63,
74, 103–6, 113, 131–35, 137, 143–45,
166
navy, 4, 214
Nazi, xviii, 205, 255, 256, 259–60, 268–
69, 271–72, 275–76, 278–79; ideology, 273–74; Germany, 257, 267;
genocide of Jews, 257–58
necessary identity. See identity, necessary
necessity, xiii, 3, 21, 24, 36, 72, 156, 165,
189, 199, 294, 311; cultural, 22; divine, 1–2; economic, 8, 19; supernatural, 2; technological, 9
Negro, 37, 43, 55, 58, 73n19, 74n19, 95,
121, 125, 129, 134, 136–39, 146–48,
166, 197, 206, 231–32, 292, 320, 322
New World, xi, 55, 60, 85, 126, 215, 321,
327
Northup, Solomon, xvii, 208; *Twelve
Years a Slave*, 204
Nozick, Robert, 124n1, 203

object, xvii, 5, 12, 81, 154, 210, 225, 294
obligation, 102, 104–5, 107–11, 113,
115–16, 118, 141, 149, 183, 190, 198,
212, 251, 290, 295, 320; legal, xv, 119,
131–33, 137–38, 146
Odyssey, 14, 23, 26
offspring, xvii–xviii, 88, 177, 204, 230,
236, 240, 246–48
oppressed, xvii, 149, 165, 172, 190, 201,
268, 271
oppression, xviii, 84, 159, 161, 172–74,
182, 187, 260, 264, 267, 271

passivity, 24, 157, 161, 238; social, 20
paternalism, xii, 103, 136, 164, 175, 182,
190, 192–93, 195, 203–6, 244, 295;
and autonomy, 191, 201; definition
of, 188; and exploitation, 202; as a
justification of slavery, 189; models
of, xvi, xvii, 194, 196–201
Patterson, Orlando, 50, 54, 117–18,

and black gestators, 230, 235, 239, 245–46; in Brazil, 294, 296; in the Caribbean, 223; comparison of slavery and gestation as commercial, 230, 233, 244, 247, 248n1; conceptual core (definition of), 173; and contracts, 229–31, 248n2; defense of, xii, 121; definition of, 113–14, 117; and dignity, 300–301 (respect), 305–6; as evil, 261; evilness of, xvii; Greek and Roman practices, 289; and human rights, 209–10; and imprisonment, 214; and incentives to cooperate, 313; injustice of, 282–83, 301, 307; justice of. See justice, of slavery; justification of. See justification, of slavery; and labor scarcity, 289–90; and material incentives, 291; modern, 11; moral assessment of, xii, xvi, 171–72; natal alienation, 263, 266, 275; natural, 9; and physical bondage, 102, 114; on plantations, 302; as practiced by Africans, 99; and rebellion, 298. See also rebellion; revolt; Spartans; religious conception of, 294; Roman, 3; as servitude, 106; theory of, 10, 49–54, 61–62, 64, 66–67, 71–72, 310, 313; as unjust, xii, 19, 72, 99, 119, 283, 312, 314; and utilitarianism, 221; and voluntary contracts, 315. See also free agreement, demise of; and war, 172; wrongness, xvii, 225–26, 313–14

Smith, Adam, 92–93, 282, 310
social: class, 14; construction, 17; contrasts, 21; distance, 4; experience, 22; issues, xv; policy, xviii; practice, xii, 19, 263, 273; practice, institutionalized, xi; scientist, xi, xvi, 282. See also injustice; institution; justice; language; world
society, 19, 22, 34, 37, 39, 43, 73, 86–87, 90, 109, 122, 133, 143, 147, 172–73, 176–79, 183, 191, 194–95, 198–99,

206, 210–11, 213, 215–16, 224, 241, 246, 257, 263, 288–89, 293, 310–11, 322; American, xv; liberal, 21, 201, 202; modern, 21; traditional, 21
sociobiology, 20
Socrates, 14
solidarity, xvii, 190
sophists, 20, 219, 220
Sophocles, 14, 28, 184; *Philoctetes*, 26n38, 184
sovereign, xv, 52, 56, 62, 103–8, 110, 113, 126, 157, 165
Spartan(s), 4, 23n9, 288, 298, 310
spirituals, 161. See also blacks, spiritual shout
Stampp, Kenneth, 197
state of nature. See nature, state of
Stoicism, 6, 152, 157, 161, 164, 166
structure, 16, 18, 20, 37, 88–89, 94, 168, 171, 174–75, 178–79, 181–82, 283, 291, 302, 305–6
Stuckey, Sterling, 277n13, 16
subjects, 3, 52, 73, 104–5, 107–8, 126, 140, 198, 294, 314
subordination, 7, 157, 165–66, 191, 282, 306, 316; of women, xiii
superiority, 6, 68, 84, 135, 169, 236, 245, 249, 251; mental, 10
supply, 4, 57, 92, 141
surrogate (surrogacy): and autonomy, 244; contracts, xviii, 229, 241, 244, 250, 252; legal and ethical questions, 229; mother, xviii, 229–31, 233–35, 237–38, 240, 243, 247–50, 254; opposition to, xvii; parenting, 229; rights, 246–47
syncretism, 294
syncretist, xix, 96

Teiresias, 16, 28
Tekmessa, 2
teleology, 20, 28
Thales, 14, 15, 17, 18
Theognis, 10, 25
theory: empirical, xiv, 60, 75; generation

of females, 27; moral, xiv, xvi, 50, 60; natural selection, 20, 311; natural-rights, xv, 122, 135; normative communitarian, xvi; political, xi, xiv–xv, 34, 67, 77, 104, 106, 108, 110, 132, 145, 318; rights-based, xvi; of slavery. *See* slavery, theory of
Thucydides, 3, 23
toil, 39, 121, 205; ceaseless, xiv, 36
Toussaint l'Ouverture, 217
tradition, xii, 14–15, 18, 20–21, 79, 120, 132, 135, 137, 144, 154, 160, 163, 170, 176, 194, 197, 199, 201, 229, 234, 244, 263–64, 266–67, 294–95, 308, 323
tragedy, 16, 18, 26, 210
treaty, xii, 23, 287
Trojan War, 1
Troy, fall of, 3
Tully, James, 74n21
Turner, Nat, 160
Two Treatises of Civil Government. See Locke, John
tyranny, 140–41

Uncle Tom, 261
United States, 49, 125, 131–33, 136–41, 145–47, 149, 179, 183, 187, 242–43, 245, 249, 251, 253–54, 264, 275, 287, 309, 322, 325; Constitution, 231; government, xv
unjust, structurally, 12
utilitarianism, xii, xvii, 194, 202, 210, 214–16, 219, 222, 226; dilemma, 223 (for utilitarians). *See also* Bentham, Jeremy
utopia, 18

victim, xviii, 2, 13, 70, 139, 195, 229, 256, 258, 260, 265–70, 273–75
view: abolitionist, xiv, 79, 82; religious, xix, 294
violence, 5, 13, 18, 52, 112, 142, 147, 161, 165–66, 212, 289–91
Voltaire, 85
voluntary, 180, 199; action, 106, 120 (contracts); enslavement, 288; exchanges and women's choice, 244–45

war, 4, 23–24, 52–53, 59, 70–72, 74, 105, 109–13, 116, 118–19, 127, 143, 145, 172, 217, 272, 278, 288, 310–11, 326; prisoners of, xii, 69, 214
white: children, 238, 247, 252n41; women, 247
will, 154, 157, 159–60, 195–203
Williams, Bernard, 221
Wollstonecraft, Mary, 90, 95, 97; *Vindication of the Rights of Women*, 90, 97
women, xii–xiii, xvii–xviii, 7, 16, 20, 22–23, 25–27, 39, 88, 104, 109, 121, 129, 172, 188, 194, 204, 229–31, 233–34, 237–40, 243–49, 259, 265, 274, 277, 282, 304; role of, 18; treatment of, 14
worker, 181
world: ancient, xii–xiii, 3–4, 18, 20–22; contemporary, 20; Greek, 1, 8, 12. *See also* Greek; modern, 19–22; social, 12, 284, 317
wrongness, xvii, 210, 225, 284, 313–14

Xenophon, 4–5, 24n17

Zeus, 1, 16
Zong case, 80, 94n4

Contributors

Anita L. Allen, Associate Dean and Professor, The Law Center, Georgetown University.

Bernard R. Boxill, Professor, Department of Philosophy, University of North Carolina, Chapel Hill.

Joshua Cohen, Professor, Department of Philosophy, Massachusetts Institute of Technology.

R. M. Hare, Professor, Department of Philosophy, University of Florida.

Bill E. Lawson, Professor, Department of Philosophy, Michigan State University.

Tommy L. Lott, Professor, Department of Philosophy, University of Missouri—St. Louis.

Howard McGary, Professor, Department of Philosophy, Rutgers University.

Julius Moravcsik, Professor, Department of Philosophy, Stanford University.

John Perry, Professor, Department of Philosophy, Stanford University.

Laurence M. Thomas, Professor, Department of Philosophy, Syracruse University.

William Uzgalis, Associate Professor, Department of Philosophy, Oregon State University.

Julie K. Ward, Associate Professor, Department of Philosophy, Loyola University, Chicago.

Cynthia Willett, Assistant Professor, Department of Philosophy, Emory University.

Bernard Williams, Professor, Department of Philosophy, University of California—Berkeley.